Mr. Potato Head™
UNPLUGGED

Mr. Potato Head™
UNPLUGGED

BY
JIM DAVIS
AND
BRETT KOTH

Andrews McMeel
Publishing

Kansas City

The **Mr. Potato Head**™ comic strip is distributed internationally by Universal Press Syndicate.

Mr. Potato Head™ *Unplugged* copyright © 2002 by Jim Davis and Brett Koth. All rights reserved. Printed in the United States of America. No part of this book may be used or reproduced in any manner whatsoever without written permission except in the case of reprints in the context of reviews. For information, write Andrews McMeel Publishing, an Andrews McMeel Universal company, 4520 Main Street, Kansas City, Missouri 64111.

MR. POTATO HEAD is a trademark of Hasbro and is used with permission. © 2002 Hasbro. All Rights Reserved.

ISBN: 0-7407-2667-6

02 03 04 05 06 BAH 10 9 8 7 6 5 4 3 2 1

Library of Congress Control Number: 2002107477

www.uComics.com

——— **ATTENTION: SCHOOLS AND BUSINESSES** ———

Andrews McMeel books are available at quantity discounts with bulk purchase for educational, business, or sales promotional use. For information, please write to: Special Sales Department, Andrews McMeel Publishing, 4520 Main Street, Kansas City, Missouri 64111.

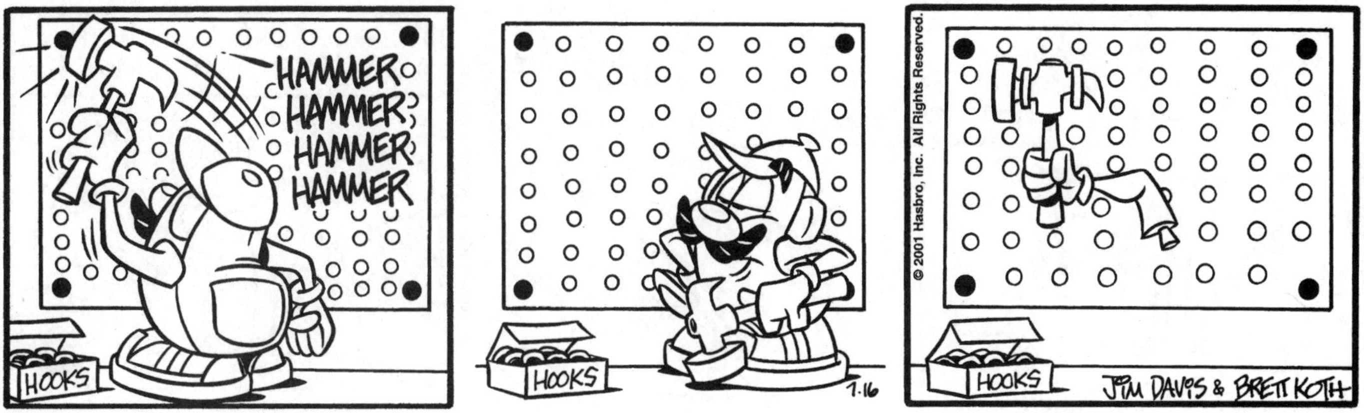
HAMMER
HAMMER
HAMMER
HAMMER
HOOKS
HOOKS
7.16
© 2001 Hasbro, Inc. All Rights Reserved.
HOOKS
JIM DAVIS & BRETT KOTH

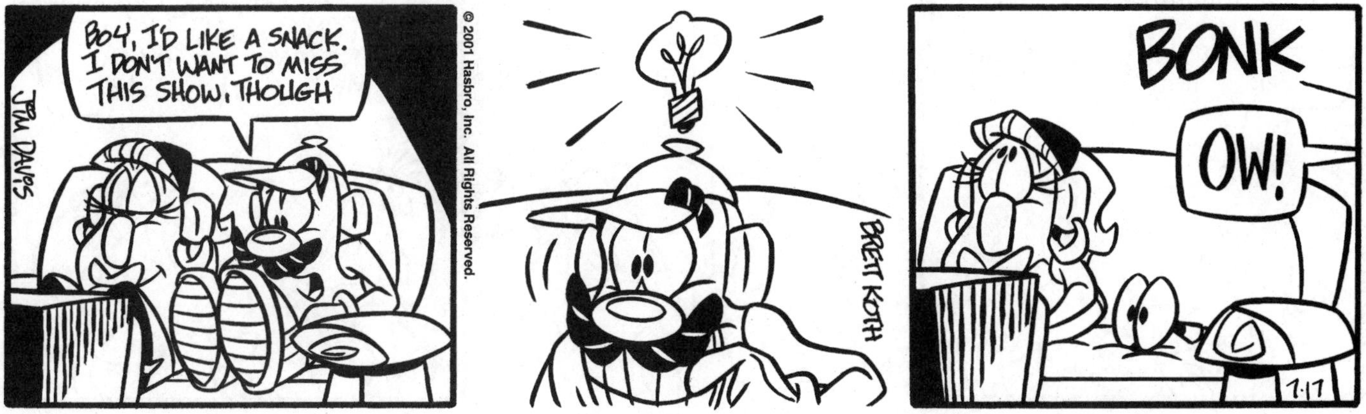
BOY, I'D LIKE A SNACK. I DON'T WANT TO MISS THIS SHOW, THOUGH
JIM DAVIS
© 2001 Hasbro, Inc. All Rights Reserved.
BRETT KOTH
BONK
OW!
7.17

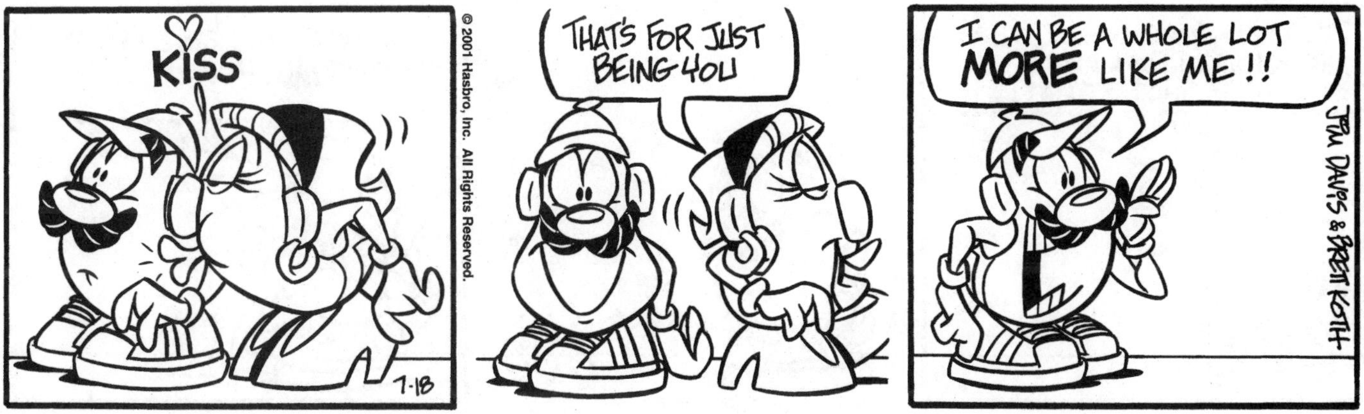
KISS
7.18
© 2001 Hasbro, Inc. All Rights Reserved.
THAT'S FOR JUST BEING YOU
I CAN BE A WHOLE LOT MORE LIKE ME!!
JIM DAVIS & BRETT KOTH

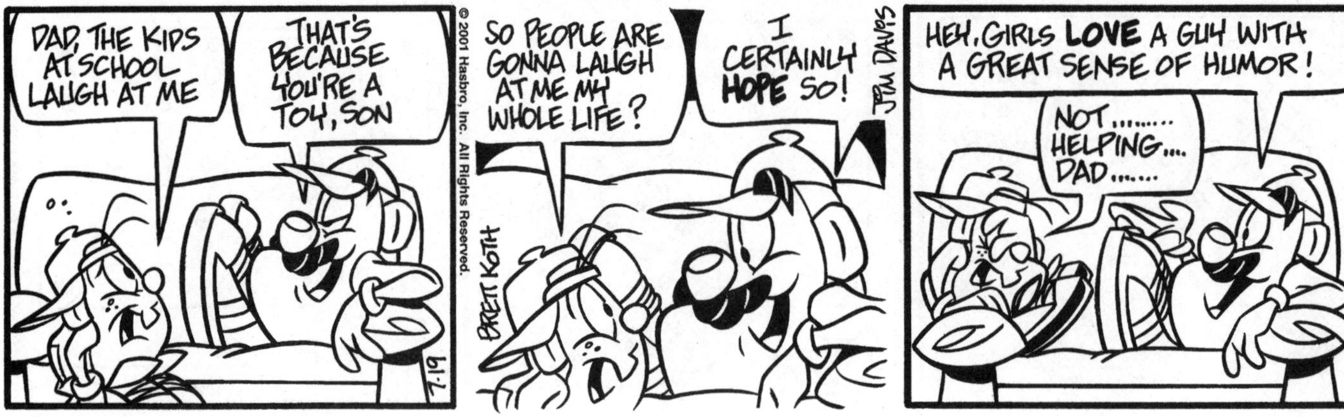
DAD, THE KIDS AT SCHOOL LAUGH AT ME
THAT'S BECAUSE YOU'RE A TOY, SON
SO PEOPLE ARE GONNA LAUGH AT ME MY WHOLE LIFE?
I CERTAINLY HOPE SO!
HEY, GIRLS LOVE A GUY WITH A GREAT SENSE OF HUMOR!
NOT........ HELPING.... DAD.......

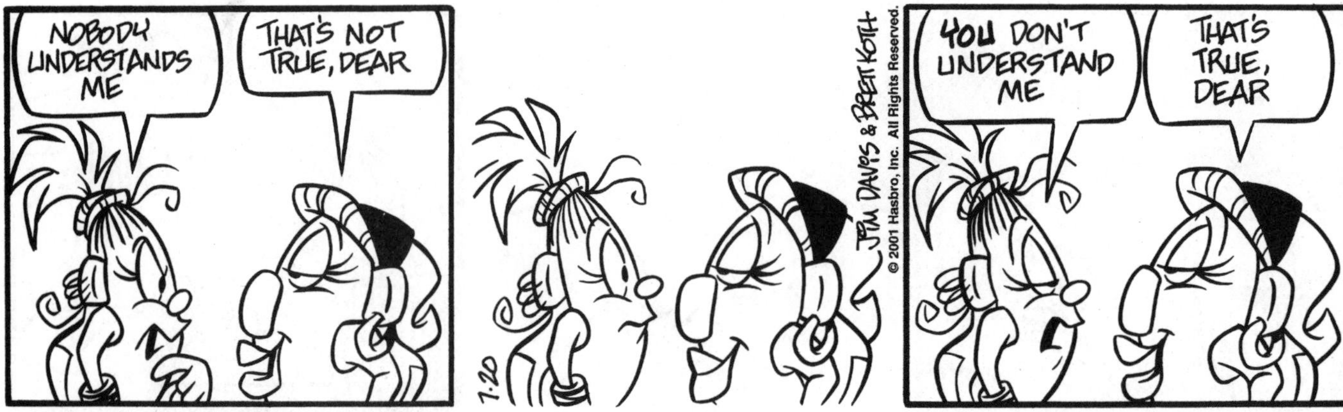
NOBODY UNDERSTANDS ME
THAT'S NOT TRUE, DEAR
YOU DON'T UNDERSTAND ME
THAT'S TRUE, DEAR

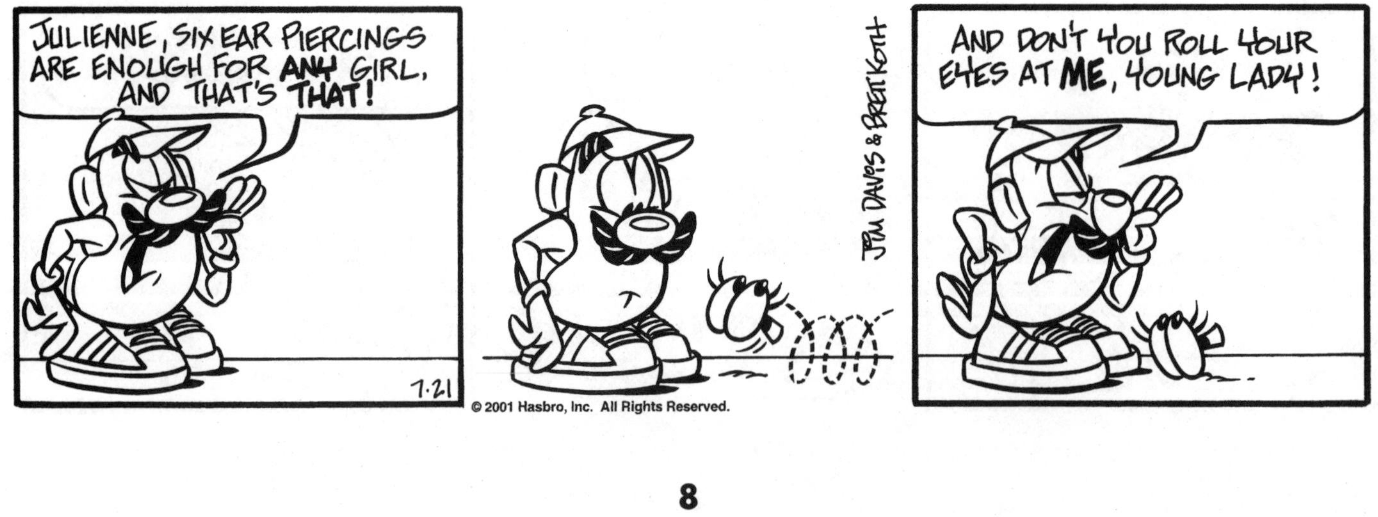
JULIENNE, SIX EAR PIERCINGS ARE ENOUGH FOR ANY GIRL, AND THAT'S THAT!
AND DON'T YOU ROLL YOUR EYES AT ME, YOUNG LADY!

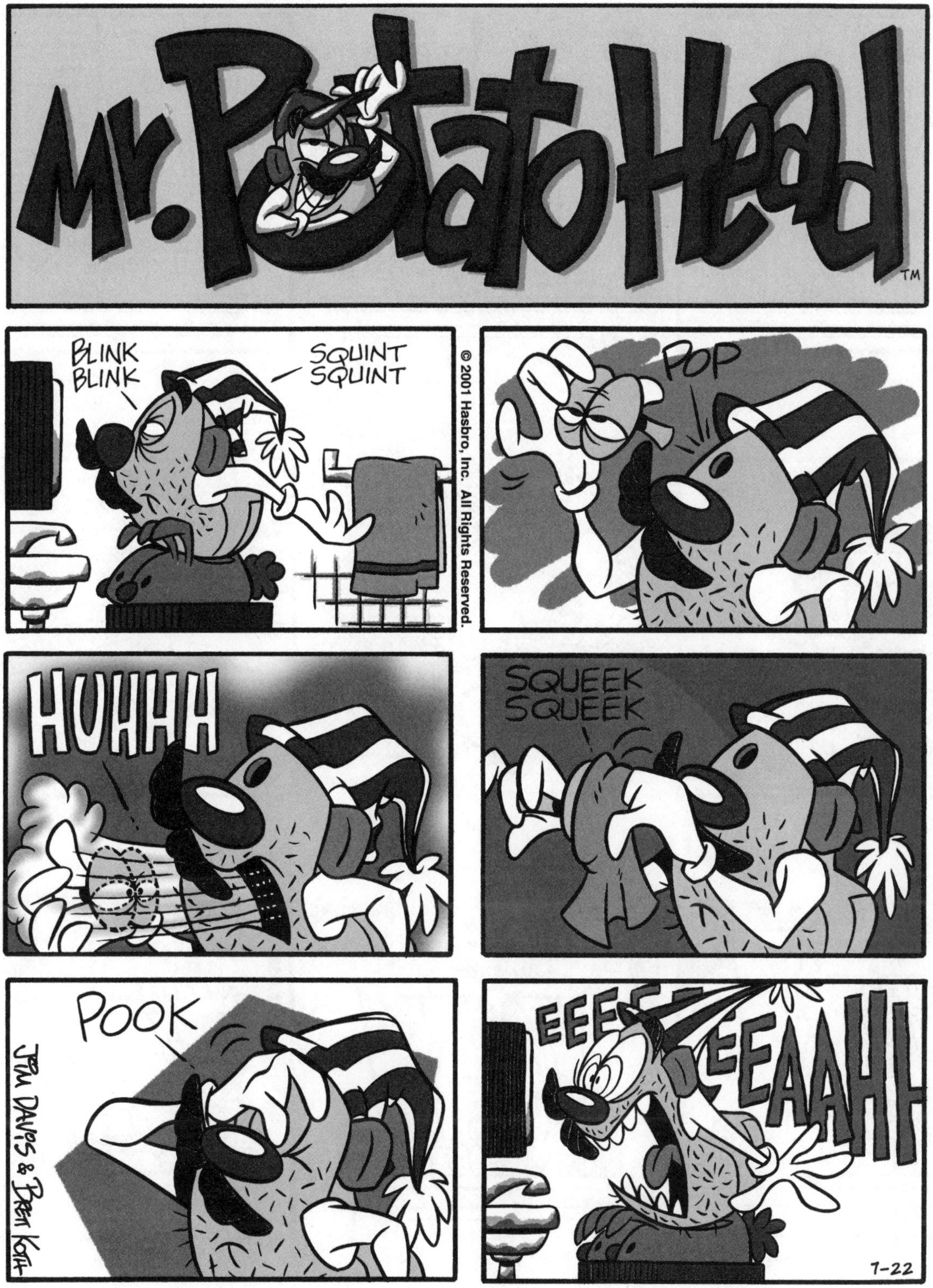
Mr. Potato Head™
BLINK BLINK
SQUINT SQUINT
© 2001 Hasbro, Inc. All Rights Reserved.
POP
HUHHH
SQUEEK SQUEEK
POOK
JIM DAVIS & BRETT KOTH
EEEEEEAAHH
7-22

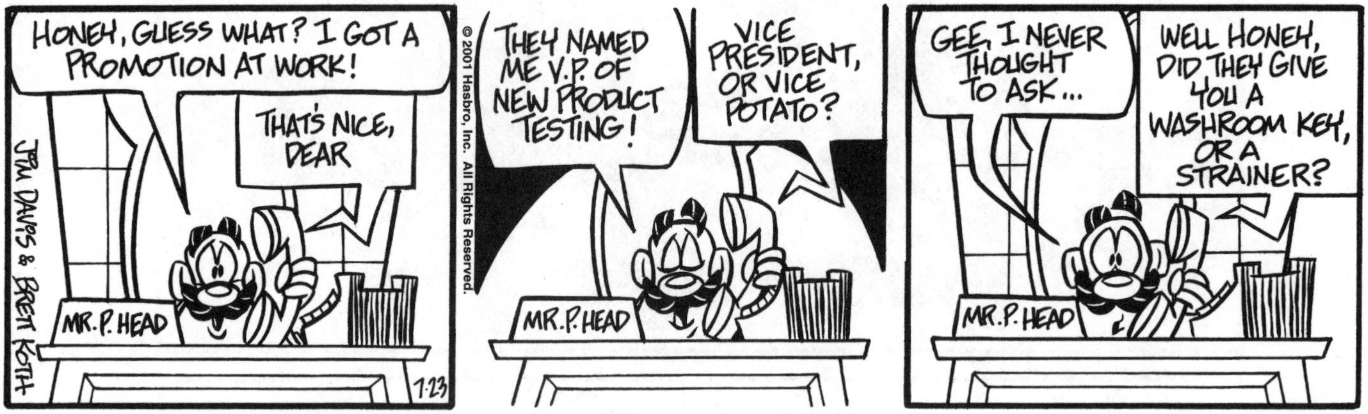
HONEY, GUESS WHAT? I GOT A PROMOTION AT WORK!
THAT'S NICE, DEAR
MR. P. HEAD
JIM DAVIS & BRETT KOTH
1·23
© 2001 Hasbro, Inc. All Rights Reserved.
THEY NAMED ME V.P. OF NEW PRODUCT TESTING!
VICE PRESIDENT, OR VICE POTATO?
MR. P. HEAD
GEE, I NEVER THOUGHT TO ASK...
WELL HONEY, DID THEY GIVE YOU A WASHROOM KEY, OR A STRAINER?
MR. P. HEAD

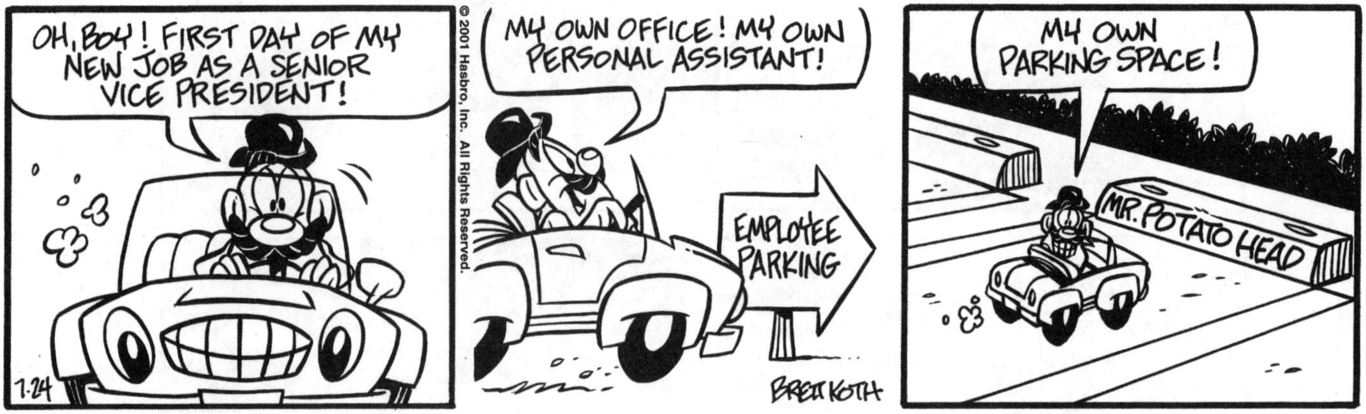
OH, BOY! FIRST DAY OF MY NEW JOB AS A SENIOR VICE PRESIDENT!
1·24
© 2001 Hasbro, Inc. All Rights Reserved.
MY OWN OFFICE! MY OWN PERSONAL ASSISTANT!
EMPLOYEE PARKING
BRETT KOTH
MY OWN PARKING SPACE!
MR. POTATO HEAD

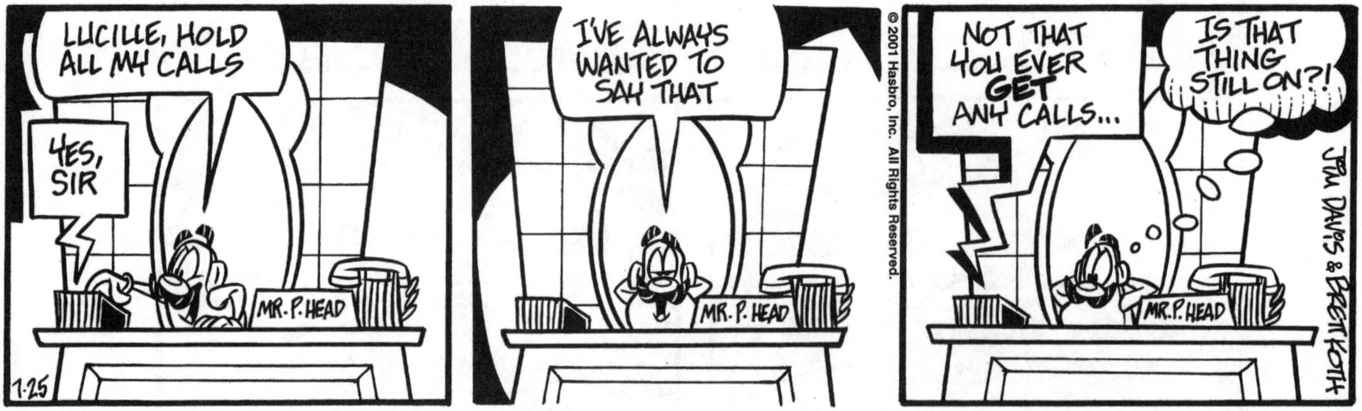
LUCILLE, HOLD ALL MY CALLS
YES, SIR
MR. P. HEAD
1·25
I'VE ALWAYS WANTED TO SAY THAT
MR. P. HEAD
© 2001 Hasbro, Inc. All Rights Reserved.
NOT THAT YOU EVER GET ANY CALLS...
IS THAT THING STILL ON?!
MR. P. HEAD
JIM DAVIS & BRETT KOTH

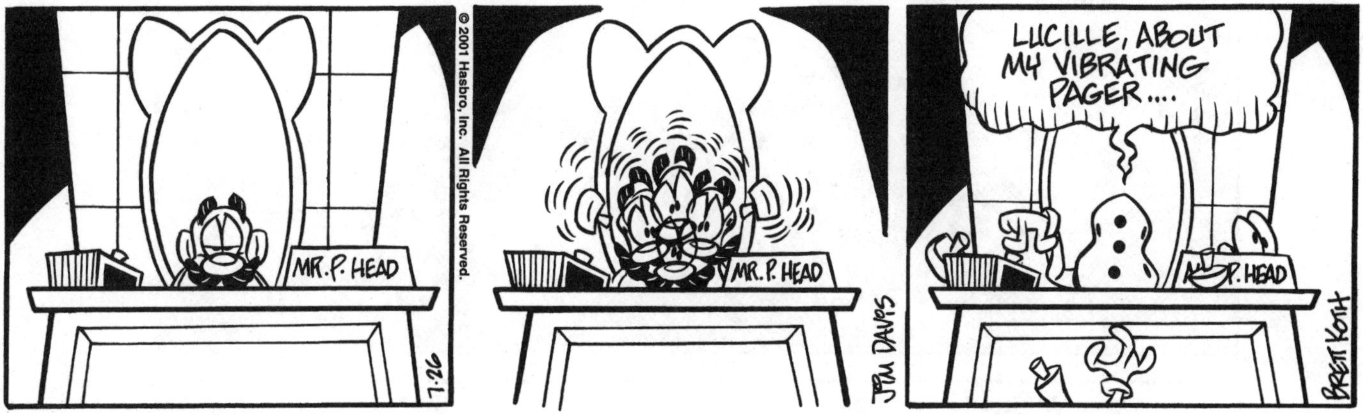
MR. P. HEAD
MR. P. HEAD
LUCILLE, ABOUT MY VIBRATING PAGER.....
7-26
JIM DAVIS
BRETT KOTH

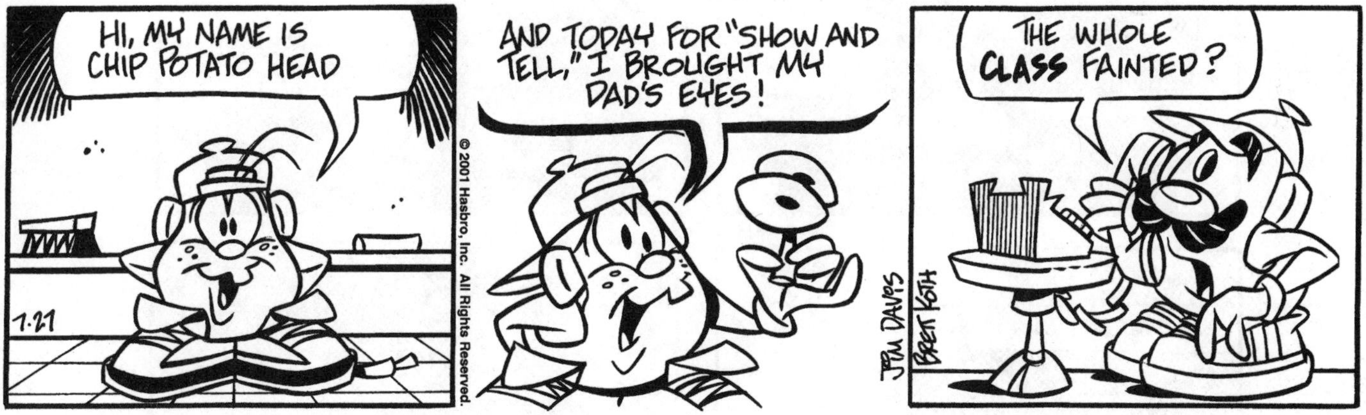
HI, MY NAME IS CHIP POTATO HEAD
AND TODAY FOR "SHOW AND TELL," I BROUGHT MY DAD'S EYES!
THE WHOLE CLASS FAINTED?
7-27
JIM DAVIS
BRETT KOTH

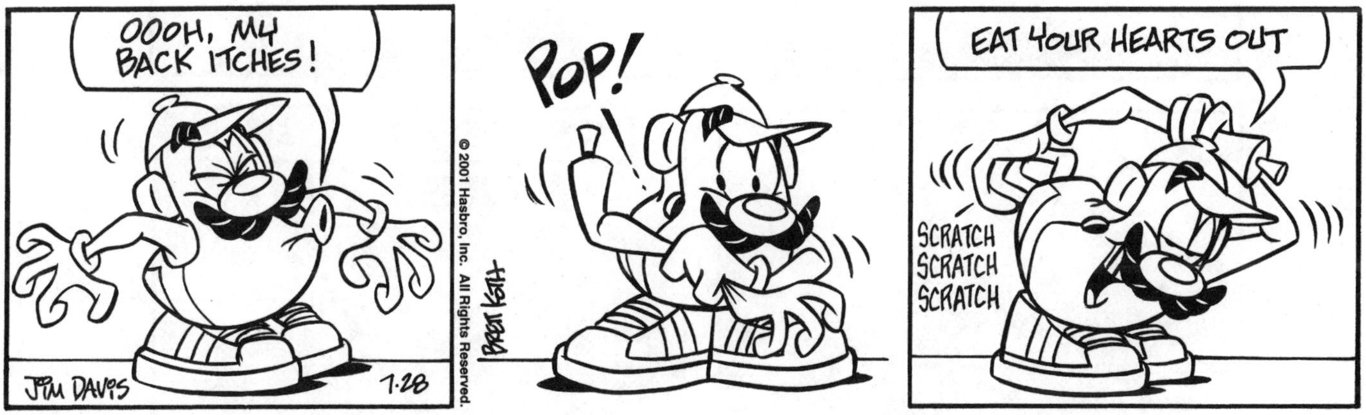
OOOH, MY BACK ITCHES!
POP!
EAT YOUR HEARTS OUT
SCRATCH SCRATCH SCRATCH
7-28
JIM DAVIS
BRETT KOTH

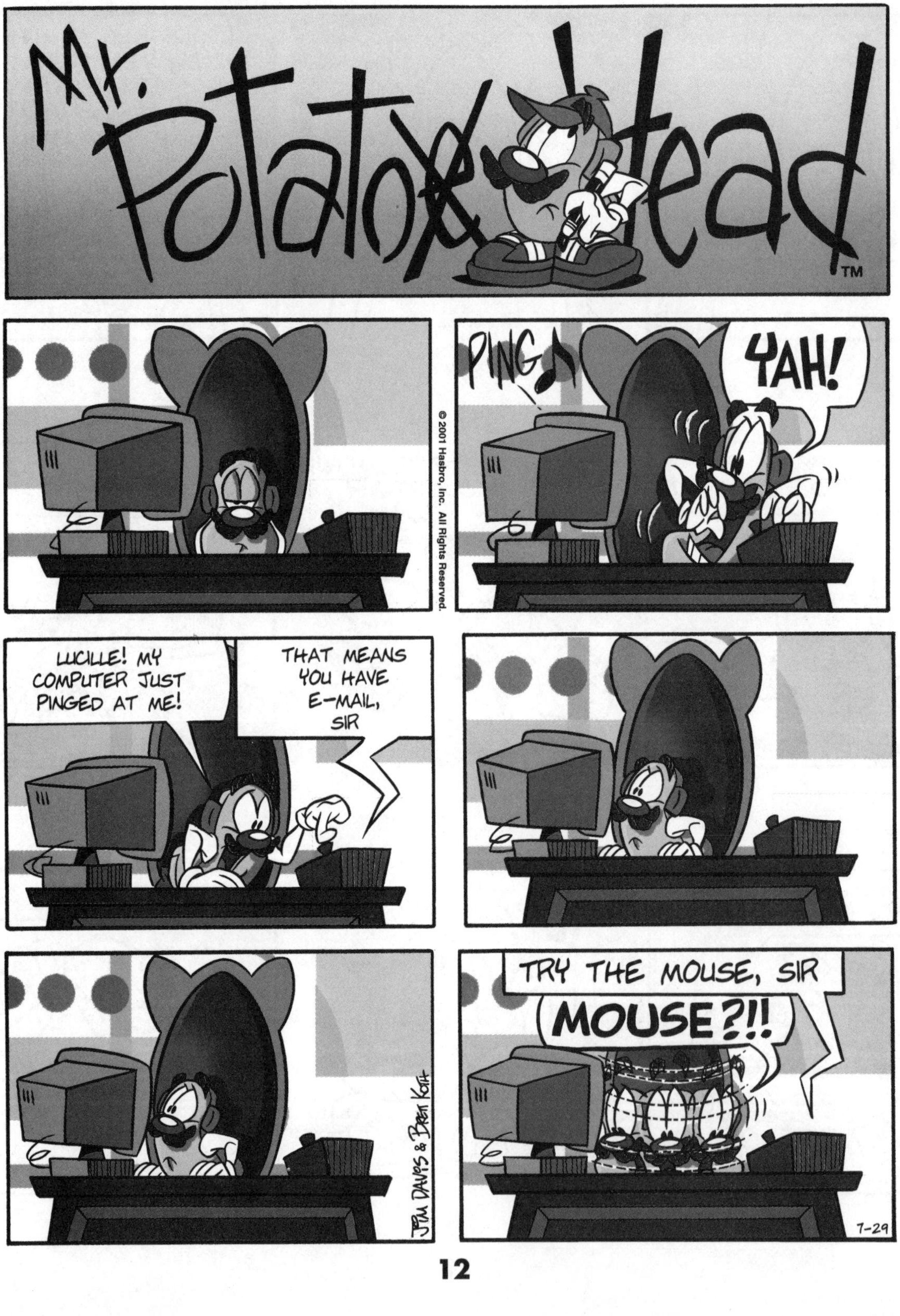
Mr. Potato Head
TM
© 2001 Hasbro, Inc. All Rights Reserved.
PING♪
YAH!
LUCILLE! MY COMPUTER JUST PINGED AT ME!
THAT MEANS YOU HAVE E-MAIL, SIR
JIM DAVIS & BRETT KOTH
TRY THE MOUSE, SIR
MOUSE?!!
7-29

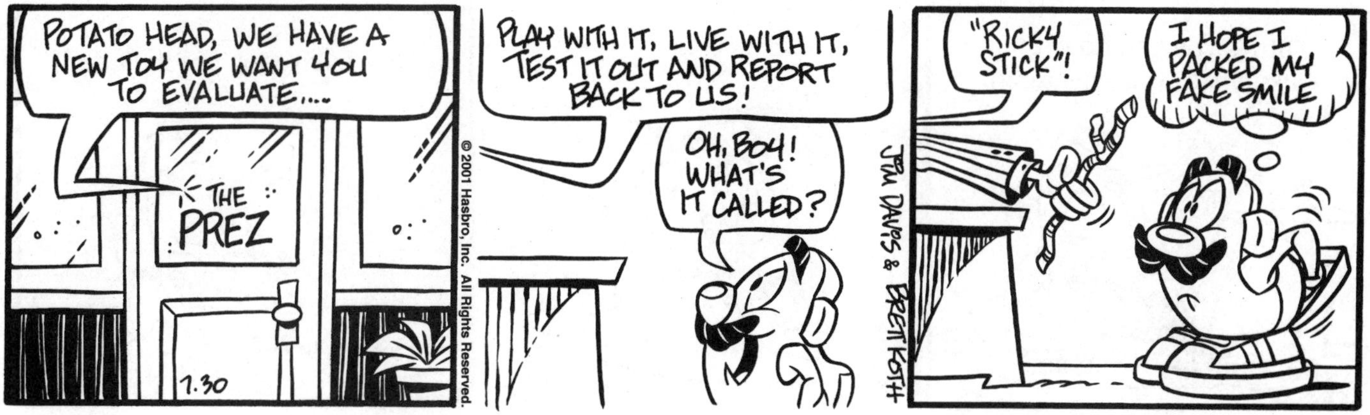
POTATO HEAD, WE HAVE A NEW TOY WE WANT YOU TO EVALUATE....
THE PREZ
7.30
© 2001 Hasbro, Inc. All Rights Reserved.
PLAY WITH IT, LIVE WITH IT, TEST IT OUT AND REPORT BACK TO US!
OH, BOY! WHAT'S IT CALLED?
JIM DAVIS & BRETT KOTH
"RICKY STICK"!
I HOPE I PACKED MY FAKE SMILE

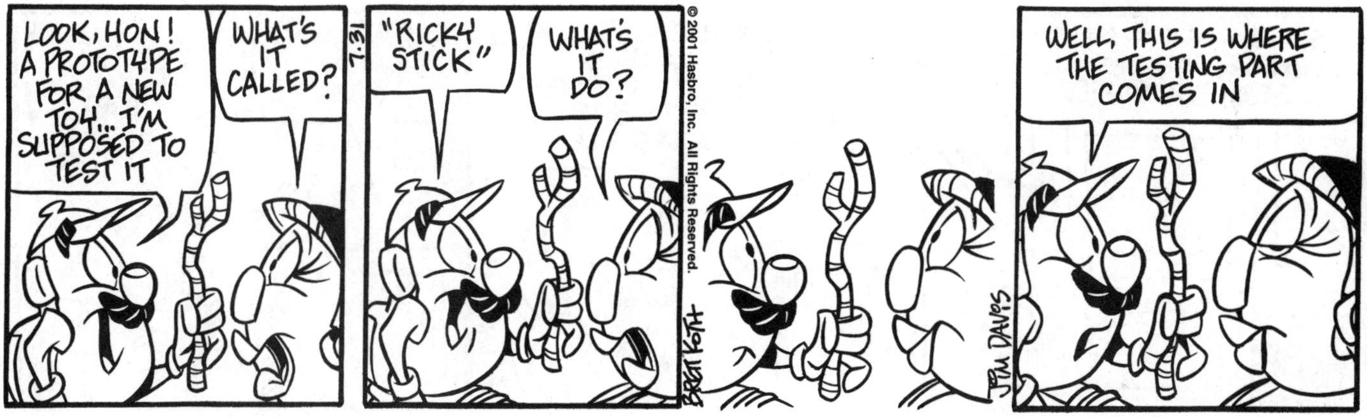
LOOK, HON! A PROTOTYPE FOR A NEW TOY... I'M SUPPOSED TO TEST IT
WHAT'S IT CALLED?
7.31
"RICKY STICK"
WHAT'S IT DO?
© 2001 Hasbro, Inc. All Rights Reserved.
BRETT KOTH
JIM DAVIS
WELL, THIS IS WHERE THE TESTING PART COMES IN

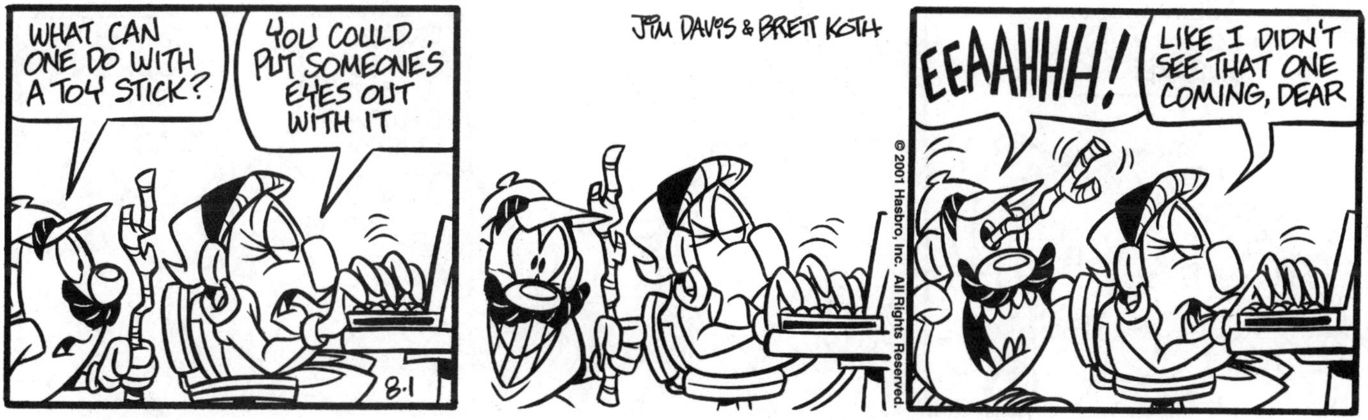
WHAT CAN ONE DO WITH A TOY STICK?
YOU COULD PUT SOMEONE'S EYES OUT WITH IT
8.1
JIM DAVIS & BRETT KOTH
© 2001 Hasbro, Inc. All Rights Reserved.
EEAAHHH!
LIKE I DIDN'T SEE THAT ONE COMING, DEAR

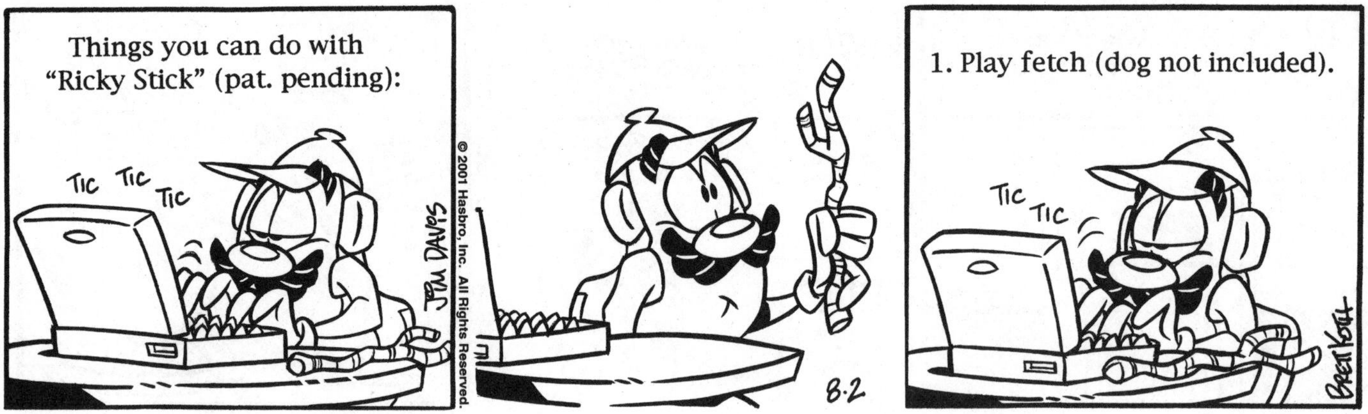
Things you can do with
"Ricky Stick" (pat. pending):
TIC TIC TIC
© 2001 Hasbro, Inc. All Rights Reserved.
JIM DAVIS
8.2
1. Play fetch (dog not included).
TIC TIC
BRETT KOTH

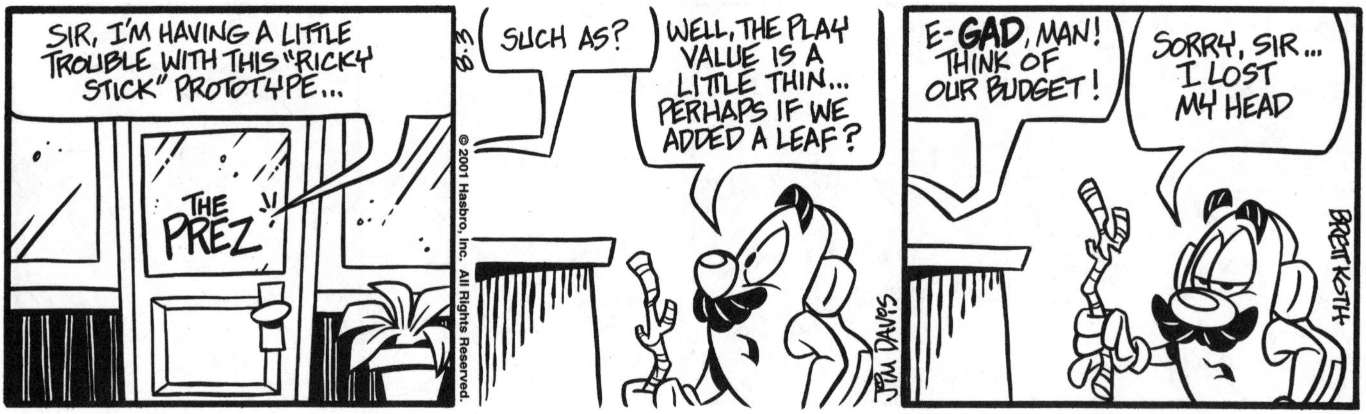
SIR, I'M HAVING A LITTLE TROUBLE WITH THIS "RICKY STICK" PROTOTYPE...
THE PREZ
8.3
© 2001 Hasbro, Inc. All Rights Reserved.
SUCH AS?
WELL, THE PLAY VALUE IS A LITTLE THIN... PERHAPS IF WE ADDED A LEAF?
JIM DAVIS
E-GAD, MAN! THINK OF OUR BUDGET!
SORRY, SIR... I LOST MY HEAD
BRETT KOTH

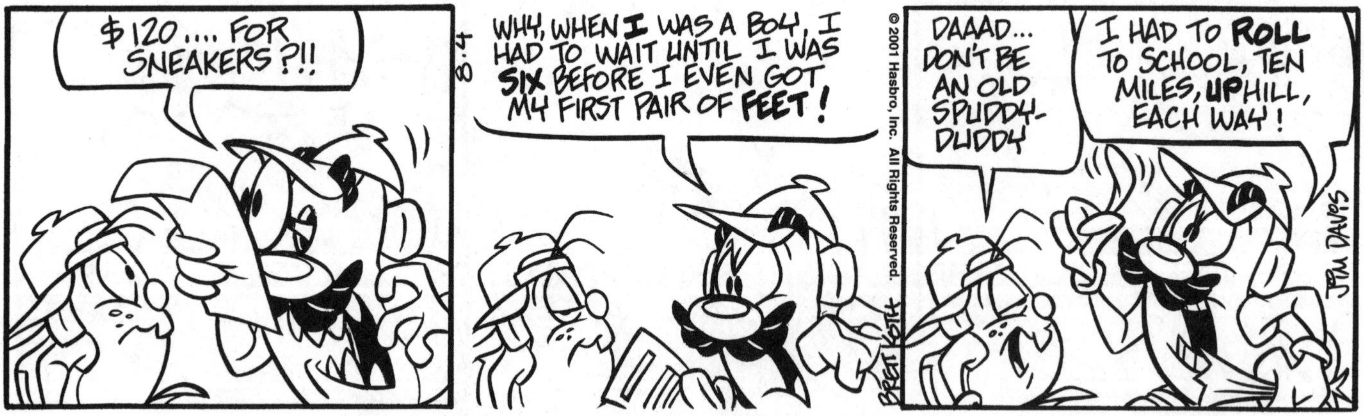
$120.... FOR SNEAKERS?!!
8.4
WHY, WHEN I WAS A BOY, I HAD TO WAIT UNTIL I WAS SIX BEFORE I EVEN GOT MY FIRST PAIR OF FEET!
BRETT KOTH
© 2001 Hasbro, Inc. All Rights Reserved.
DAAAD... DON'T BE AN OLD SPUDDY-DUDDY
I HAD TO ROLL TO SCHOOL, TEN MILES, UPHILL, EACH WAY!
JIM DAVIS

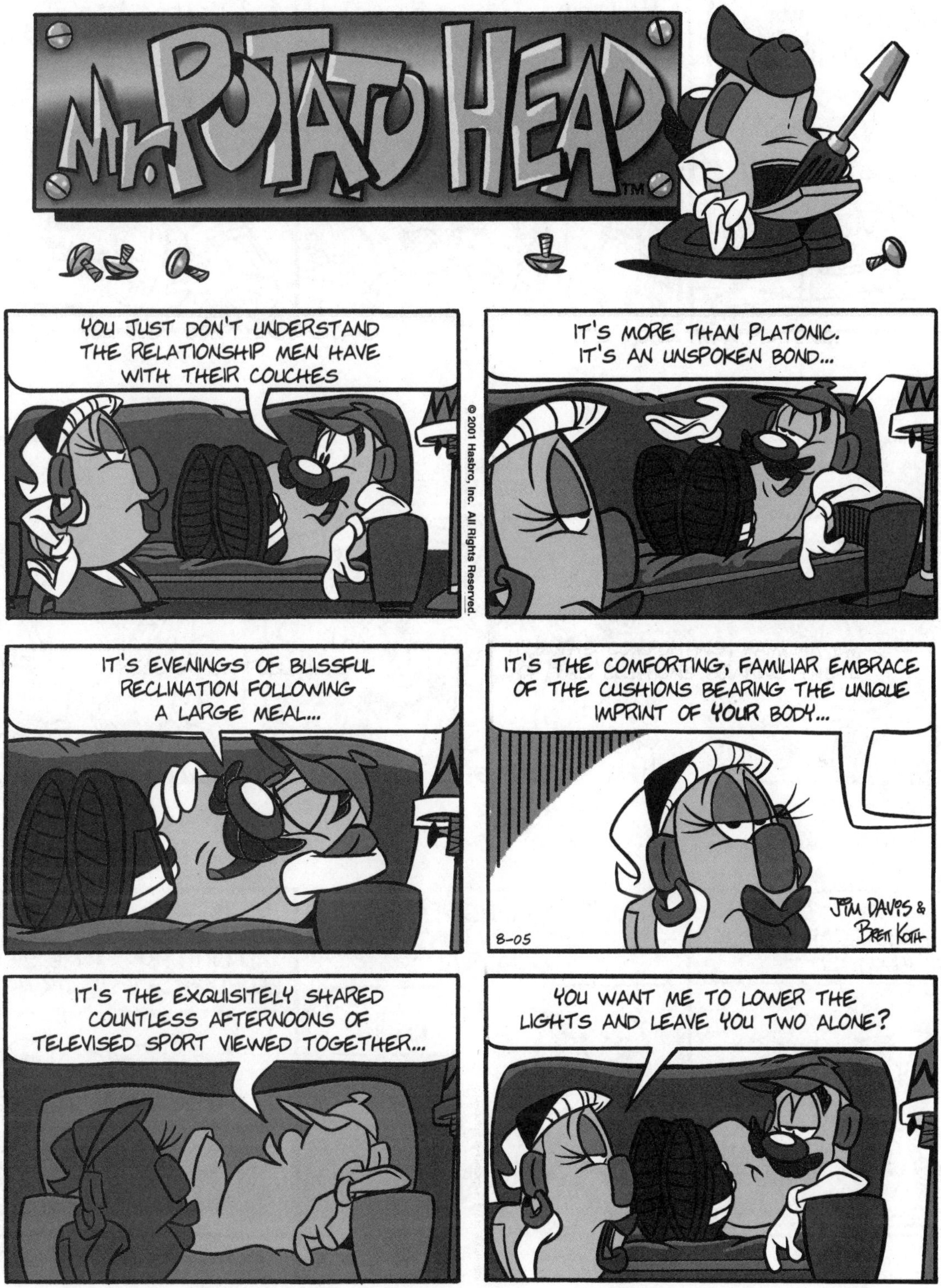
Mr. POTATO HEAD™
YOU JUST DON'T UNDERSTAND THE RELATIONSHIP MEN HAVE WITH THEIR COUCHES
IT'S MORE THAN PLATONIC. IT'S AN UNSPOKEN BOND...
IT'S EVENINGS OF BLISSFUL RECLINATION FOLLOWING A LARGE MEAL...
IT'S THE COMFORTING, FAMILIAR EMBRACE OF THE CUSHIONS BEARING THE UNIQUE IMPRINT OF YOUR BODY...
8-05
JIM DAVIS & BRETT KOTH
IT'S THE EXQUISITELY SHARED COUNTLESS AFTERNOONS OF TELEVISED SPORT VIEWED TOGETHER...
YOU WANT ME TO LOWER THE LIGHTS AND LEAVE YOU TWO ALONE?

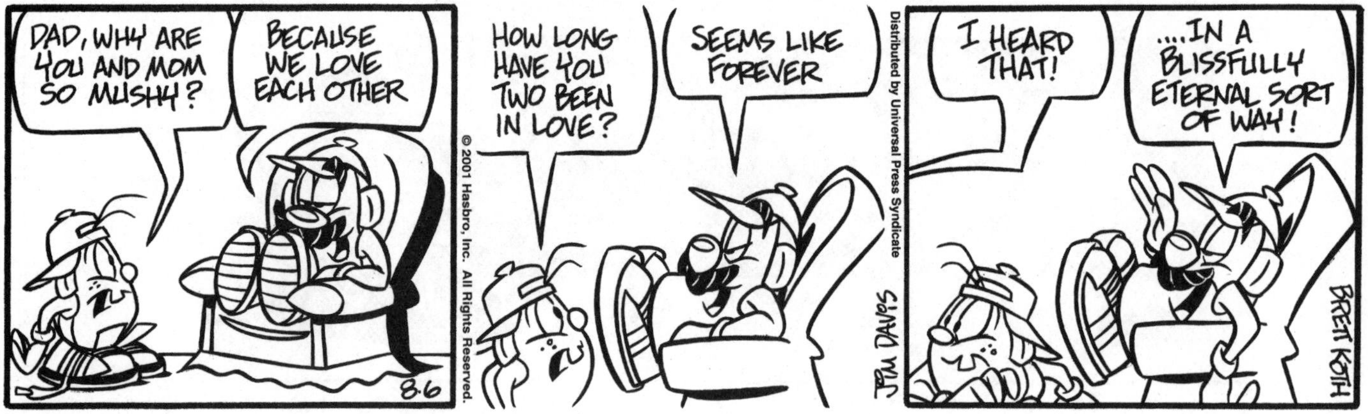
DAD, WHY ARE YOU AND MOM SO MUSHY?
BECAUSE WE LOVE EACH OTHER
8-6
© 2001 Hasbro, Inc. All Rights Reserved.
HOW LONG HAVE YOU TWO BEEN IN LOVE?
SEEMS LIKE FOREVER
Distributed by Universal Press Syndicate
JIM DAVIS
I HEARD THAT!
....IN A BLISSFULLY ETERNAL SORT OF WAY!
BRETT KOTH

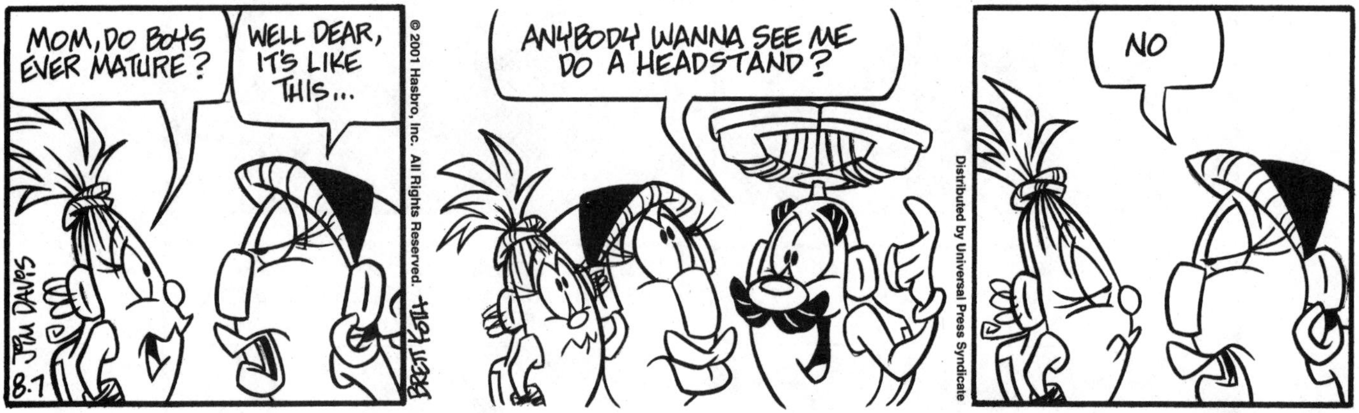
MOM, DO BOYS EVER MATURE?
WELL DEAR, IT'S LIKE THIS...
JIM DAVIS
8-7
© 2001 Hasbro, Inc. All Rights Reserved.
BRETT KOTH
ANYBODY WANNA SEE ME DO A HEADSTAND?
Distributed by Universal Press Syndicate
NO

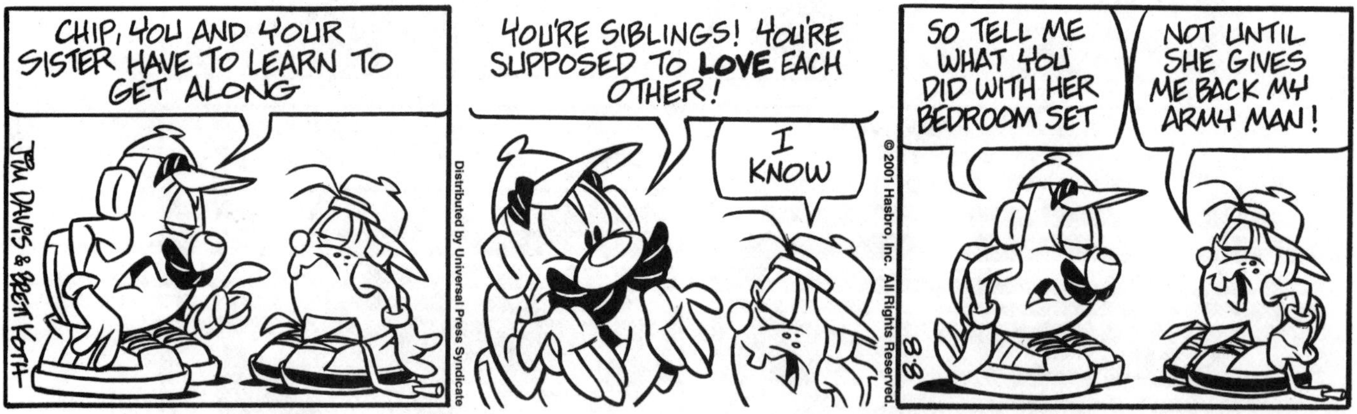
CHIP, YOU AND YOUR SISTER HAVE TO LEARN TO GET ALONG
JIM DAVIS & BRETT KOTH
Distributed by Universal Press Syndicate
YOU'RE SIBLINGS! YOU'RE SUPPOSED TO **LOVE** EACH OTHER!
I KNOW
© 2001 Hasbro, Inc. All Rights Reserved.
8-8
SO TELL ME WHAT YOU DID WITH HER BEDROOM SET
NOT UNTIL SHE GIVES ME BACK MY ARMY MAN!

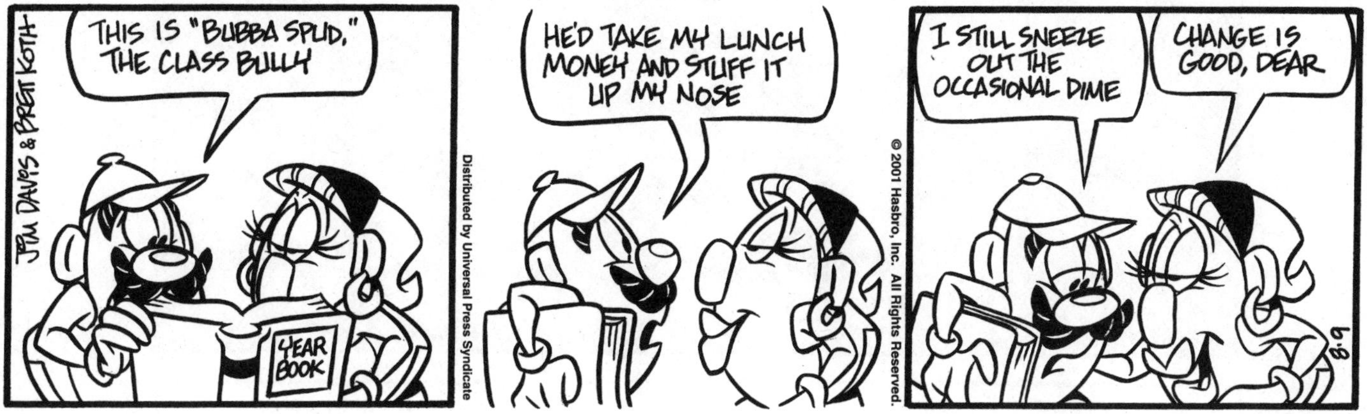
JIM DAVIS & BRETT KOTH
THIS IS "BUBBA SPUD," THE CLASS BULLY
YEAR BOOK
Distributed by Universal Press Syndicate
HE'D TAKE MY LUNCH MONEY AND STUFF IT UP MY NOSE
© 2001 Hasbro, Inc. All Rights Reserved.
I STILL SNEEZE OUT THE OCCASIONAL DIME
CHANGE IS GOOD, DEAR
8.9

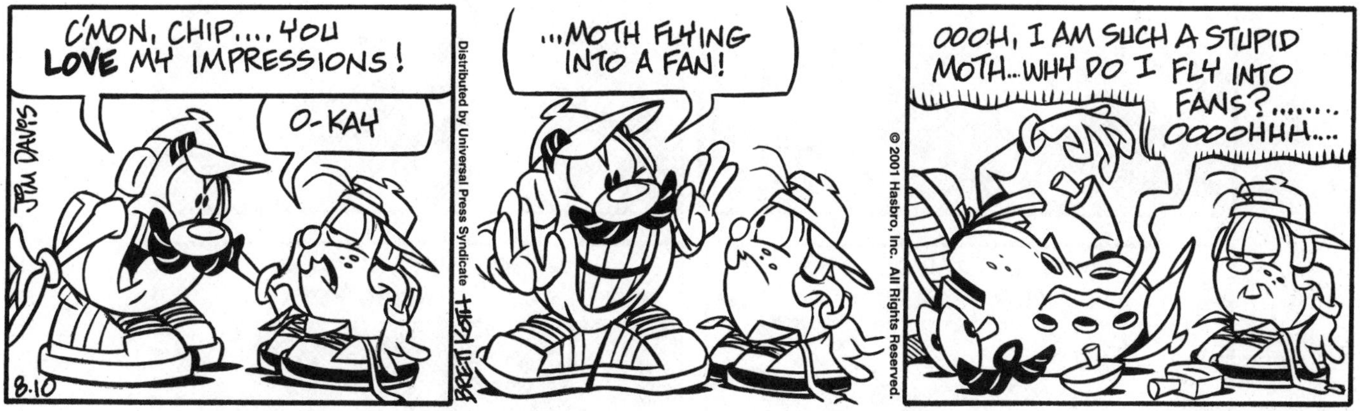
JIM DAVIS
C'MON, CHIP...., YOU **LOVE** MY IMPRESSIONS!
O-KAY
8.10
Distributed by Universal Press Syndicate
BRETT KOTH
...MOTH FLYING INTO A FAN!
© 2001 Hasbro, Inc. All Rights Reserved.
OOOH, I AM SUCH A STUPID MOTH...WHY DO I FLY INTO FANS?........ OOOOHHH....

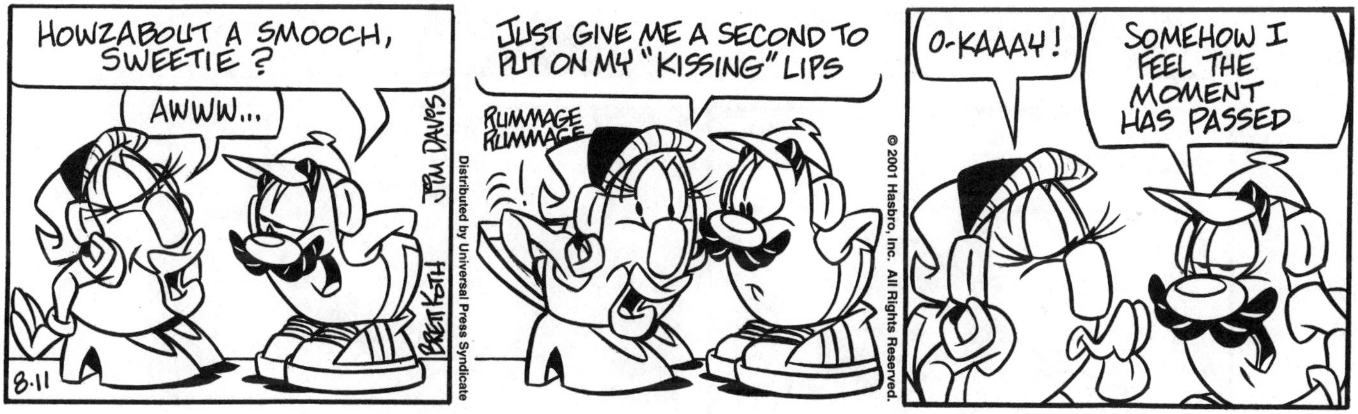
HOWZABOUT A SMOOCH, SWEETIE?
AWWW...
JIM DAVIS
BRETT KOTH
8.11
Distributed by Universal Press Syndicate
JUST GIVE ME A SECOND TO PUT ON MY "KISSING" LIPS
RUMMAGE RUMMAGE
© 2001 Hasbro, Inc. All Rights Reserved.
O-KAAAY!
SOMEHOW I FEEL THE MOMENT HAS PASSED

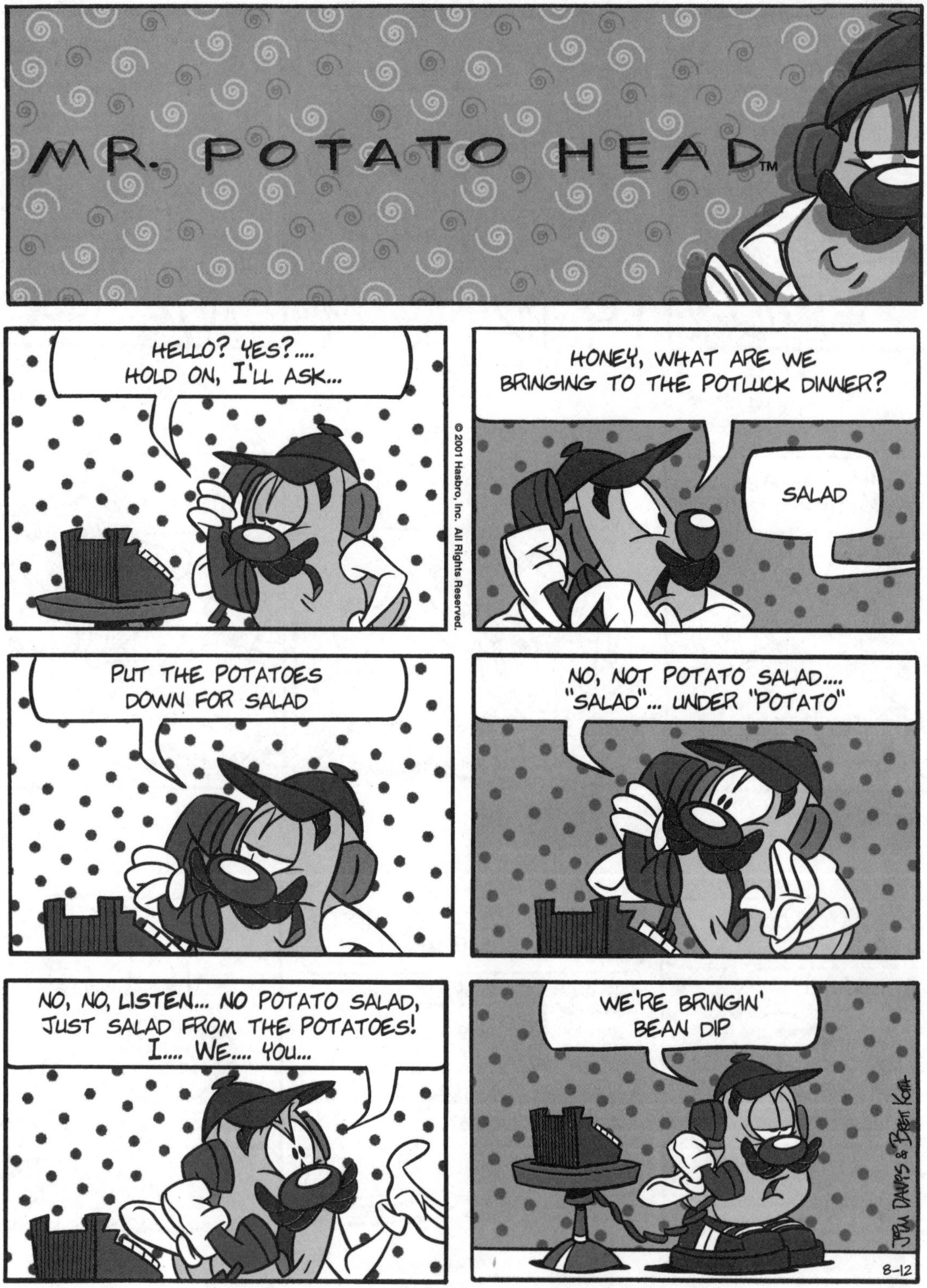
MR. POTATO HEAD™
HELLO? YES?.... HOLD ON, I'LL ASK...
HONEY, WHAT ARE WE BRINGING TO THE POTLUCK DINNER?
SALAD
PUT THE POTATOES DOWN FOR SALAD
NO, NOT POTATO SALAD.... "SALAD"... UNDER "POTATO"
NO, NO, LISTEN... NO POTATO SALAD, JUST SALAD FROM THE POTATOES! I.... WE.... YOU...
WE'RE BRINGIN' BEAN DIP
8-12

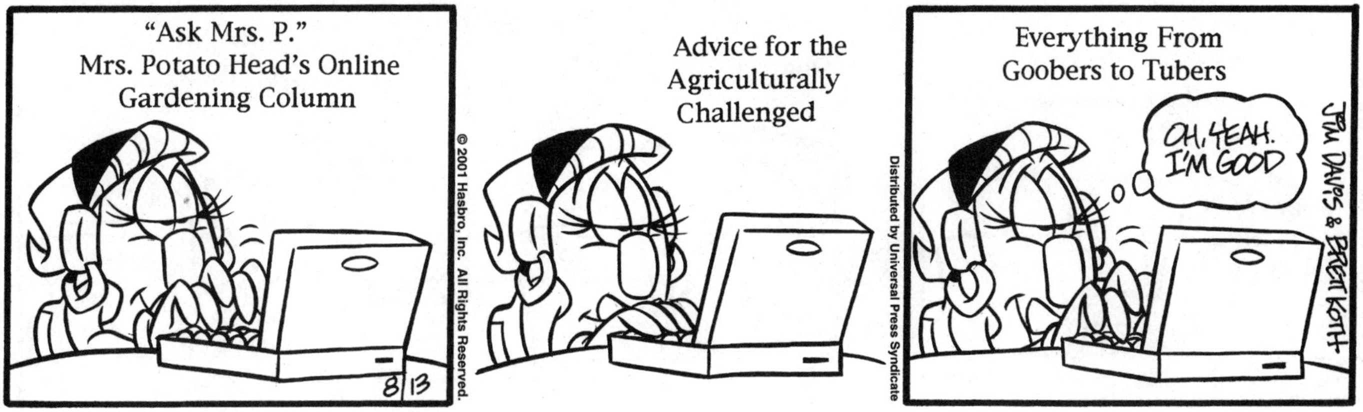
"Ask Mrs. P."
Mrs. Potato Head's Online Gardening Column
© 2001 Hasbro, Inc. All Rights Reserved.
8/13
Advice for the Agriculturally Challenged
Distributed by Universal Press Syndicate
Everything From Goobers to Tubers
OH, YEAH. I'M GOOD
JIM DAVIS & BRETT KOTH

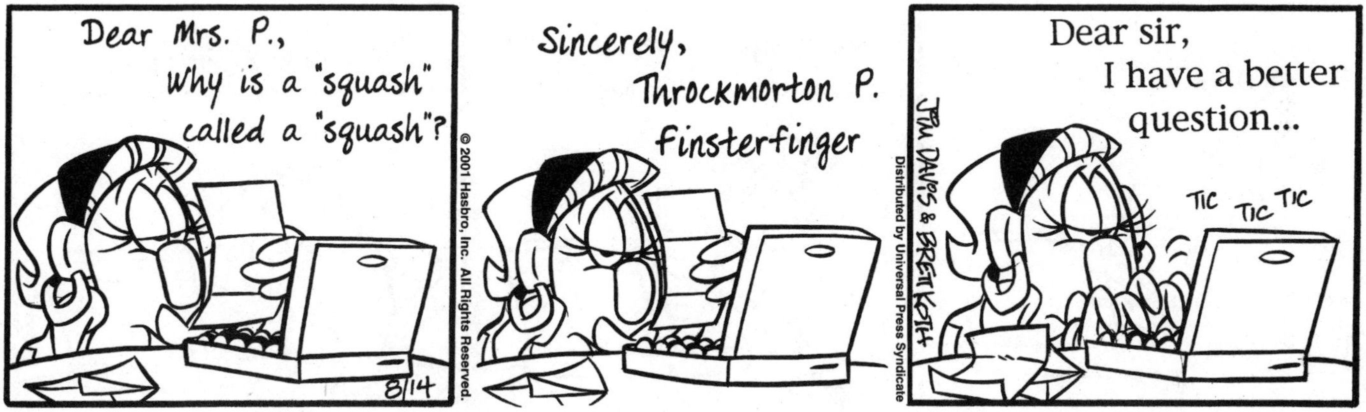
Dear Mrs. P.,
Why is a "squash" called a "squash"?
8/14
© 2001 Hasbro, Inc. All Rights Reserved.
Sincerely,
Throckmorton P. Finsterfinger
Distributed by Universal Press Syndicate
JIM DAVIS & BRETT KOTH
Dear sir,
I have a better question...
TIC TIC TIC

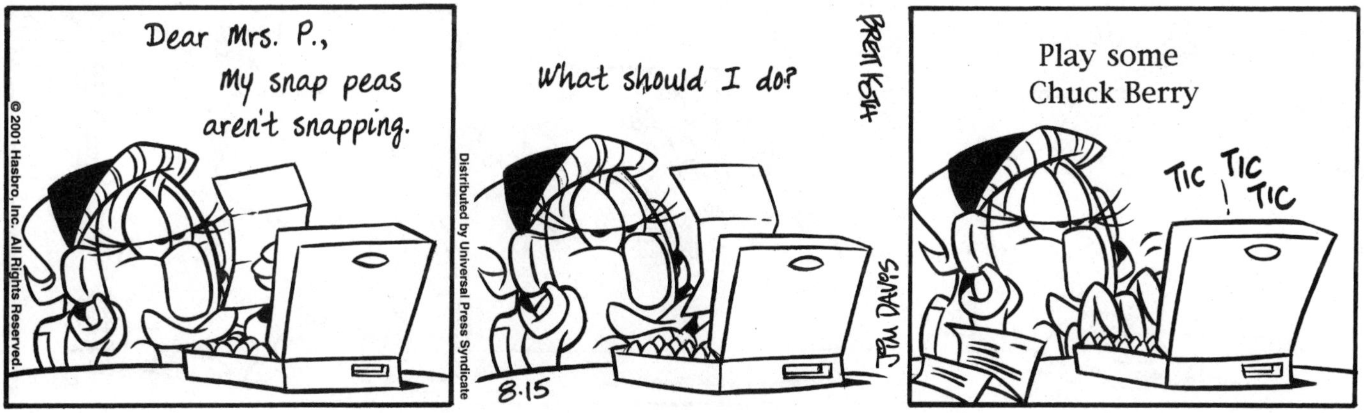
© 2001 Hasbro, Inc. All Rights Reserved.
Dear Mrs. P.,
My snap peas aren't snapping.
Distributed by Universal Press Syndicate
What should I do?
8.15
BRETT KOTH
JIM DAVIS
Play some Chuck Berry
TIC TIC TIC

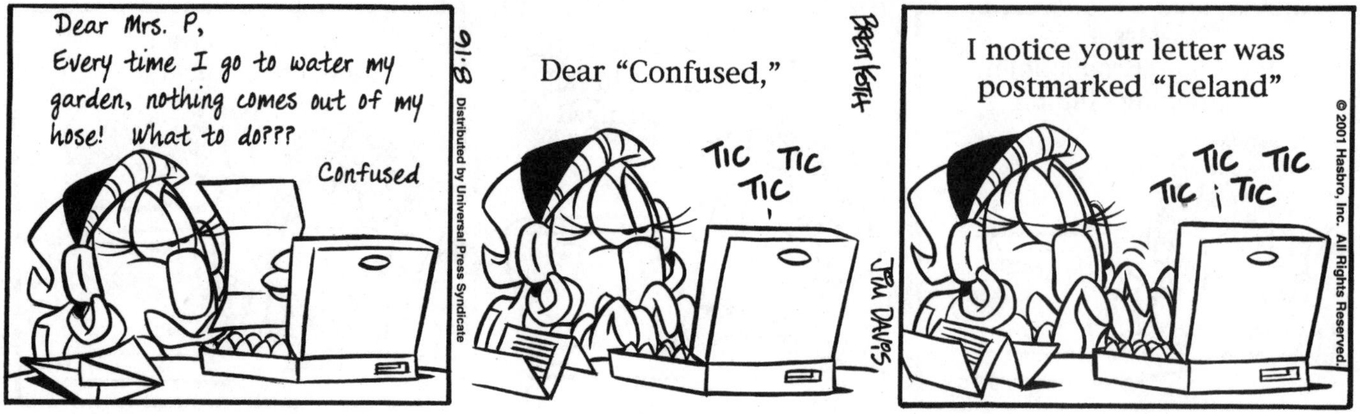
Dear Mrs. P,
Every time I go to water my garden, nothing comes out of my hose! What to do???
Confused
8.16
Distributed by Universal Press Syndicate
Dear "Confused,"
TIC TIC TIC
BRETT KOTH
JIM DAVIS
I notice your letter was postmarked "Iceland"
TIC TIC TIC TIC
© 2001 Hasbro, Inc. All Rights Reserved.

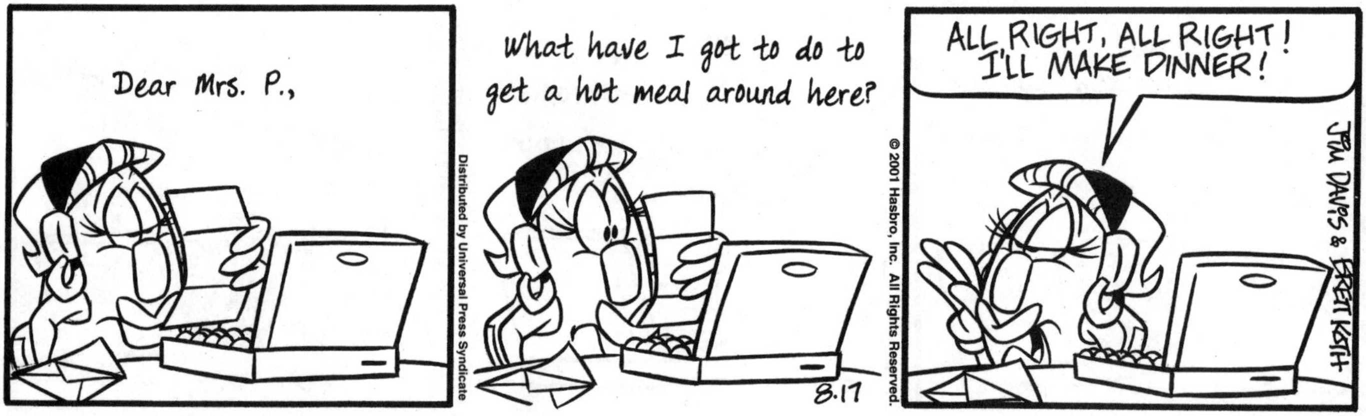
Dear Mrs. P.,
Distributed by Universal Press Syndicate
What have I got to do to get a hot meal around here?
8.17
© 2001 Hasbro, Inc. All Rights Reserved.
ALL RIGHT, ALL RIGHT! I'LL MAKE DINNER!
JIM DAVIS & BRETT KOTH

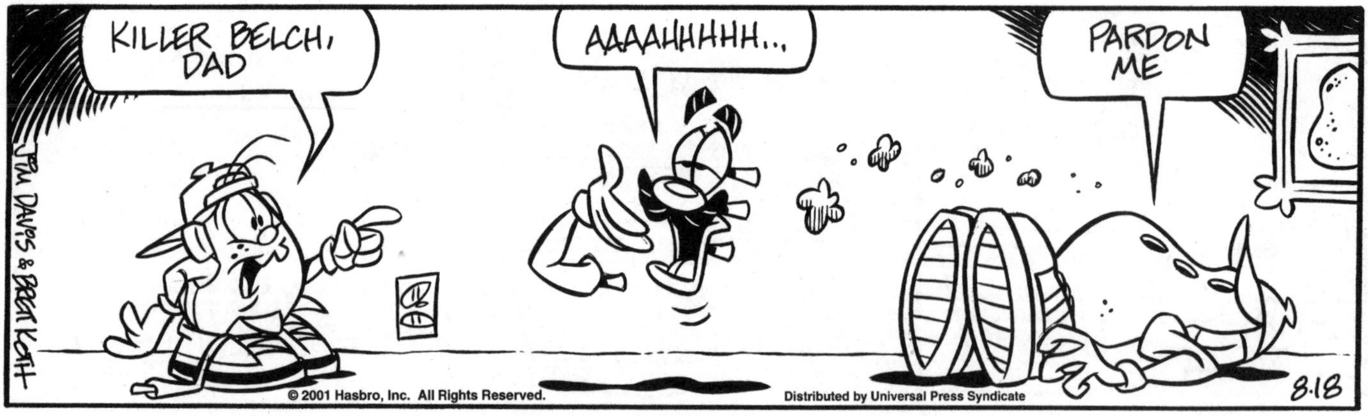
JIM DAVIS & BRETT KOTH
KILLER BELCH, DAD
AAAAHHHHH...
PARDON ME
© 2001 Hasbro, Inc. All Rights Reserved.
Distributed by Universal Press Syndicate
8.18

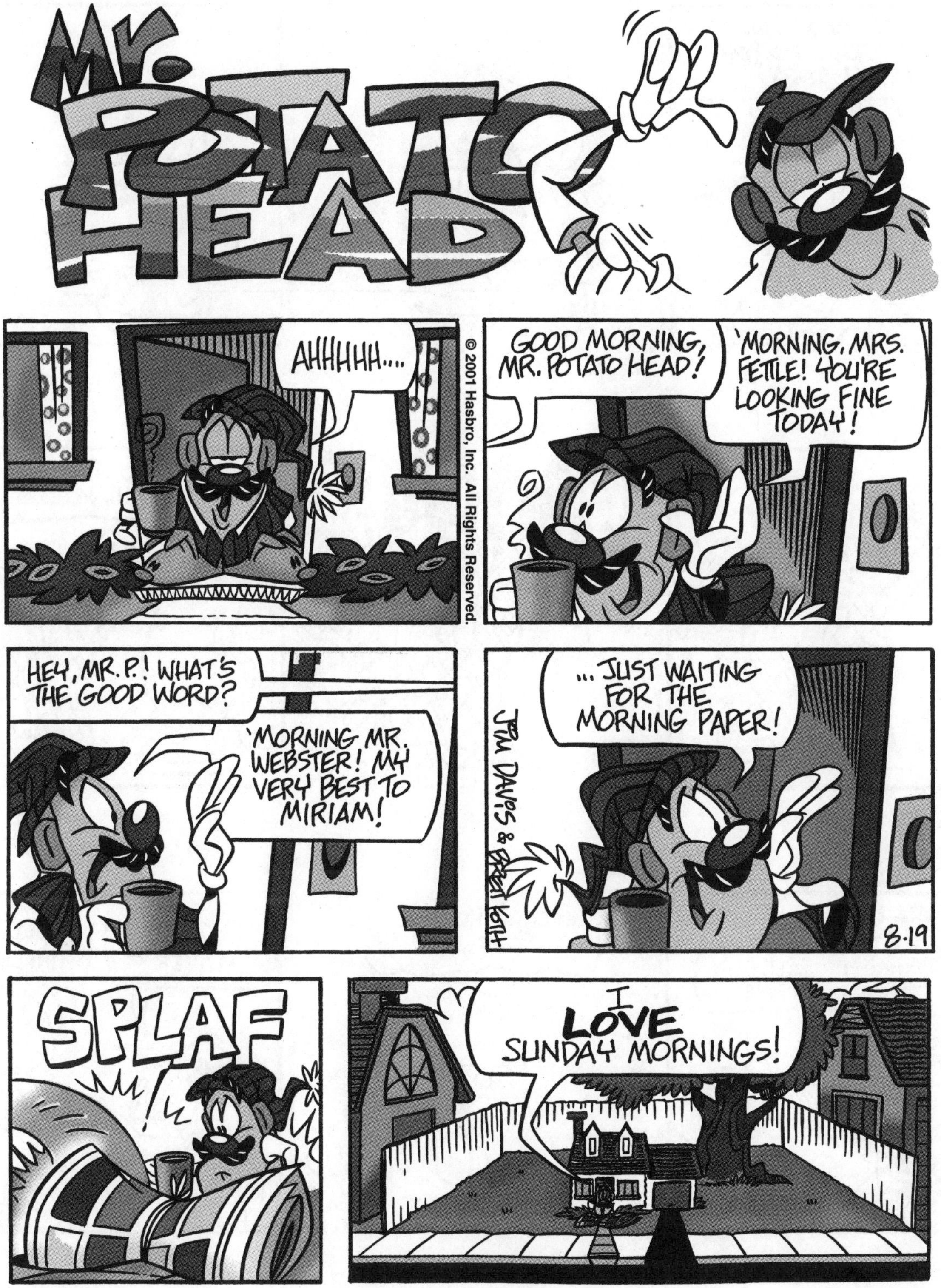
MR. POTATO HEAD
© 2001 Hasbro, Inc. All Rights Reserved.
AHHHHH....
GOOD MORNING, MR. POTATO HEAD!
'MORNING, MRS. FETTLE! YOU'RE LOOKING FINE TODAY!
HEY, MR. P.! WHAT'S THE GOOD WORD?
'MORNING MR. WEBSTER! MY VERY BEST TO MIRIAM!
JIM DAVIS & BRETT KOTH
...JUST WAITING FOR THE MORNING PAPER!
8.19
SPLAF
I LOVE SUNDAY MORNINGS!

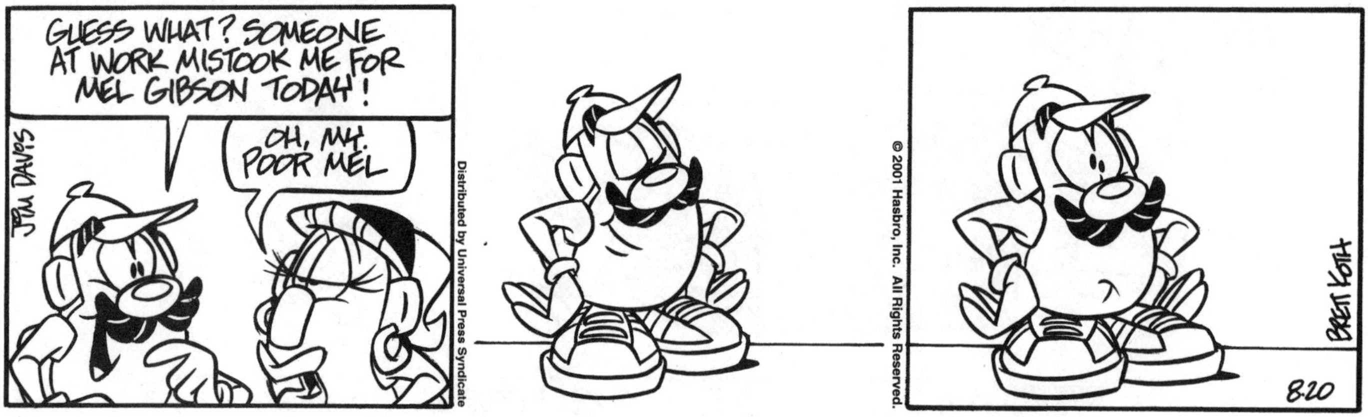
GUESS WHAT? SOMEONE AT WORK MISTOOK ME FOR MEL GIBSON TODAY!
OH, MY. POOR MEL
JIM DAVIS
Distributed by Universal Press Syndicate
© 2001 Hasbro, Inc. All Rights Reserved.
BRETT KOTH
8·20

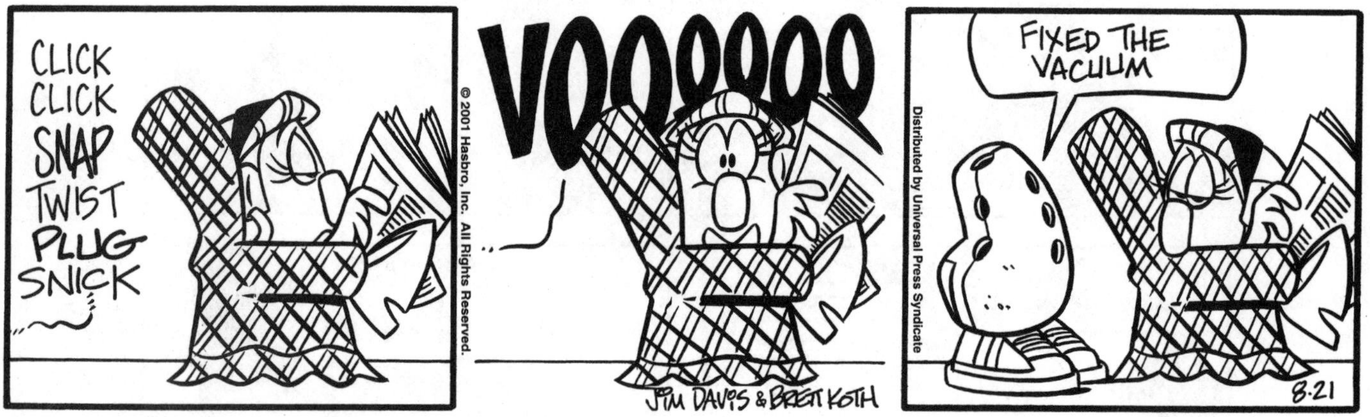
CLICK
CLICK
SNAP
TWIST
PLUG
SNICK
© 2001 Hasbro, Inc. All Rights Reserved.
VOOOOOO
JIM DAVIS & BRETT KOTH
Distributed by Universal Press Syndicate
FIXED THE VACUUM
8·21

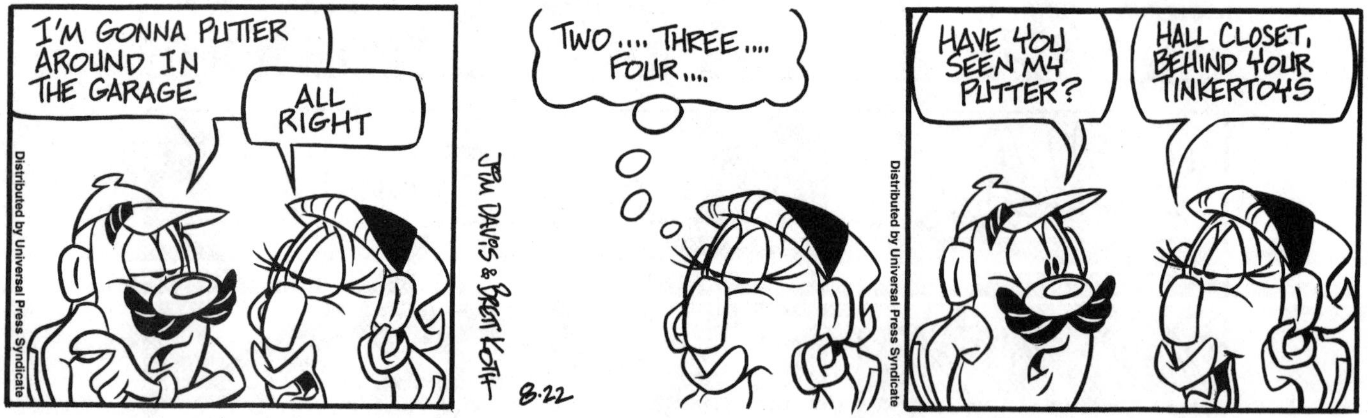
I'M GONNA PUTTER AROUND IN THE GARAGE
ALL RIGHT
Distributed by Universal Press Syndicate
JIM DAVIS & BRETT KOTH
8·22
TWO.... THREE.... FOUR....
Distributed by Universal Press Syndicate
HAVE YOU SEEN MY PUTTER?
HALL CLOSET, BEHIND YOUR TINKERTOYS

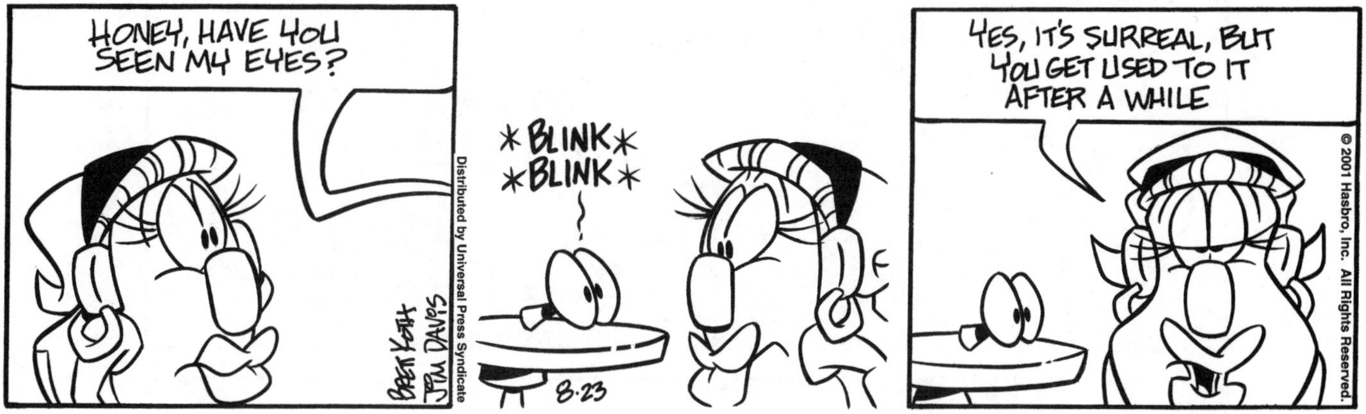
HONEY, HAVE YOU SEEN MY EYES?
BLINK *BLINK*
YES, IT'S SURREAL, BUT YOU GET USED TO IT AFTER A WHILE
Distributed by Universal Press Syndicate
© 2001 Hasbro, Inc. All Rights Reserved.

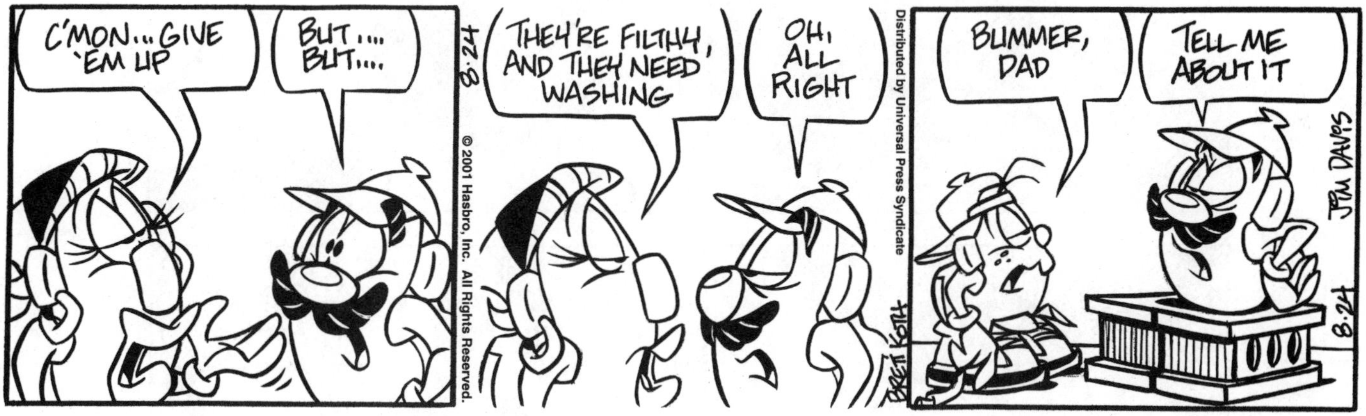
C'MON... GIVE 'EM UP
BUT.... BUT....
THEY'RE FILTHY, AND THEY NEED WASHING
OH, ALL RIGHT
BUMMER, DAD
TELL ME ABOUT IT
© 2001 Hasbro, Inc. All Rights Reserved.
Distributed by Universal Press Syndicate

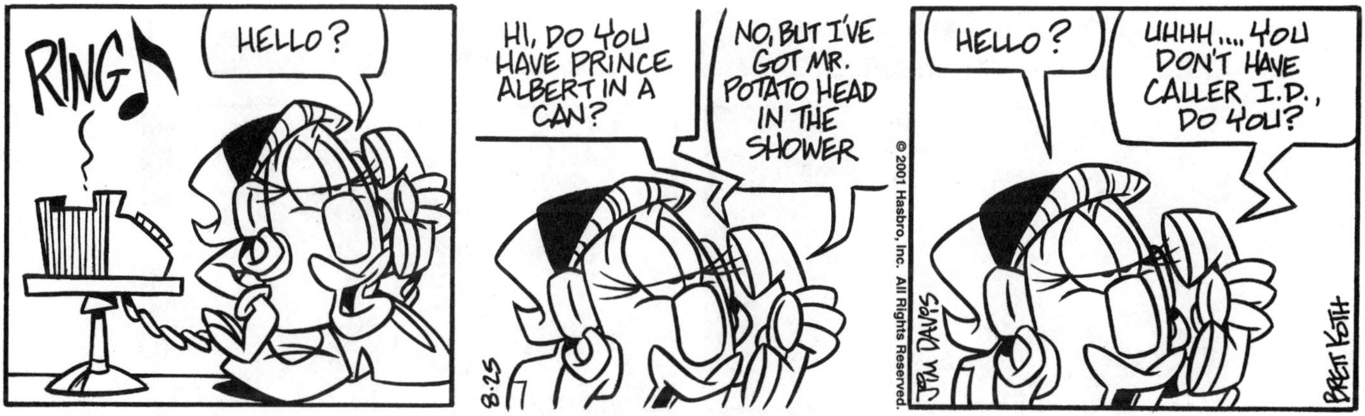
RING
HELLO?
HI, DO YOU HAVE PRINCE ALBERT IN A CAN?
NO, BUT I'VE GOT MR. POTATO HEAD IN THE SHOWER
HELLO?
UHHH.... YOU DON'T HAVE CALLER I.D., DO YOU?
© 2001 Hasbro, Inc. All Rights Reserved.

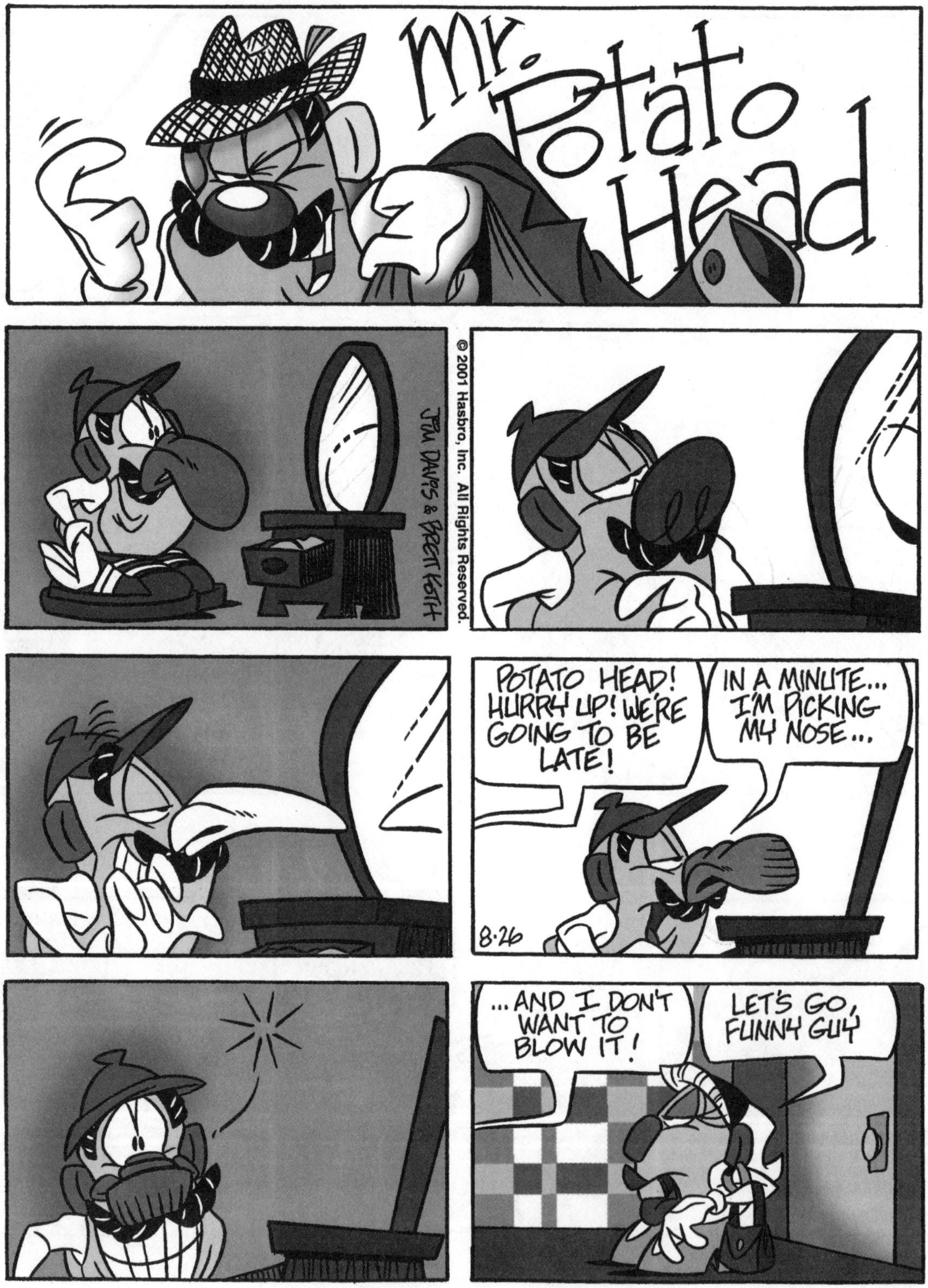
Mr. Potato Head
© 2001 Hasbro, Inc. All Rights Reserved.
JIM DAVIS & BRETT KOTH
POTATO HEAD! HURRY UP! WE'RE GOING TO BE LATE!
IN A MINUTE... I'M PICKING MY NOSE...
8·26
...AND I DON'T WANT TO BLOW IT!
LET'S GO, FUNNY GUY

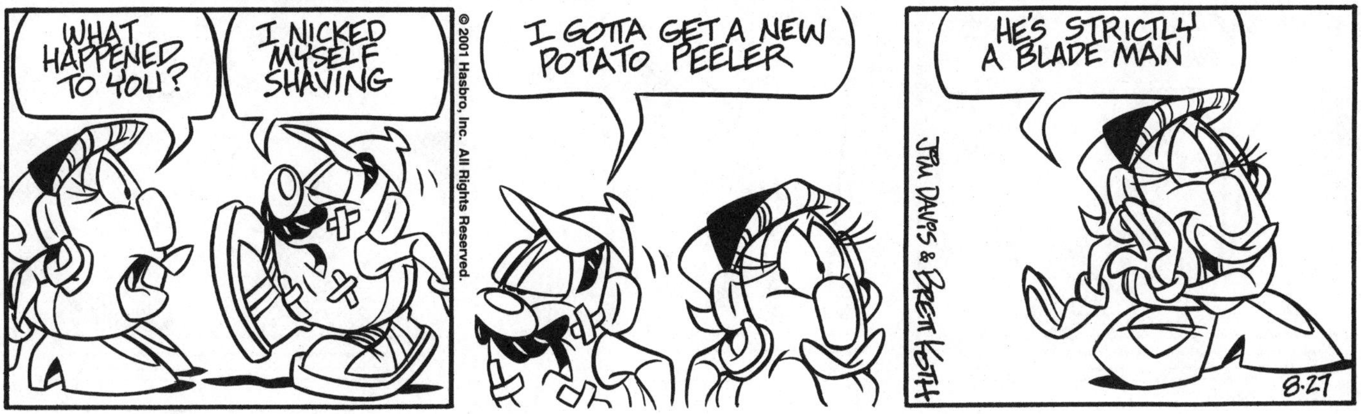
WHAT HAPPENED TO YOU?
I NICKED MYSELF SHAVING
© 2001 Hasbro, Inc. All Rights Reserved.
I GOTTA GET A NEW POTATO PEELER
JIM DAVIS & BRETT KOTH
HE'S STRICTLY A BLADE MAN
8-27

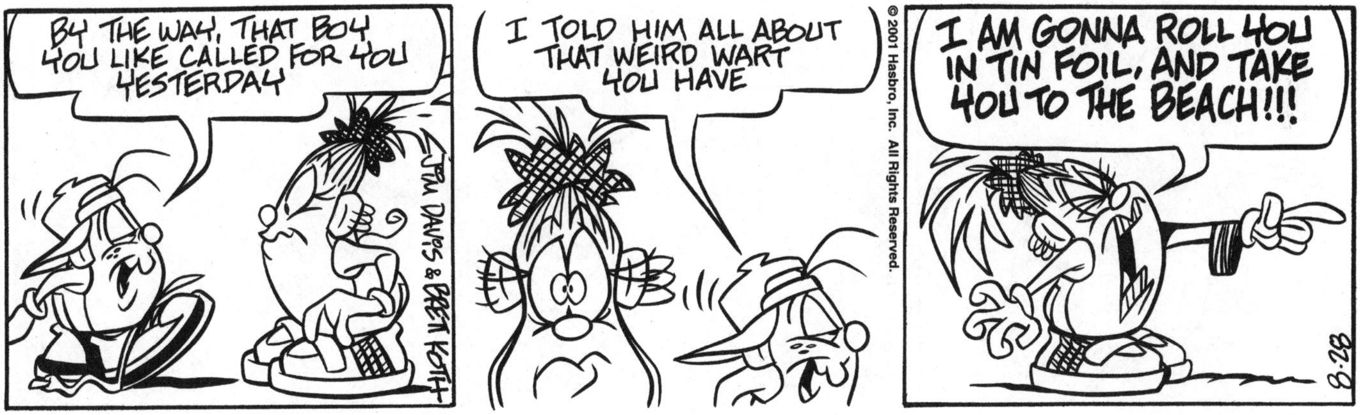
BY THE WAY, THAT BOY YOU LIKE CALLED FOR YOU YESTERDAY
JIM DAVIS & BRETT KOTH
I TOLD HIM ALL ABOUT THAT WEIRD WART YOU HAVE
© 2001 Hasbro, Inc. All Rights Reserved.
I AM GONNA ROLL YOU IN TIN FOIL, AND TAKE YOU TO THE BEACH!!!
8-28

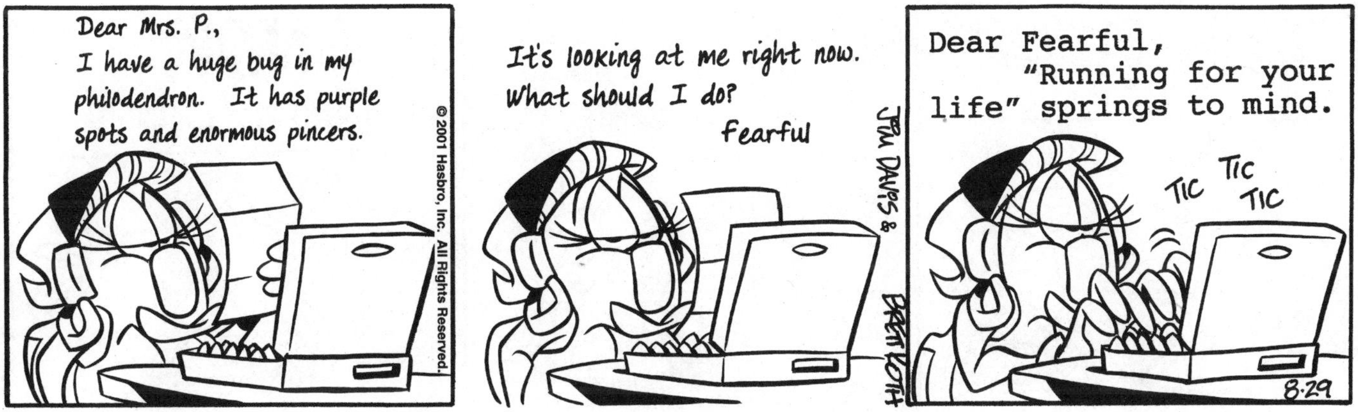
Dear Mrs. P.,
I have a huge bug in my philodendron. It has purple spots and enormous pincers.
© 2001 Hasbro, Inc. All Rights Reserved.
It's looking at me right now. What should I do?
Fearful
JIM DAVIS & BRETT KOTH
Dear Fearful,
"Running for your life" springs to mind.
TIC TIC TIC
8-29

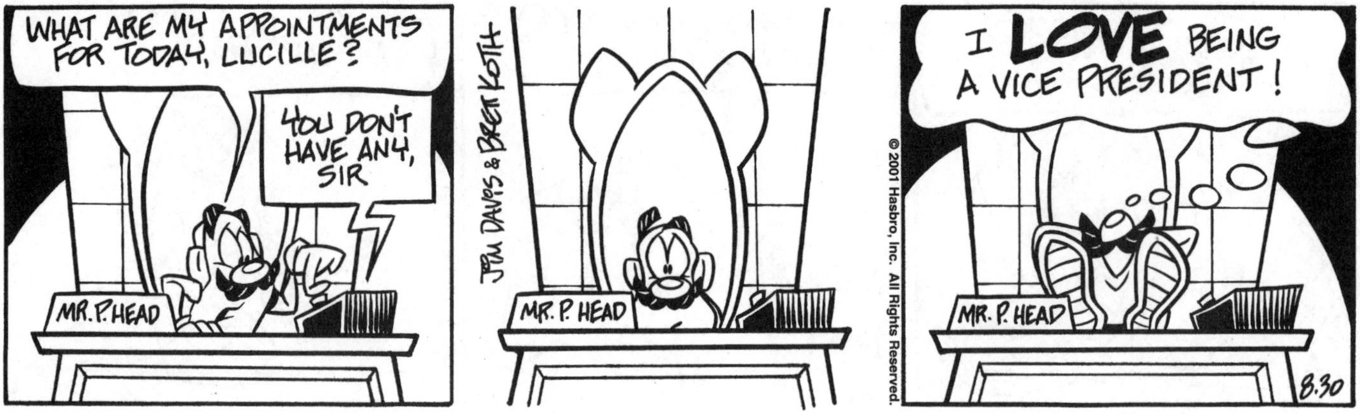
WHAT ARE MY APPOINTMENTS FOR TODAY, LUCILLE?
YOU DON'T HAVE ANY, SIR
MR. P. HEAD
JIM DAVIS & BRETT KOTH
MR. P. HEAD
© 2001 Hasbro, Inc. All Rights Reserved.
I LOVE BEING A VICE PRESIDENT!
MR. P. HEAD
8.30

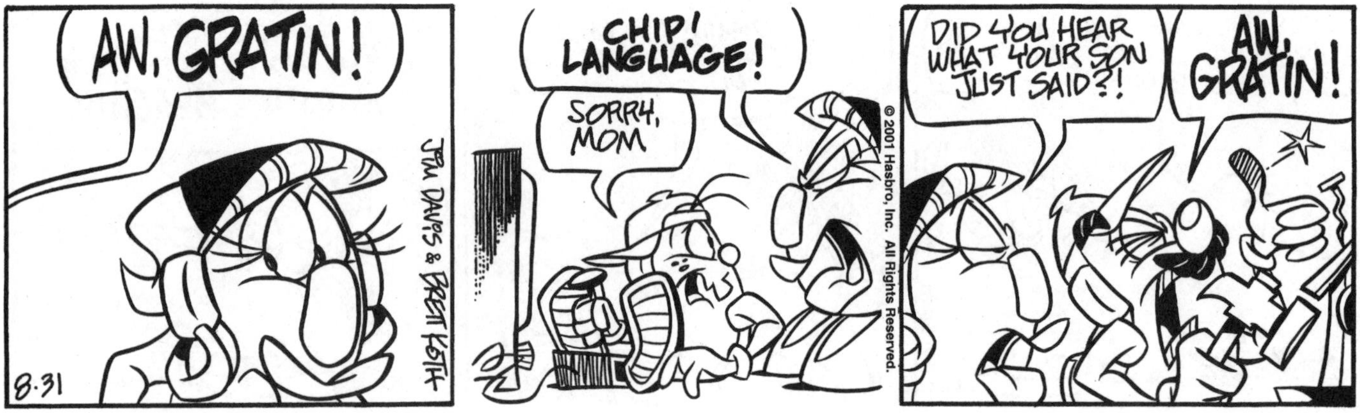
AW, GRATIN!
8.31
JIM DAVIS & BRETT KOTH
CHIP! LANGUAGE!
SORRY, MOM
© 2001 Hasbro, Inc. All Rights Reserved.
DID YOU HEAR WHAT YOUR SON JUST SAID?!
AW, GRATIN!

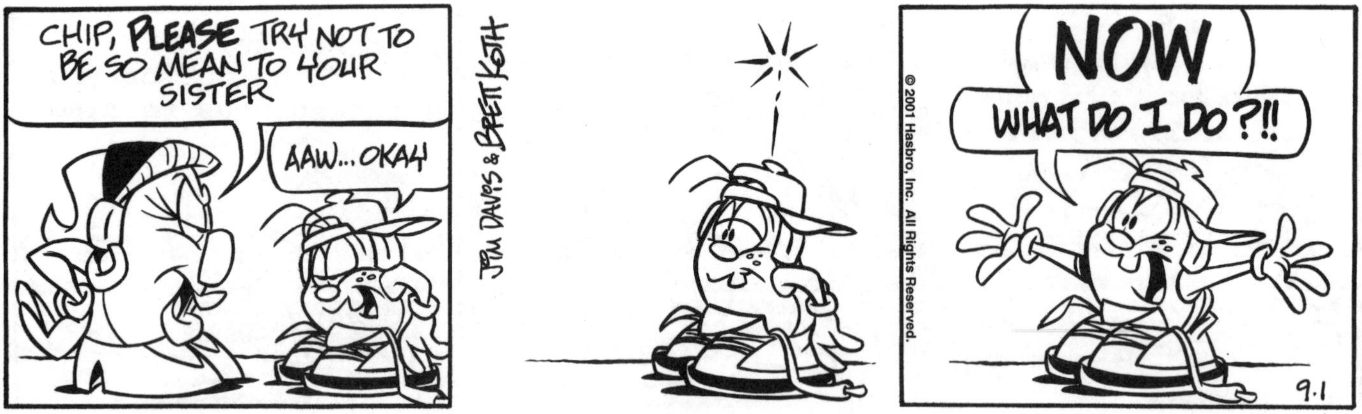
CHIP, PLEASE TRY NOT TO BE SO MEAN TO YOUR SISTER
AAW... OKAY
JIM DAVIS & BRETT KOTH
© 2001 Hasbro, Inc. All Rights Reserved.
NOW WHAT DO I DO?!!
9.1

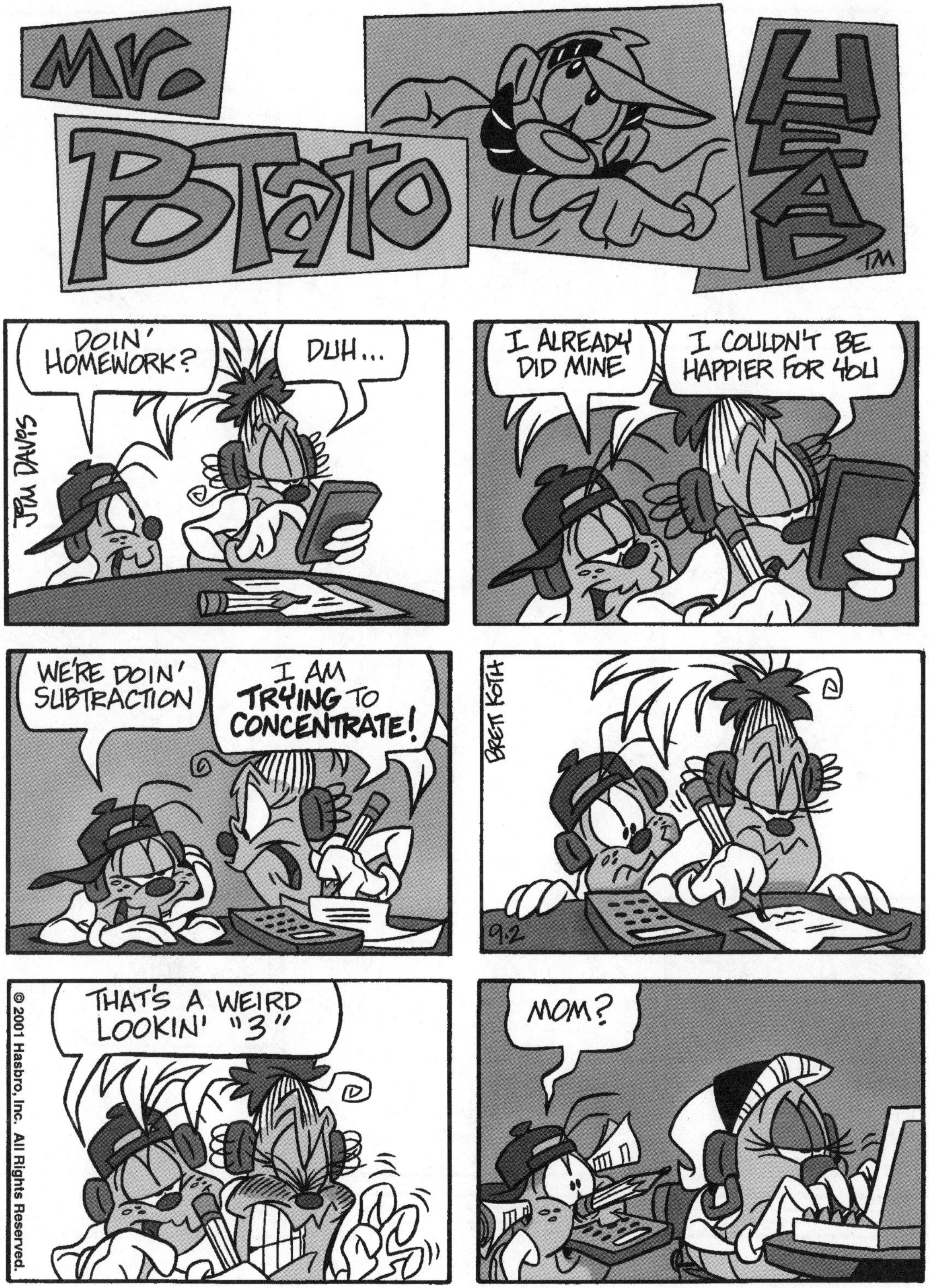
MR. POTATO HEAD™
JIM DAVIS
DOIN' HOMEWORK?
DUH...
I ALREADY DID MINE
I COULDN'T BE HAPPIER FOR YOU
WE'RE DOIN' SUBTRACTION
I AM TRYING TO CONCENTRATE!
BRETT KOTH
9.2
© 2001 Hasbro, Inc. All Rights Reserved.
THAT'S A WEIRD LOOKIN' "3"
MOM?

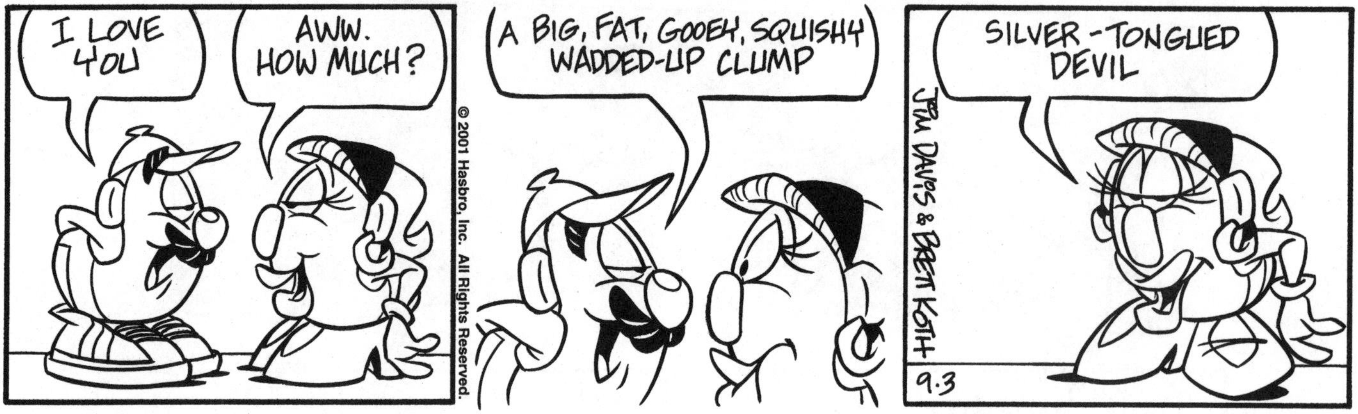
I LOVE YOU
AWW. HOW MUCH?
A BIG, FAT, GOOEY, SQUISHY WADDED-UP CLUMP
SILVER-TONGUED DEVIL
© 2001 Hasbro, Inc. All Rights Reserved.
JIM DAVIS & BRETT KOTH
9.3

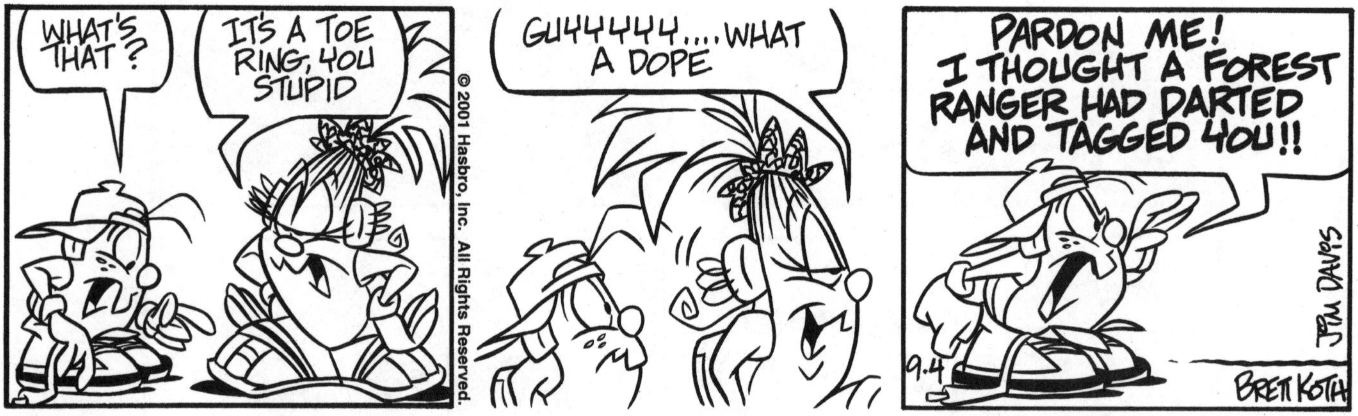
WHAT'S THAT?
IT'S A TOE RING, YOU STUPID
GUYYYYY.... WHAT A DOPE
PARDON ME! I THOUGHT A FOREST RANGER HAD DARTED AND TAGGED YOU!!
© 2001 Hasbro, Inc. All Rights Reserved.
JIM DAVIS
BRETT KOTH
9.4

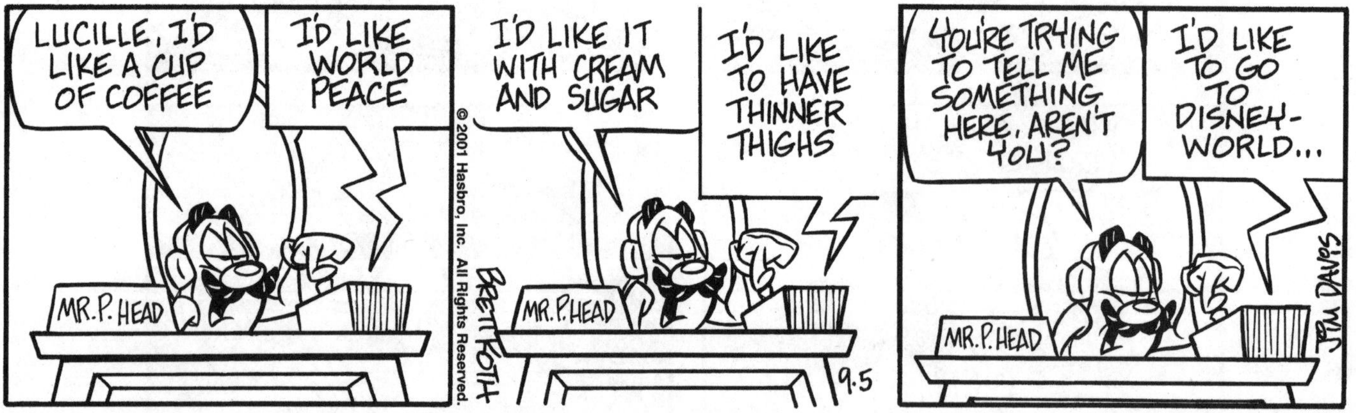
LUCILLE, I'D LIKE A CUP OF COFFEE
I'D LIKE WORLD PEACE
MR. P. HEAD
I'D LIKE IT WITH CREAM AND SUGAR
I'D LIKE TO HAVE THINNER THIGHS
YOU'RE TRYING TO TELL ME SOMETHING HERE, AREN'T YOU?
I'D LIKE TO GO TO DISNEY-WORLD...
© 2001 Hasbro, Inc. All Rights Reserved.
BRETT KOTH
JIM DAVIS
9.5

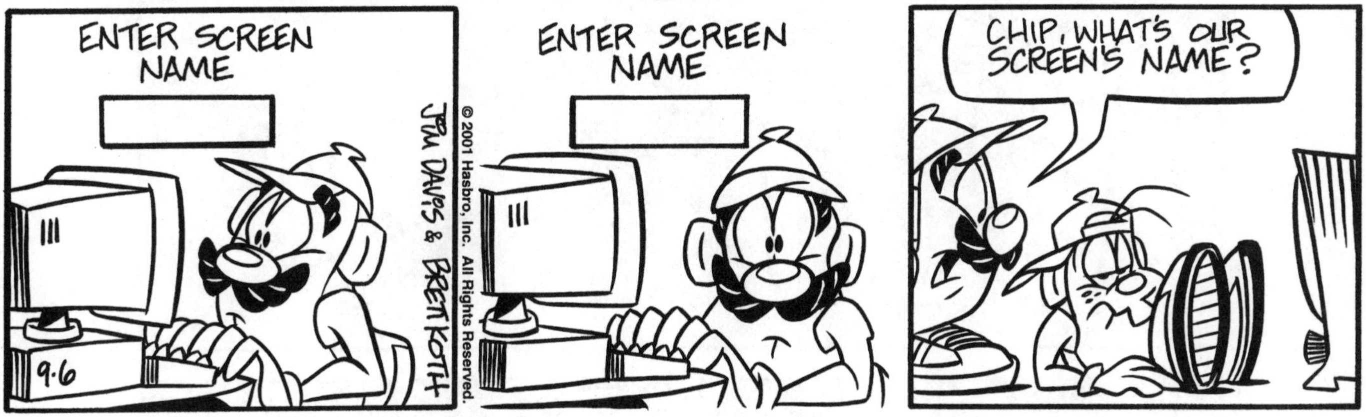
ENTER SCREEN NAME
ENTER SCREEN NAME
CHIP, WHAT'S OUR SCREEN'S NAME?
9·6
JIM DAVIS & BRETT KOTH

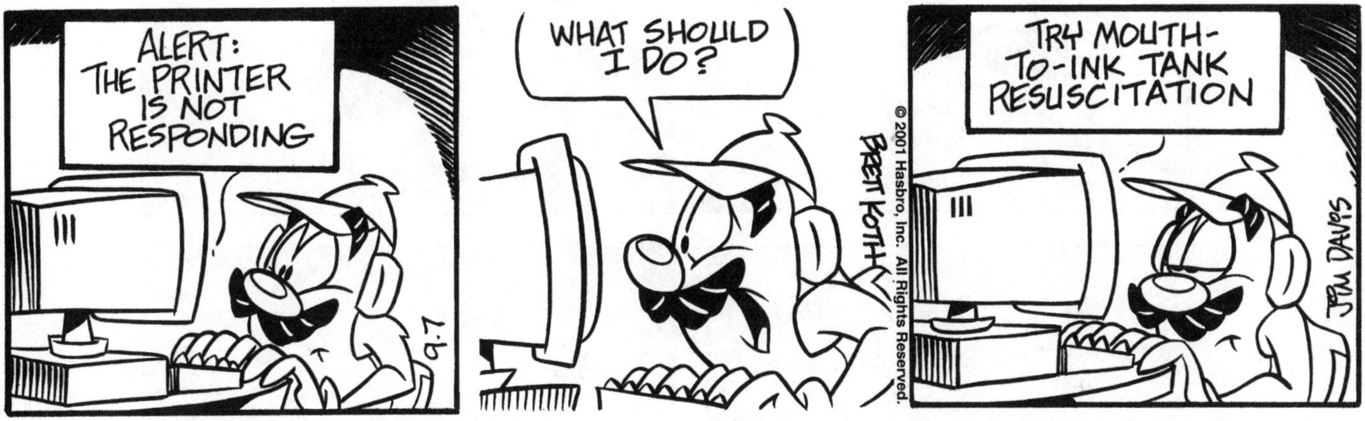
ALERT: THE PRINTER IS NOT RESPONDING
WHAT SHOULD I DO?
TRY MOUTH-TO-INK TANK RESUSCITATION
9·7
BRETT KOTH
JIM DAVIS

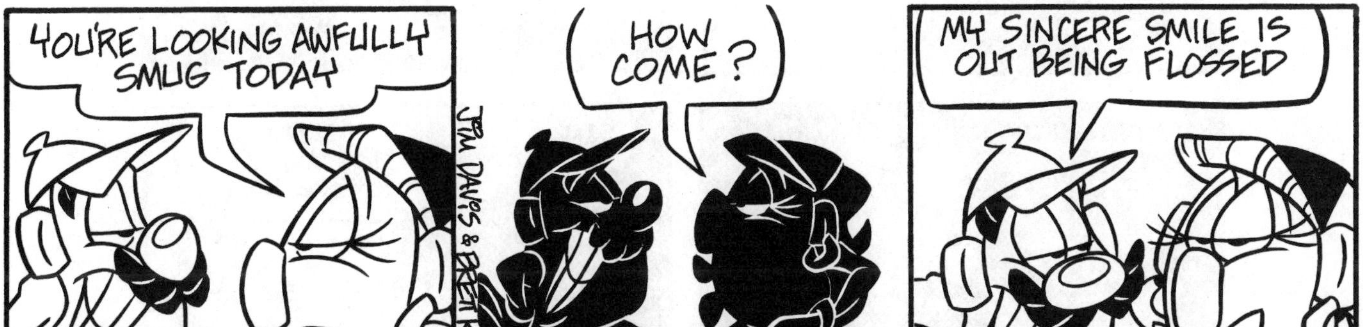
YOU'RE LOOKING AWFULLY SMUG TODAY
HOW COME?
MY SINCERE SMILE IS OUT BEING FLOSSED
JIM DAVIS & BRETT KOTH
9·8

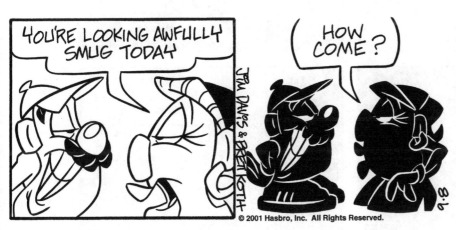

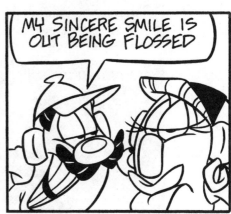

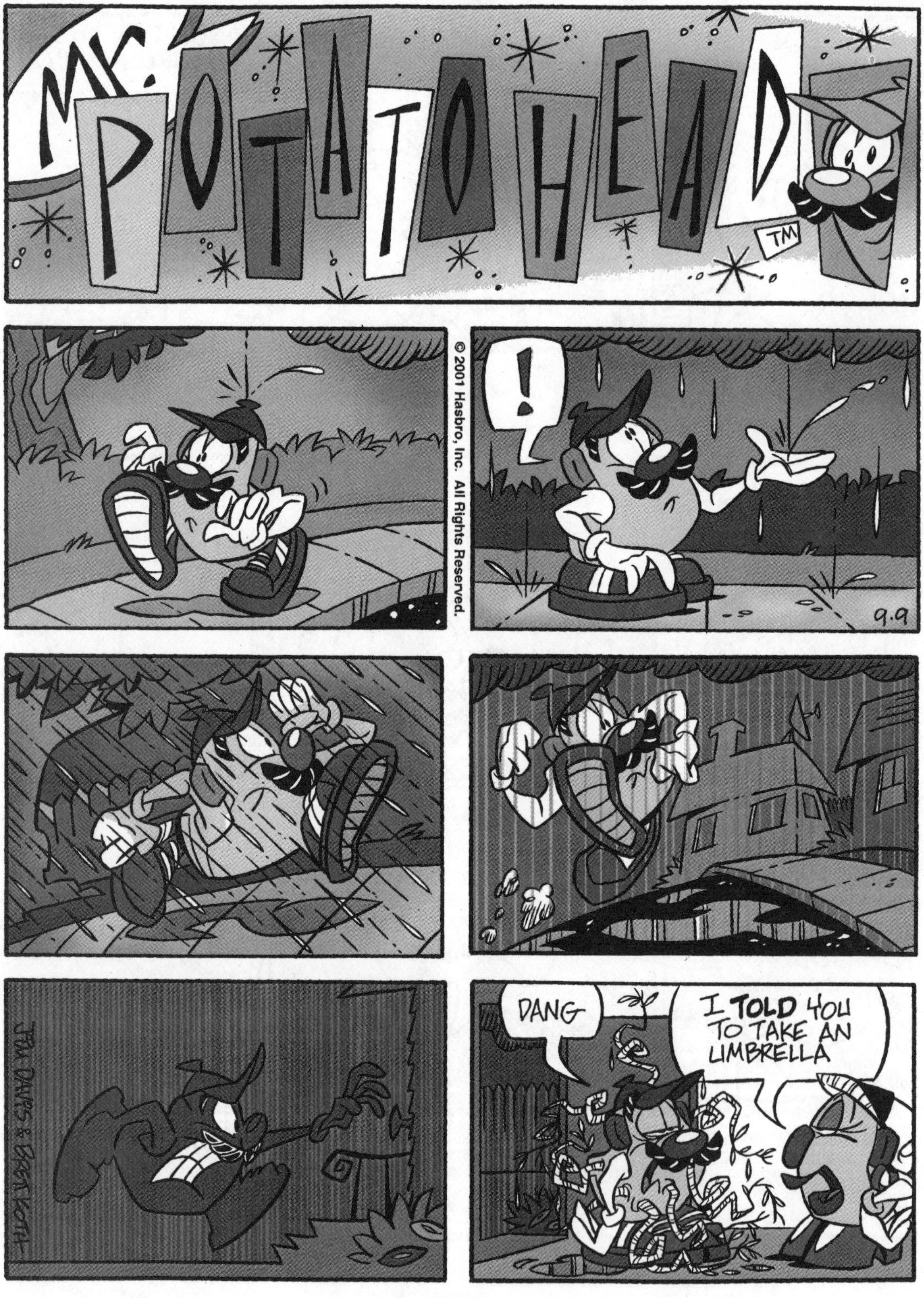
MR. POTATO HEAD TM
© 2001 Hasbro, Inc. All Rights Reserved.
!
9.9
JIM DAVIS & BRETT KOTH
DANG
I TOLD YOU TO TAKE AN UMBRELLA

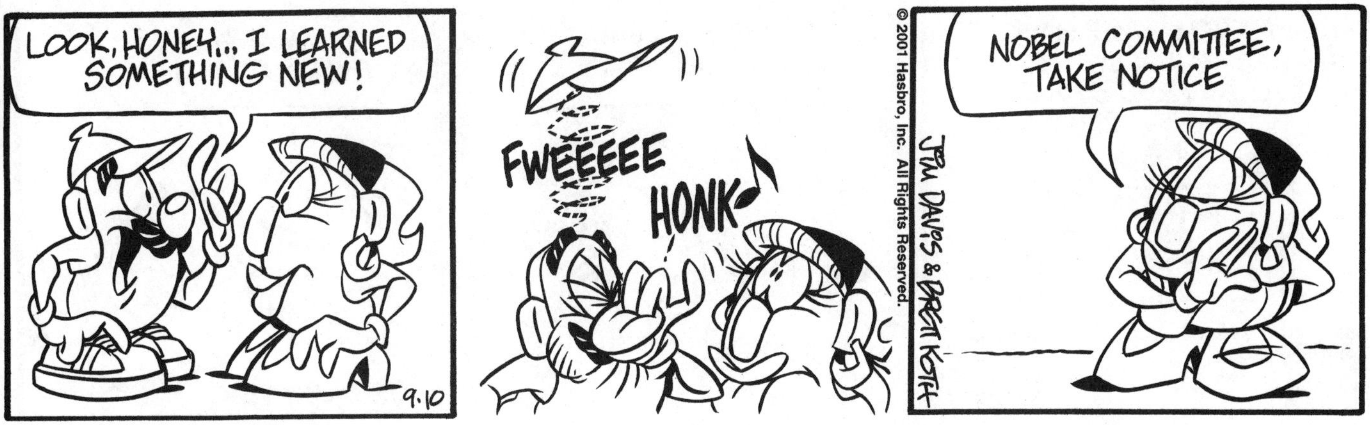
LOOK, HONEY... I LEARNED SOMETHING NEW!
9.10
FWEEEEE
HONK
© 2001 Hasbro, Inc. All Rights Reserved.
JIM DAVIS & BRETT KOTH
NOBEL COMMITTEE, TAKE NOTICE

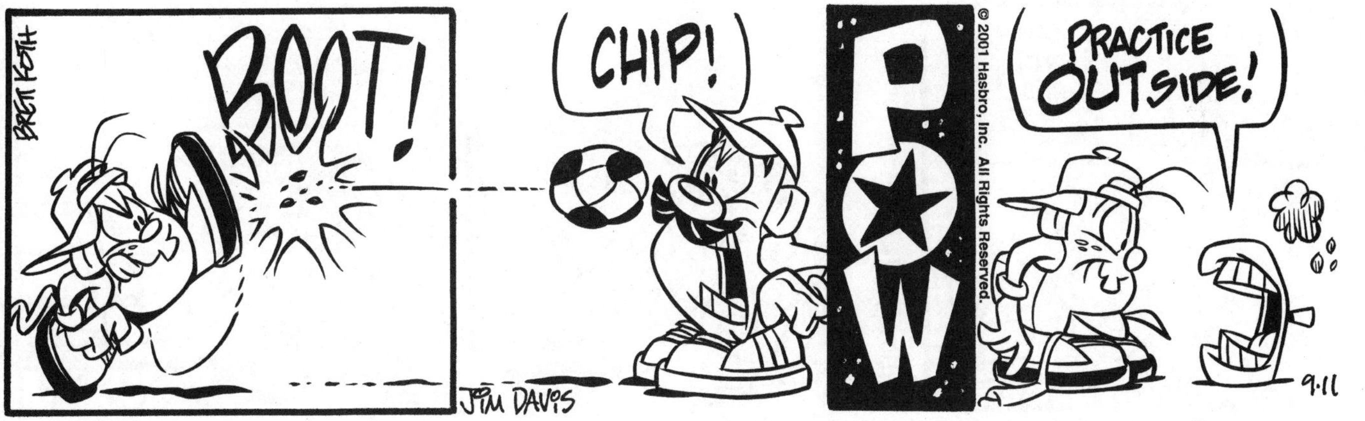
BRETT KOTH
BOOT!
JIM DAVIS
CHIP!
POW
© 2001 Hasbro, Inc. All Rights Reserved.
PRACTICE OUTSIDE!
9.11

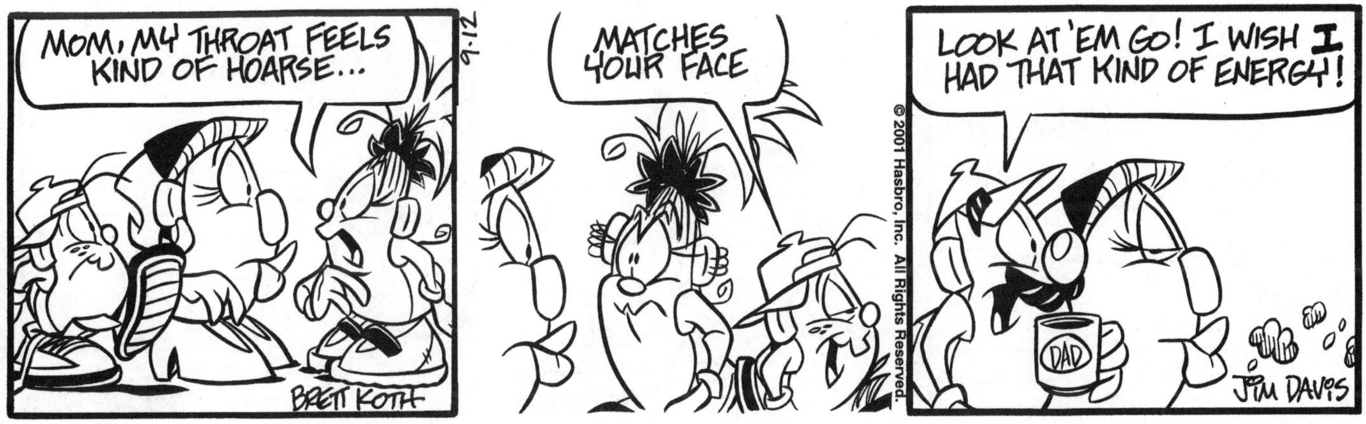
MOM, MY THROAT FEELS KIND OF HOARSE...
9.12
BRETT KOTH
MATCHES YOUR FACE
© 2001 Hasbro, Inc. All Rights Reserved.
LOOK AT 'EM GO! I WISH I HAD THAT KIND OF ENERGY!
DAD
JIM DAVIS

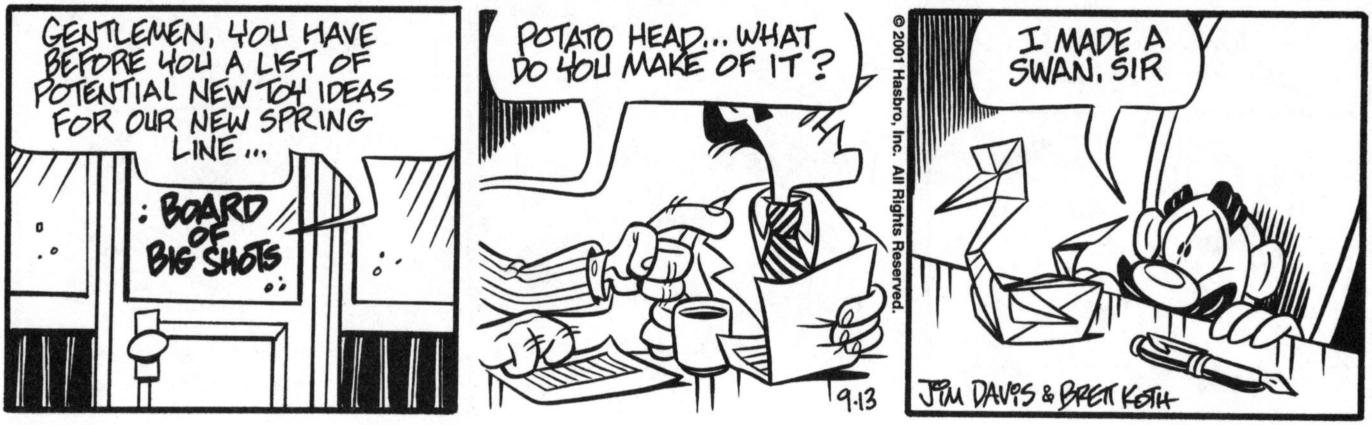
GENTLEMEN, YOU HAVE BEFORE YOU A LIST OF POTENTIAL NEW TOY IDEAS FOR OUR NEW SPRING LINE...
BOARD OF BIG SHOTS
POTATO HEAD... WHAT DO YOU MAKE OF IT?
© 2001 Hasbro, Inc. All Rights Reserved.
9.13
I MADE A SWAN, SIR
JIM DAVIS & BRETT KOTH

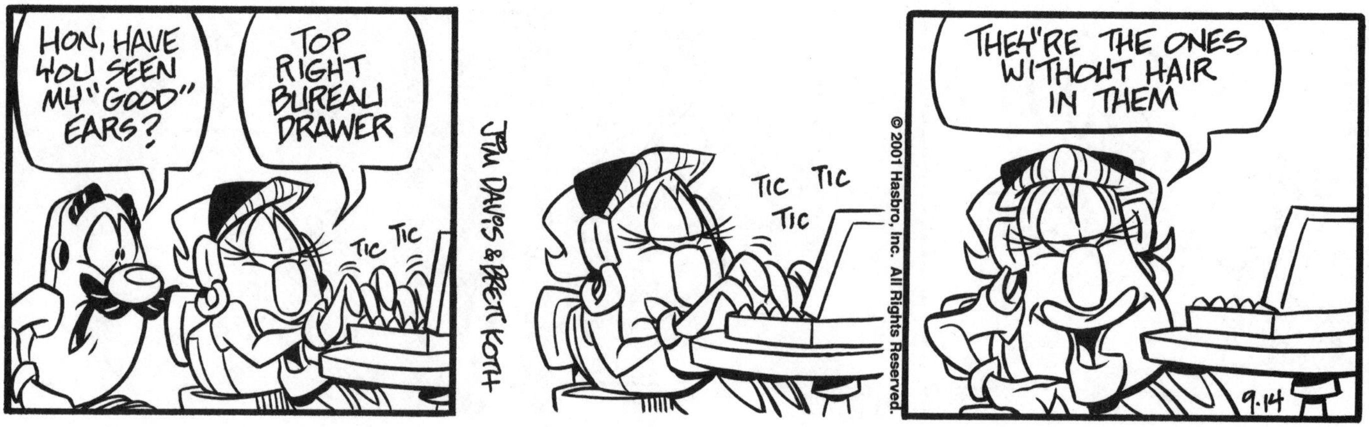
HON, HAVE YOU SEEN MY "GOOD" EARS?
TOP RIGHT BUREAU DRAWER
TIC TIC
JIM DAVIS & BRETT KOTH
TIC TIC TIC
© 2001 Hasbro, Inc. All Rights Reserved.
THEY'RE THE ONES WITHOUT HAIR IN THEM
9.14

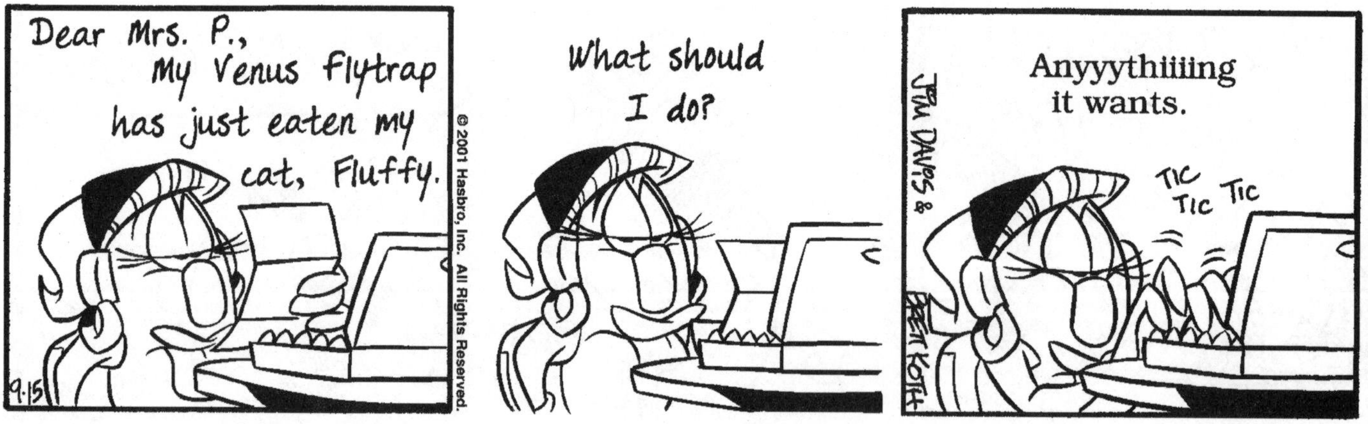
Dear Mrs. P.,
My Venus flytrap has just eaten my cat, Fluffy.
9.15
© 2001 Hasbro, Inc. All Rights Reserved.
What should I do?
JIM DAVIS & BRETT KOTH
Anyyythiiiing it wants.
TIC TIC TIC

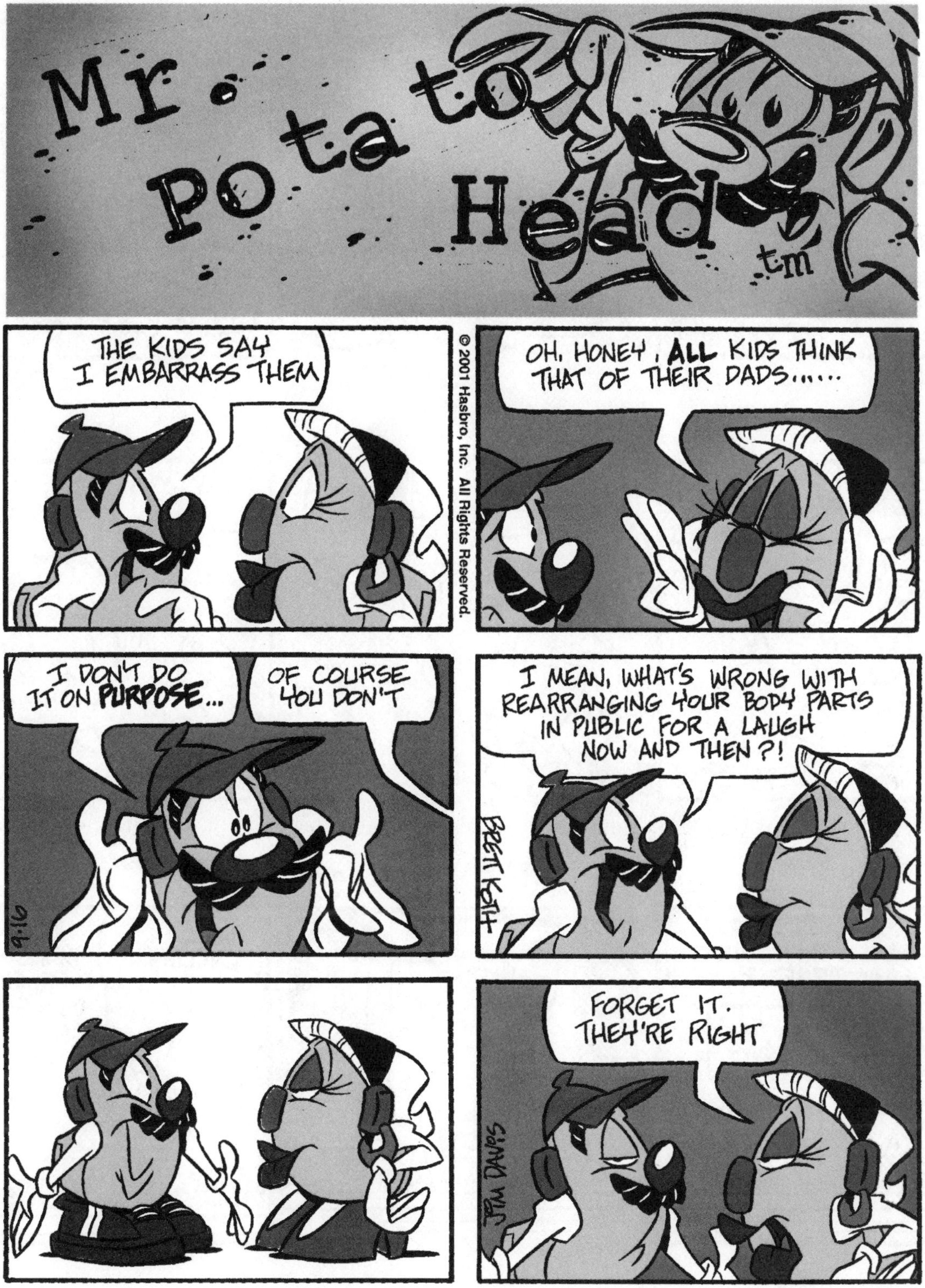
Mr. Potato Head
tm
THE KIDS SAY I EMBARRASS THEM
© 2001 Hasbro, Inc. All Rights Reserved.
OH, HONEY, ALL KIDS THINK THAT OF THEIR DADS......
I DON'T DO IT ON PURPOSE...
OF COURSE YOU DON'T
9·16
I MEAN, WHAT'S WRONG WITH REARRANGING YOUR BODY PARTS IN PUBLIC FOR A LAUGH NOW AND THEN?!
BRETT KOTH
JIM DAVIS
FORGET IT. THEY'RE RIGHT

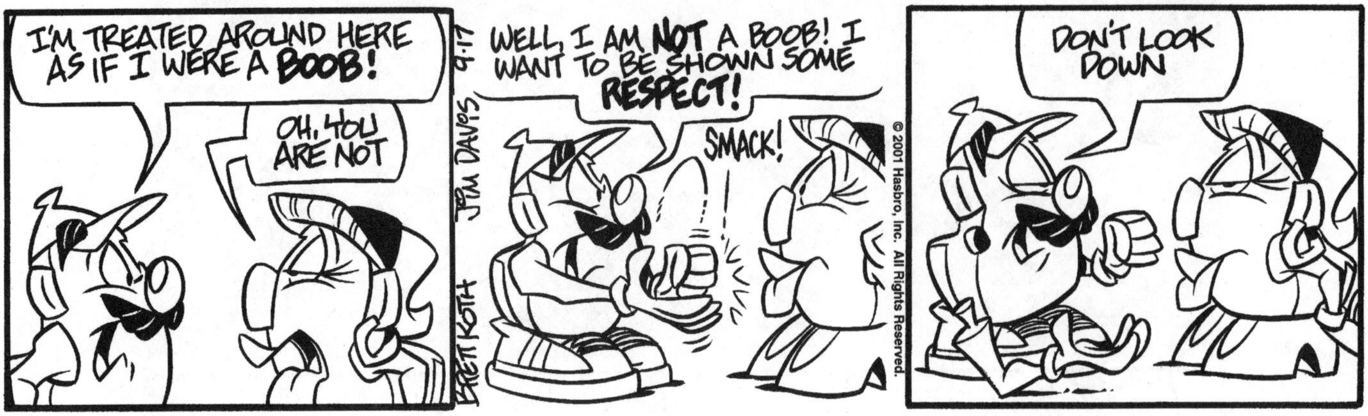
I'M TREATED AROUND HERE AS IF I WERE A BOOB!
OH, YOU ARE NOT
9.17
JIM DAVIS
BRETT KOTH
WELL, I AM NOT A BOOB! I WANT TO BE SHOWN SOME RESPECT!
SMACK!
© 2001 Hasbro, Inc. All Rights Reserved.
DON'T LOOK DOWN

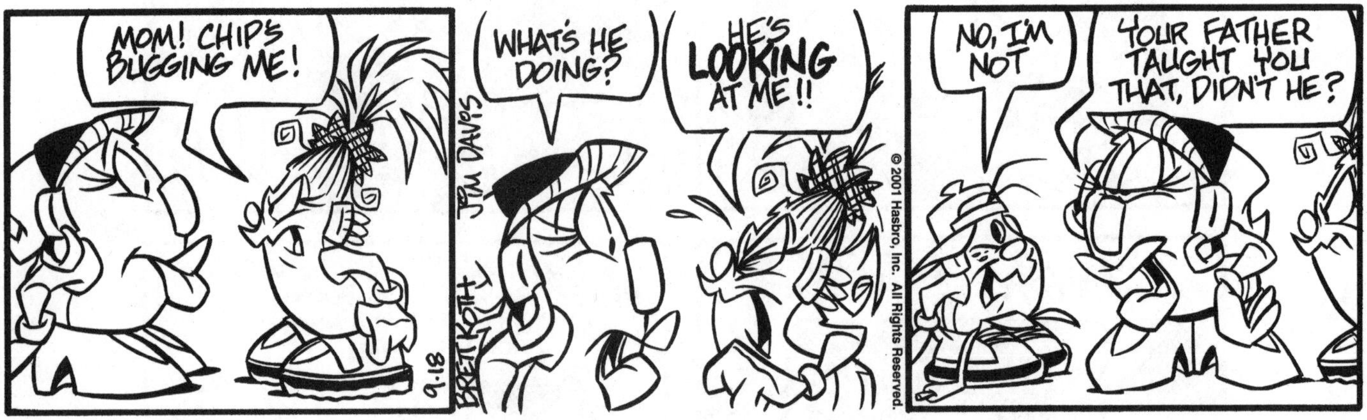
MOM! CHIP'S BUGGING ME!
9.18
JIM DAVIS
BRETT KOTH
WHAT'S HE DOING?
HE'S LOOKING AT ME!!
© 2001 Hasbro, Inc. All Rights Reserved.
NO, I'M NOT
YOUR FATHER TAUGHT YOU THAT, DIDN'T HE?

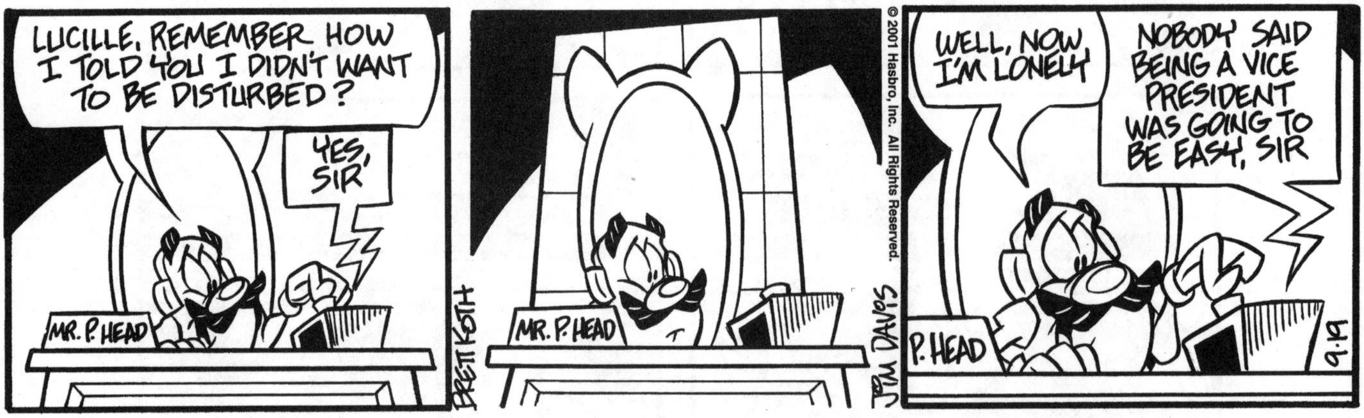
LUCILLE, REMEMBER HOW I TOLD YOU I DIDN'T WANT TO BE DISTURBED?
YES, SIR
MR. P. HEAD
BRETT KOTH
MR. P. HEAD
JIM DAVIS
© 2001 Hasbro, Inc. All Rights Reserved.
WELL, NOW I'M LONELY
NOBODY SAID BEING A VICE PRESIDENT WAS GOING TO BE EASY, SIR
P. HEAD
9.19

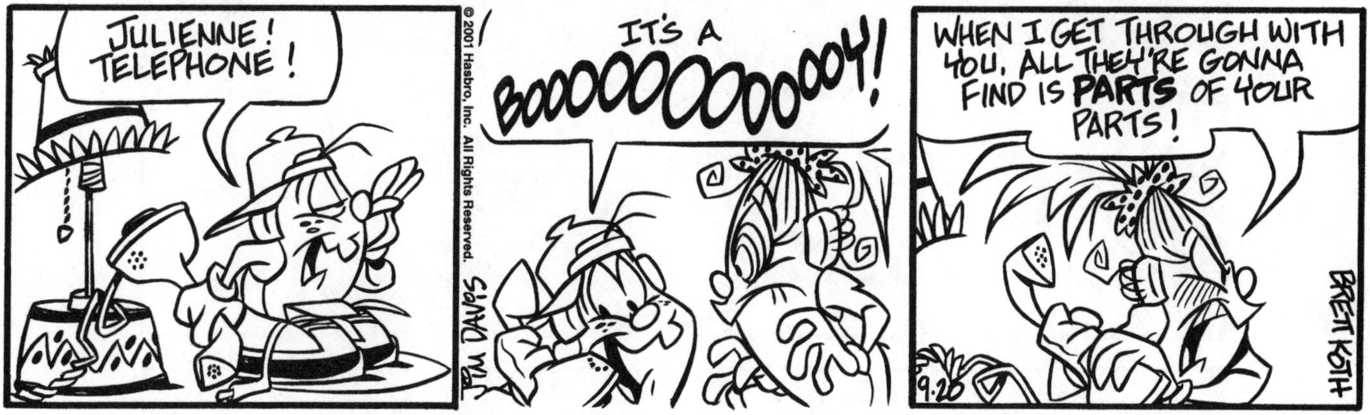
JULIENNE! TELEPHONE!
IT'S A BOOOOOOOOOOOOY!
WHEN I GET THROUGH WITH YOU, ALL THEY'RE GONNA FIND IS **PARTS** OF YOUR PARTS!
© 2001 Hasbro, Inc. All Rights Reserved.
JIM DAVIS
BRETT KOTH
9·20

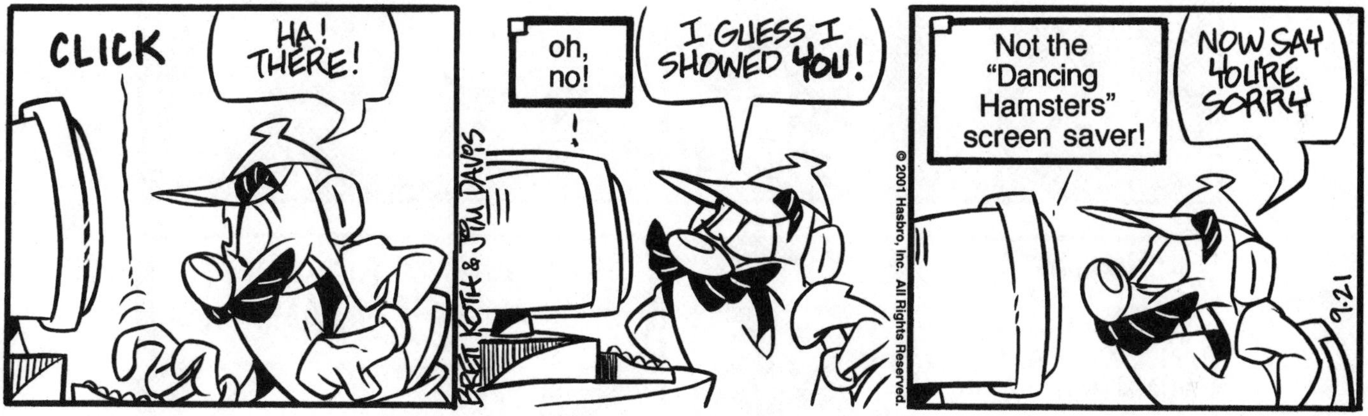
CLICK
HA! THERE!
oh, no!
I GUESS I SHOWED **YOU**!
Not the "Dancing Hamsters" screen saver!
NOW SAY YOU'RE SORRY
BRETT KOTH & JIM DAVIS
© 2001 Hasbro, Inc. All Rights Reserved.
9·21

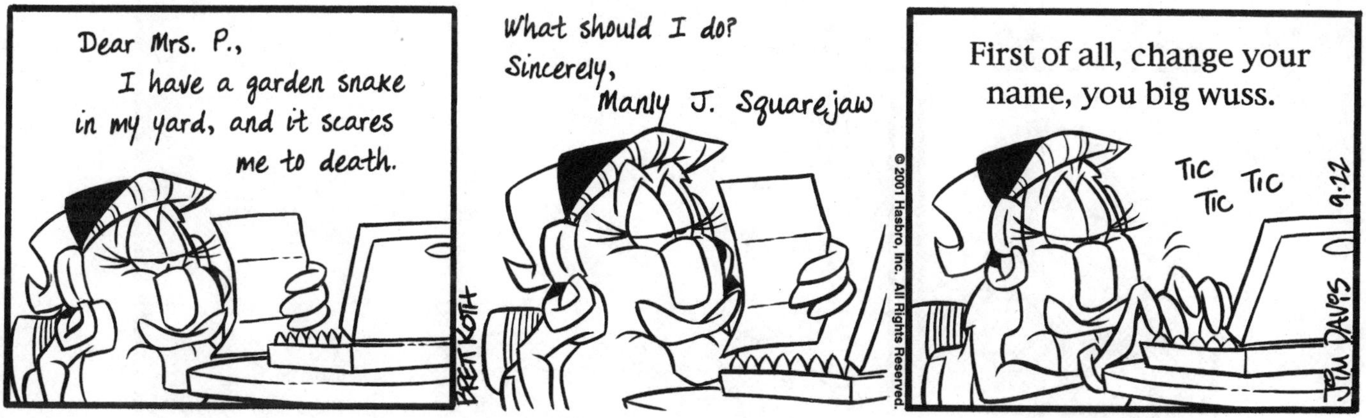
Dear Mrs. P.,
I have a garden snake in my yard, and it scares me to death.
What should I do?
Sincerely,
Manly J. Squarejaw
First of all, change your name, you big wuss.
TIC TIC TIC
BRETT KOTH
© 2001 Hasbro, Inc. All Rights Reserved.
JIM DAVIS
9·22

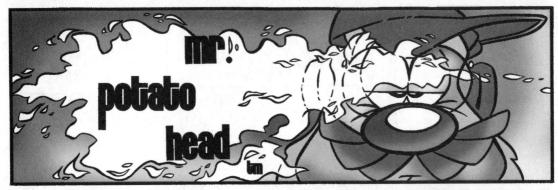

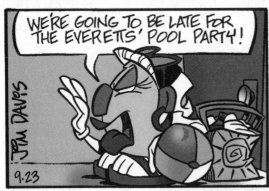

mr. potato head tm
WE'RE GOING TO BE LATE FOR THE EVERETTS' POOL PARTY!
© 2001 Hasbro, Inc. All Rights Reserved.
JIM DAVIS
9.23
...I CAN'T FIND MY BARE FEET!
I THOUGHT I PUT THEM IN... -OH... OH... WAIT A MINUTE...
BRETT KOTH
-HERE THEY ARE, RIGHT NEXT TO MY- SAAAAAAAAY....
HUH?... HUH?
THE REST OF US HAVE TO FIT INTO THE POOL, TOO, YOU KNOW

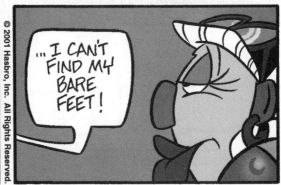

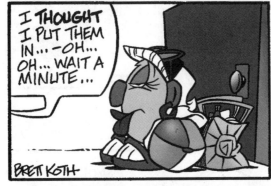

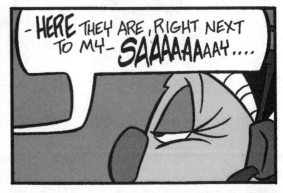

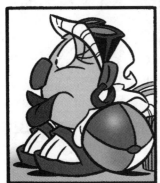

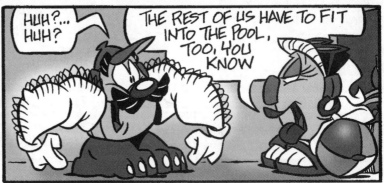

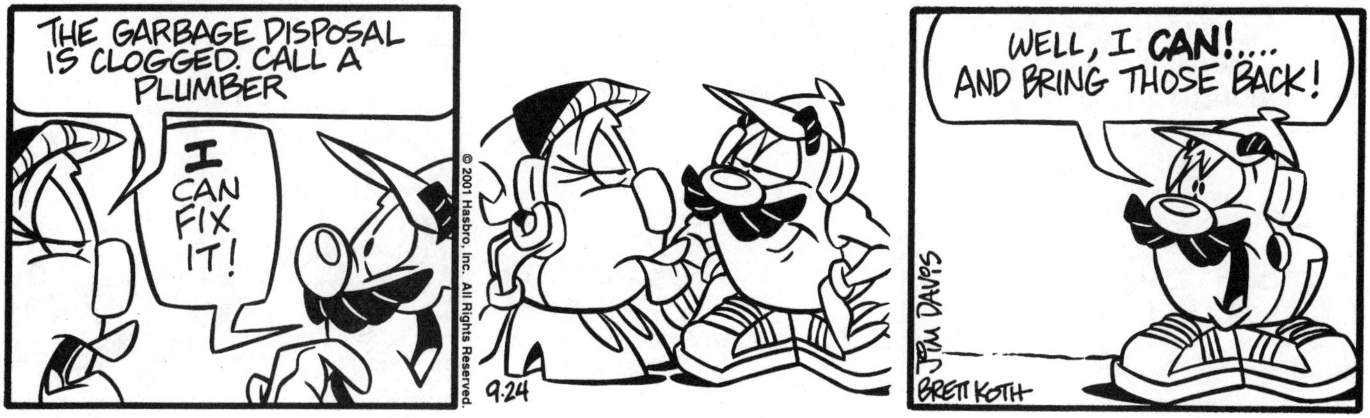
THE GARBAGE DISPOSAL IS CLOGGED. CALL A PLUMBER
I CAN FIX IT!
© 2001 Hasbro, Inc. All Rights Reserved.
9.24
WELL, I CAN!.... AND BRING THOSE BACK!
JIM DAVIS
BRETT KOTH

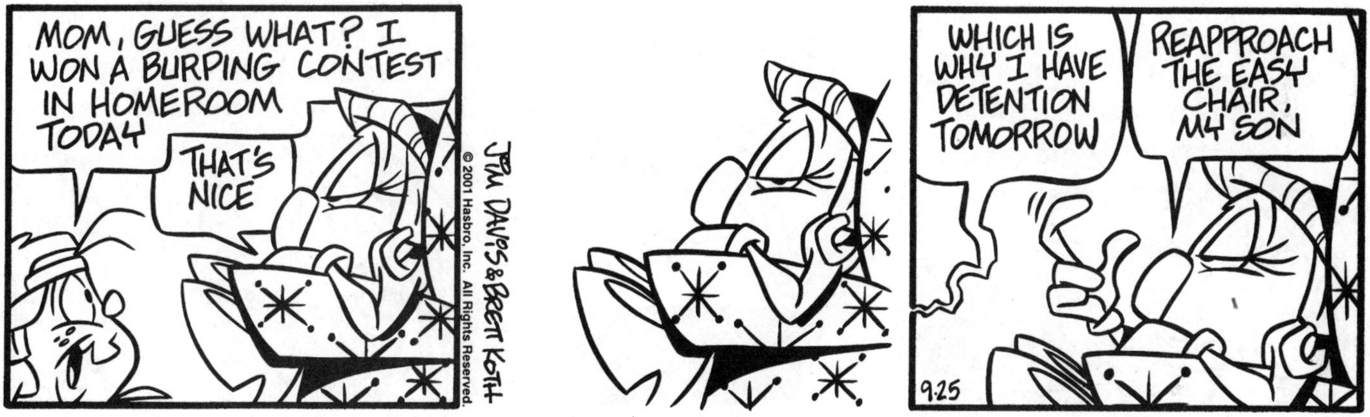
MOM, GUESS WHAT? I WON A BURPING CONTEST IN HOMEROOM TODAY
THAT'S NICE
JIM DAVIS & BRETT KOTH
© 2001 Hasbro, Inc. All Rights Reserved.
WHICH IS WHY I HAVE DETENTION TOMORROW
REAPPROACH THE EASY CHAIR, MY SON
9.25

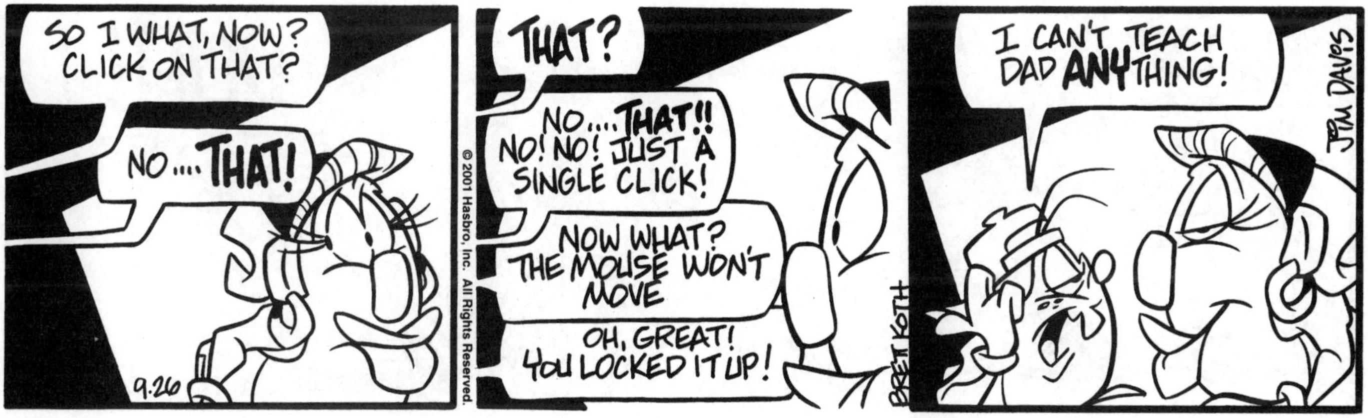
SO I WHAT, NOW? CLICK ON THAT?
NO.... THAT!
9.26
© 2001 Hasbro, Inc. All Rights Reserved.
THAT?
NO.... THAT!! NO! NO! JUST A SINGLE CLICK!
NOW WHAT? THE MOUSE WON'T MOVE
OH, GREAT! YOU LOCKED IT UP!
BRETT KOTH
I CAN'T TEACH DAD ANYTHING!
JIM DAVIS

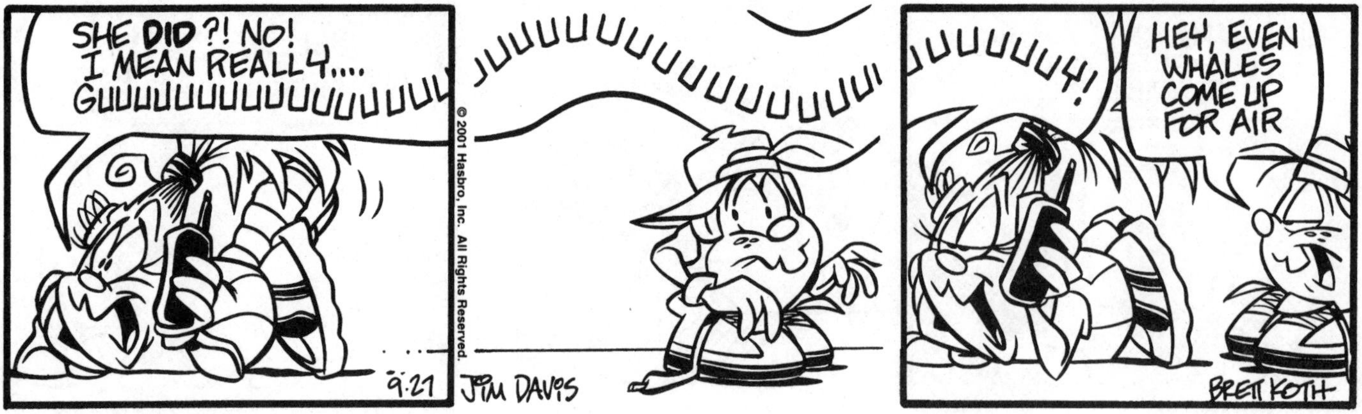
SHE DID?! NO! I MEAN REALLY.... GUUUUUUUUUUUUUUUU
9·27
© 2001 Hasbro, Inc. All Rights Reserved.
JIM DAVIS
UUUUUUUUUUUUUUUUUUUUUUUUU
UUUUUUUY!
HEY, EVEN WHALES COME UP FOR AIR
BRETT KOTH

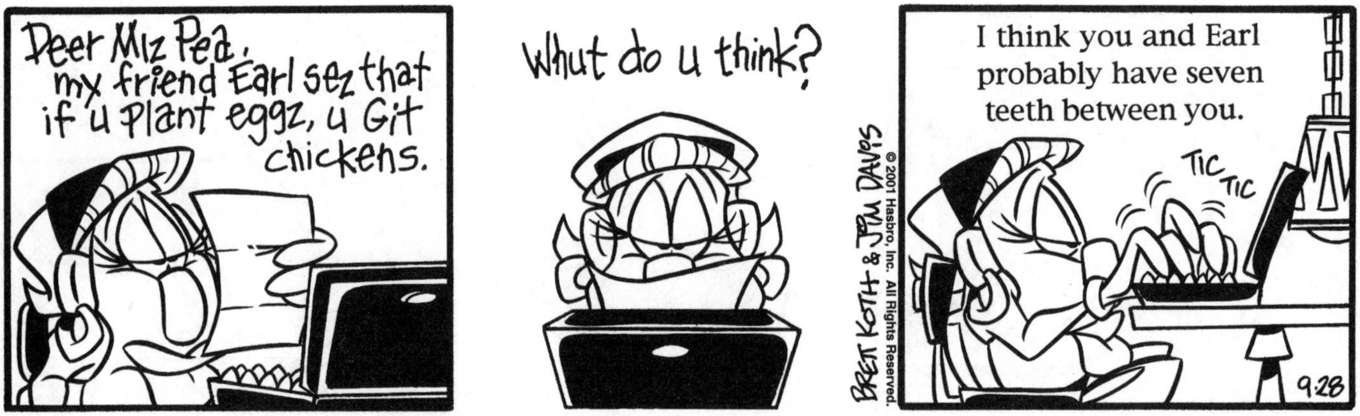
Deer Miz Pea, my friend Earl sez that if u plant eggz, u Git chickens.
Whut do u think?
BRETT KOTH & JIM DAVIS
© 2001 Hasbro, Inc. All Rights Reserved.
I think you and Earl probably have seven teeth between you.
TIC TIC
9·28

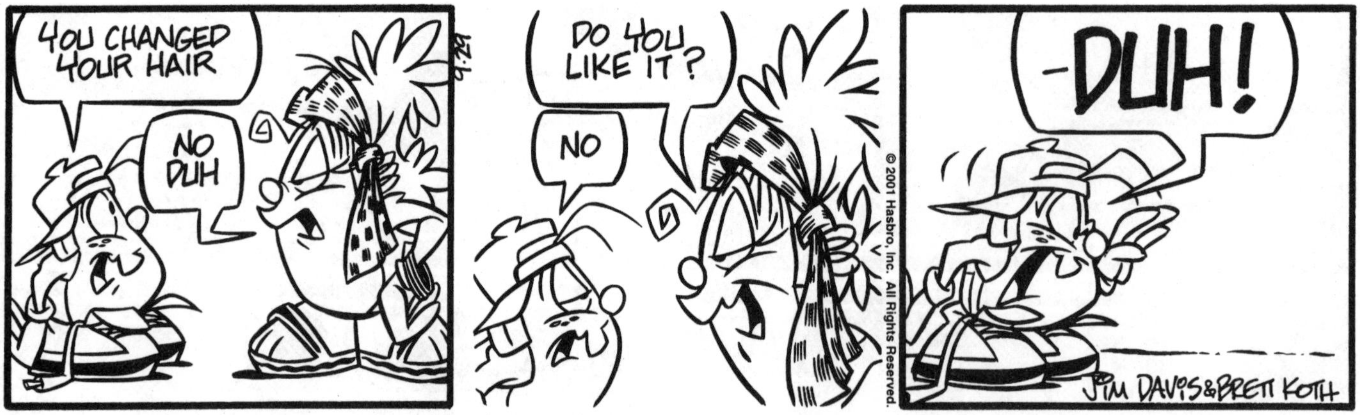
YOU CHANGED YOUR HAIR
NO DUH
9·29
DO YOU LIKE IT?
NO
© 2001 Hasbro, Inc. All Rights Reserved.
-DUH!
JIM DAVIS & BRETT KOTH

MR. POTATO HEAD
TM
9.30
HUH HUH. HUH HUH
WHOO!
ZONK
GREAT PLAY, SON!
THANKS, DAD...

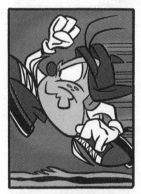

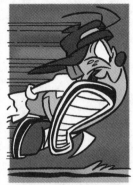

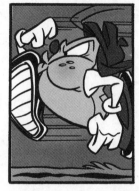

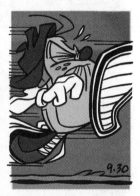

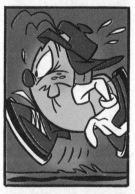

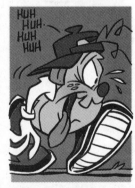

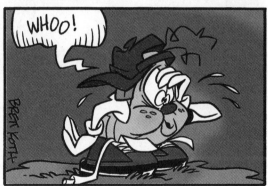

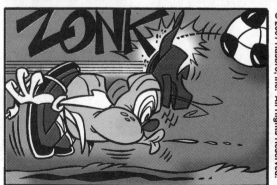

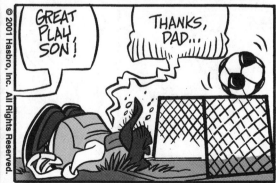

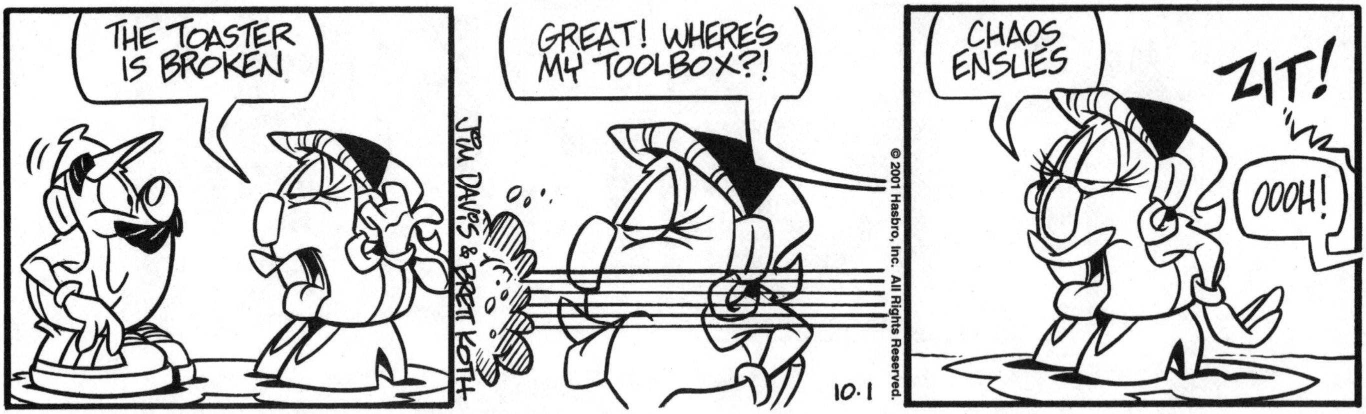
THE TOASTER IS BROKEN
GREAT! WHERE'S MY TOOLBOX?!
CHAOS ENSUES
ZIT!
OOOH!
JIM DAVIS & BRETT KOTH
10·1
© 2001 Hasbro, Inc. All Rights Reserved.

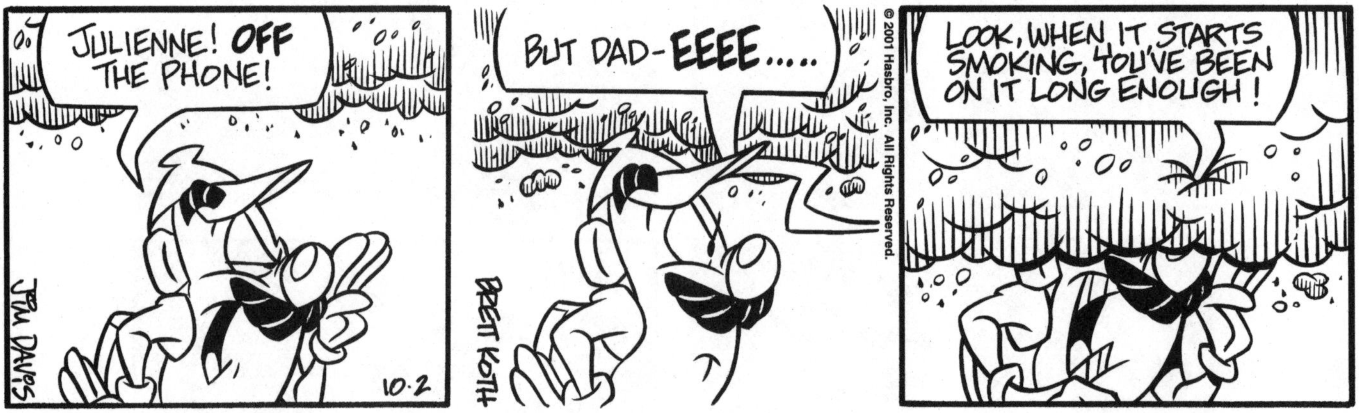
JULIENNE! OFF THE PHONE!
BUT DAD-EEEE.....
LOOK, WHEN IT STARTS SMOKING, YOU'VE BEEN ON IT LONG ENOUGH!
JIM DAVIS
BRETT KOTH
10·2
© 2001 Hasbro, Inc. All Rights Reserved.

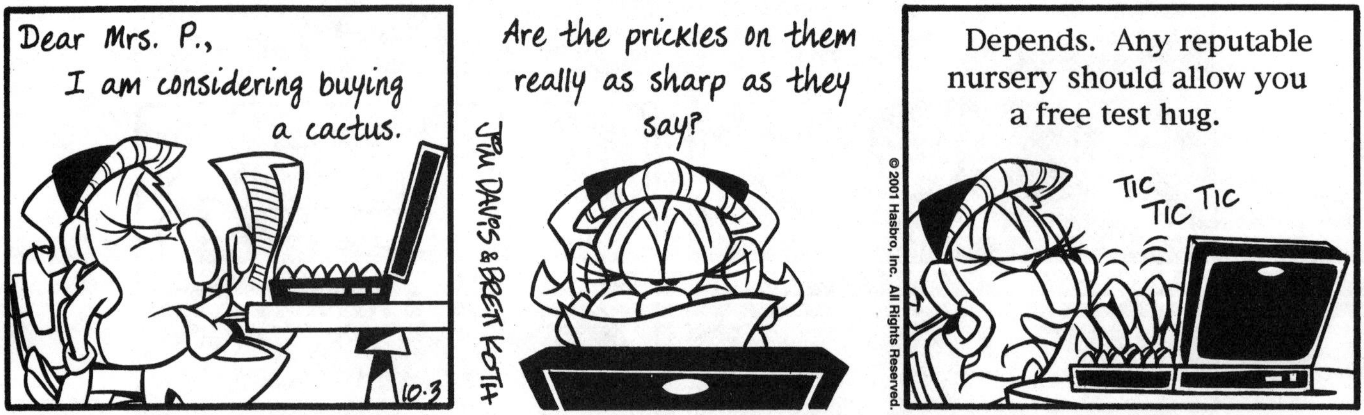
Dear Mrs. P., I am considering buying a cactus.
Are the prickles on them really as sharp as they say?
Depends. Any reputable nursery should allow you a free test hug.
TIC TIC TIC
JIM DAVIS & BRETT KOTH
10·3
© 2001 Hasbro, Inc. All Rights Reserved.

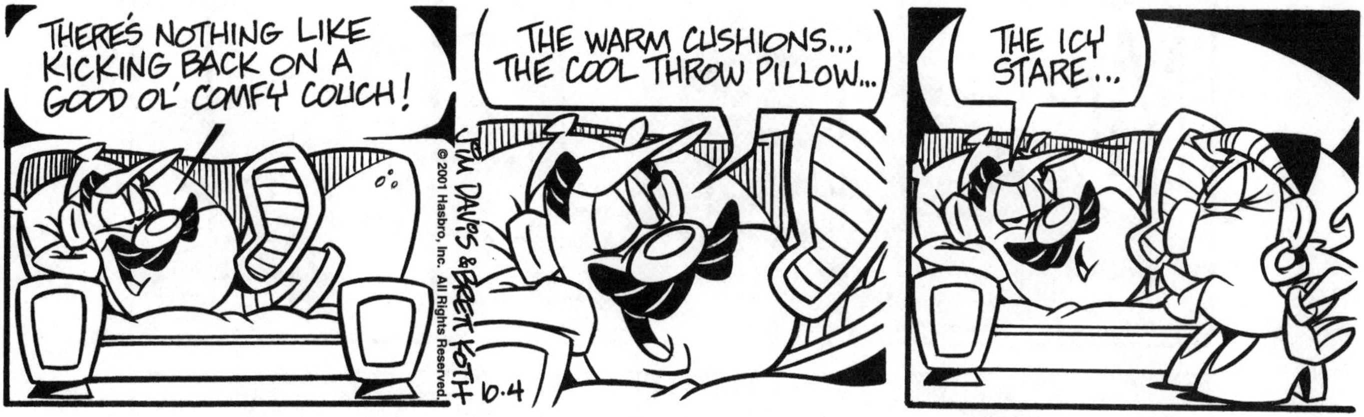
THERE'S NOTHING LIKE KICKING BACK ON A GOOD OL' COMFY COUCH!
THE WARM CUSHIONS... THE COOL THROW PILLOW...
THE ICY STARE...
JIM DAVIS & BRETT KOTH
10.4
© 2001 Hasbro, Inc. All Rights Reserved.

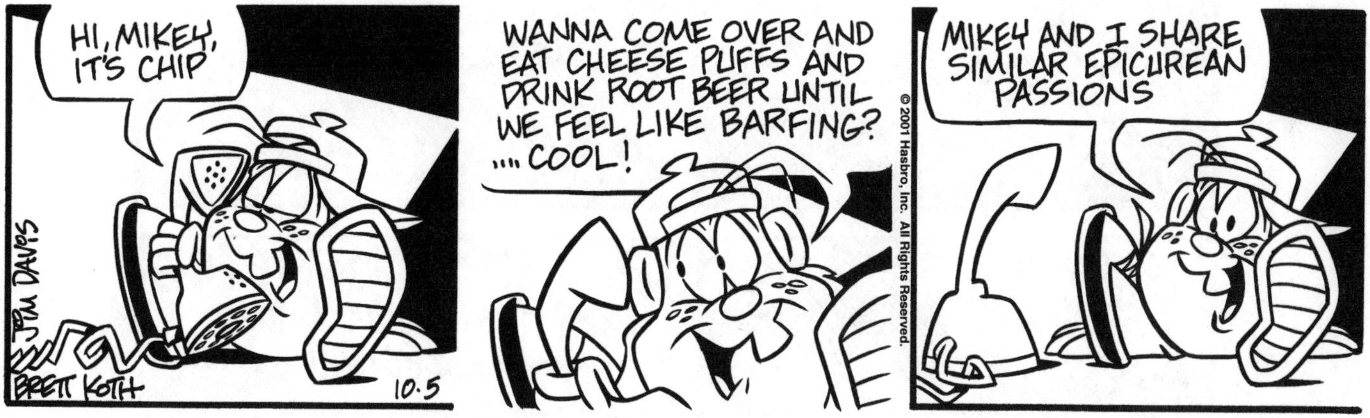
HI, MIKEY, IT'S CHIP
WANNA COME OVER AND EAT CHEESE PUFFS AND DRINK ROOT BEER UNTIL WE FEEL LIKE BARFING? .... COOL!
MIKEY AND I SHARE SIMILAR EPICUREAN PASSIONS
JIM DAVIS
BRETT KOTH
10.5
© 2001 Hasbro, Inc. All Rights Reserved.

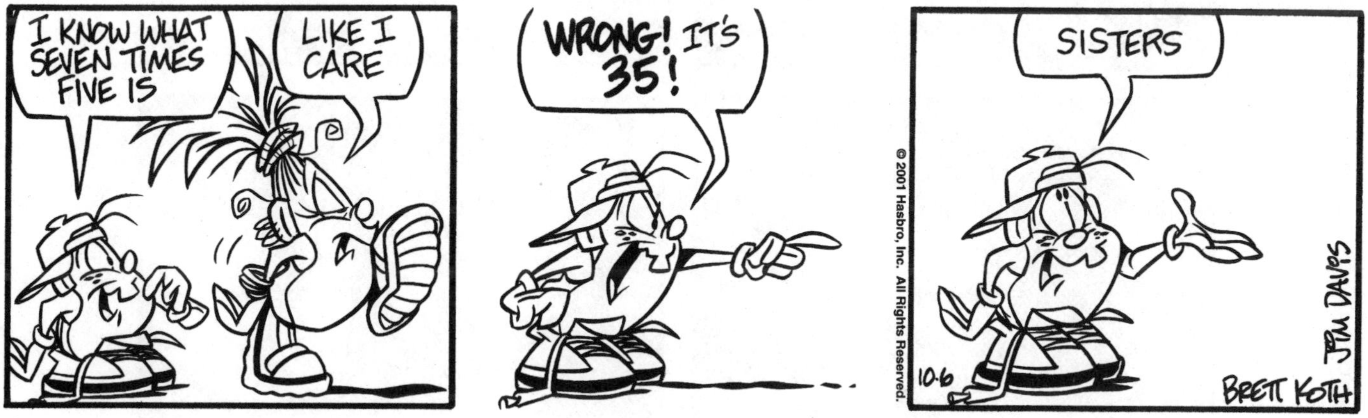
I KNOW WHAT SEVEN TIMES FIVE IS
LIKE I CARE
WRONG! IT'S 35!
SISTERS
JIM DAVIS
BRETT KOTH
10.6
© 2001 Hasbro, Inc. All Rights Reserved.

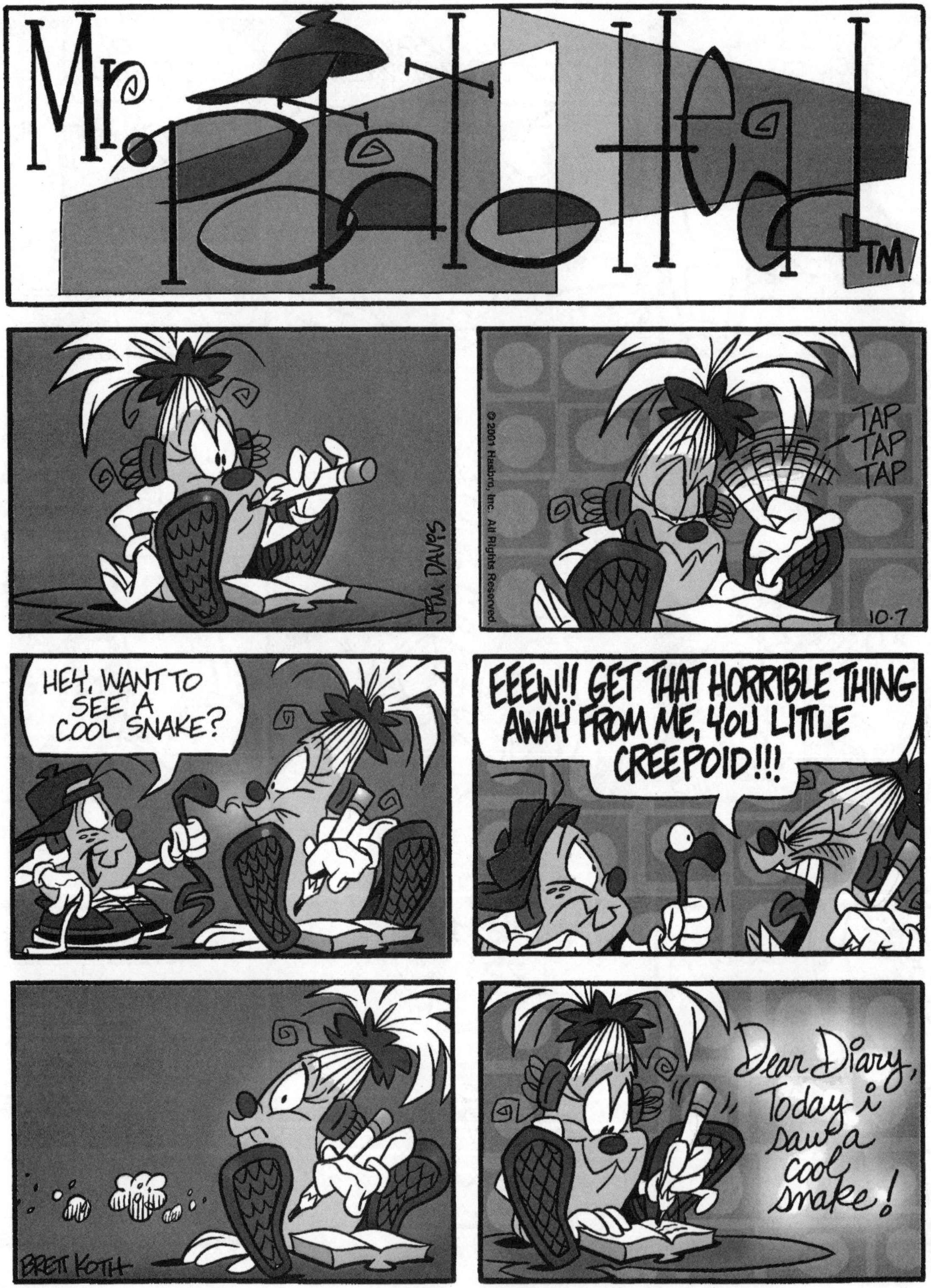

Mr. Potato Head TM
JIM DAVIS
© 2001 Hasbro, Inc. All Rights Reserved.
TAP TAP TAP
10-7
HEY, WANT TO SEE A COOL SNAKE?
EEEW!! GET THAT HORRIBLE THING AWAY FROM ME, YOU LITTLE CREEPOID!!!
BRETT KOTH
Dear Diary, Today i saw a cool snake!

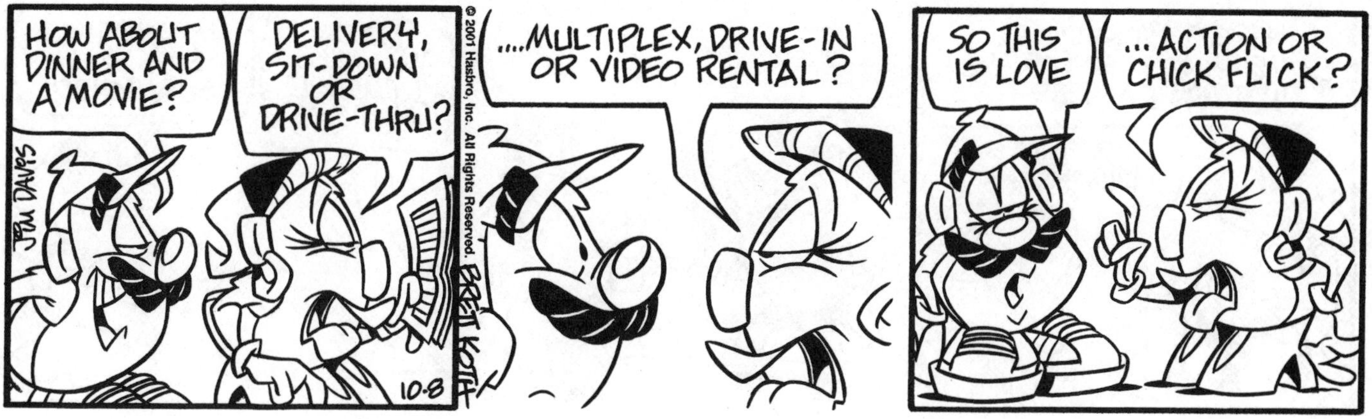
HOW ABOUT DINNER AND A MOVIE?
DELIVERY, SIT-DOWN OR DRIVE-THRU?
....MULTIPLEX, DRIVE-IN OR VIDEO RENTAL?
SO THIS IS LOVE
...ACTION OR CHICK FLICK?
JIM DAVIS
BRETT KOTH
10-8
© 2001 Hasbro, Inc. All Rights Reserved.

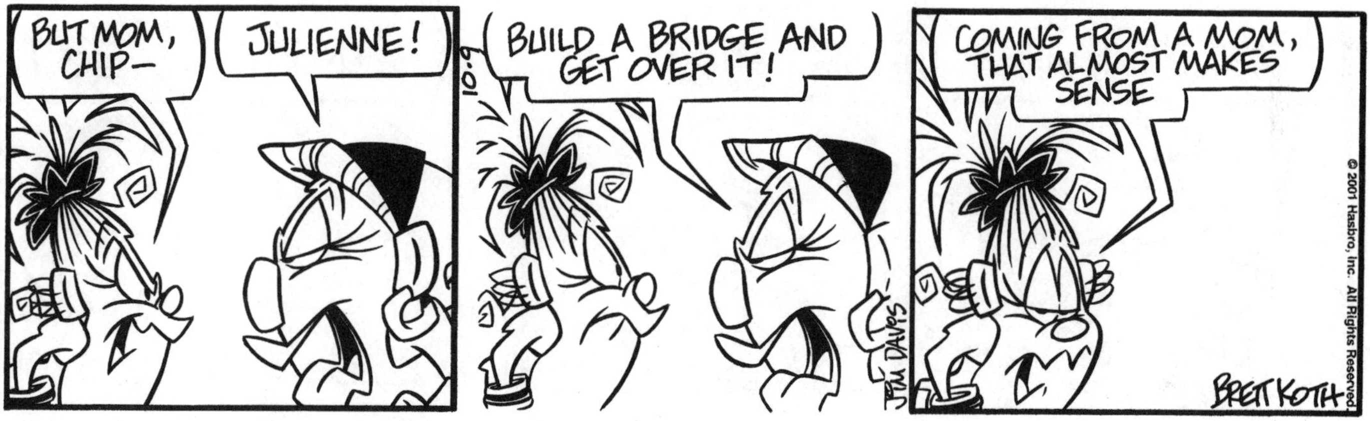
BUT MOM, CHIP—
JULIENNE!
BUILD A BRIDGE AND GET OVER IT!
COMING FROM A MOM, THAT ALMOST MAKES SENSE
10-9
JIM DAVIS
BRETT KOTH
© 2001 Hasbro, Inc. All Rights Reserved.

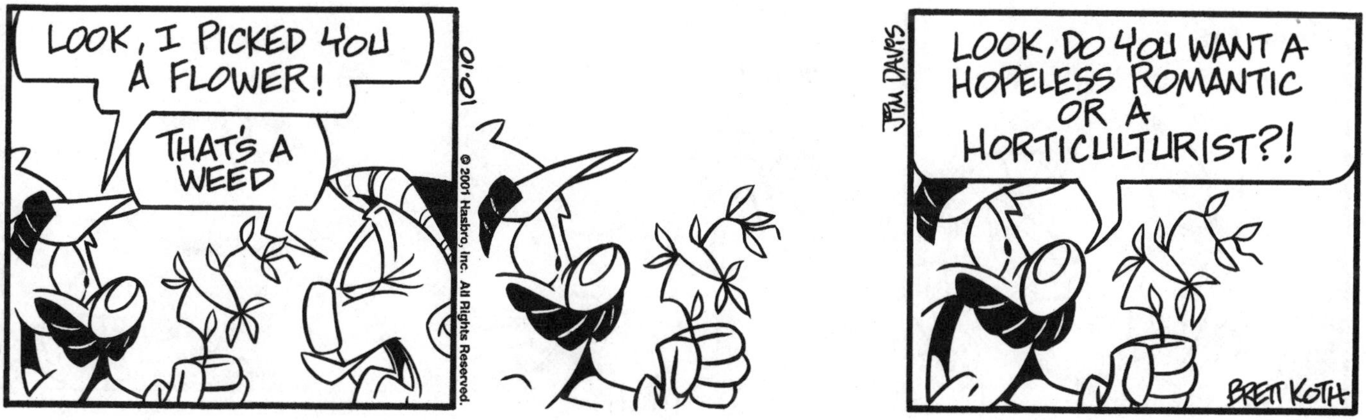
LOOK, I PICKED YOU A FLOWER!
THAT'S A WEED
LOOK, DO YOU WANT A HOPELESS ROMANTIC OR A HORTICULTURIST?!
10-10
JIM DAVIS
BRETT KOTH
© 2001 Hasbro, Inc. All Rights Reserved.

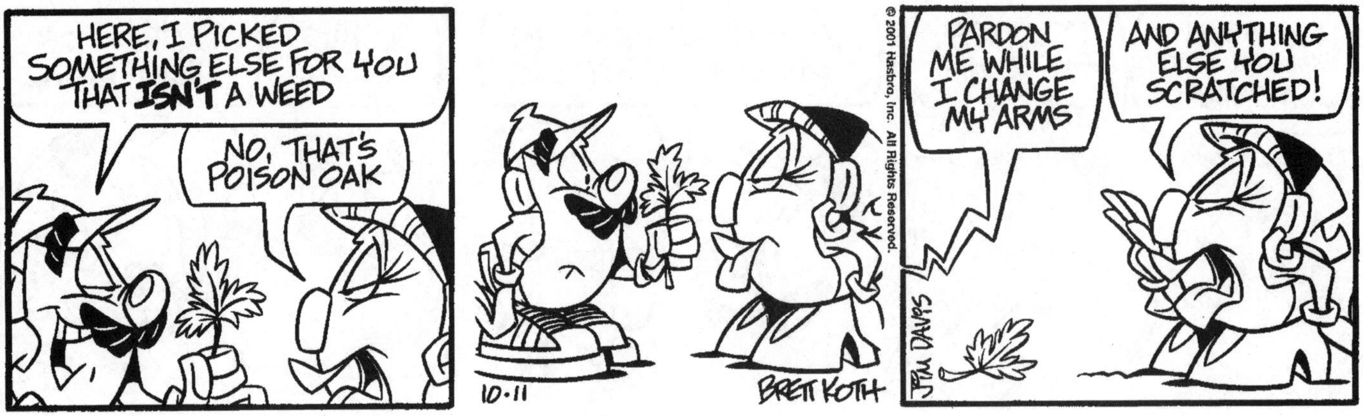
HERE, I PICKED SOMETHING ELSE FOR YOU THAT ISN'T A WEED
NO, THAT'S POISON OAK
© 2001 Hasbro, Inc. All Rights Reserved.
PARDON ME WHILE I CHANGE MY ARMS
AND ANYTHING ELSE YOU SCRATCHED!
10·11
BRETT KOTH
JIM DAVIS

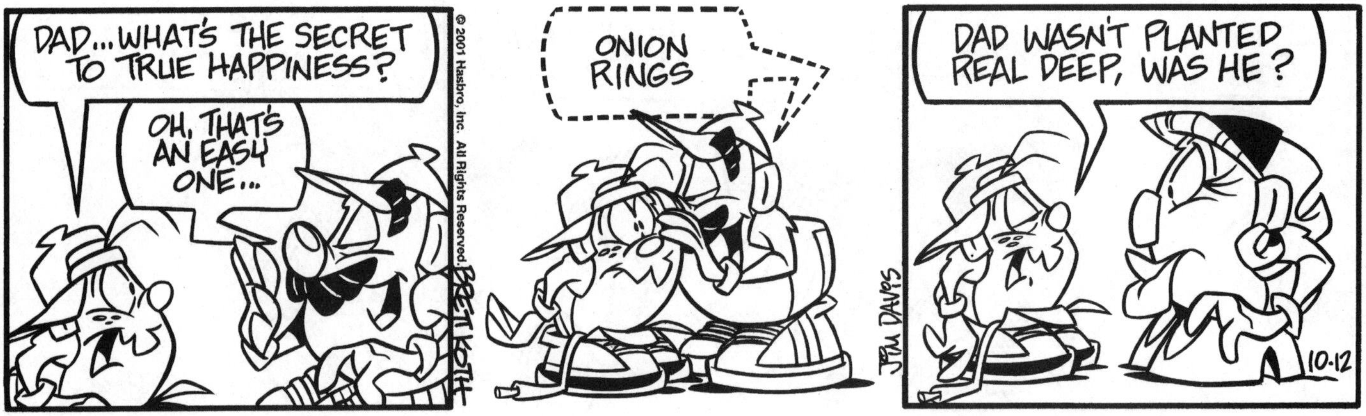
DAD...WHAT'S THE SECRET TO TRUE HAPPINESS?
OH, THAT'S AN EASY ONE...
© 2001 Hasbro, Inc. All Rights Reserved.
BRETT KOTH
ONION RINGS
JIM DAVIS
DAD WASN'T PLANTED REAL DEEP, WAS HE?
10·12

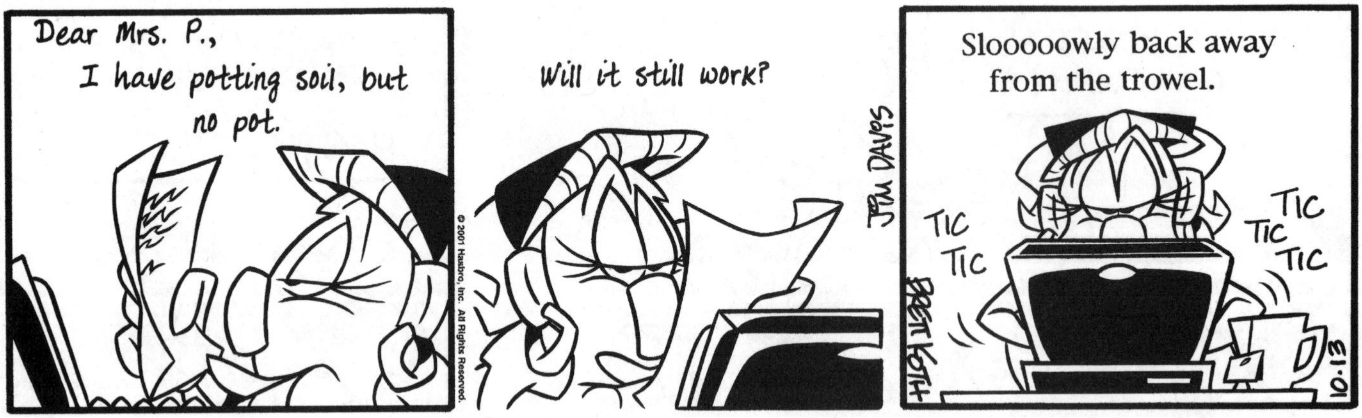
Dear Mrs. P.,
I have potting soil, but no pot.
© 2001 Hasbro, Inc. All Rights Reserved.
Will it still work?
JIM DAVIS
Sloooooowly back away from the trowel.
TIC
TIC
TIC
TIC
TIC
BRETT KOTH
10·13

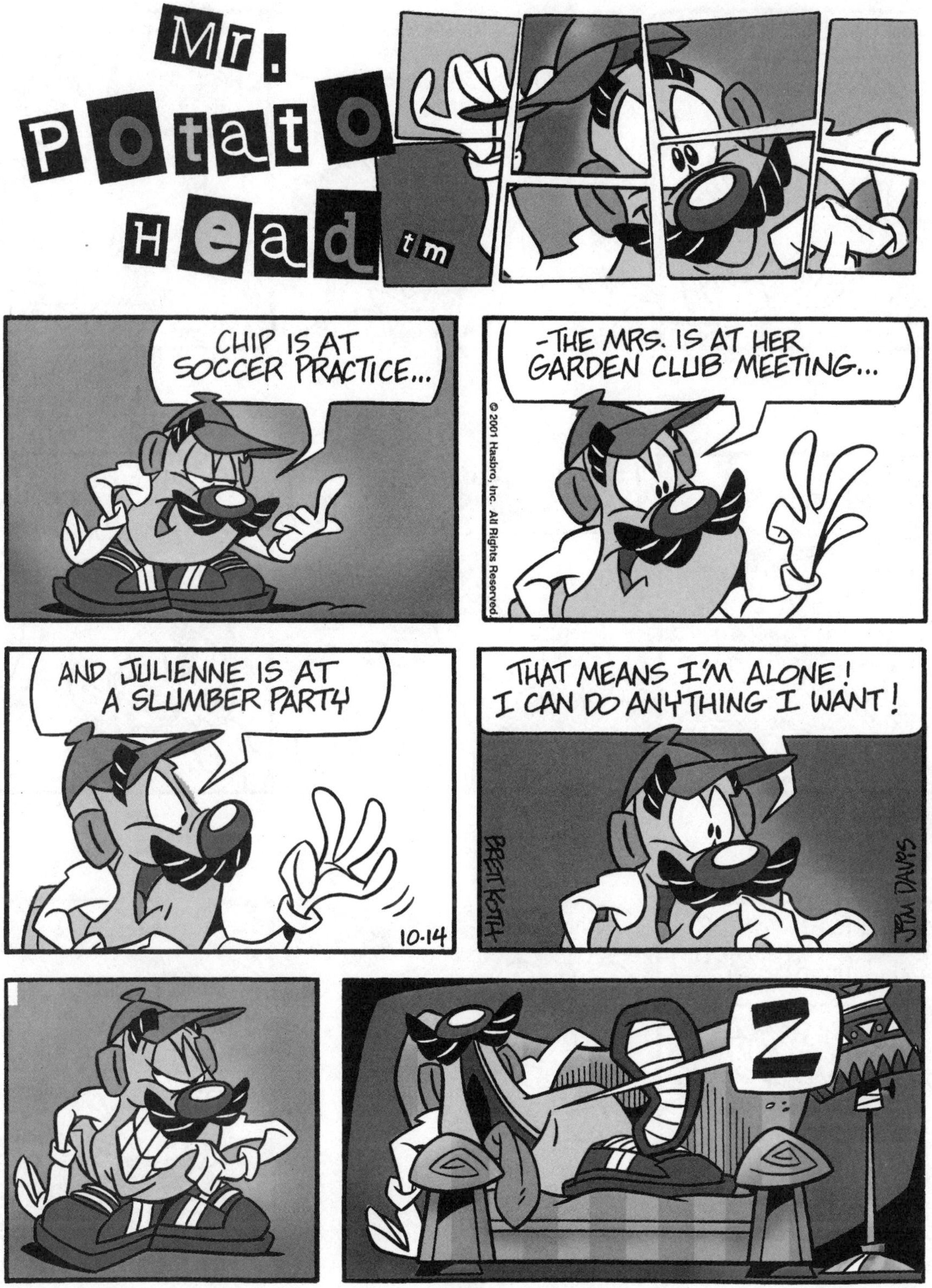
Mr. Potato Head tm
CHIP IS AT SOCCER PRACTICE...
-THE MRS. IS AT HER GARDEN CLUB MEETING...
© 2001 Hasbro, Inc. All Rights Reserved.
AND JULIENNE IS AT A SLUMBER PARTY
10-14
BRETT KOTH
THAT MEANS I'M ALONE! I CAN DO ANYTHING I WANT!
JIM DAVIS
Z

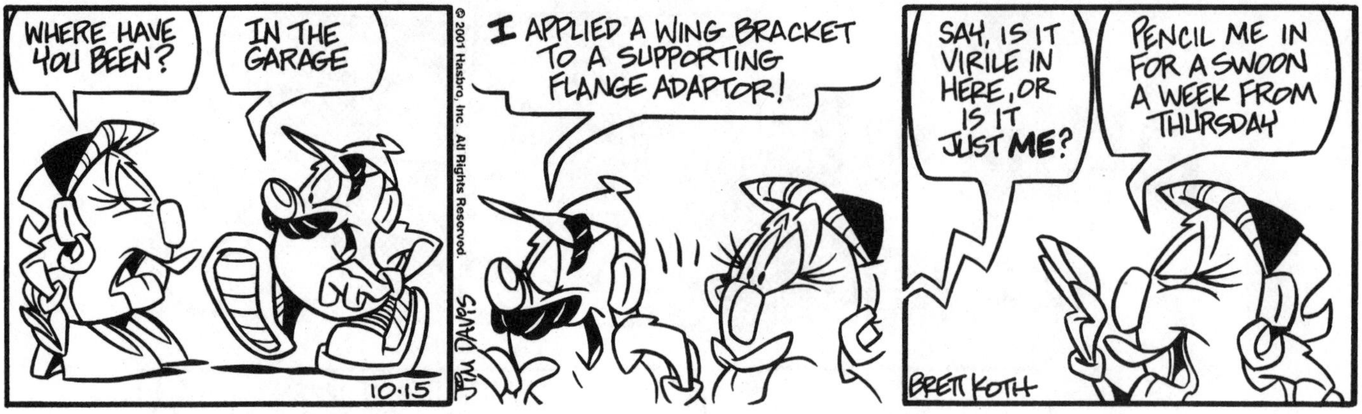
WHERE HAVE YOU BEEN?
IN THE GARAGE
10·15
© 2001 Hasbro, Inc. All Rights Reserved.
JIM DAVIS
I APPLIED A WING BRACKET TO A SUPPORTING FLANGE ADAPTOR!
SAY, IS IT VIRILE IN HERE, OR IS IT JUST ME?
PENCIL ME IN FOR A SWOON A WEEK FROM THURSDAY
BRETT KOTH

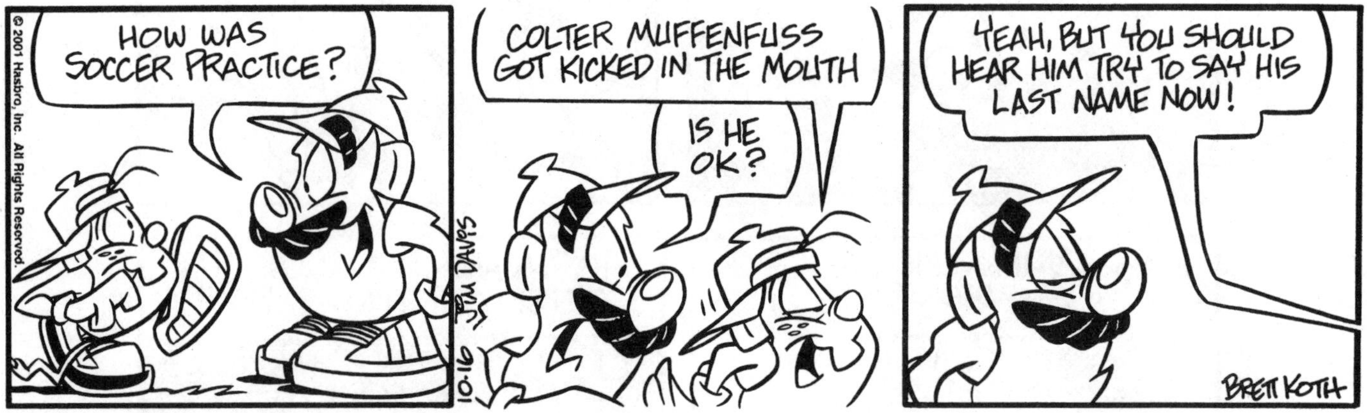
© 2001 Hasbro, Inc. All Rights Reserved.
HOW WAS SOCCER PRACTICE?
JIM DAVIS
10·16
COLTER MUFFENFUSS GOT KICKED IN THE MOUTH
IS HE OK?
YEAH, BUT YOU SHOULD HEAR HIM TRY TO SAY HIS LAST NAME NOW!
BRETT KOTH

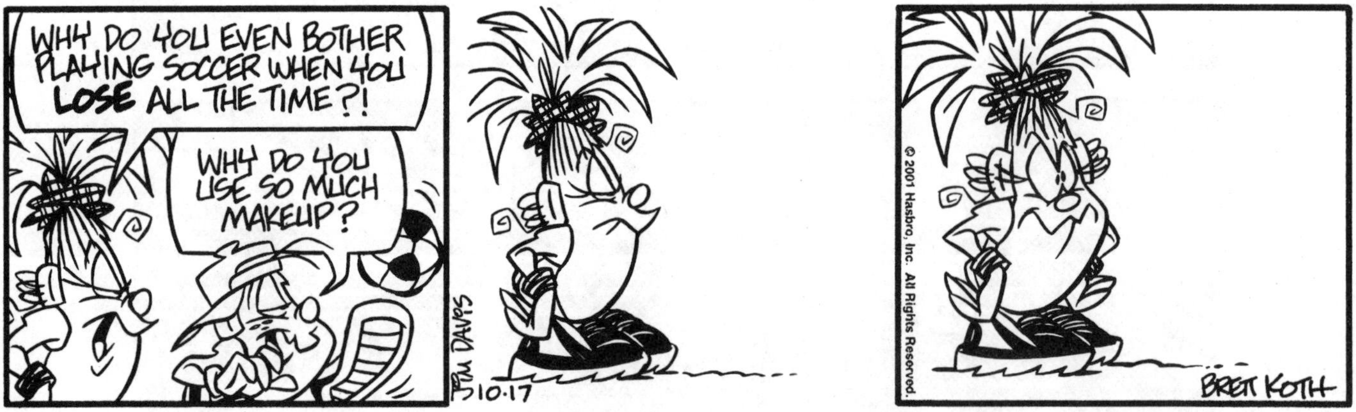
WHY DO YOU EVEN BOTHER PLAYING SOCCER WHEN YOU **LOSE** ALL THE TIME?!
WHY DO YOU USE SO MUCH MAKEUP?
JIM DAVIS
10·17
© 2001 Hasbro, Inc. All Rights Reserved.
BRETT KOTH

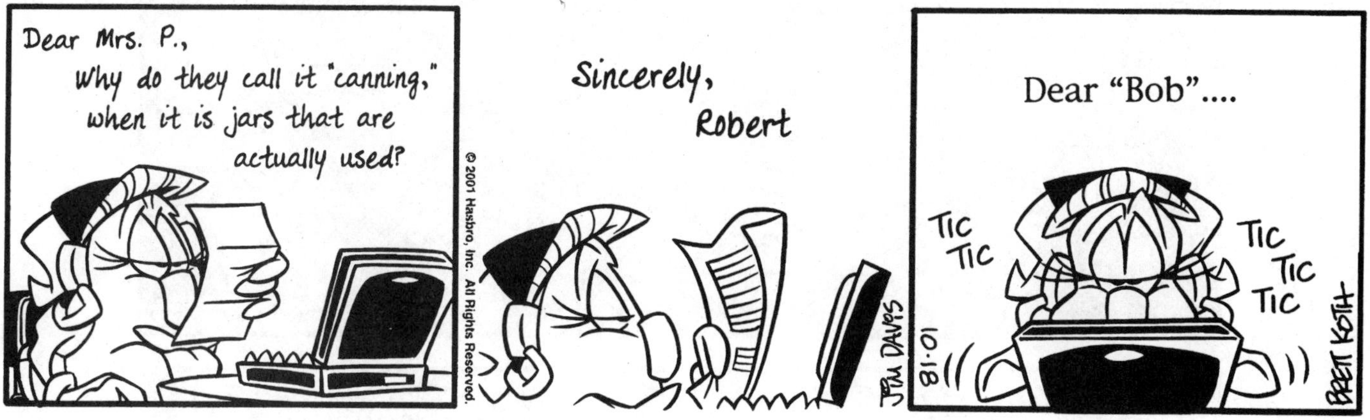
Dear Mrs. P.,
Why do they call it "canning," when it is jars that are actually used?
Sincerely,
Robert
Dear "Bob"....
TIC TIC
TIC TIC TIC
© 2001 Hasbro, Inc. All Rights Reserved.
JIM DAVIS 10.18
BRETT KOTH

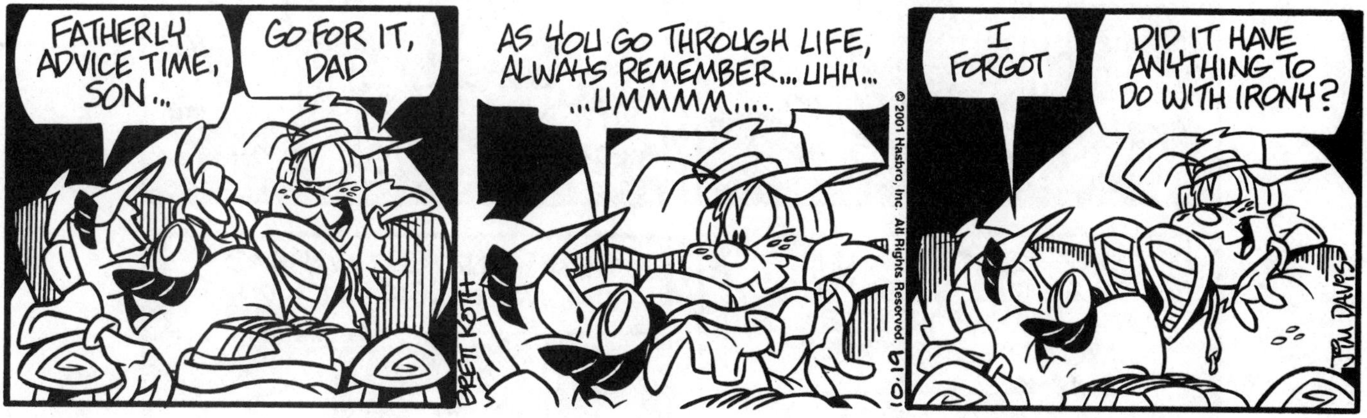
FATHERLY ADVICE TIME, SON...
GO FOR IT, DAD
AS YOU GO THROUGH LIFE, ALWAYS REMEMBER... UHH... ...UMMMM.....
I FORGOT
DID IT HAVE ANYTHING TO DO WITH IRONY?
© 2001 Hasbro, Inc. All Rights Reserved. 10.19
BRETT KOTH
JIM DAVIS

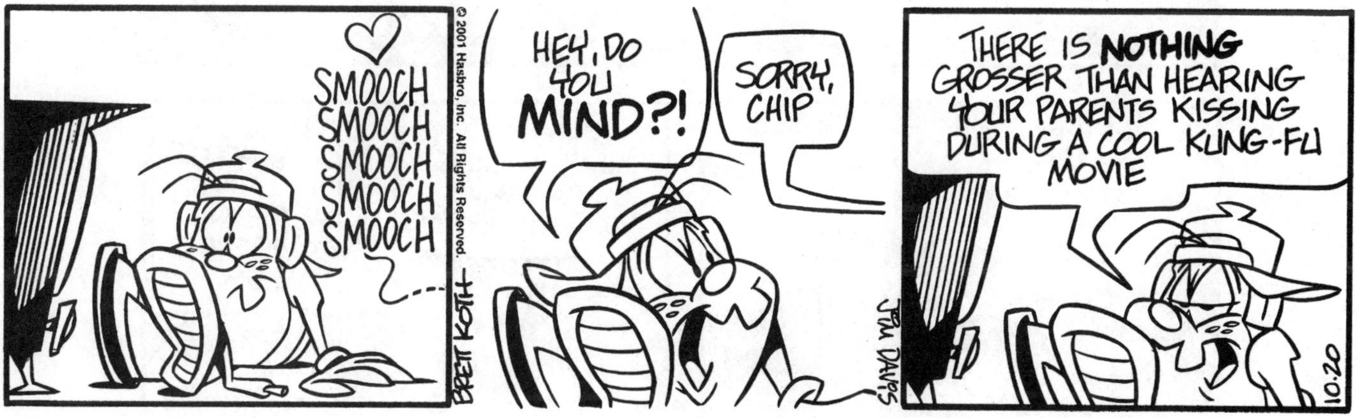
SMOOCH
SMOOCH
SMOOCH
SMOOCH
SMOOCH
HEY, DO YOU MIND?!
SORRY, CHIP
THERE IS NOTHING GROSSER THAN HEARING YOUR PARENTS KISSING DURING A COOL KUNG-FU MOVIE
© 2001 Hasbro, Inc. All Rights Reserved.
BRETT KOTH
JIM DAVIS
10.20

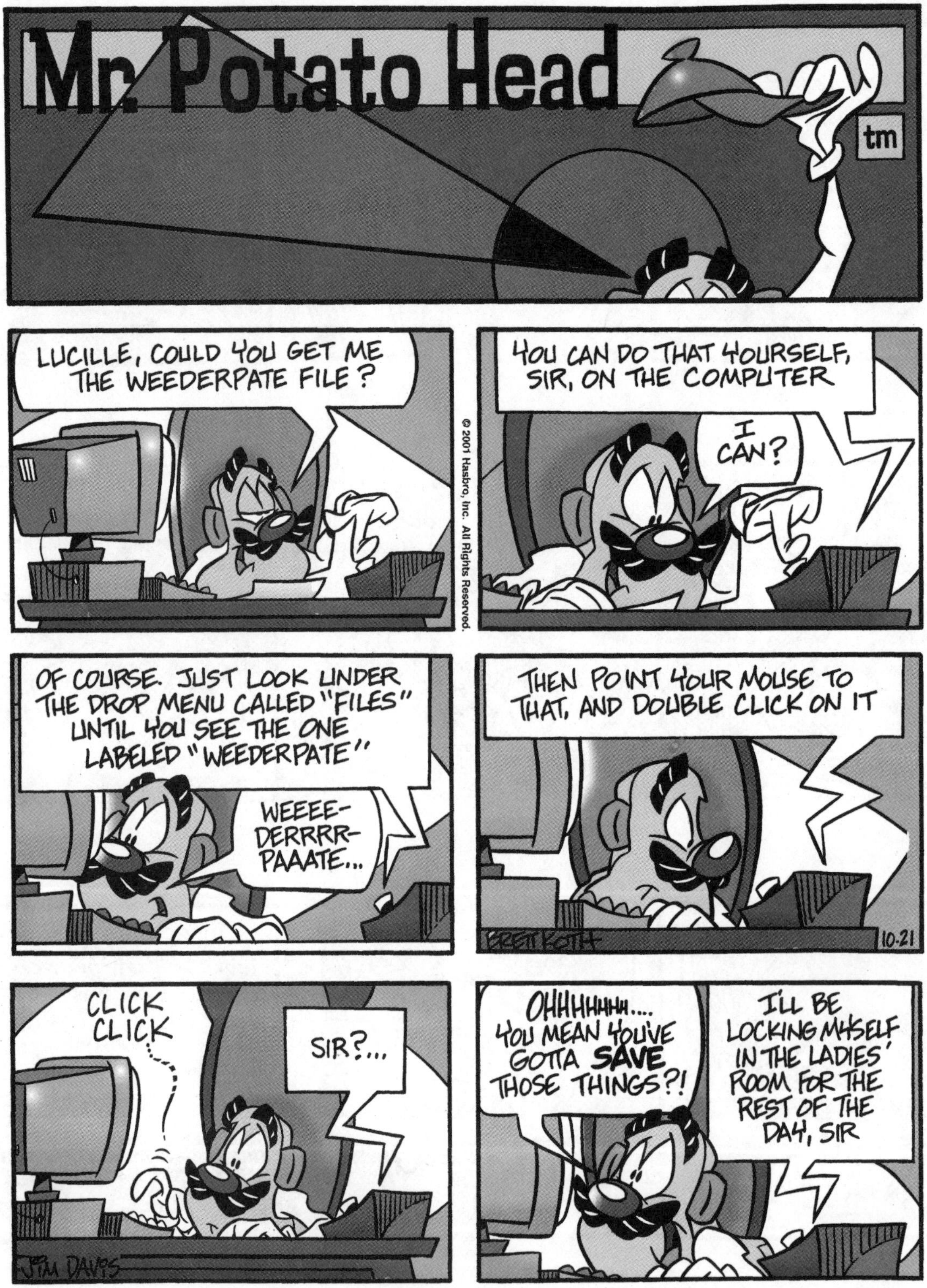
Mr. Potato Head
tm
LUCILLE, COULD YOU GET ME THE WEEDERPATE FILE?
© 2001 Hasbro, Inc. All Rights Reserved.
YOU CAN DO THAT YOURSELF, SIR, ON THE COMPUTER
I CAN?
OF COURSE. JUST LOOK UNDER THE DROP MENU CALLED "FILES" UNTIL YOU SEE THE ONE LABELED "WEEDERPATE"
WEEEE-DERRRR-PAAATE...
THEN POINT YOUR MOUSE TO THAT, AND DOUBLE CLICK ON IT
BRETT KOTH
10-21
CLICK CLICK
SIR?...
JIM DAVIS
OHHHHHH.... YOU MEAN YOU'VE GOTTA SAVE THOSE THINGS?!
I'LL BE LOCKING MYSELF IN THE LADIES' ROOM FOR THE REST OF THE DAY, SIR

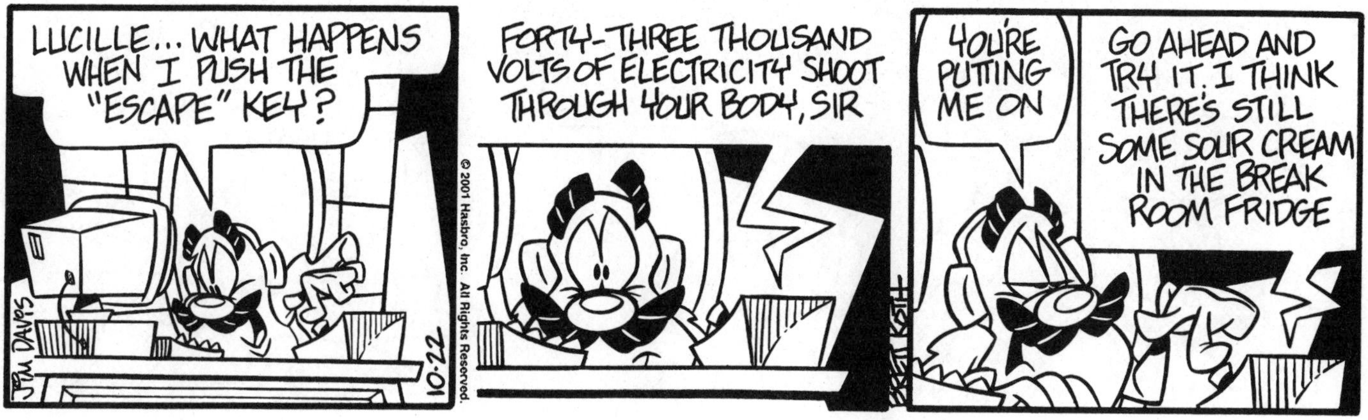
LUCILLE... WHAT HAPPENS WHEN I PUSH THE "ESCAPE" KEY?
JIM DAVIS
10-22
© 2001 Hasbro, Inc. All Rights Reserved.
FORTY-THREE THOUSAND VOLTS OF ELECTRICITY SHOOT THROUGH YOUR BODY, SIR
BRETT KOTH
YOU'RE PUTTING ME ON
GO AHEAD AND TRY IT. I THINK THERE'S STILL SOME SOUR CREAM IN THE BREAK ROOM FRIDGE

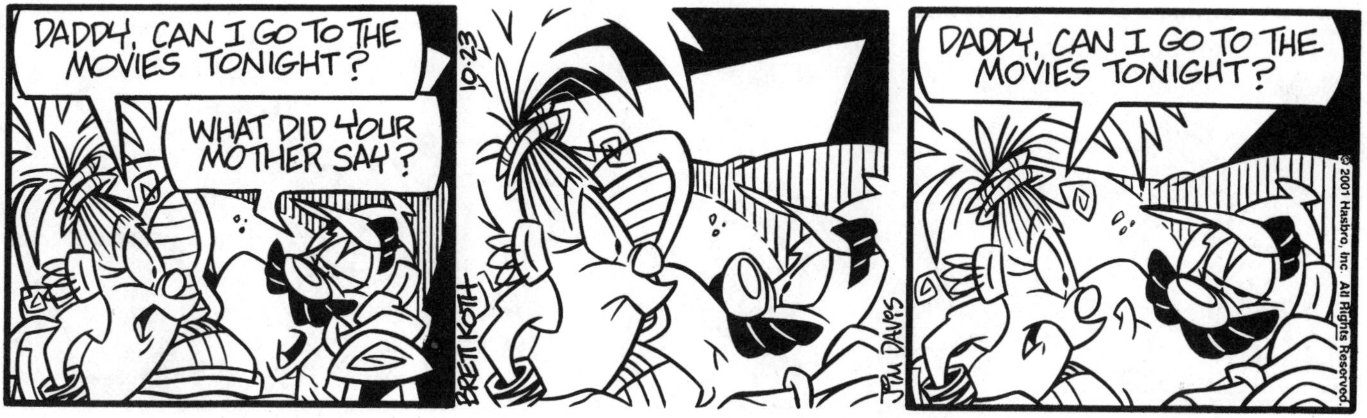
DADDY, CAN I GO TO THE MOVIES TONIGHT?
WHAT DID YOUR MOTHER SAY?
10-23
BRETT KOTH
JIM DAVIS
DADDY, CAN I GO TO THE MOVIES TONIGHT?
© 2001 Hasbro, Inc. All Rights Reserved.

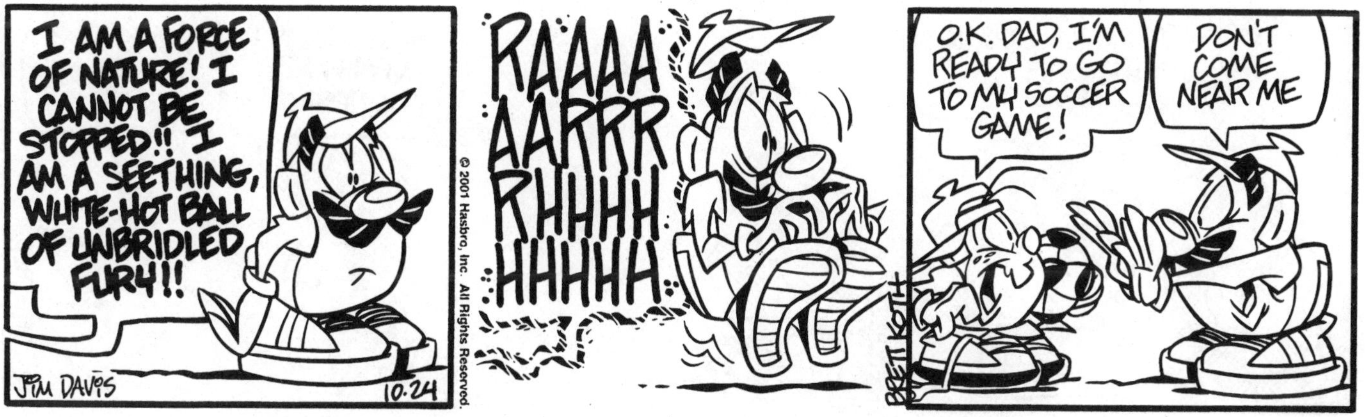
I AM A FORCE OF NATURE! I CANNOT BE STOPPED!! I AM A SEETHING, WHITE-HOT BALL OF UNBRIDLED FURY!!
JIM DAVIS
10-24
© 2001 Hasbro, Inc. All Rights Reserved.
RAAAAAARRRRHHHHHHHHA
BRETT KOTH
O.K. DAD, I'M READY TO GO TO MY SOCCER GAME!
DON'T COME NEAR ME

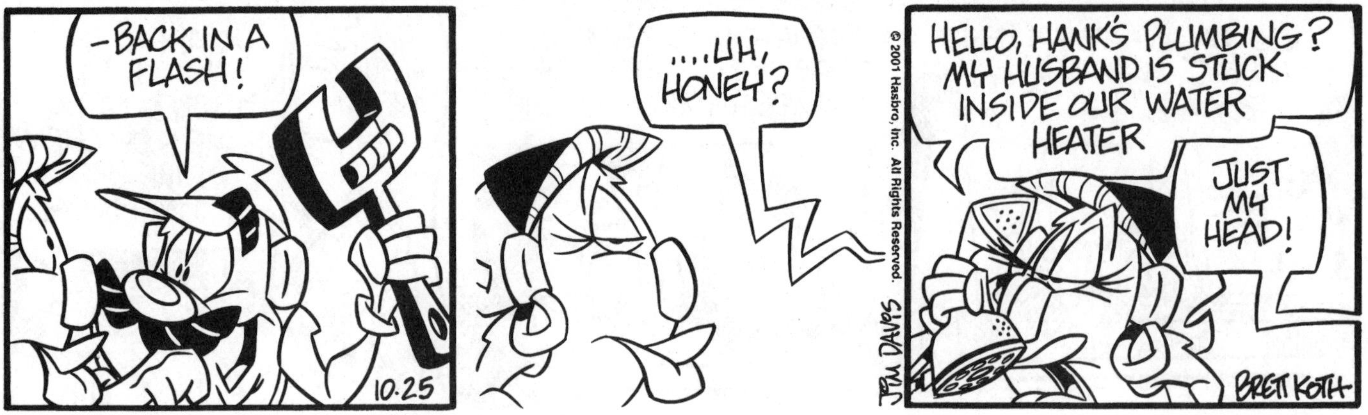

-BACK IN A FLASH!
10.25
....UH, HONEY?
HELLO, HANK'S PLUMBING? MY HUSBAND IS STUCK INSIDE OUR WATER HEATER
JUST MY HEAD!
© 2001 Hasbro, Inc. All Rights Reserved.
JIM DAVIS
BRETT KOTH

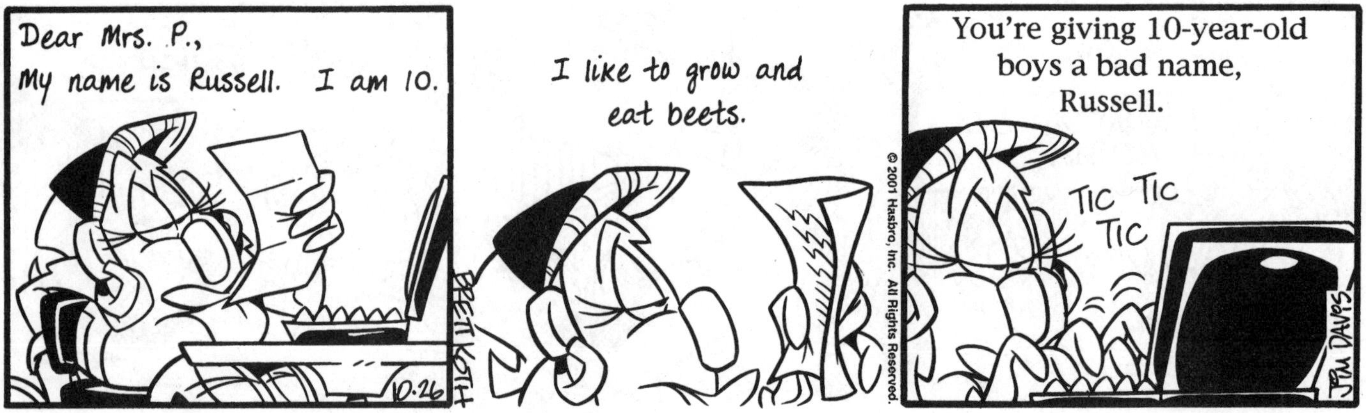

Dear Mrs. P.,
My name is Russell. I am 10.
10.26
BRETT KOTH
I like to grow and eat beets.
© 2001 Hasbro, Inc. All Rights Reserved.
You're giving 10-year-old boys a bad name, Russell.
TIC TIC TIC
JIM DAVIS

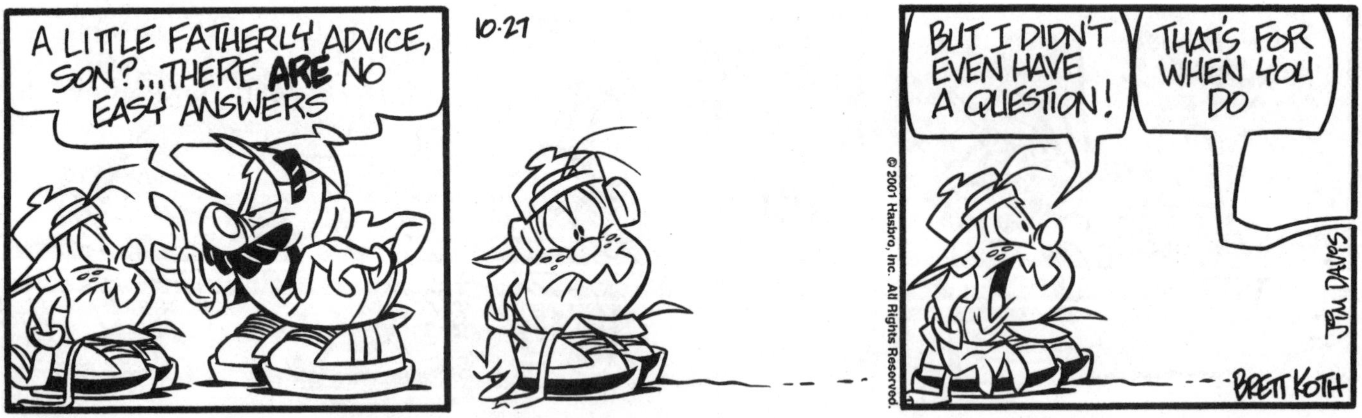

A LITTLE FATHERLY ADVICE, SON?...THERE **ARE** NO EASY ANSWERS
10.27
© 2001 Hasbro, Inc. All Rights Reserved.
BUT I DIDN'T EVEN HAVE A QUESTION!
THAT'S FOR WHEN YOU DO
JIM DAVIS
BRETT KOTH

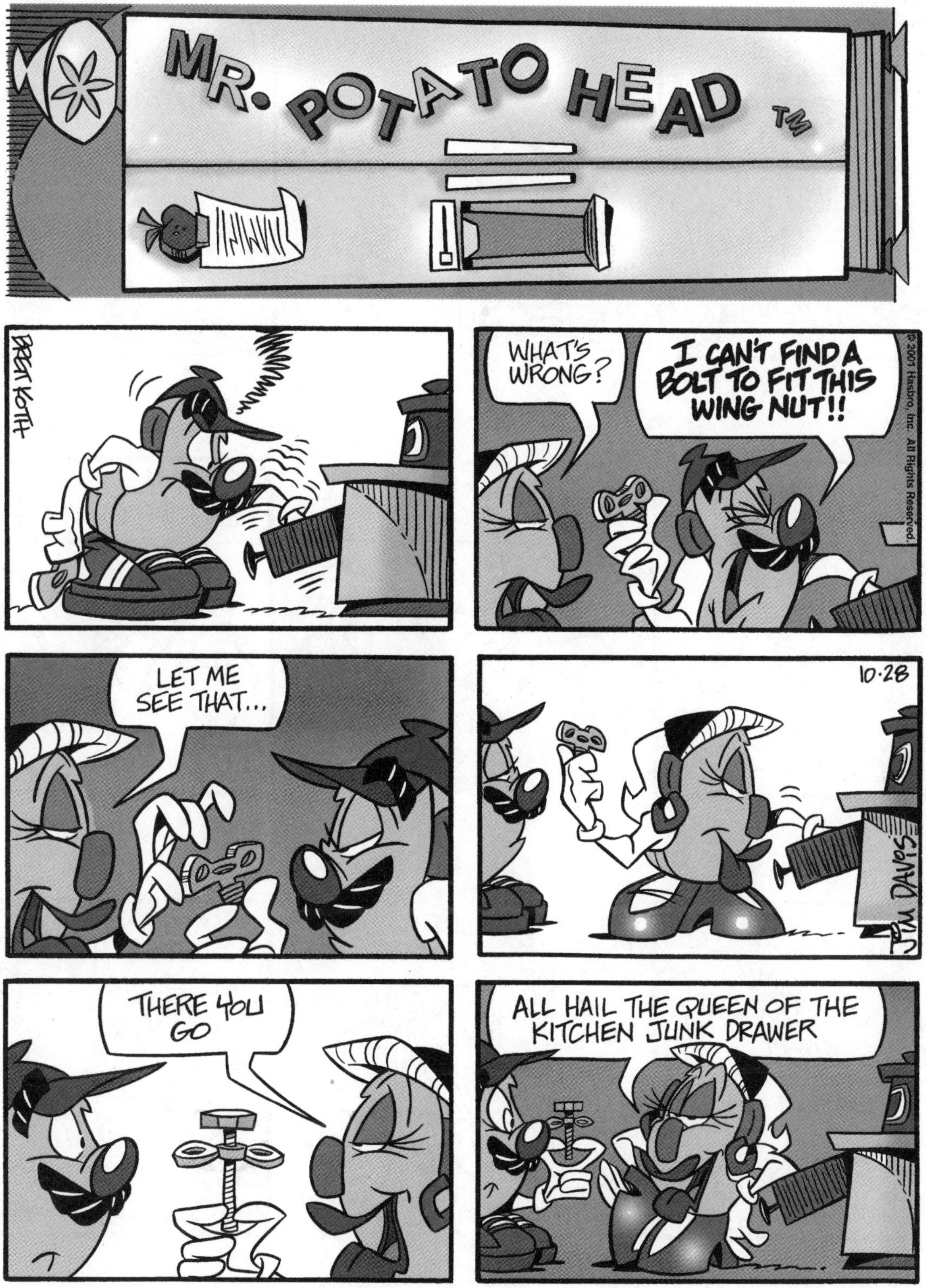
MR. POTATO HEAD TM
BRETT KOTH
© 2001 Hasbro, Inc. All Rights Reserved.
WHAT'S WRONG?
I CAN'T FIND A BOLT TO FIT THIS WING NUT!!
LET ME SEE THAT...
10·28
JIM DAVIS
THERE YOU GO
ALL HAIL THE QUEEN OF THE KITCHEN JUNK DRAWER

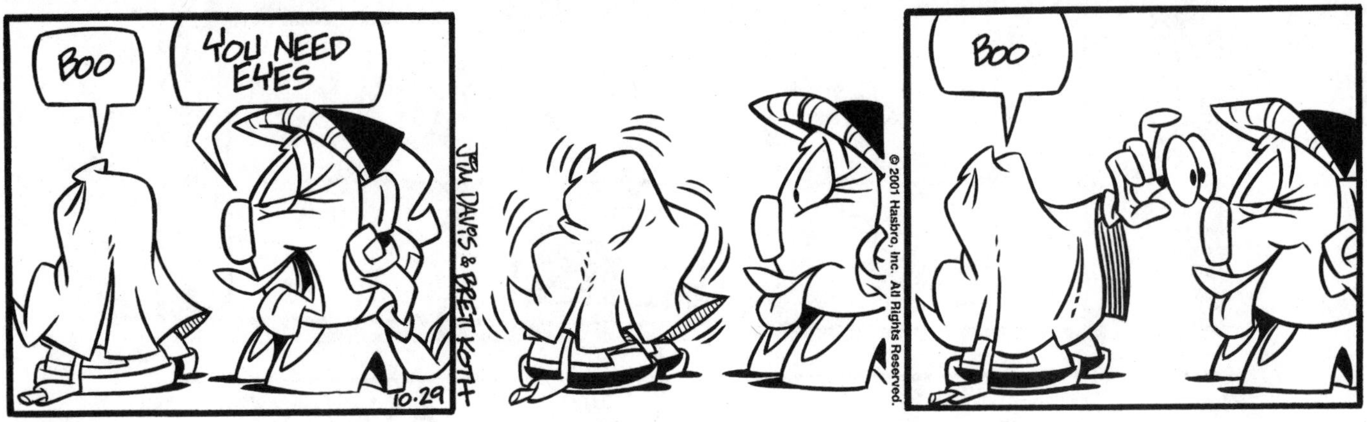
BOO
YOU NEED EYES
JIM DAVIS & BRETT KOTH
10.29
© 2001 Hasbro, Inc. All Rights Reserved.
BOO

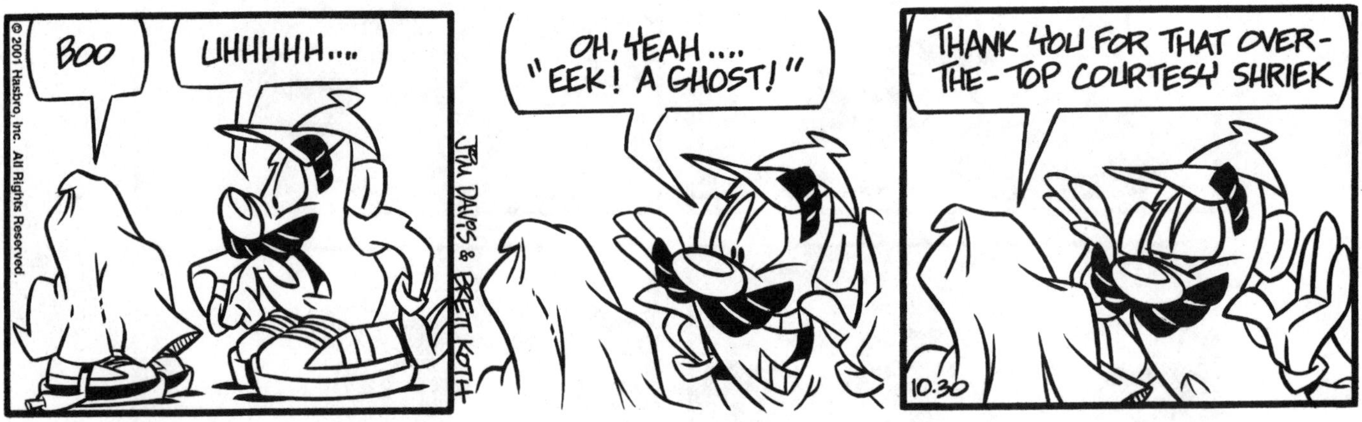
© 2001 Hasbro, Inc. All Rights Reserved.
BOO
UHHHHH....
JIM DAVIS & BRETT KOTH
OH, YEAH.... "EEK! A GHOST!"
THANK YOU FOR THAT OVER-THE-TOP COURTESY SHRIEK
10.30

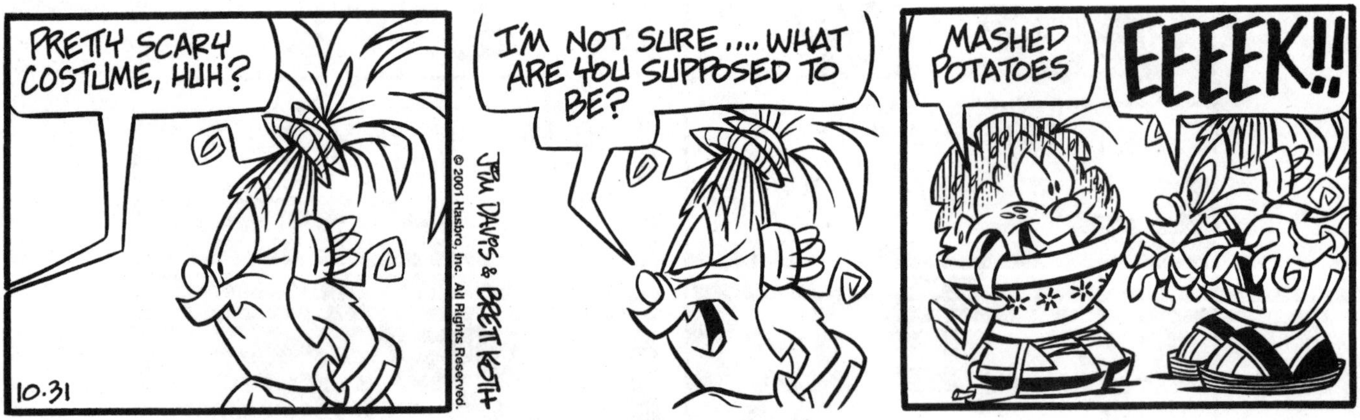
PRETTY SCARY COSTUME, HUH?
10.31
JIM DAVIS & BRETT KOTH
© 2001 Hasbro, Inc. All Rights Reserved.
I'M NOT SURE.... WHAT ARE YOU SUPPOSED TO BE?
MASHED POTATOES
EEEEK!!

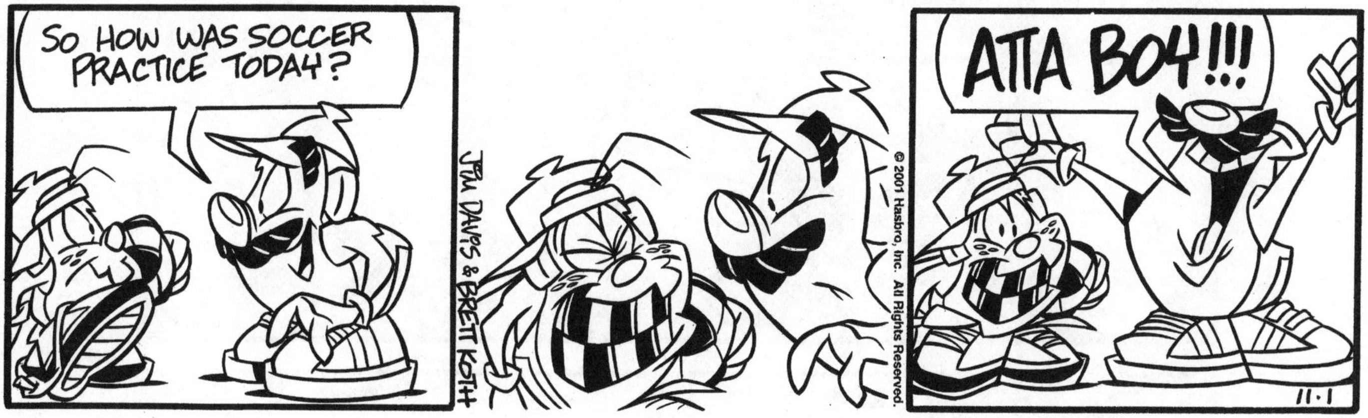
SO HOW WAS SOCCER PRACTICE TODAY?
JIM DAVIS & BRETT KOTH
© 2001 Hasbro, Inc. All Rights Reserved.
ATTA BOY!!!
11·1

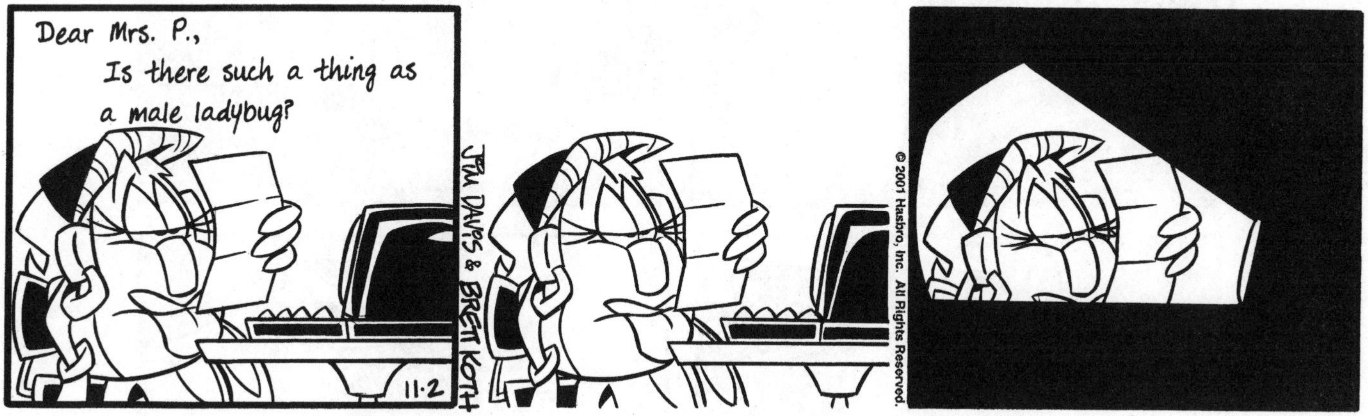
Dear Mrs. P.,
Is there such a thing as a male ladybug?
11·2
JIM DAVIS & BRETT KOTH
© 2001 Hasbro, Inc. All Rights Reserved.

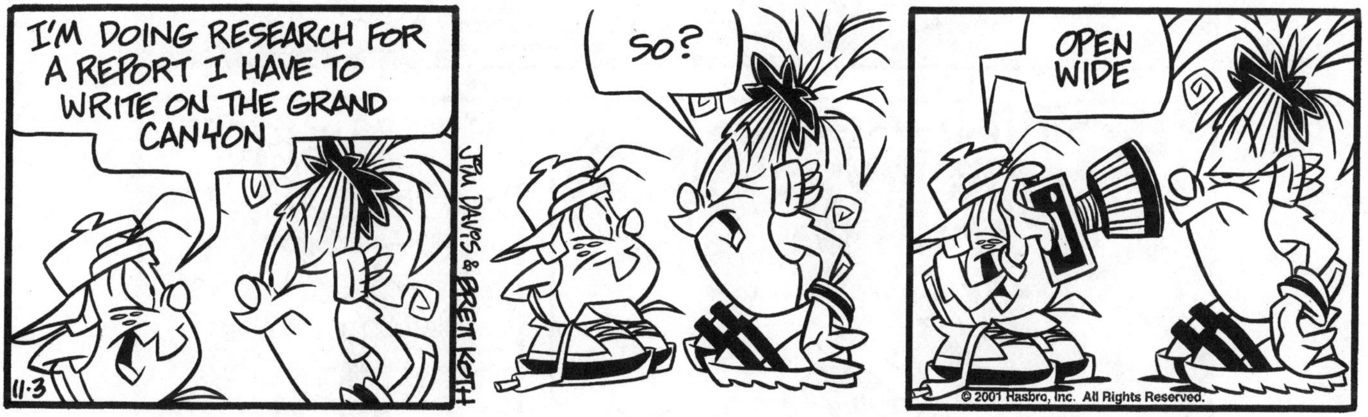
I'M DOING RESEARCH FOR A REPORT I HAVE TO WRITE ON THE GRAND CANYON
11·3
JIM DAVIS & BRETT KOTH
SO?
OPEN WIDE
© 2001 Hasbro, Inc. All Rights Reserved.

Mr. Potato Head! tm
11-4
Z
© 2001 Hasbro, Inc. All Rights Reserved.
Z
Z
JIM DAVIS
Z
BOiiiiNNNG
HOOOOOOOOOO
BRETT KOTH
A "DAD BELLY BOUNCE." .... THE ULTIMATE THRILL RIDE!
GASSSP
GAAASSP
GAASSSP

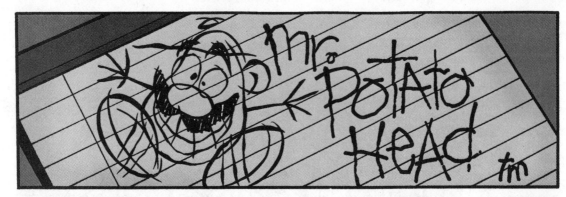

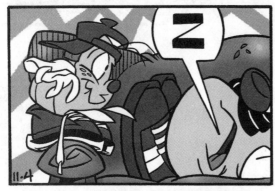

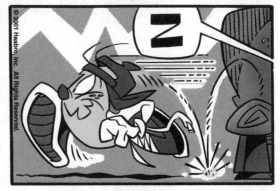

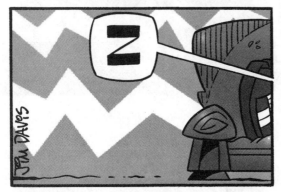

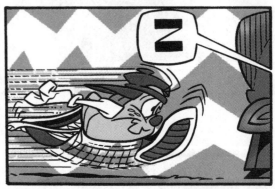

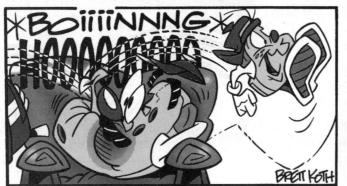

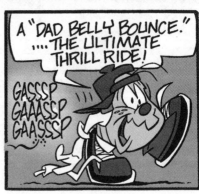

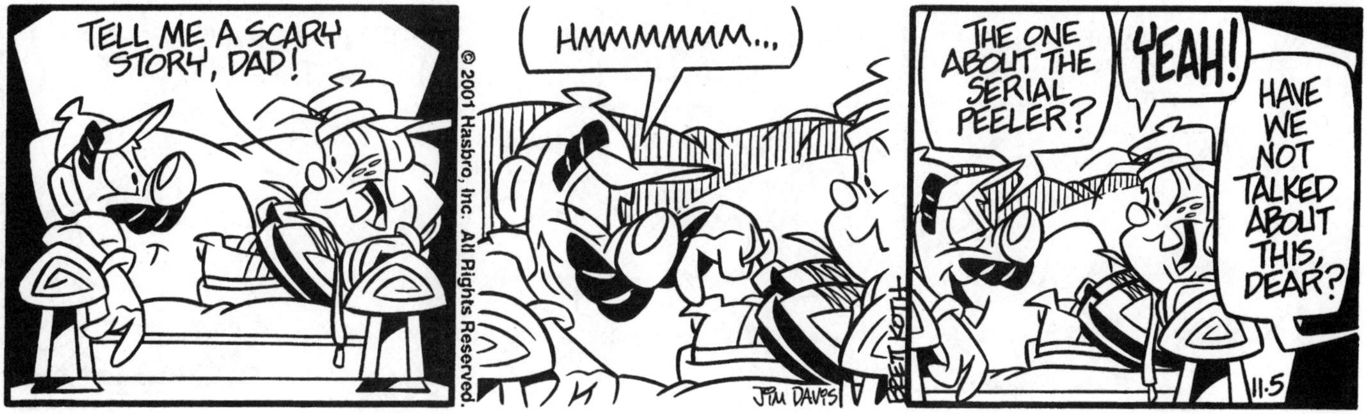
TELL ME A SCARY STORY, DAD!
© 2001 Hasbro, Inc. All Rights Reserved.
HMMMMMM...
JIM DAVIS
BRETT KOTH
THE ONE ABOUT THE SERIAL PEELER?
YEAH!
HAVE WE NOT TALKED ABOUT THIS, DEAR?
11·5

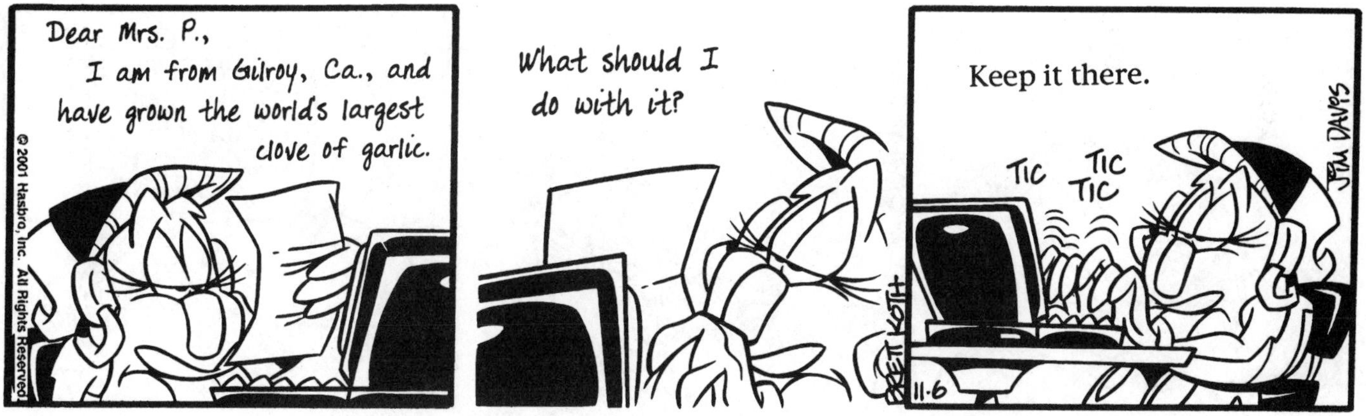
Dear Mrs. P.,
I am from Gilroy, Ca., and have grown the world's largest clove of garlic.
© 2001 Hasbro, Inc. All Rights Reserved.
What should I do with it?
BRETT KOTH
Keep it there.
TIC
TIC
TIC
JIM DAVIS
11·6

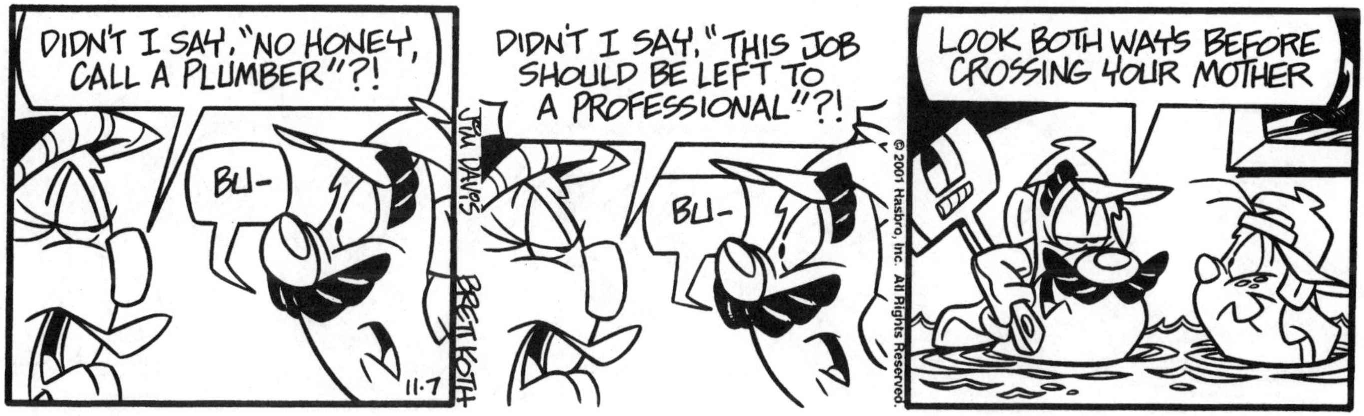
DIDN'T I SAY, "NO HONEY, CALL A PLUMBER"?!
BU-
JIM DAVIS
BRETT KOTH
11·7
DIDN'T I SAY, "THIS JOB SHOULD BE LEFT TO A PROFESSIONAL"?!
BU-
© 2001 Hasbro, Inc. All Rights Reserved.
LOOK BOTH WAYS BEFORE CROSSING YOUR MOTHER

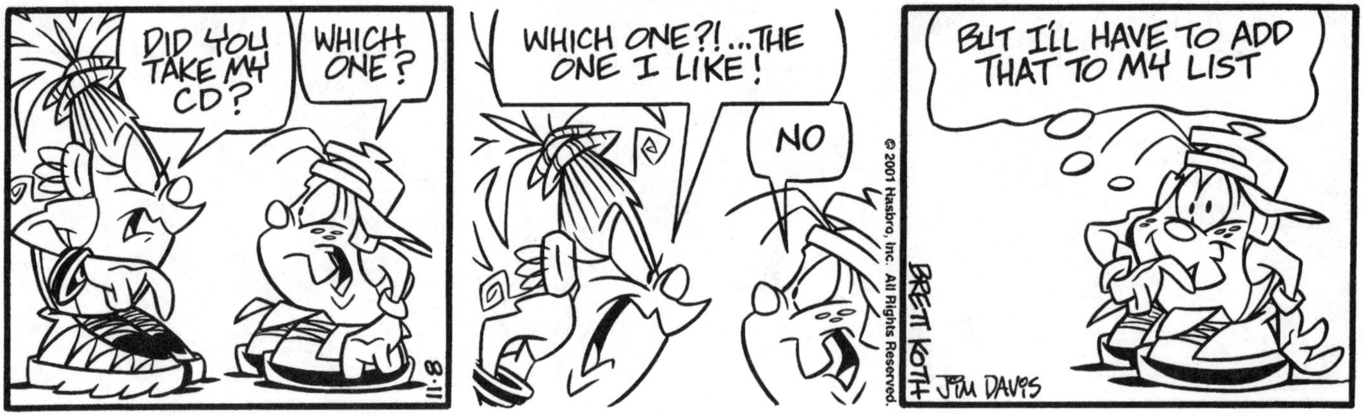
DID YOU TAKE MY CD?
WHICH ONE?
WHICH ONE?! ...THE ONE I LIKE!
NO
BUT I'LL HAVE TO ADD THAT TO MY LIST
© 2001 Hasbro, Inc. All Rights Reserved.
BRETT KOTH
JIM DAVIS

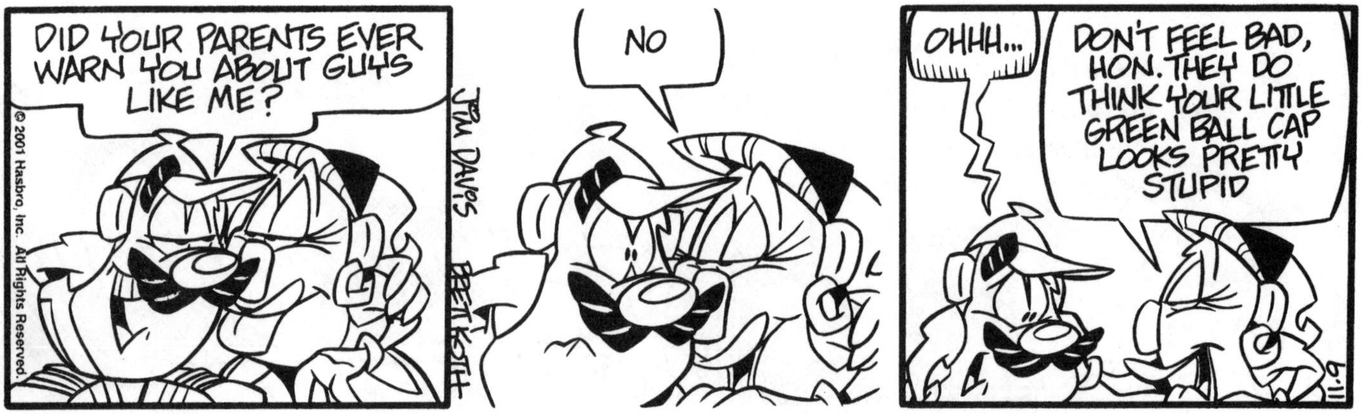
DID YOUR PARENTS EVER WARN YOU ABOUT GUYS LIKE ME?
© 2001 Hasbro, Inc. All Rights Reserved.
JIM DAVIS
BRETT KOTH
NO
OHHH...
DON'T FEEL BAD, HON. THEY DO THINK YOUR LITTLE GREEN BALL CAP LOOKS PRETTY STUPID

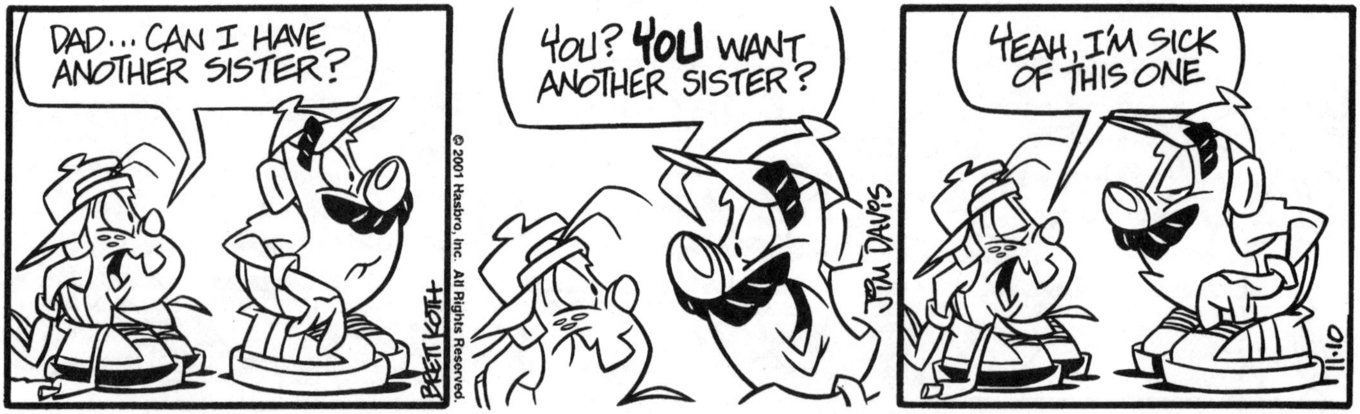
DAD... CAN I HAVE ANOTHER SISTER?
BRETT KOTH
© 2001 Hasbro, Inc. All Rights Reserved.
YOU? YOU WANT ANOTHER SISTER?
JIM DAVIS
YEAH, I'M SICK OF THIS ONE

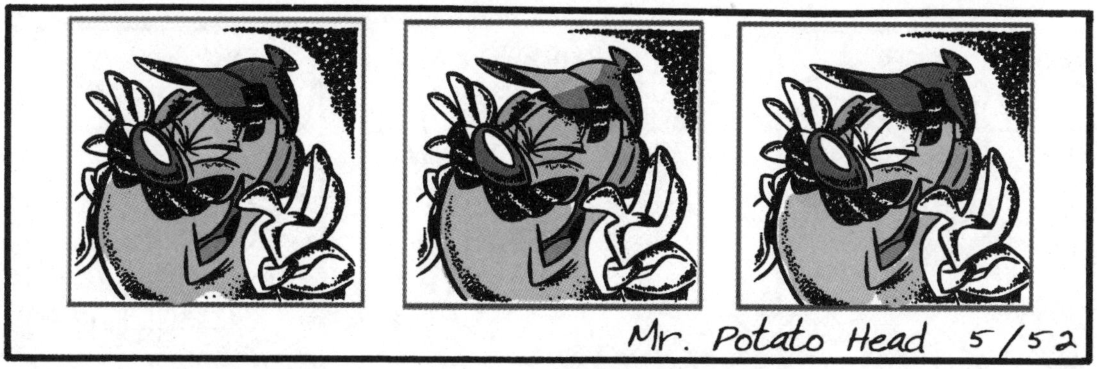
Mr. Potato Head 5/52

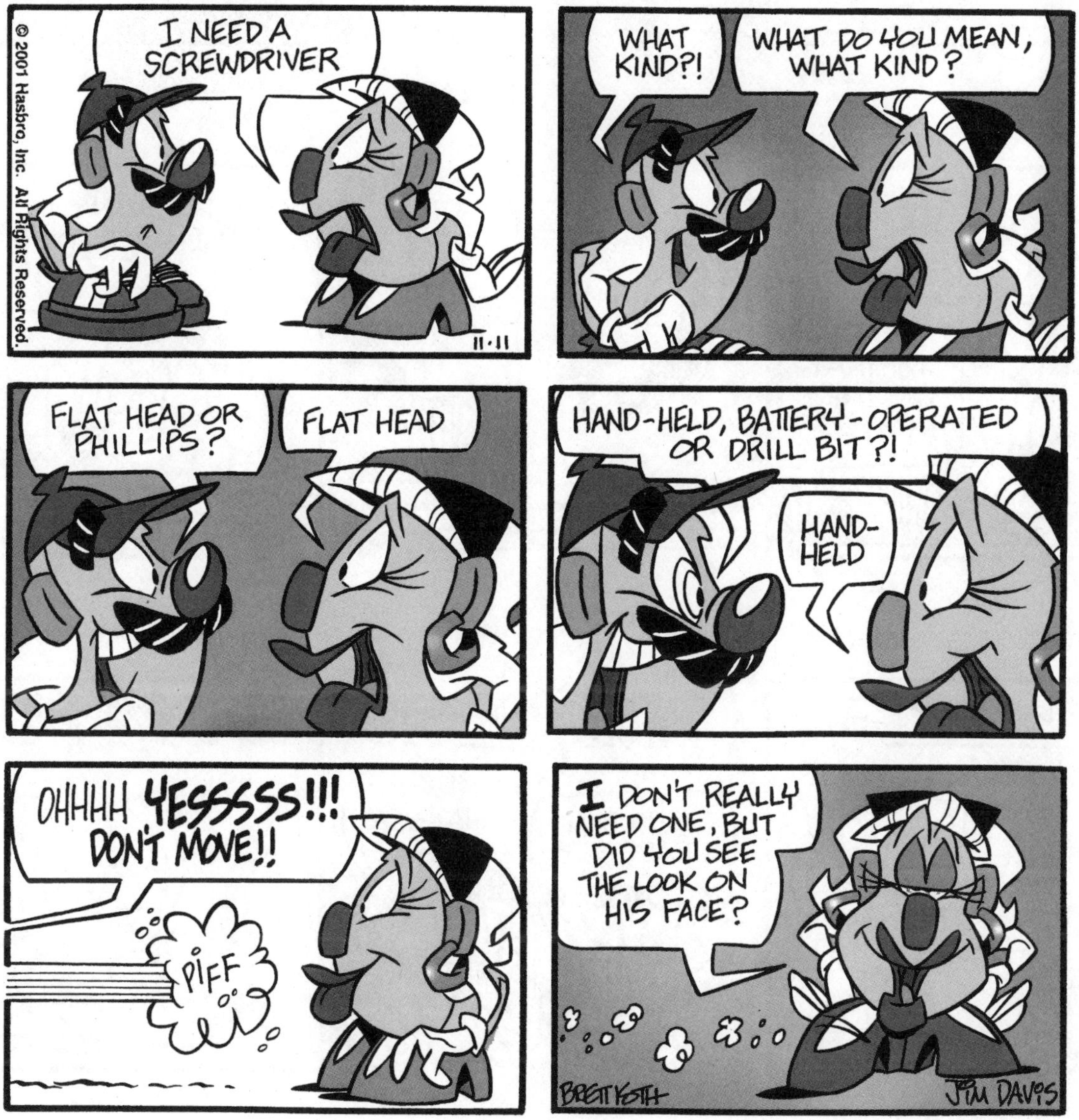
© 2001 Hasbro, Inc. All Rights Reserved.
I NEED A SCREWDRIVER
11·11
WHAT KIND?!
WHAT DO YOU MEAN, WHAT KIND?
FLAT HEAD OR PHILLIPS?
FLAT HEAD
HAND-HELD, BATTERY-OPERATED OR DRILL BIT?!
HAND-HELD
OHHHH YESSSSS!!! DON'T MOVE!!
PIFF
I DON'T REALLY NEED ONE, BUT DID YOU SEE THE LOOK ON HIS FACE?
BRETT KOTH
JIM DAVIS

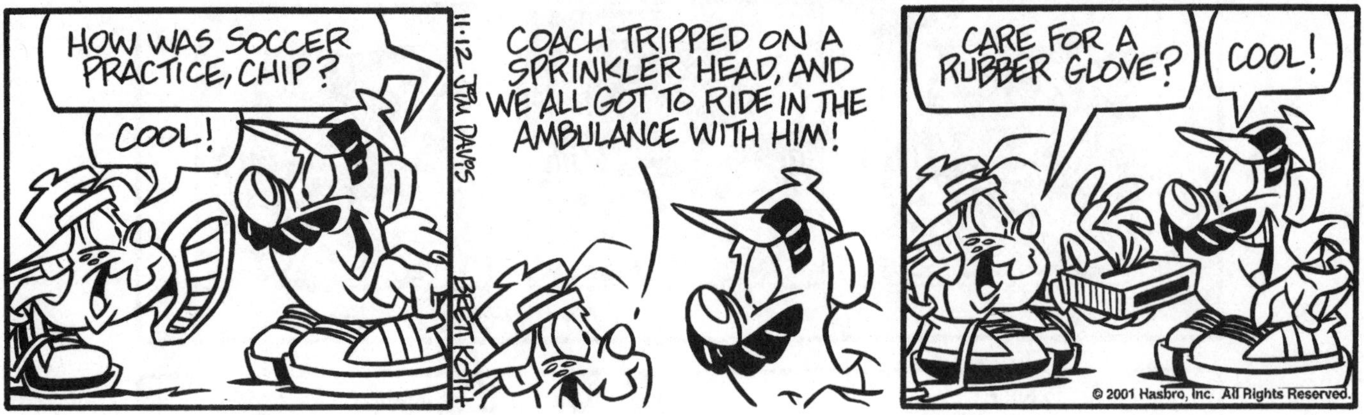
HOW WAS SOCCER PRACTICE, CHIP?
COOL!
11·12 JIM DAVIS BRETT KOTH
COACH TRIPPED ON A SPRINKLER HEAD, AND WE ALL GOT TO RIDE IN THE AMBULANCE WITH HIM!
CARE FOR A RUBBER GLOVE?
COOL!
© 2001 Hasbro, Inc. All Rights Reserved.

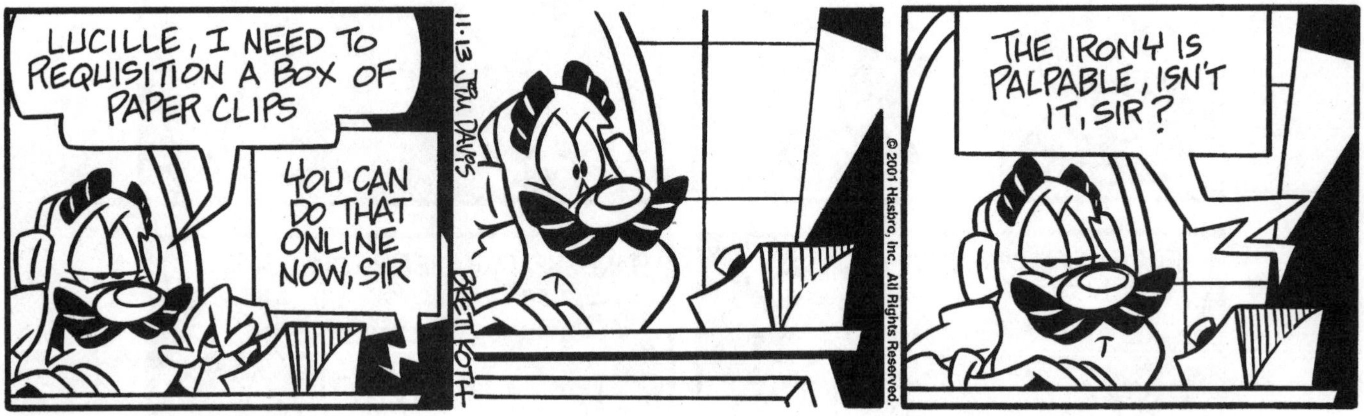
LUCILLE, I NEED TO REQUISITION A BOX OF PAPER CLIPS
YOU CAN DO THAT ONLINE NOW, SIR
11·13 JIM DAVIS BRETT KOTH
© 2001 Hasbro, Inc. All Rights Reserved.
THE IRONY IS PALPABLE, ISN'T IT, SIR?

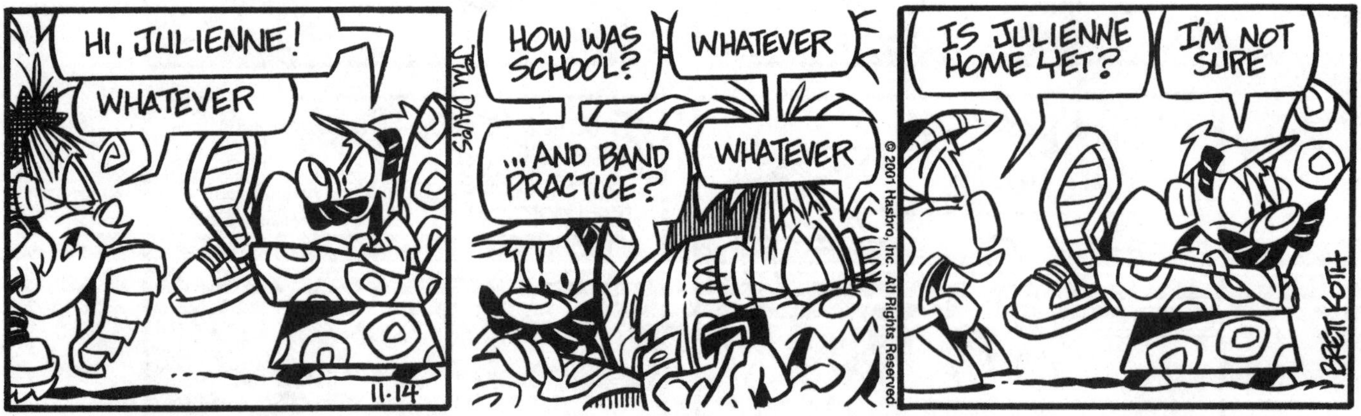
HI, JULIENNE!
WHATEVER
JIM DAVIS
11·14
HOW WAS SCHOOL?
WHATEVER
...AND BAND PRACTICE?
WHATEVER
© 2001 Hasbro, Inc. All Rights Reserved.
IS JULIENNE HOME YET?
I'M NOT SURE
BRETT KOTH

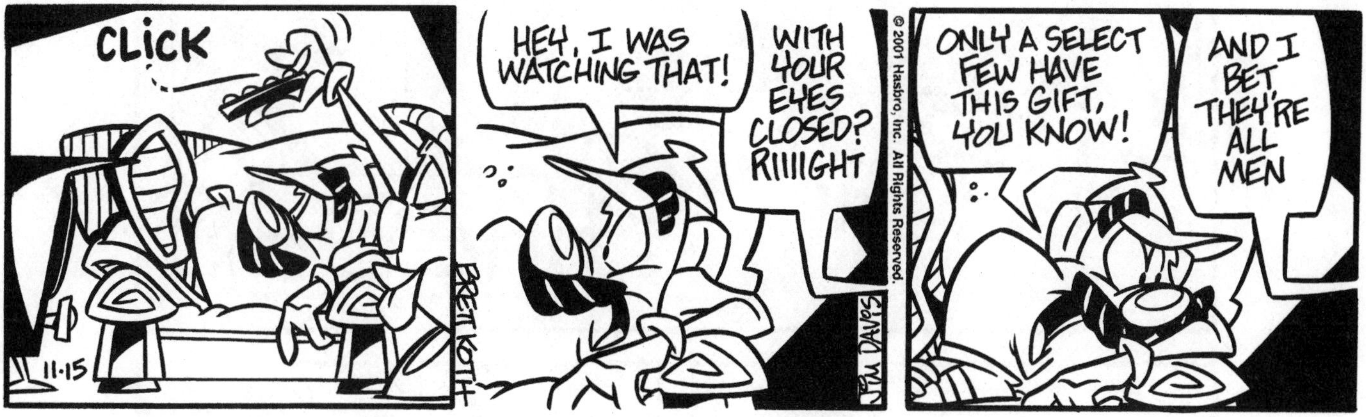
CLICK
11·15
BRETT KOTH
HEY, I WAS WATCHING THAT!
WITH YOUR EYES CLOSED? RIIIIGHT
JIM DAVIS
© 2001 Hasbro, Inc. All Rights Reserved.
ONLY A SELECT FEW HAVE THIS GIFT, YOU KNOW!
AND I BET THEY'RE ALL MEN

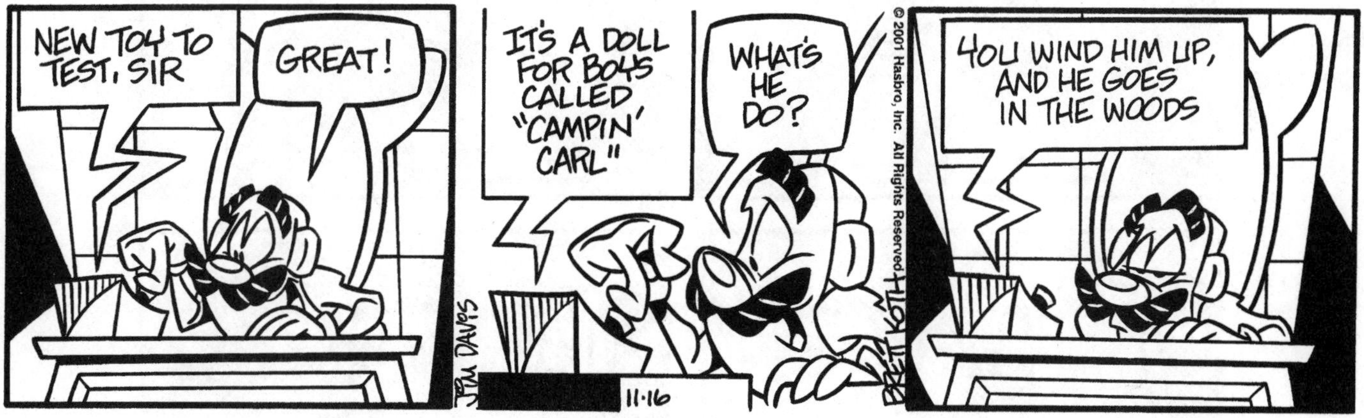
NEW TOY TO TEST, SIR
GREAT!
JIM DAVIS
IT'S A DOLL FOR BOYS CALLED "CAMPIN' CARL"
WHAT'S HE DO?
11·16
BRETT KOTH
© 2001 Hasbro, Inc. All Rights Reserved.
YOU WIND HIM UP, AND HE GOES IN THE WOODS

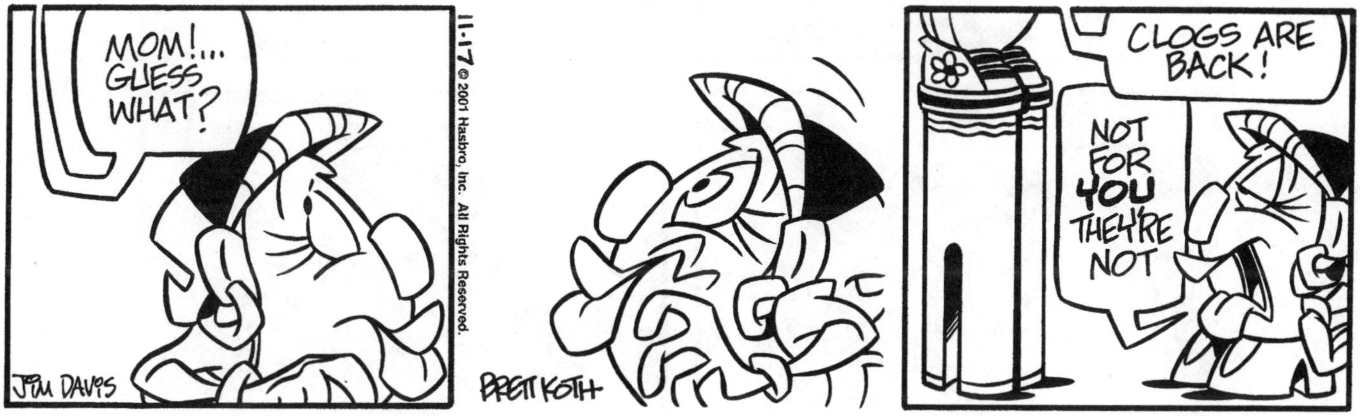
MOM!... GUESS WHAT?
JIM DAVIS
11·17 © 2001 Hasbro, Inc. All Rights Reserved.
BRETT KOTH
CLOGS ARE BACK!
NOT FOR YOU THEY'RE NOT

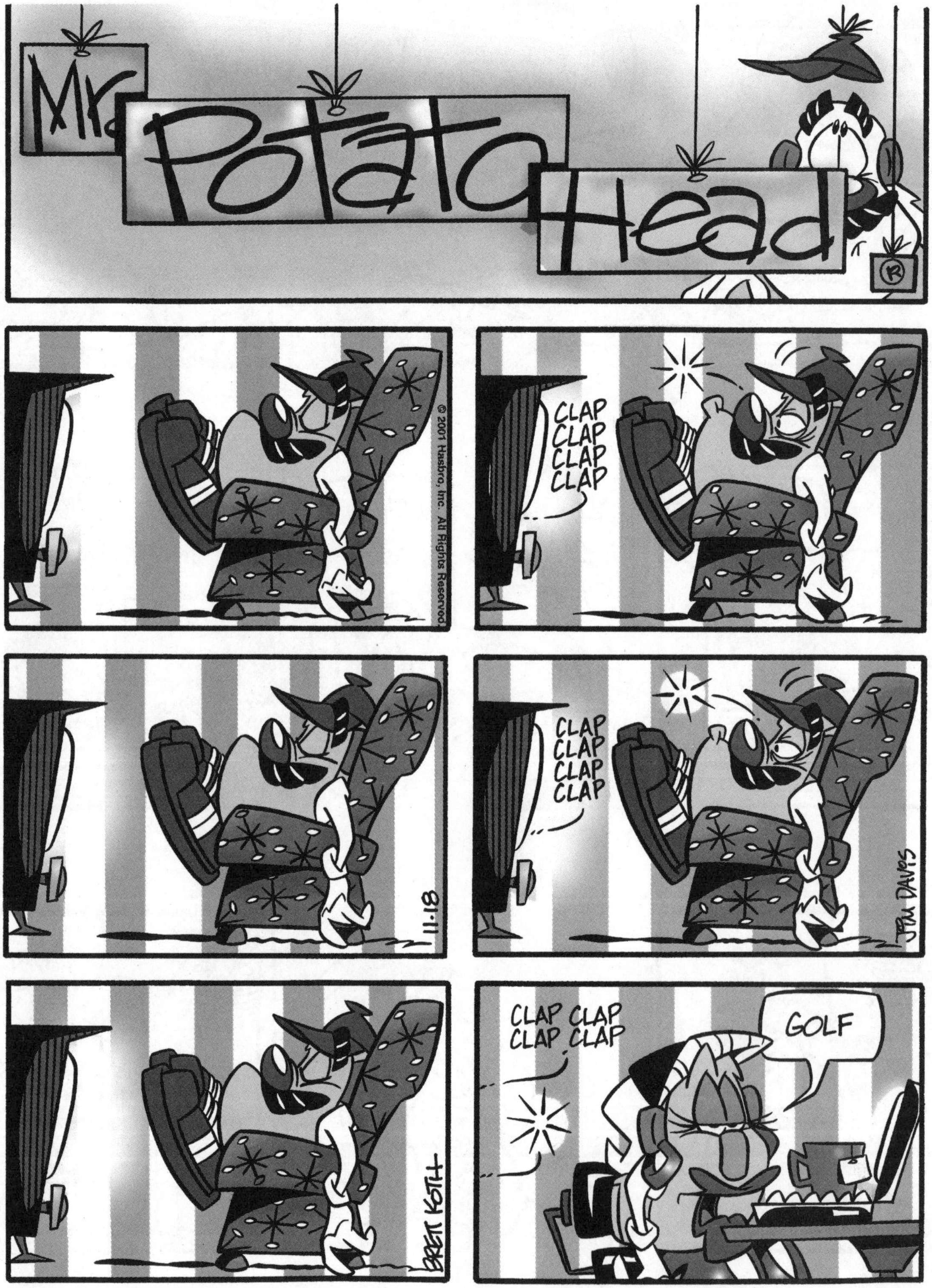

Mr. Potato Head
© 2001 Hasbro, Inc. All Rights Reserved
CLAP
CLAP
CLAP
CLAP
11-18
CLAP
CLAP
CLAP
CLAP
JIM DAVIS
BRETT KOTH
CLAP CLAP
CLAP CLAP
GOLF

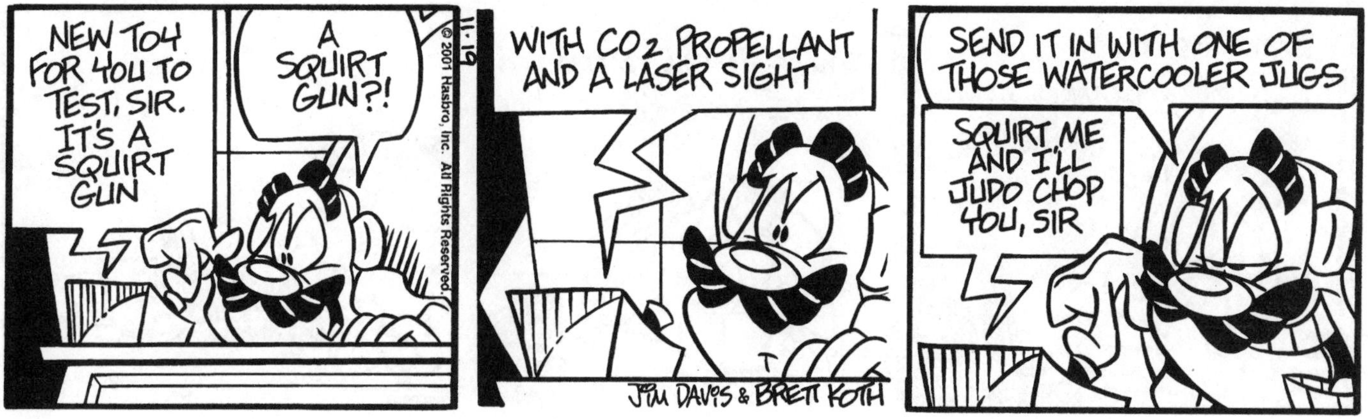
NEW TOY FOR YOU TO TEST, SIR. IT'S A SQUIRT GUN
A SQUIRT GUN?!
11-19
WITH CO2 PROPELLANT AND A LASER SIGHT
JIM DAVIS & BRETT KOTH
SEND IT IN WITH ONE OF THOSE WATERCOOLER JUGS
SQUIRT ME AND I'LL JUDO CHOP YOU, SIR

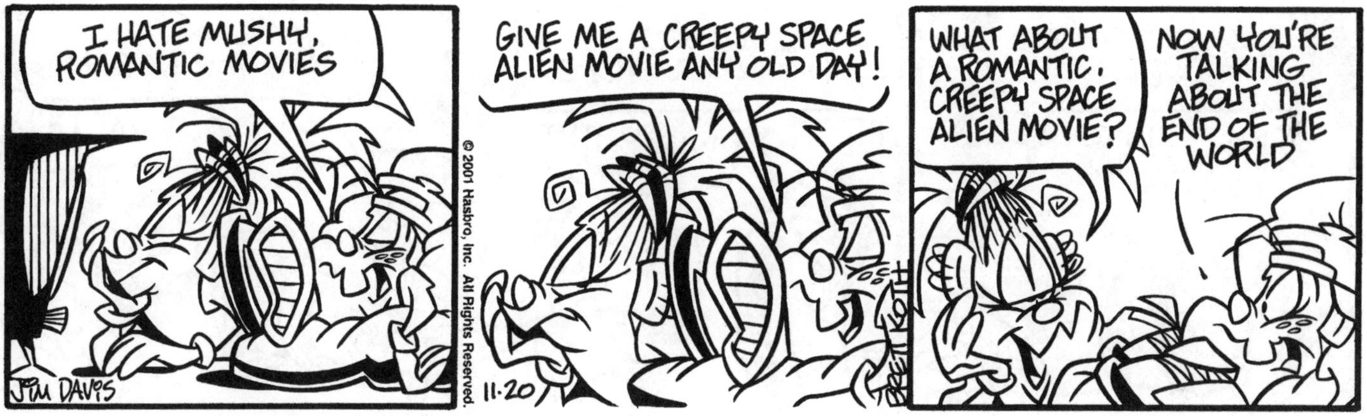
I HATE MUSHY, ROMANTIC MOVIES
JIM DAVIS
11-20
GIVE ME A CREEPY SPACE ALIEN MOVIE ANY OLD DAY!
BRETT KOTH
WHAT ABOUT A ROMANTIC, CREEPY SPACE ALIEN MOVIE?
NOW YOU'RE TALKING ABOUT THE END OF THE WORLD

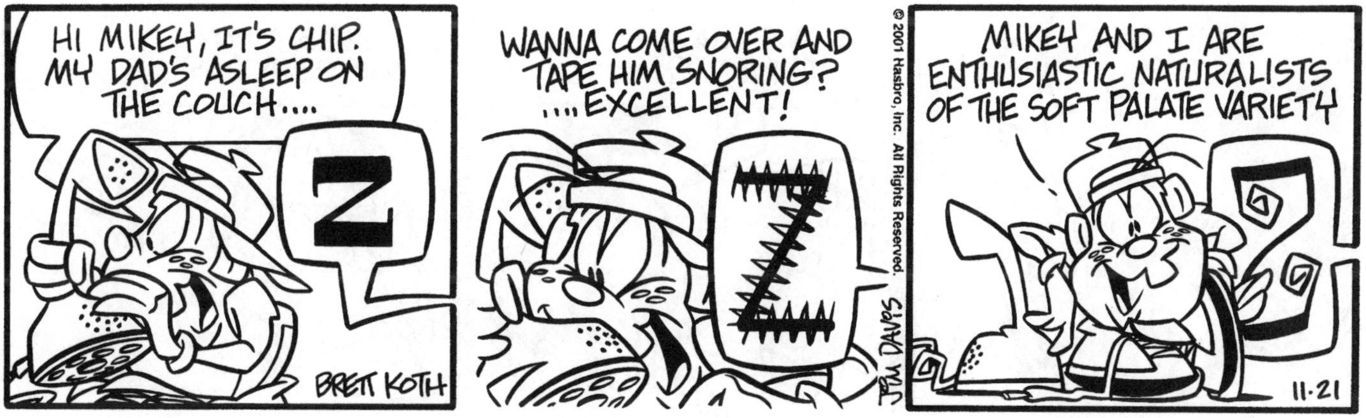
HI MIKEY, IT'S CHIP. MY DAD'S ASLEEP ON THE COUCH....
Z
BRETT KOTH
WANNA COME OVER AND TAPE HIM SNORING? ....EXCELLENT!
Z
JIM DAVIS
MIKEY AND I ARE ENTHUSIASTIC NATURALISTS OF THE SOFT PALATE VARIETY
11-21

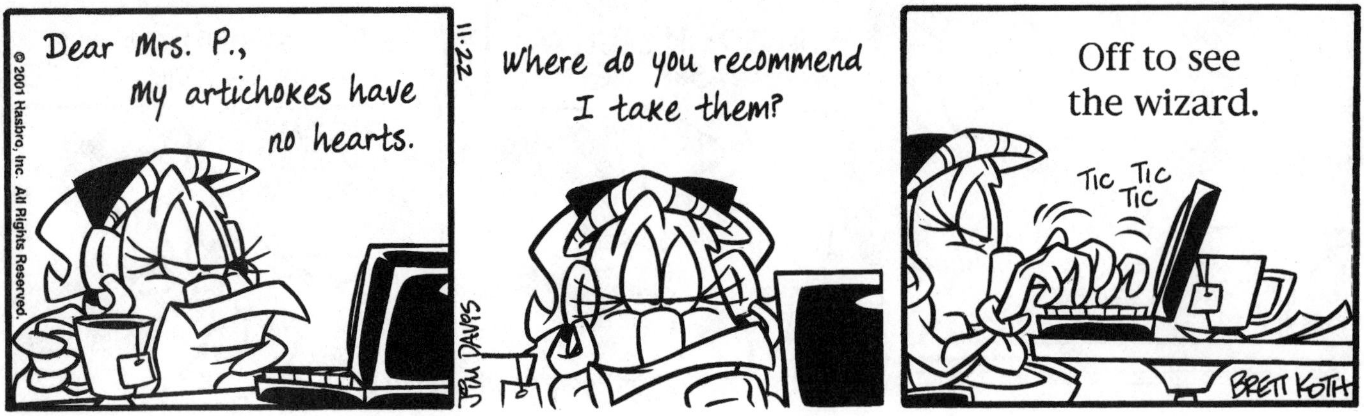
© 2001 Hasbro, Inc. All Rights Reserved.
Dear Mrs. P.,
My artichokes have no hearts.
11.22
JIM DAVIS
Where do you recommend I take them?
Off to see the wizard.
TIC TIC TIC
BRETT KOTH

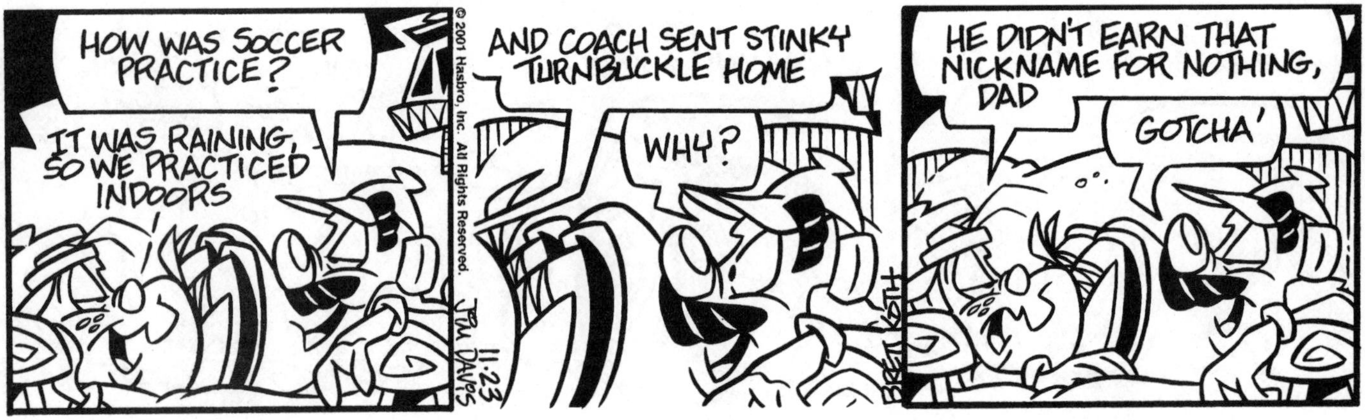
HOW WAS SOCCER PRACTICE?
IT WAS RAINING, SO WE PRACTICED INDOORS
© 2001 Hasbro, Inc. All Rights Reserved.
JIM DAVIS
11.23
AND COACH SENT STINKY TURNBUCKLE HOME
WHY?
BRETT KOTH
HE DIDN'T EARN THAT NICKNAME FOR NOTHING, DAD
GOTCHA'

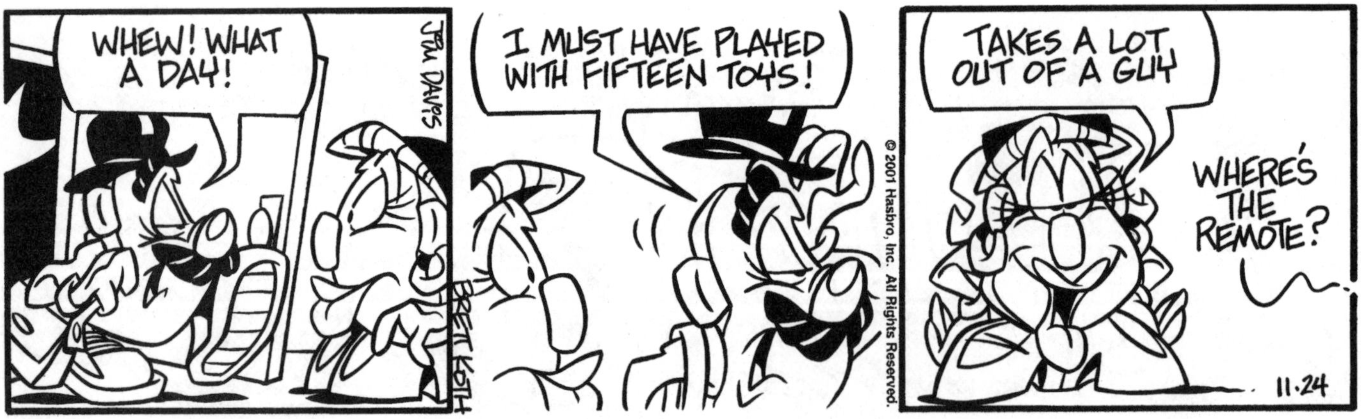
WHEW! WHAT A DAY!
JIM DAVIS
BRETT KOTH
I MUST HAVE PLAYED WITH FIFTEEN TOYS!
© 2001 Hasbro, Inc. All Rights Reserved.
TAKES A LOT OUT OF A GUY
WHERE'S THE REMOTE?
11.24

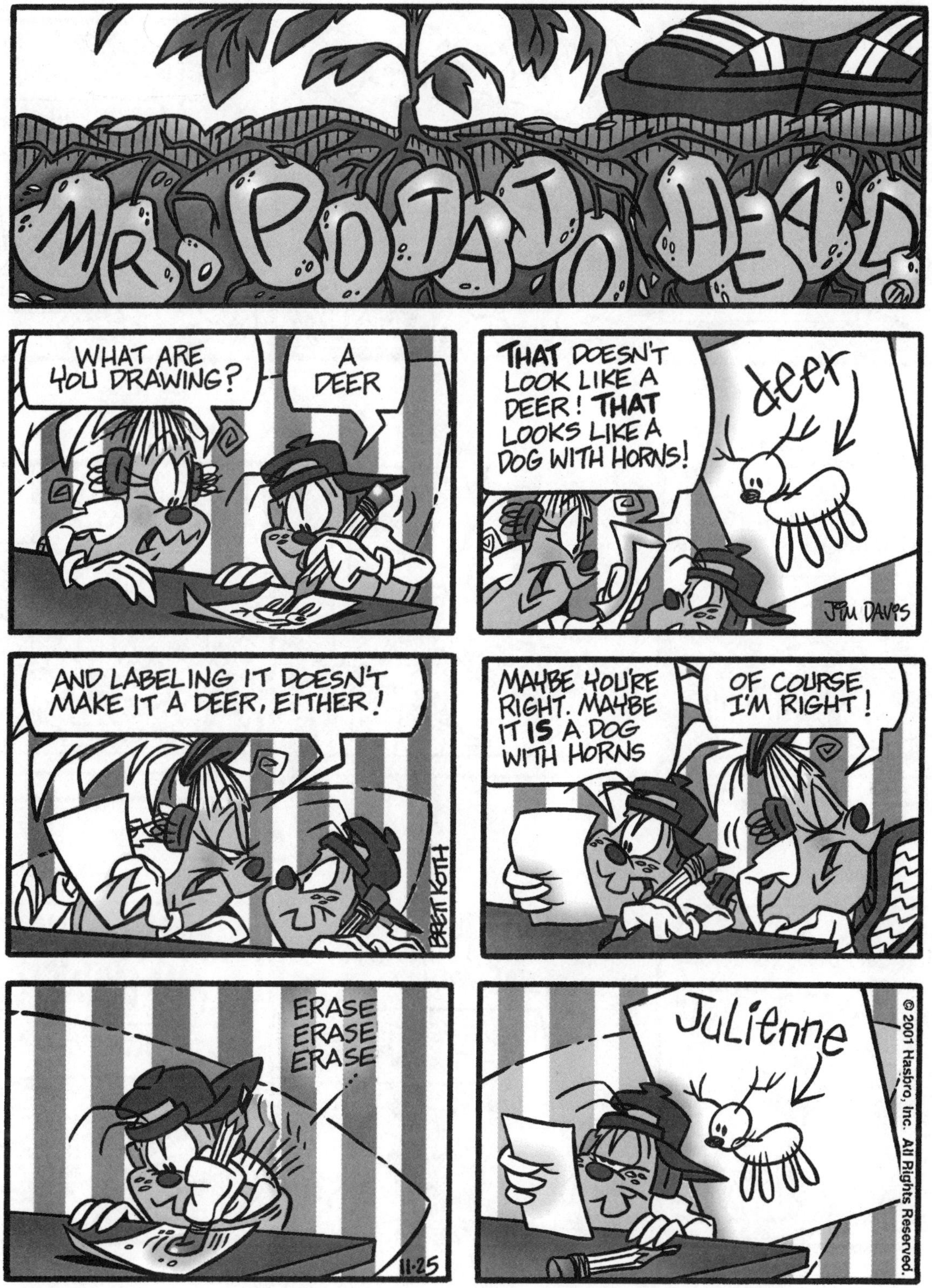
MR. POTATO HEAD
WHAT ARE YOU DRAWING?
A DEER
THAT DOESN'T LOOK LIKE A DEER! THAT LOOKS LIKE A DOG WITH HORNS!
deer
JIM DAVIS
AND LABELING IT DOESN'T MAKE IT A DEER, EITHER!
BRETT KOTH
MAYBE YOU'RE RIGHT. MAYBE IT IS A DOG WITH HORNS
OF COURSE I'M RIGHT!
ERASE ERASE ERASE
11·25
Julienne
© 2001 Hasbro, Inc. All Rights Reserved.

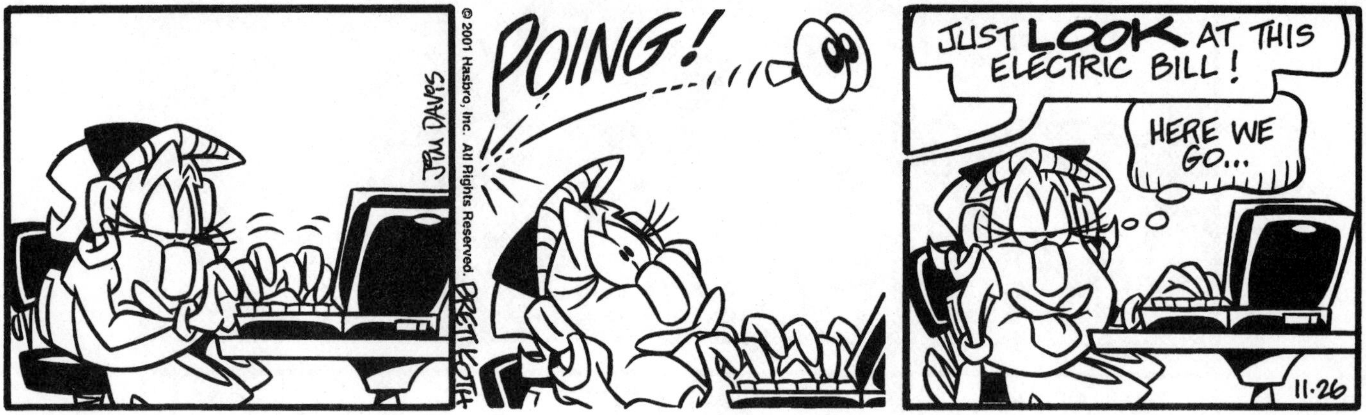
© 2001 Hasbro, Inc. All Rights Reserved.
JIM DAVIS
BRETT KOTH
POING!
JUST LOOK AT THIS ELECTRIC BILL!
HERE WE GO...
11·26

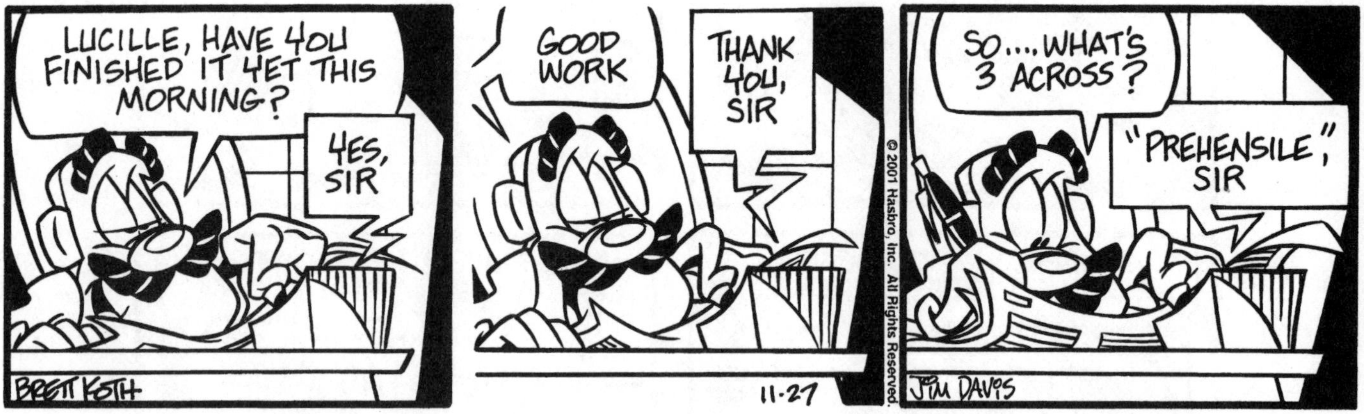
LUCILLE, HAVE YOU FINISHED IT YET THIS MORNING?
YES, SIR
BRETT KOTH
GOOD WORK
THANK YOU, SIR
11·27
© 2001 Hasbro, Inc. All Rights Reserved.
SO.... WHAT'S 3 ACROSS?
"PREHENSILE," SIR
JIM DAVIS

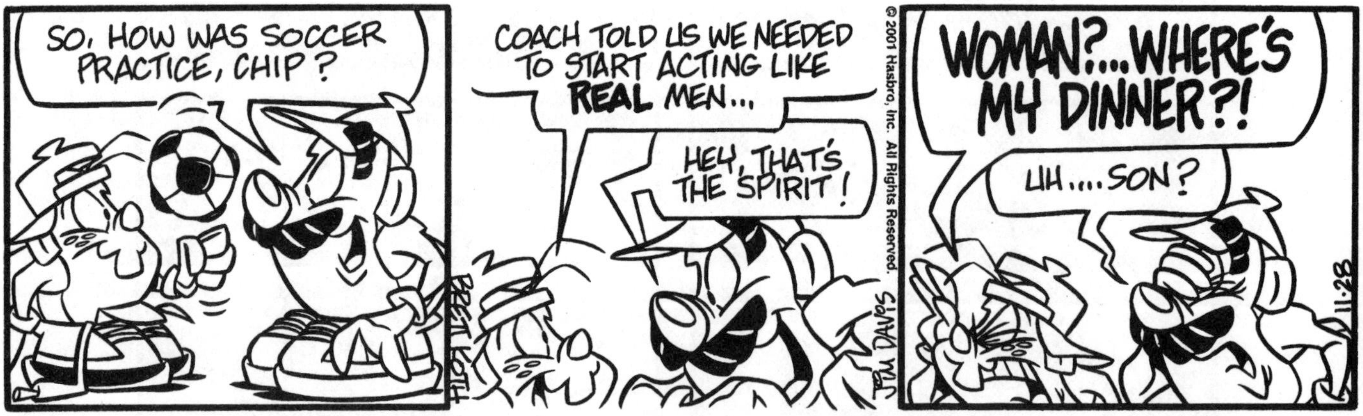
SO, HOW WAS SOCCER PRACTICE, CHIP?
BRETT KOTH
COACH TOLD US WE NEEDED TO START ACTING LIKE REAL MEN...
HEY, THAT'S THE SPIRIT!
JIM DAVIS
© 2001 Hasbro, Inc. All Rights Reserved.
WOMAN?...WHERE'S MY DINNER?!
UH.... SON?
11·28

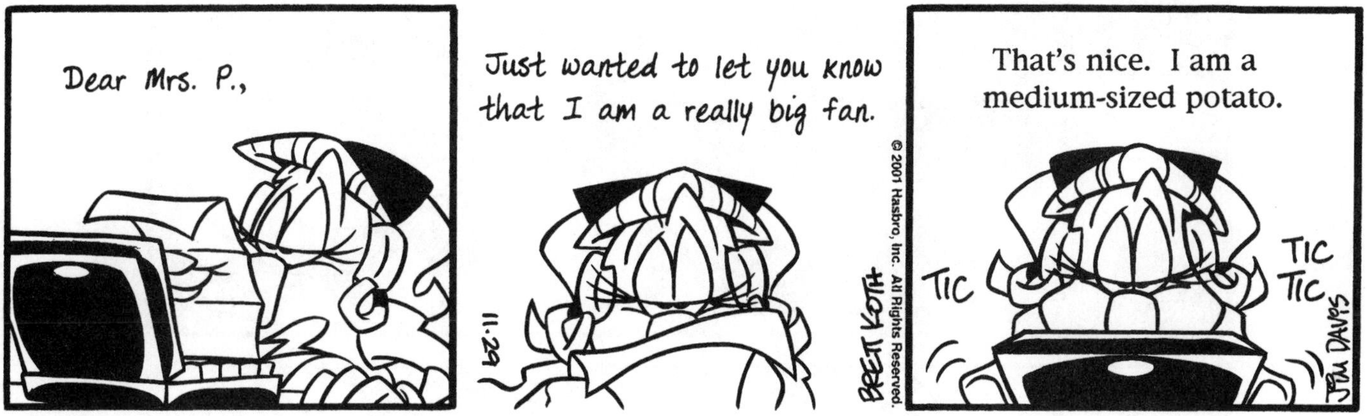
Dear Mrs. P.,
Just wanted to let you know that I am a really big fan.
11.29
That's nice. I am a medium-sized potato.
TIC
TIC
TIC
© 2001 Hasbro, Inc. All Rights Reserved.

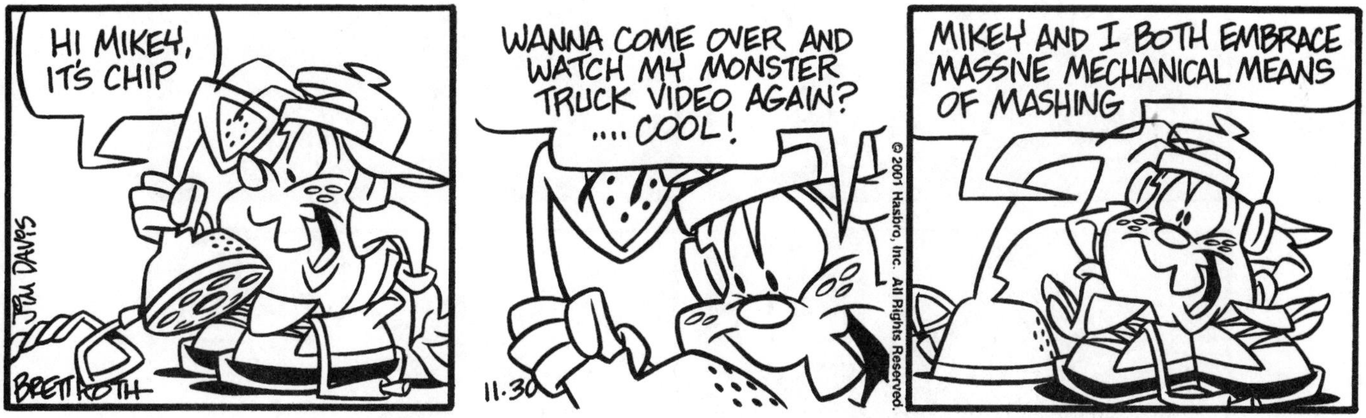
HI MIKEY, IT'S CHIP
WANNA COME OVER AND WATCH MY MONSTER TRUCK VIDEO AGAIN? ....COOL!
11.30
MIKEY AND I BOTH EMBRACE MASSIVE MECHANICAL MEANS OF MASHING
© 2001 Hasbro, Inc. All Rights Reserved.

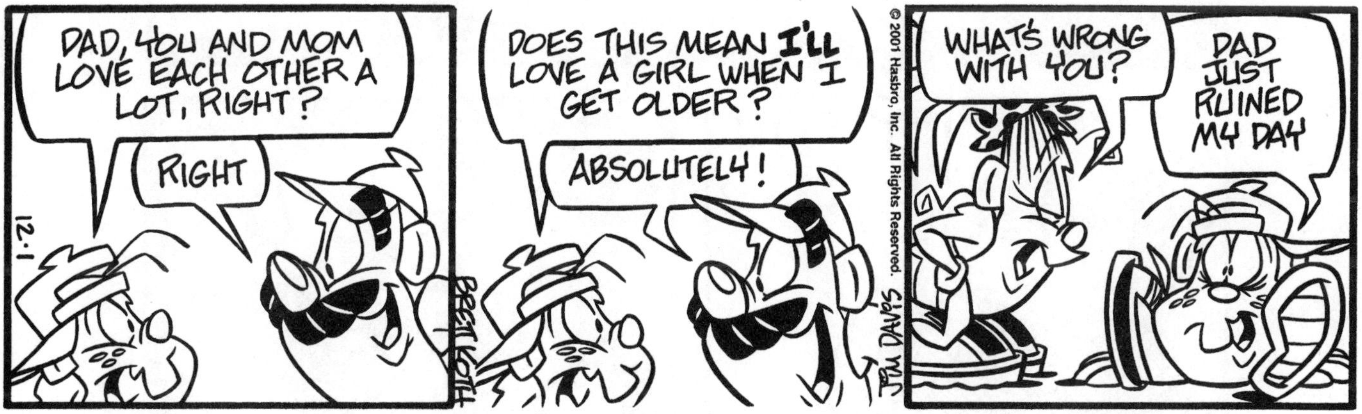
DAD, YOU AND MOM LOVE EACH OTHER A LOT, RIGHT?
RIGHT
12.1
DOES THIS MEAN I'LL LOVE A GIRL WHEN I GET OLDER?
ABSOLUTELY!
WHAT'S WRONG WITH YOU?
DAD JUST RUINED MY DAY
© 2001 Hasbro, Inc. All Rights Reserved.

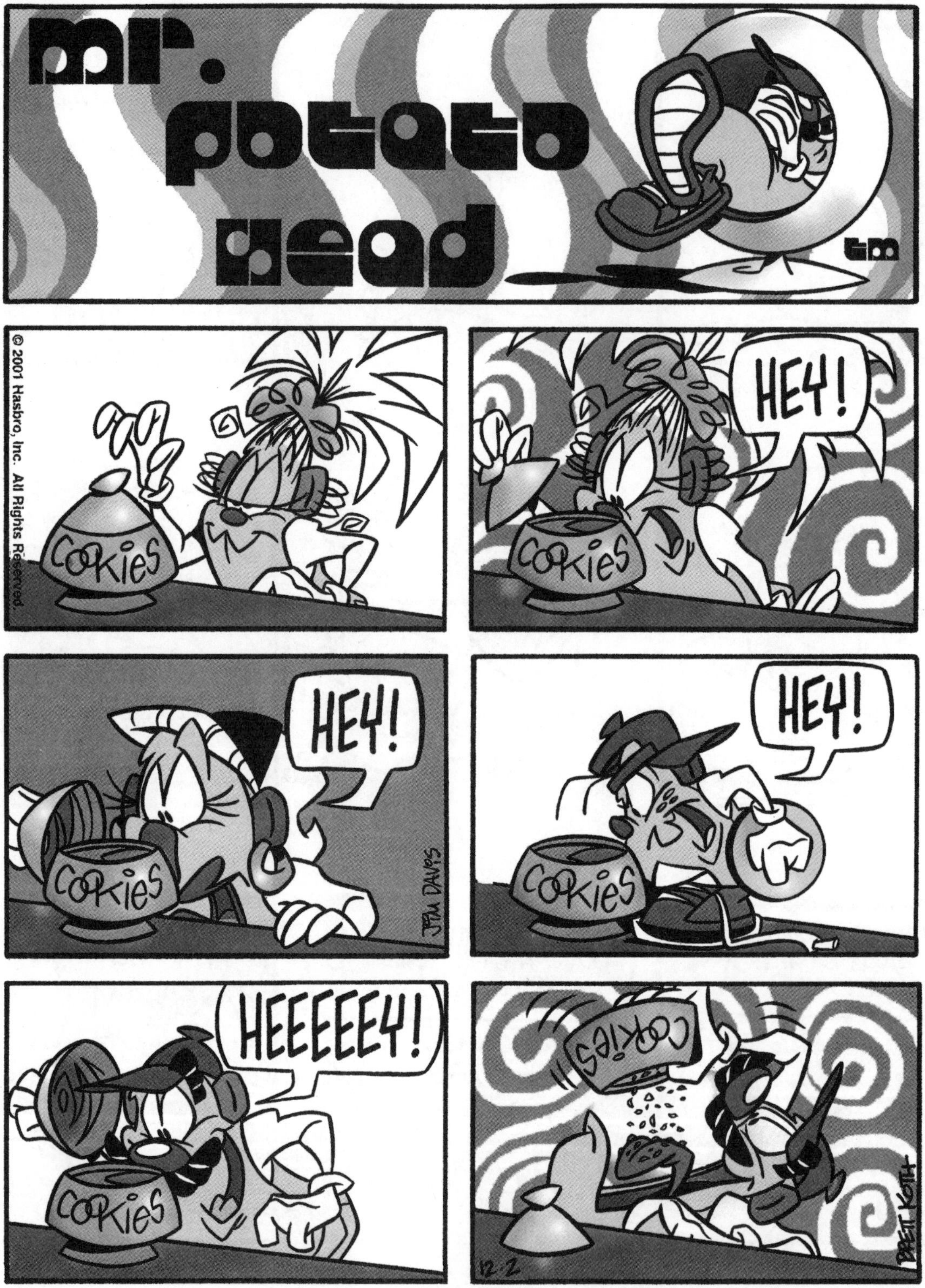
Mr. Potato Head
tm
© 2001 Hasbro, Inc. All Rights Reserved.
COOKIES
HEY!
COOKIES
HEY!
COOKIES
JIM DAVIS
HEY!
COOKIES
HEEEEEY!
COOKIES
COOKIES
BRETT KOTH
12-2

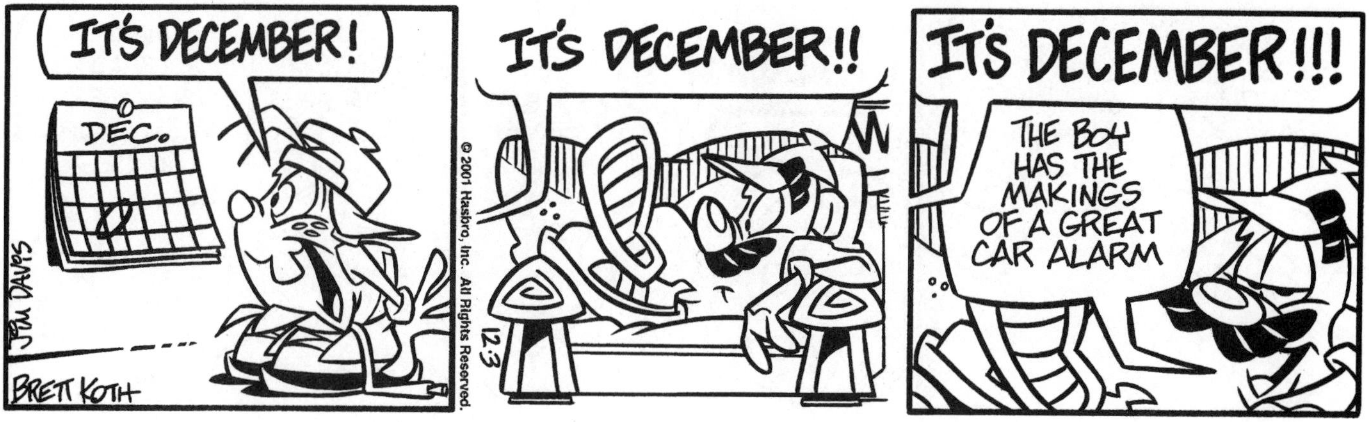
IT'S DECEMBER!
DEC.
IT'S DECEMBER!!
IT'S DECEMBER!!!
THE BOY HAS THE MAKINGS OF A GREAT CAR ALARM
JIM DAVIS
BRETT KOTH
12.3
© 2001 Hasbro, Inc. All Rights Reserved.

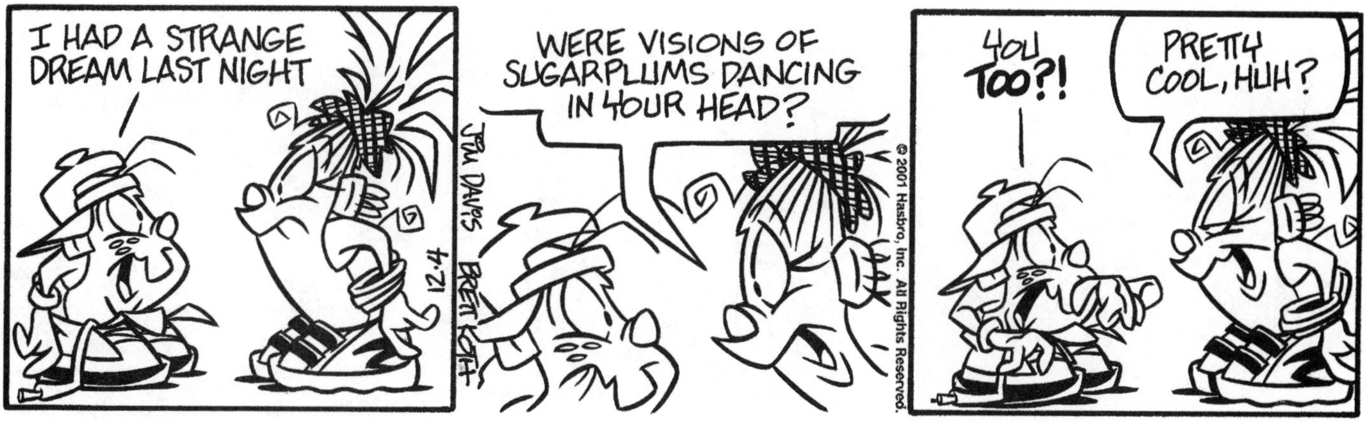
I HAD A STRANGE DREAM LAST NIGHT
WERE VISIONS OF SUGARPLUMS DANCING IN YOUR HEAD?
YOU TOO?!
PRETTY COOL, HUH?
JIM DAVIS
BRETT KOTH
12.4
© 2001 Hasbro, Inc. All Rights Reserved.

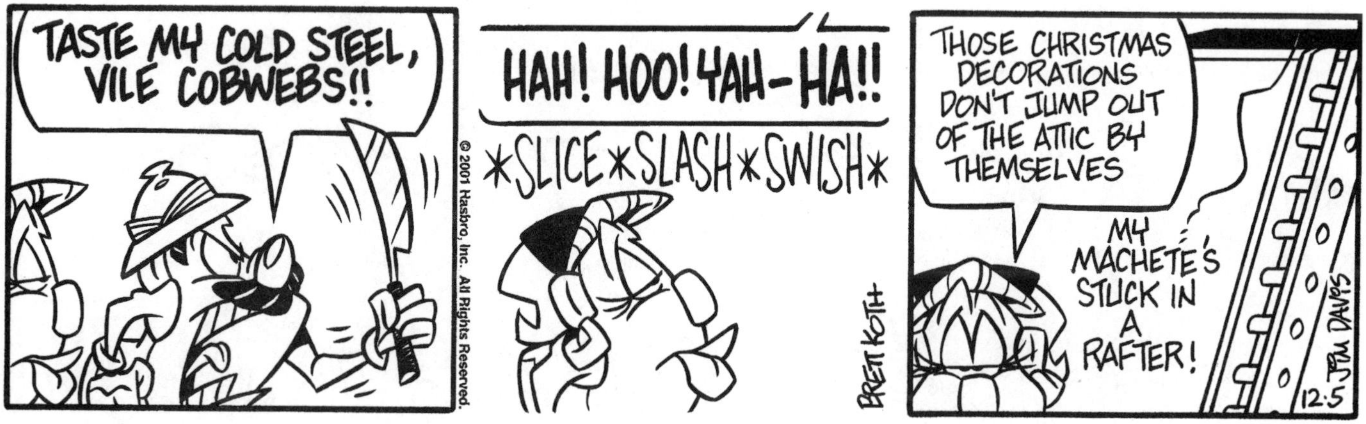
TASTE MY COLD STEEL, VILE COBWEBS!!
HAH! HOO! YAH-HA!!
*SLICE*SLASH*SWISH*
THOSE CHRISTMAS DECORATIONS DON'T JUMP OUT OF THE ATTIC BY THEMSELVES
MY MACHETE'S STUCK IN A RAFTER!
BRETT KOTH
JIM DAVIS
12.5
© 2001 Hasbro, Inc. All Rights Reserved.

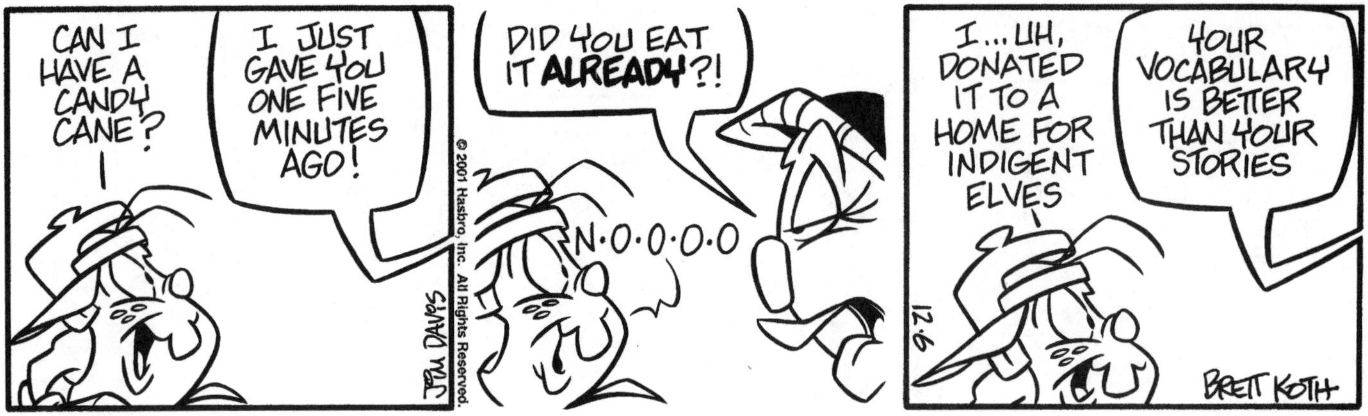
CAN I HAVE A CANDY CANE?
I JUST GAVE YOU ONE FIVE MINUTES AGO!
© 2001 Hasbro, Inc. All Rights Reserved.
JIM DAVIS
DID YOU EAT IT **ALREADY**?!
N·O·O·O·O·O
I... UH, DONATED IT TO A HOME FOR INDIGENT ELVES
YOUR VOCABULARY IS BETTER THAN YOUR STORIES
12·6
BRETT KOTH

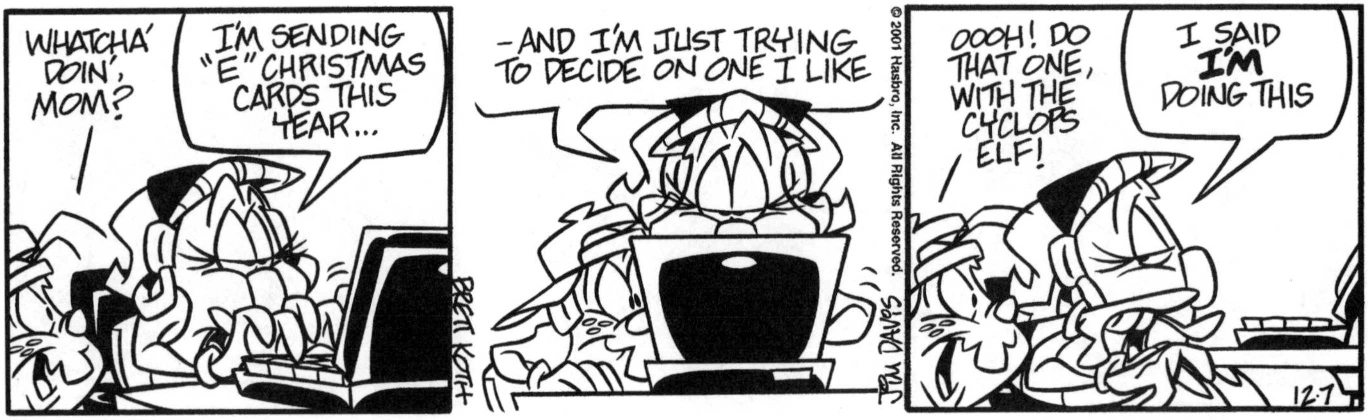
WHATCHA' DOIN', MOM?
I'M SENDING "E" CHRISTMAS CARDS THIS YEAR...
BRETT KOTH
–AND I'M JUST TRYING TO DECIDE ON ONE I LIKE
JIM DAVIS
© 2001 Hasbro, Inc. All Rights Reserved.
OOOH! DO THAT ONE, WITH THE CYCLOPS ELF!
I SAID **I'M** DOING THIS
12·7

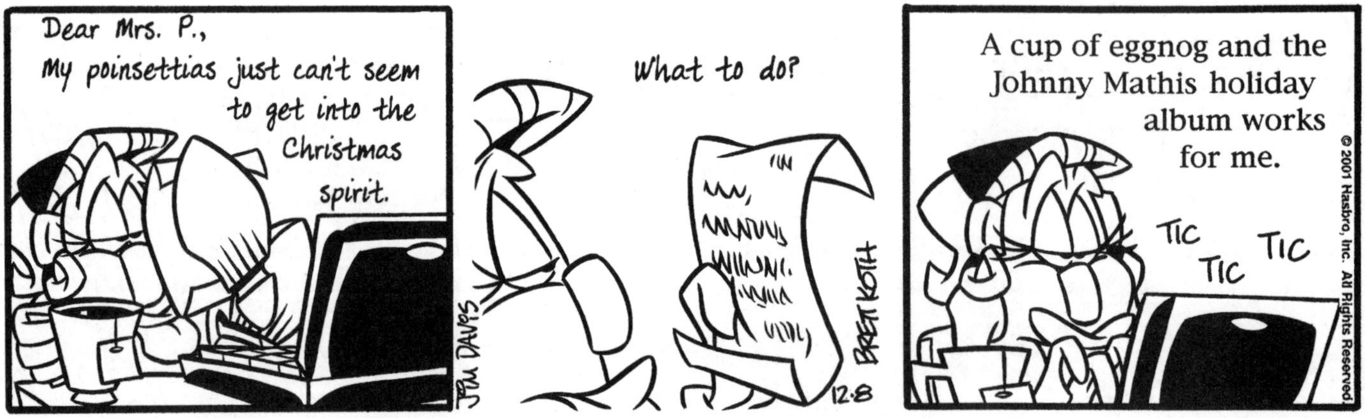
Dear Mrs. P.,
My poinsettias just can't seem to get into the Christmas spirit.
JIM DAVIS
What to do?
BRETT KOTH
12·8
A cup of eggnog and the Johnny Mathis holiday album works for me.
TIC TIC TIC
© 2001 Hasbro, Inc. All Rights Reserved.

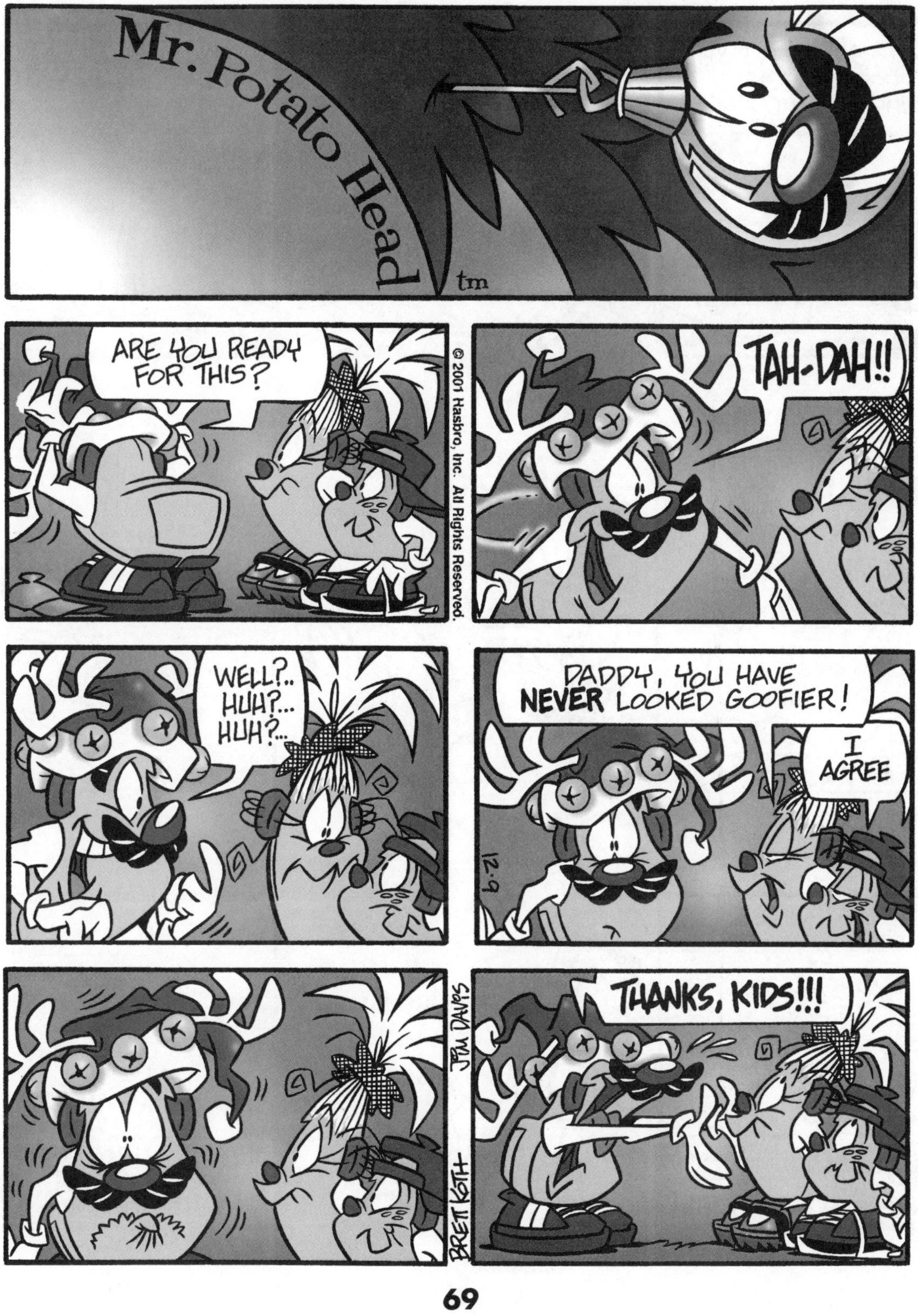
Mr. Potato Head
tm
© 2001 Hasbro, Inc. All Rights Reserved.
ARE YOU READY FOR THIS?
TAH-DAH!!
WELL?.. HUH?... HUH?...
DADDY, YOU HAVE **NEVER** LOOKED GOOFIER!
I AGREE
12.9
JIM DAVIS
BRETT KOTH
THANKS, KIDS!!!

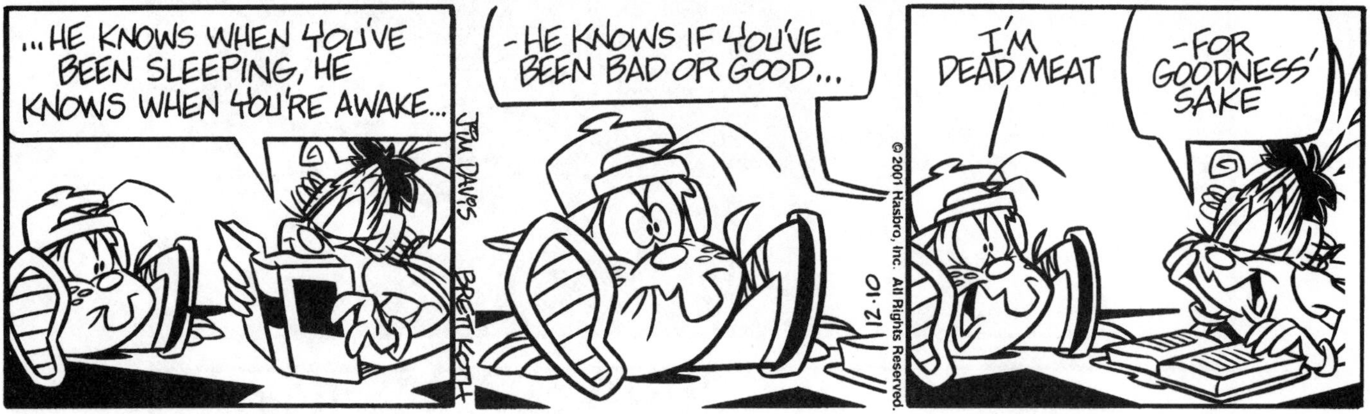
...HE KNOWS WHEN YOU'VE BEEN SLEEPING, HE KNOWS WHEN YOU'RE AWAKE...
-HE KNOWS IF YOU'VE BEEN BAD OR GOOD...
I'M DEAD MEAT
-FOR GOODNESS' SAKE
© 2001 Hasbro, Inc. All Rights Reserved.

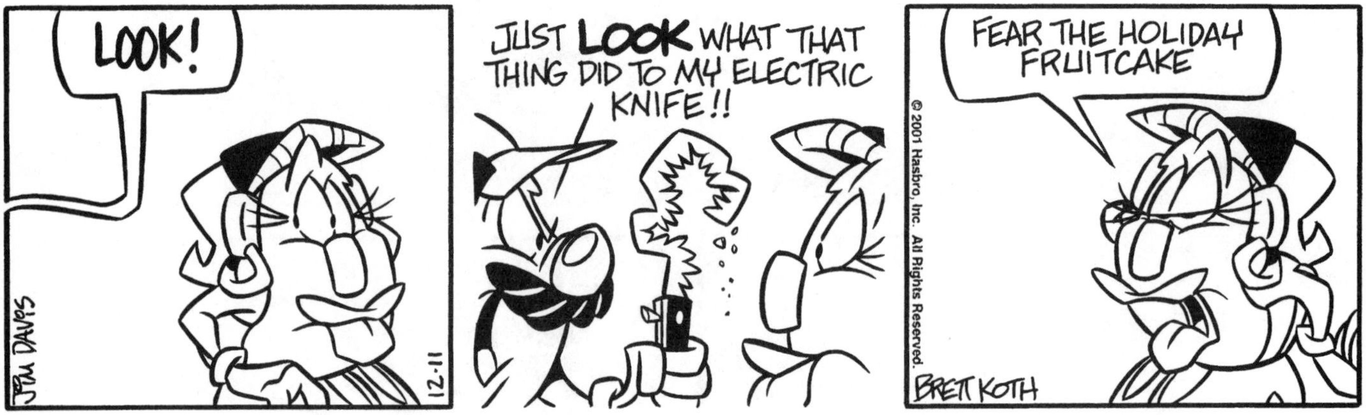
LOOK!
JUST LOOK WHAT THAT THING DID TO MY ELECTRIC KNIFE!!
FEAR THE HOLIDAY FRUITCAKE
© 2001 Hasbro, Inc. All Rights Reserved.

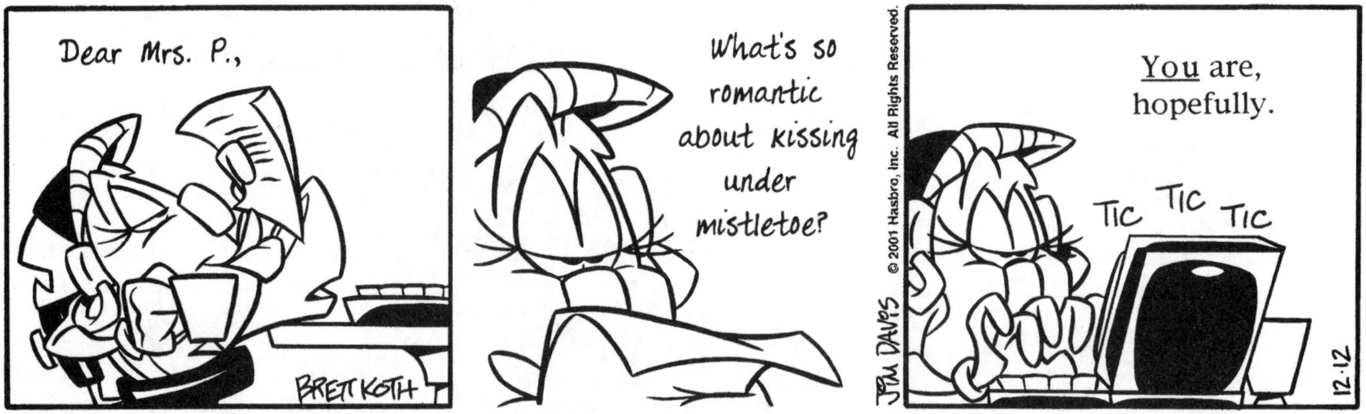
Dear Mrs. P.,
What's so romantic about kissing under mistletoe?
You are, hopefully.
TIC TIC TIC
© 2001 Hasbro, Inc. All Rights Reserved.

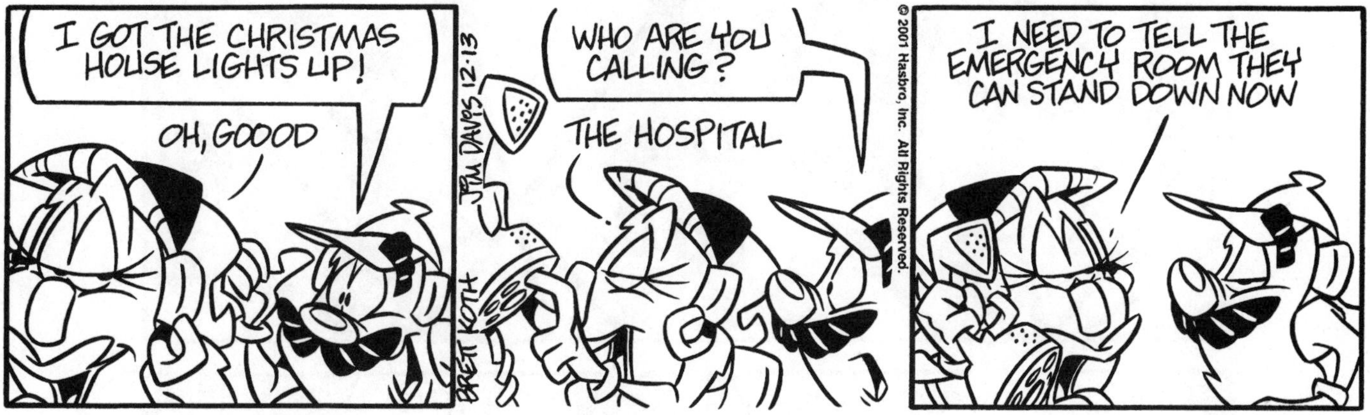
I GOT THE CHRISTMAS HOUSE LIGHTS UP!
OH, GOOOD
JIM DAVIS 12·13
BRETT KOTH
WHO ARE YOU CALLING?
THE HOSPITAL
© 2001 Hasbro, Inc. All Rights Reserved.
I NEED TO TELL THE EMERGENCY ROOM THEY CAN STAND DOWN NOW

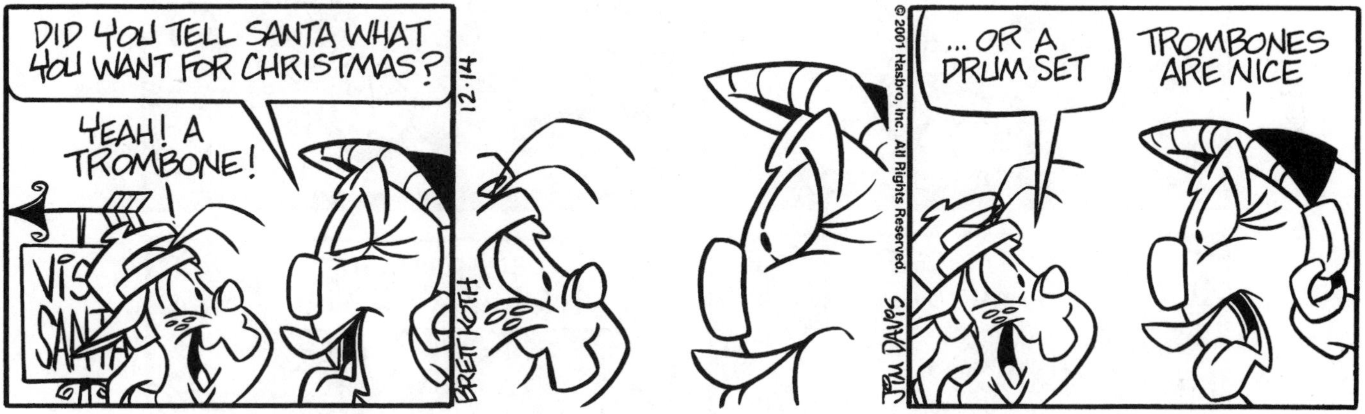
DID YOU TELL SANTA WHAT YOU WANT FOR CHRISTMAS?
YEAH! A TROMBONE!
12·14
BRETT KOTH
© 2001 Hasbro, Inc. All Rights Reserved.
JIM DAVIS
...OR A DRUM SET
TROMBONES ARE NICE

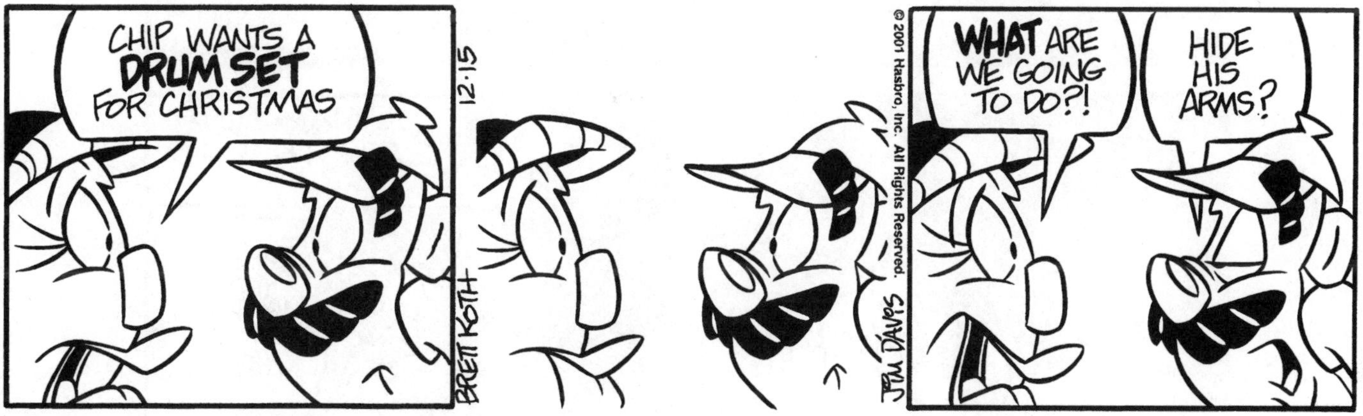
CHIP WANTS A DRUM SET FOR CHRISTMAS
12·15
BRETT KOTH
© 2001 Hasbro, Inc. All Rights Reserved.
JIM DAVIS
WHAT ARE WE GOING TO DO?!
HIDE HIS ARMS?

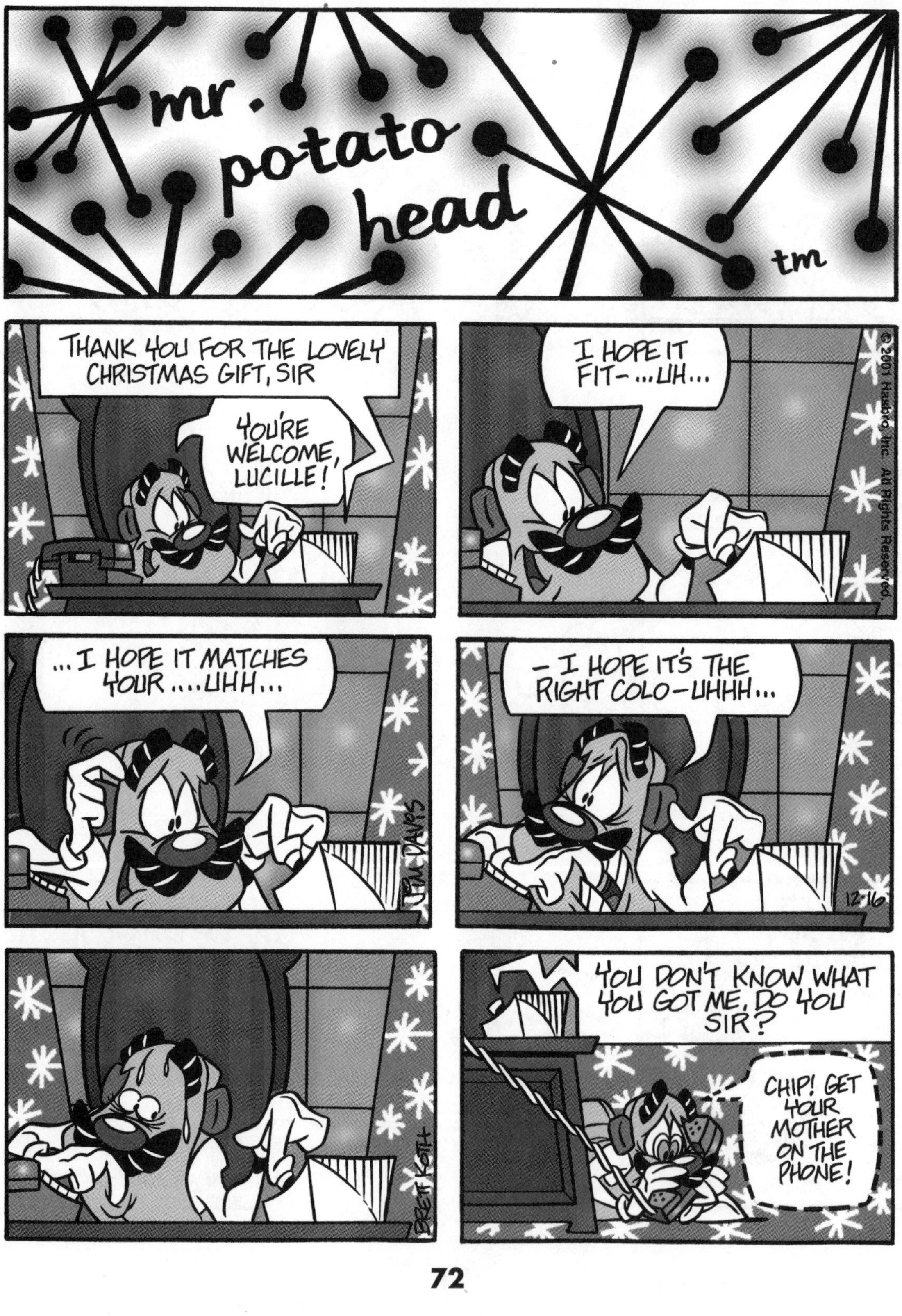
mr. potato head
tm
THANK YOU FOR THE LOVELY CHRISTMAS GIFT, SIR
YOU'RE WELCOME, LUCILLE!
I HOPE IT FIT- ...UH...
© 2001 Hasbro, Inc. All Rights Reserved.
... I HOPE IT MATCHES YOUR .... UHH...
JIM DAVIS
- I HOPE IT'S THE RIGHT COLO-UHHH...
12-16
BRETT KOTH
YOU DON'T KNOW WHAT YOU GOT ME, DO YOU SIR?
CHIP! GET YOUR MOTHER ON THE PHONE!

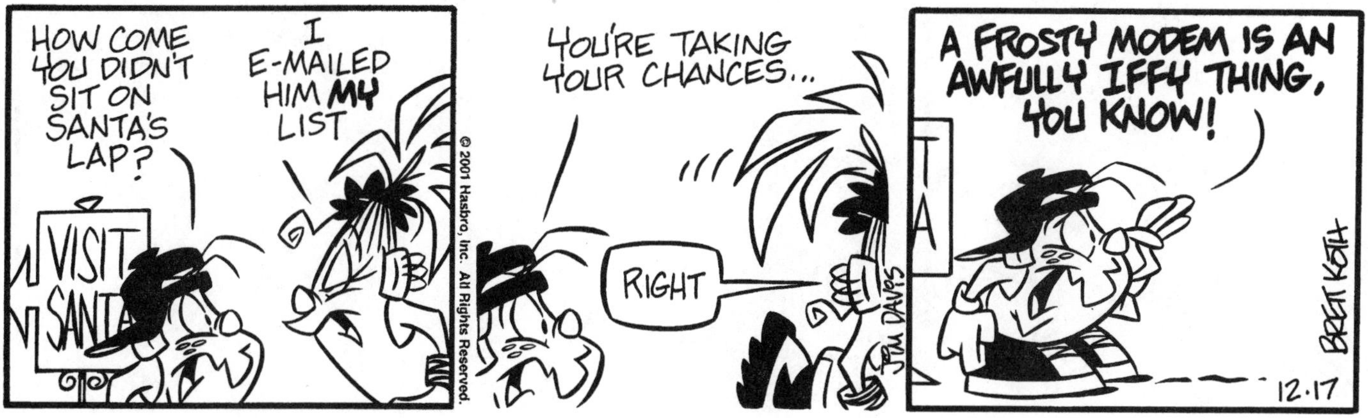
HOW COME YOU DIDN'T SIT ON SANTA'S LAP?
VISIT SANTA
I E-MAILED HIM MY LIST
© 2001 Hasbro, Inc. All Rights Reserved.
YOU'RE TAKING YOUR CHANCES...
RIGHT
JIM DAVIS
A FROSTY MODEM IS AN AWFULLY IFFY THING, YOU KNOW!
BRETT KOTH
12·17

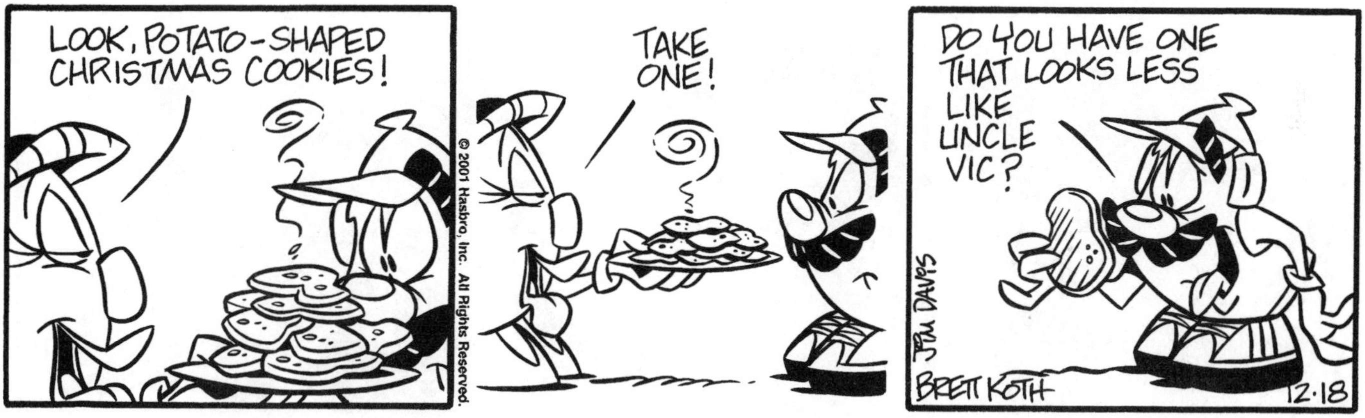
LOOK, POTATO-SHAPED CHRISTMAS COOKIES!
© 2001 Hasbro, Inc. All Rights Reserved.
TAKE ONE!
DO YOU HAVE ONE THAT LOOKS LESS LIKE UNCLE VIC?
JIM DAVIS
BRETT KOTH
12·18

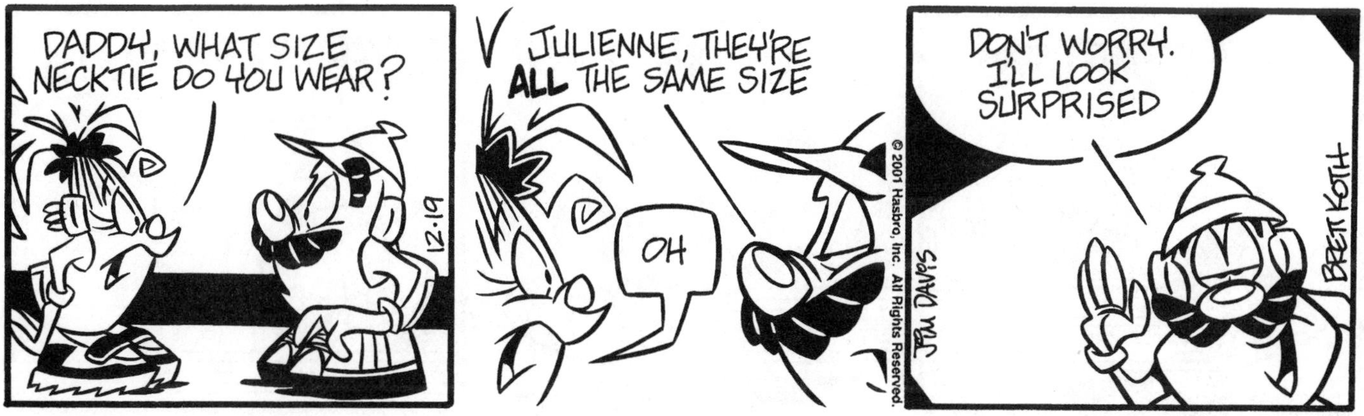
DADDY, WHAT SIZE NECKTIE DO YOU WEAR?
12·19
JULIENNE, THEY'RE ALL THE SAME SIZE
OH
© 2001 Hasbro, Inc. All Rights Reserved.
JIM DAVIS
DON'T WORRY. I'LL LOOK SURPRISED
BRETT KOTH

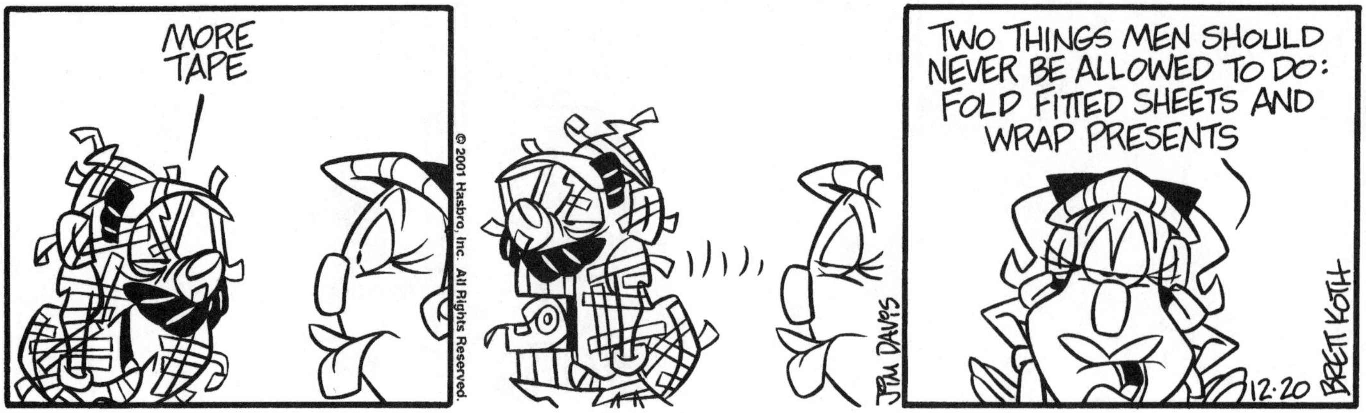
MORE TAPE
© 2001 Hasbro, Inc. All Rights Reserved.
TWO THINGS MEN SHOULD NEVER BE ALLOWED TO DO: FOLD FITTED SHEETS AND WRAP PRESENTS
JIM DAVIS
12·20 BRETT KOTH

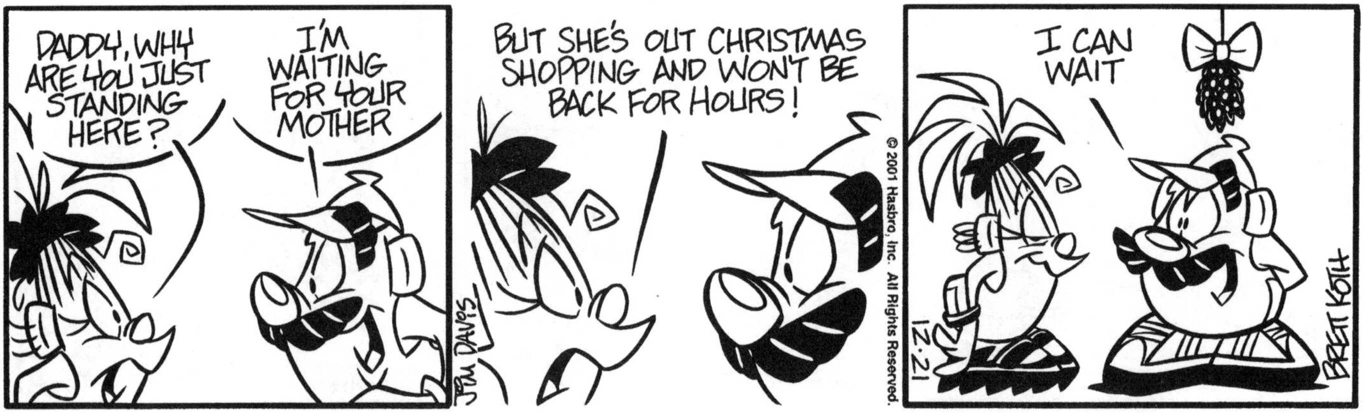
DADDY, WHY ARE YOU JUST STANDING HERE?
I'M WAITING FOR YOUR MOTHER
BUT SHE'S OUT CHRISTMAS SHOPPING AND WON'T BE BACK FOR HOURS!
I CAN WAIT
© 2001 Hasbro, Inc. All Rights Reserved.
JIM DAVIS
12·21 BRETT KOTH

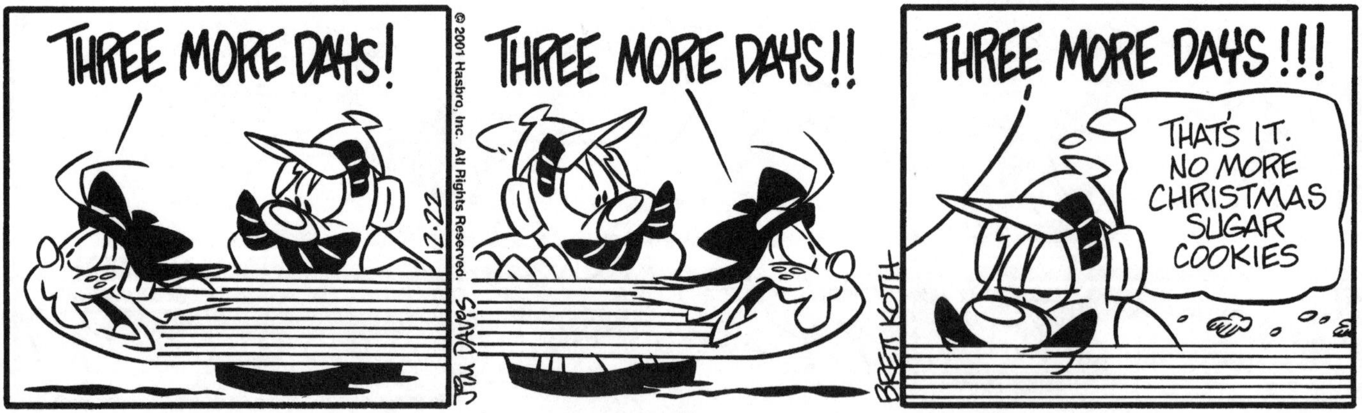
THREE MORE DAYS!
THREE MORE DAYS!!
THREE MORE DAYS!!!
THAT'S IT. NO MORE CHRISTMAS SUGAR COOKIES
© 2001 Hasbro, Inc. All Rights Reserved.
12·22
JIM DAVIS
BRETT KOTH

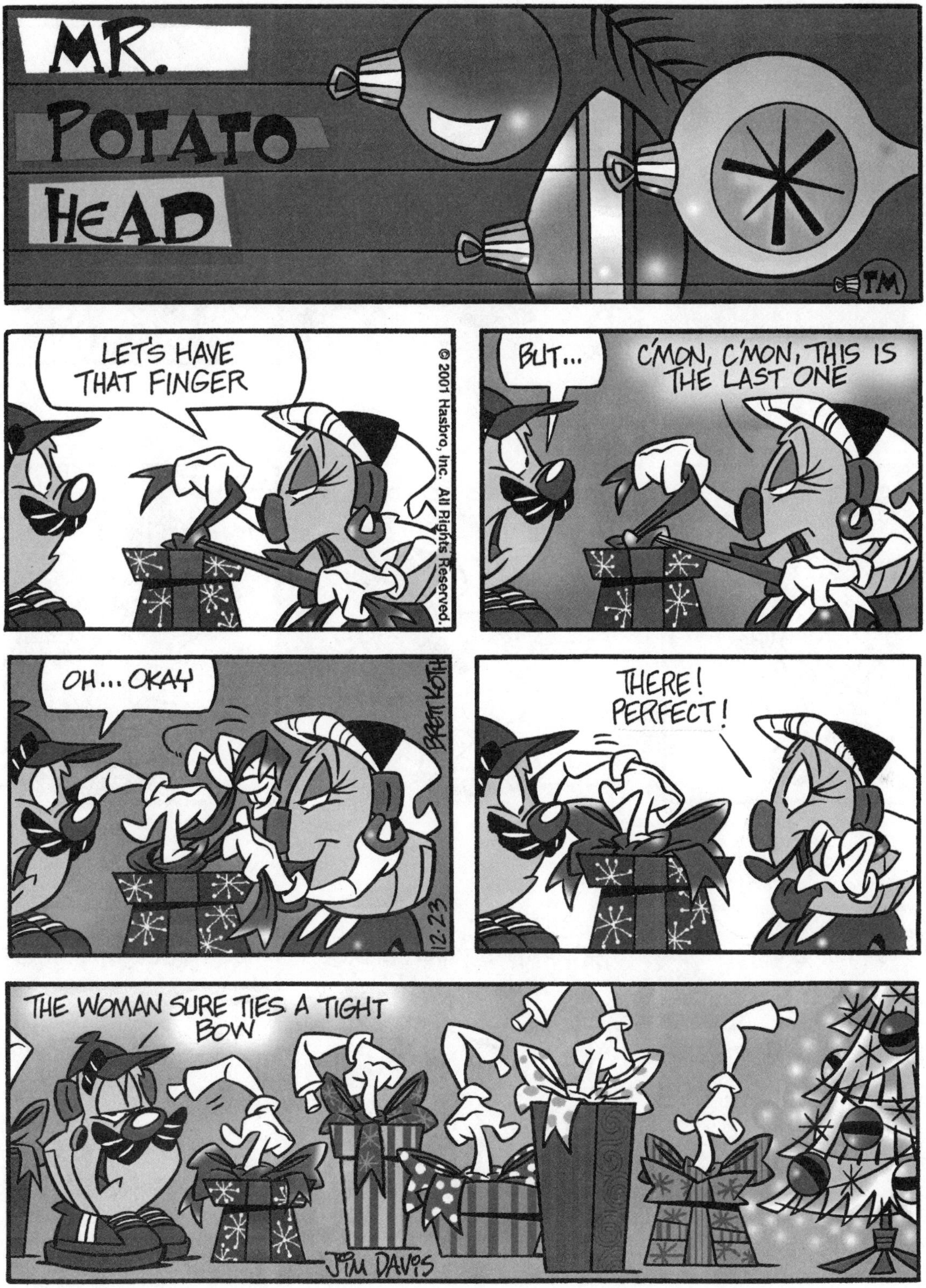

MR. POTATO HEAD
TM
LET'S HAVE THAT FINGER
© 2001 Hasbro, Inc. All Rights Reserved.
BUT...
C'MON, C'MON, THIS IS THE LAST ONE
OH... OKAY
BRETT KOTH
12-23
THERE! PERFECT!
THE WOMAN SURE TIES A TIGHT BOW
JIM DAVIS

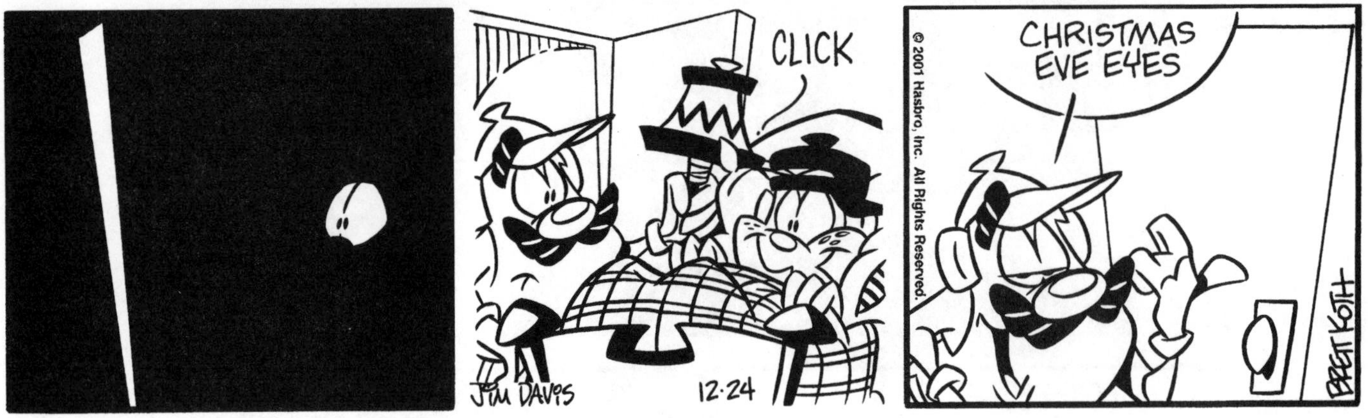
CLICK
CHRISTMAS EVE EYES

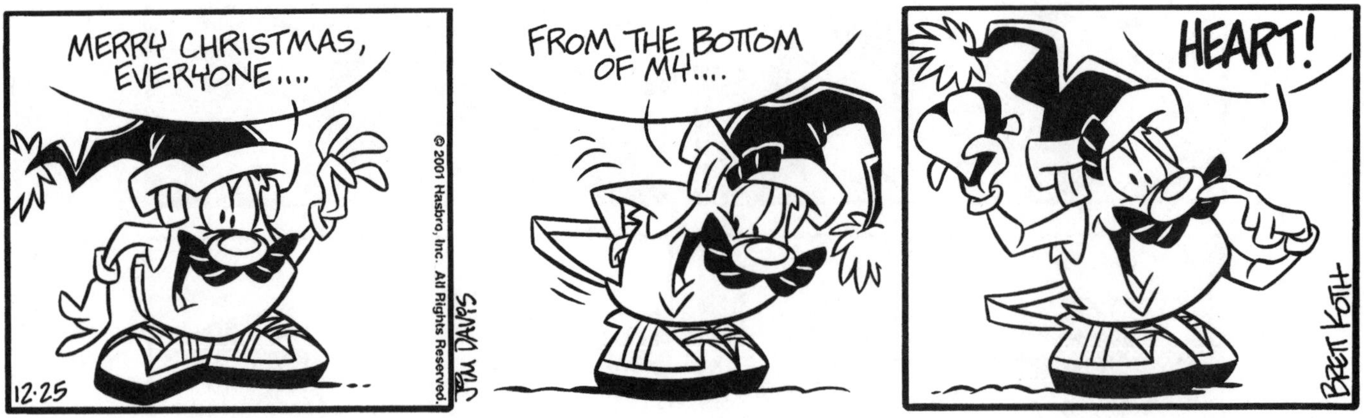
MERRY CHRISTMAS, EVERYONE....
FROM THE BOTTOM OF MY....
HEART!

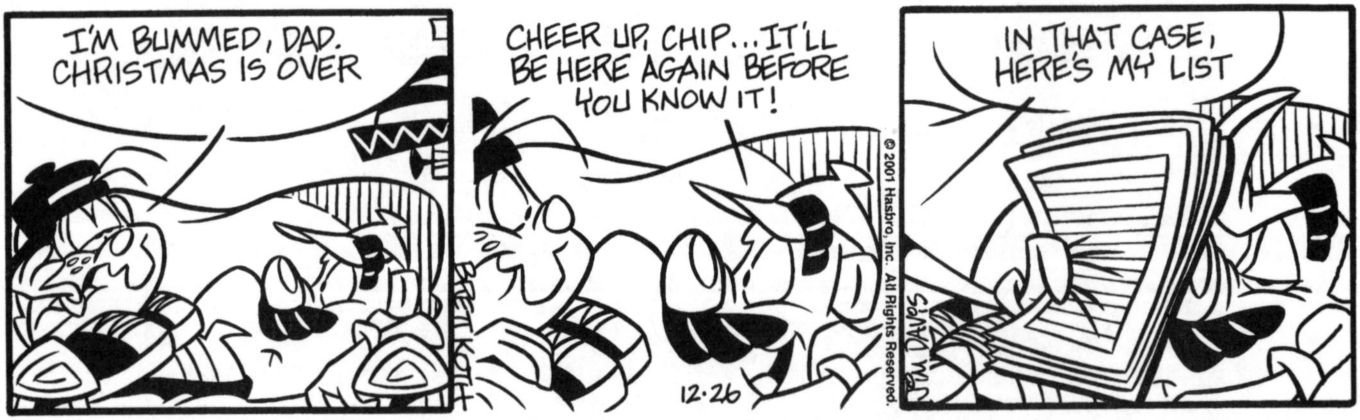
I'M BUMMED, DAD. CHRISTMAS IS OVER
CHEER UP, CHIP... IT'LL BE HERE AGAIN BEFORE YOU KNOW IT!
IN THAT CASE, HERE'S MY LIST

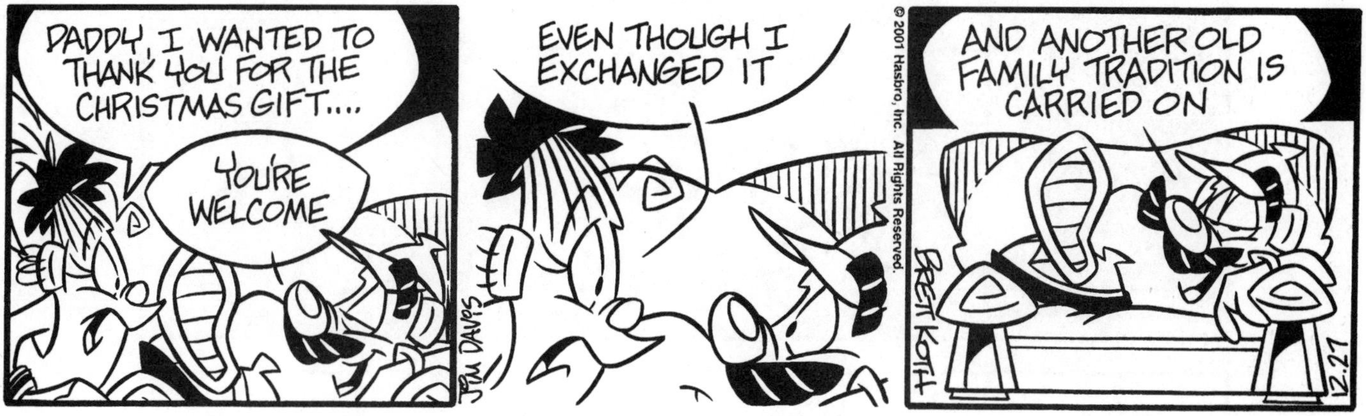
DADDY, I WANTED TO THANK YOU FOR THE CHRISTMAS GIFT....
YOU'RE WELCOME
EVEN THOUGH I EXCHANGED IT
AND ANOTHER OLD FAMILY TRADITION IS CARRIED ON
© 2001 Hasbro, Inc. All Rights Reserved.
12.27

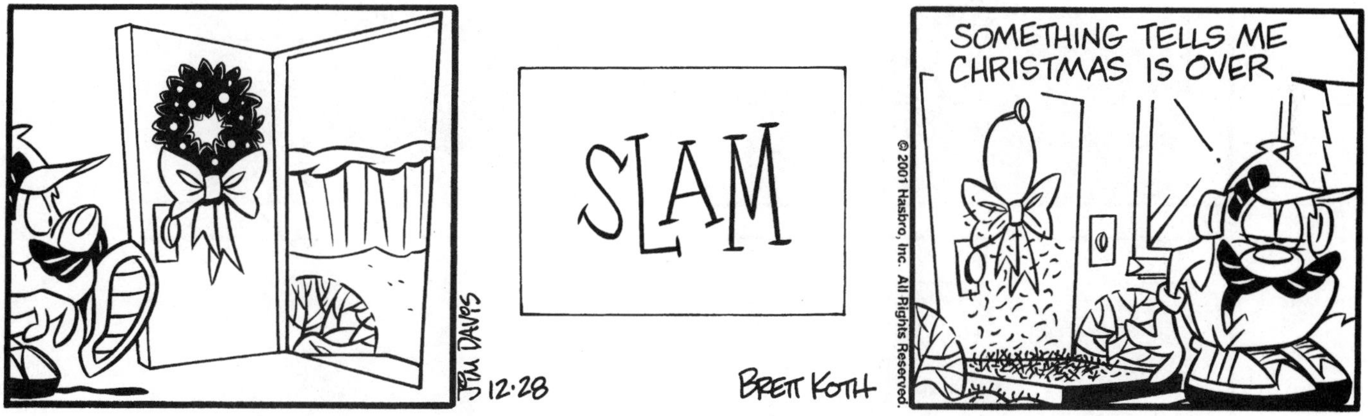
12.28
SLAM
SOMETHING TELLS ME CHRISTMAS IS OVER
© 2001 Hasbro, Inc. All Rights Reserved.

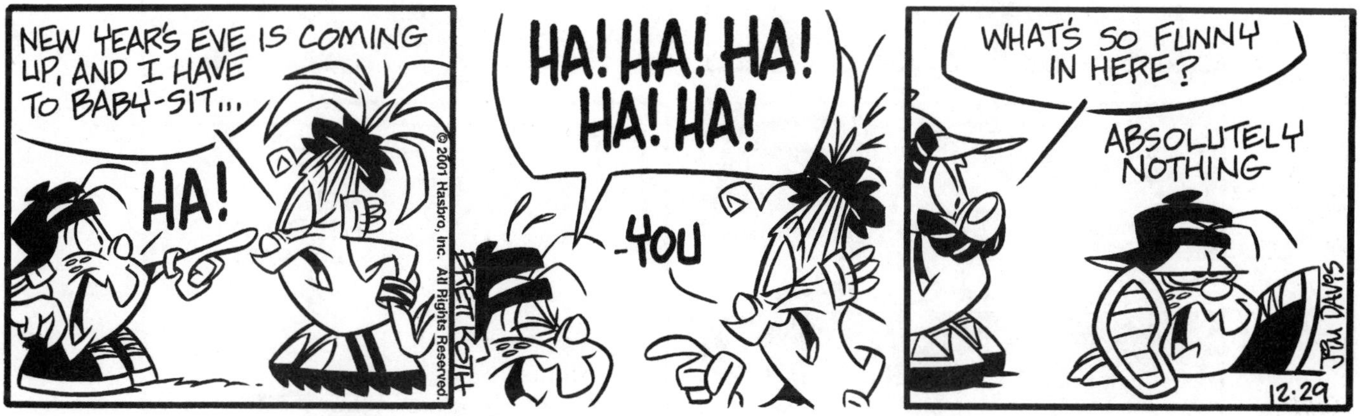
NEW YEAR'S EVE IS COMING UP, AND I HAVE TO BABY-SIT...
HA!
© 2001 Hasbro, Inc. All Rights Reserved.
HA! HA! HA! HA! HA!
-YOU
WHAT'S SO FUNNY IN HERE?
ABSOLUTELY NOTHING
12.29

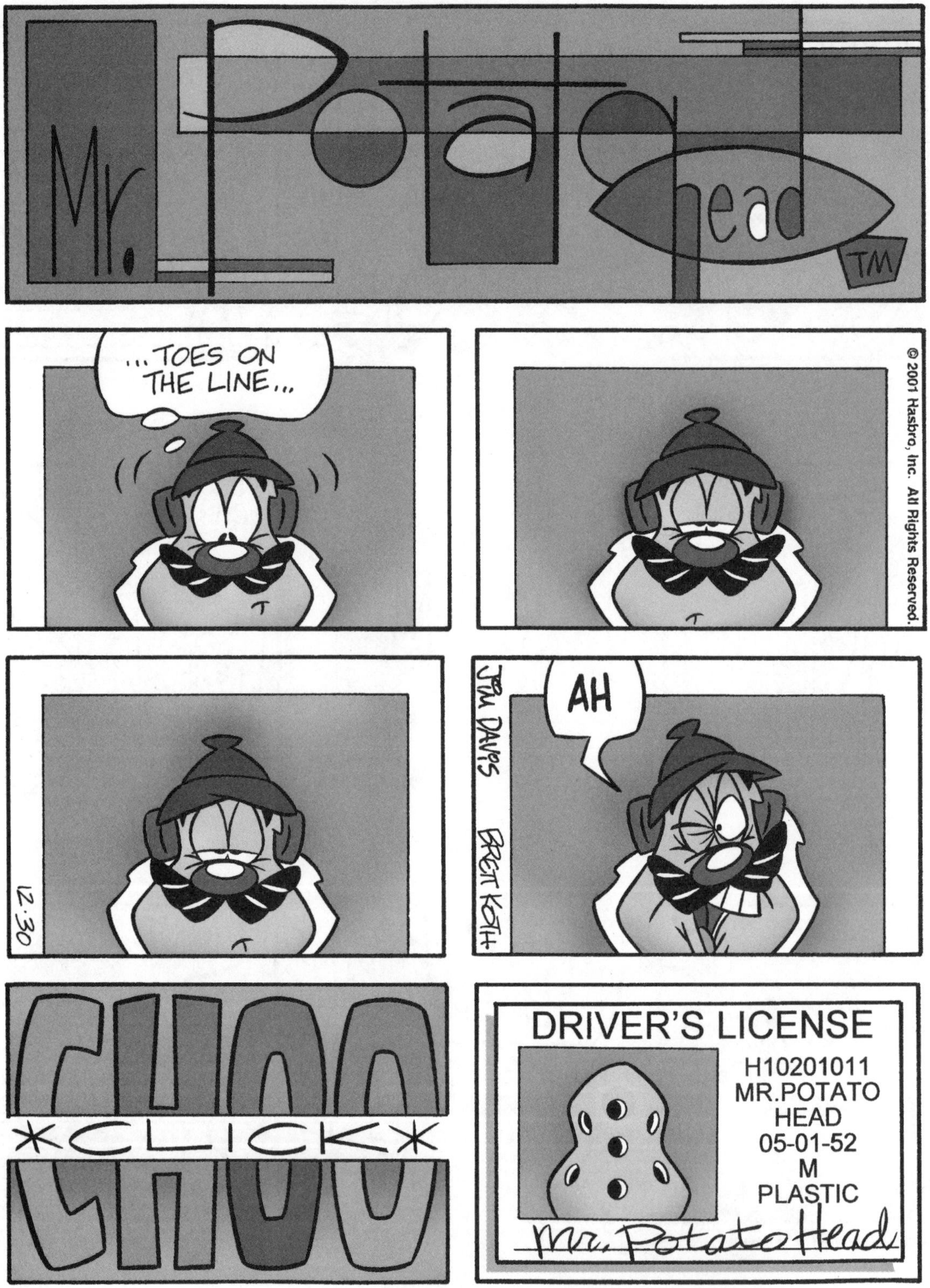
Mr. Potato Head
TM
...TOES ON THE LINE...
© 2001 Hasbro, Inc. All Rights Reserved.
JIM DAVIS
BRETT KOTH
12-30
AH
CHOO
CLICK
DRIVER'S LICENSE
H10201011
MR.POTATO
HEAD
05-01-52
M
PLASTIC
Mr. Potato Head

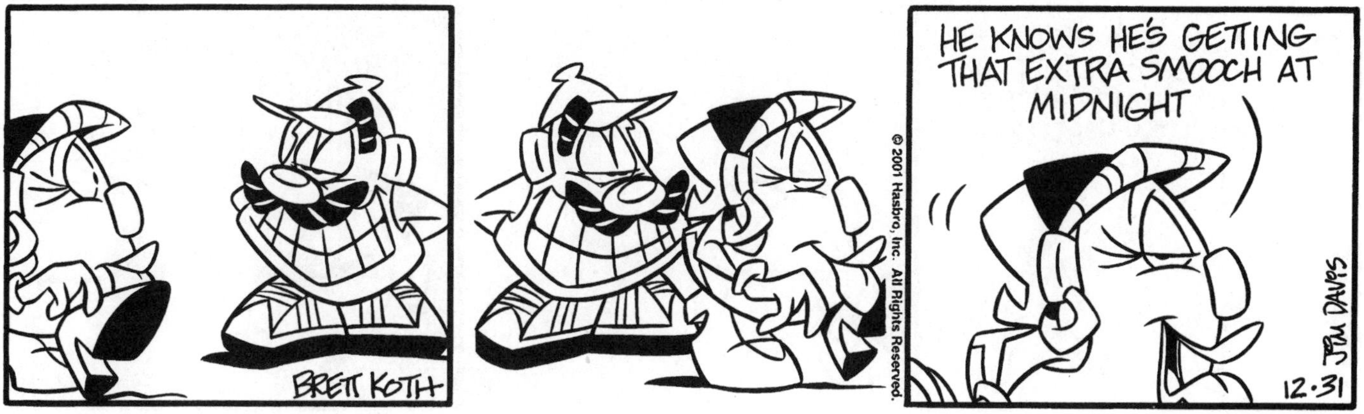
BRETT KOTH
© 2001 Hasbro, Inc. All Rights Reserved.
HE KNOWS HE'S GETTING THAT EXTRA SMOOCH AT MIDNIGHT
JIM DAVIS
12·31

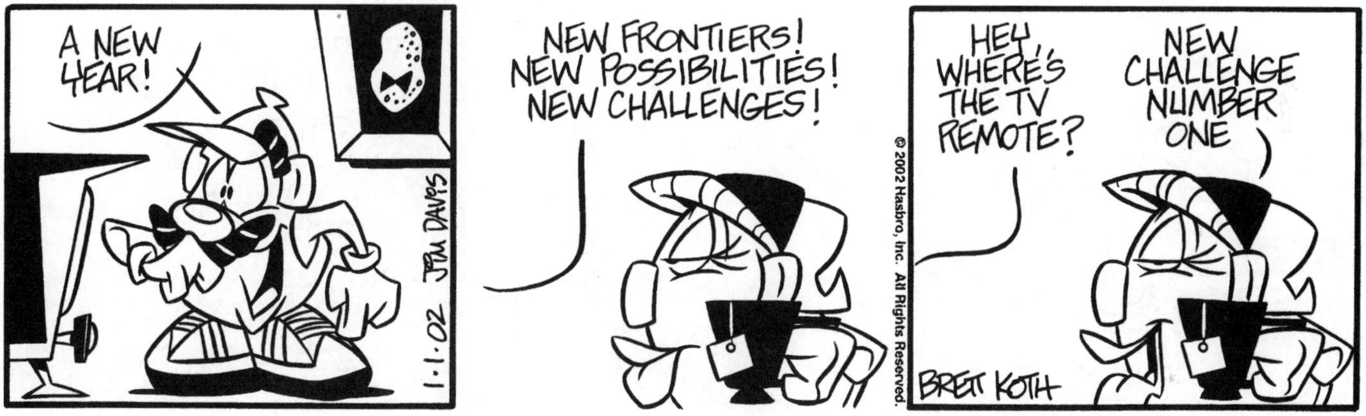
A NEW YEAR!
JIM DAVIS
1·1·02
NEW FRONTIERS! NEW POSSIBILITIES! NEW CHALLENGES!
© 2002 Hasbro, Inc. All Rights Reserved.
HEY, WHERE'S THE TV REMOTE?
NEW CHALLENGE NUMBER ONE
BRETT KOTH

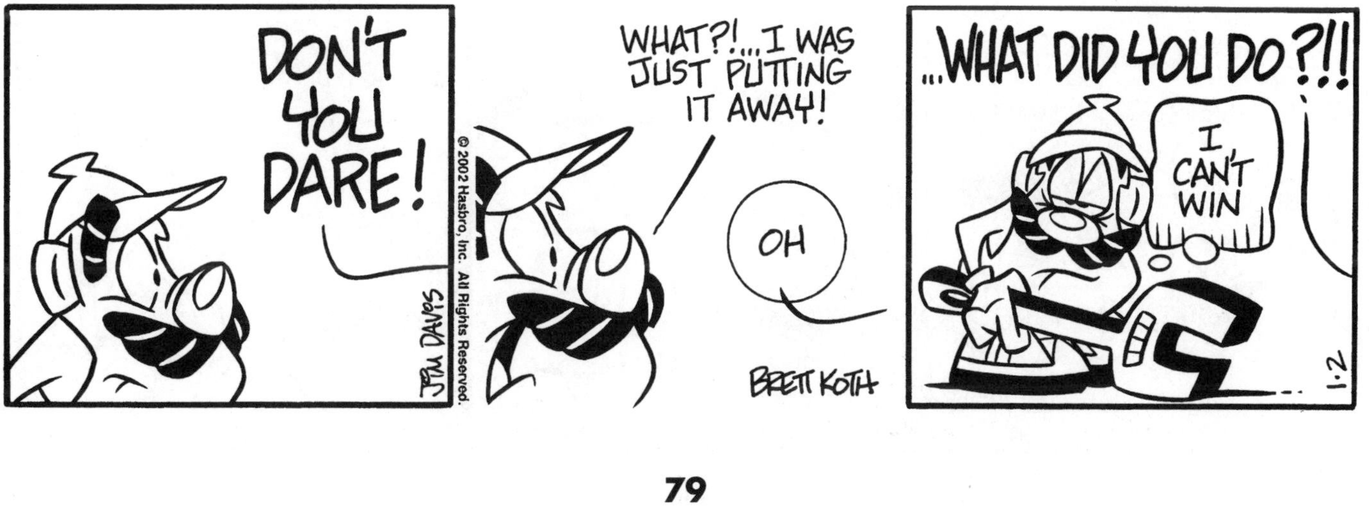
DON'T YOU DARE!
JIM DAVIS
© 2002 Hasbro, Inc. All Rights Reserved.
WHAT?!...I WAS JUST PUTTING IT AWAY!
OH
BRETT KOTH
...WHAT DID YOU DO?!!
I CAN'T WIN
1·2

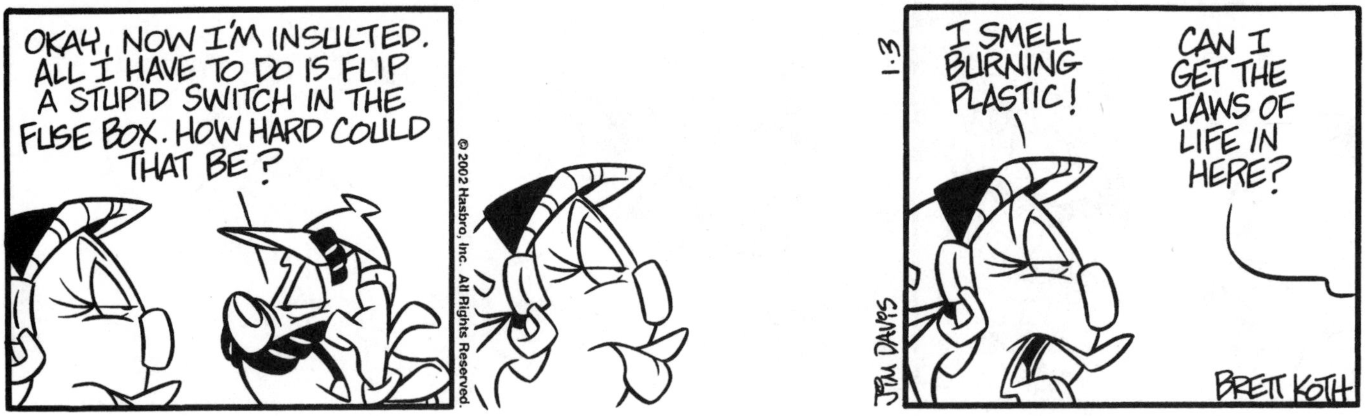
OKAY, NOW I'M INSULTED. ALL I HAVE TO DO IS FLIP A STUPID SWITCH IN THE FUSE BOX. HOW HARD COULD THAT BE?
© 2002 Hasbro, Inc. All Rights Reserved.
1.3
I SMELL BURNING PLASTIC!
CAN I GET THE JAWS OF LIFE IN HERE?
JIM DAVIS
BRETT KOTH

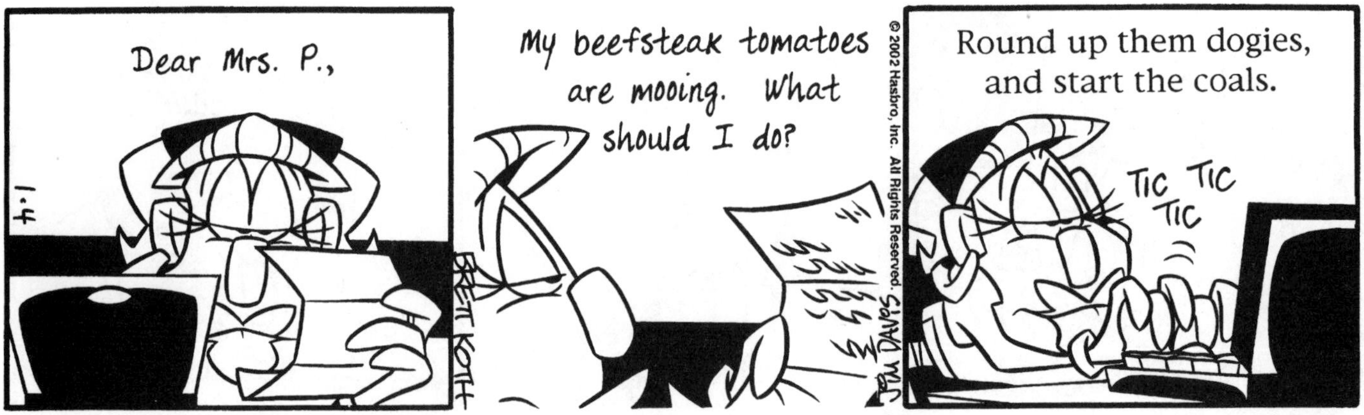
1.4
Dear Mrs. P.,
BRETT KOTH
My beefsteak tomatoes are mooing. What should I do?
© 2002 Hasbro, Inc. All Rights Reserved.
JIM DAVIS
Round up them dogies, and start the coals.
TIC TIC TIC

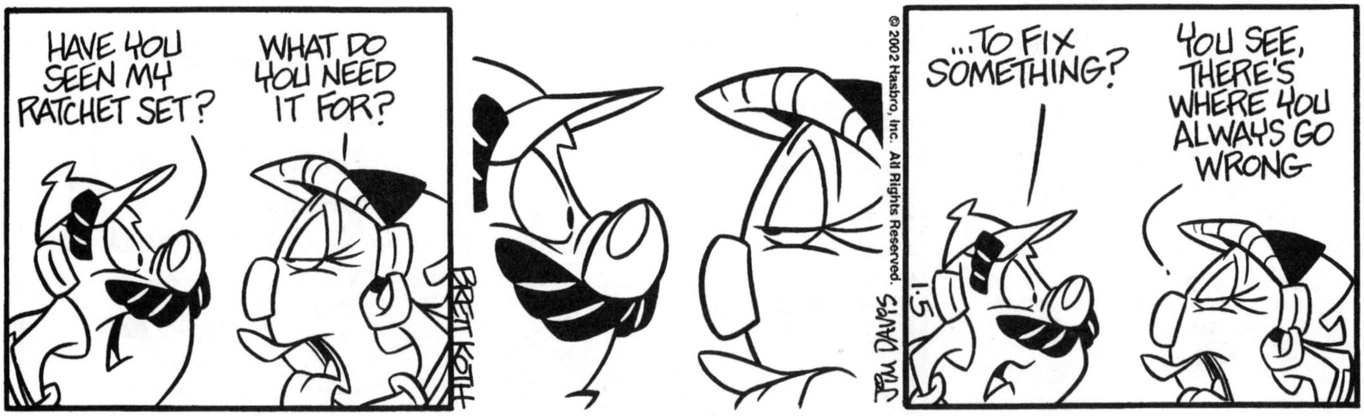
HAVE YOU SEEN MY RATCHET SET?
WHAT DO YOU NEED IT FOR?
BRETT KOTH
© 2002 Hasbro, Inc. All Rights Reserved.
JIM DAVIS
1.5
...TO FIX SOMETHING?
YOU SEE, THERE'S WHERE YOU ALWAYS GO WRONG

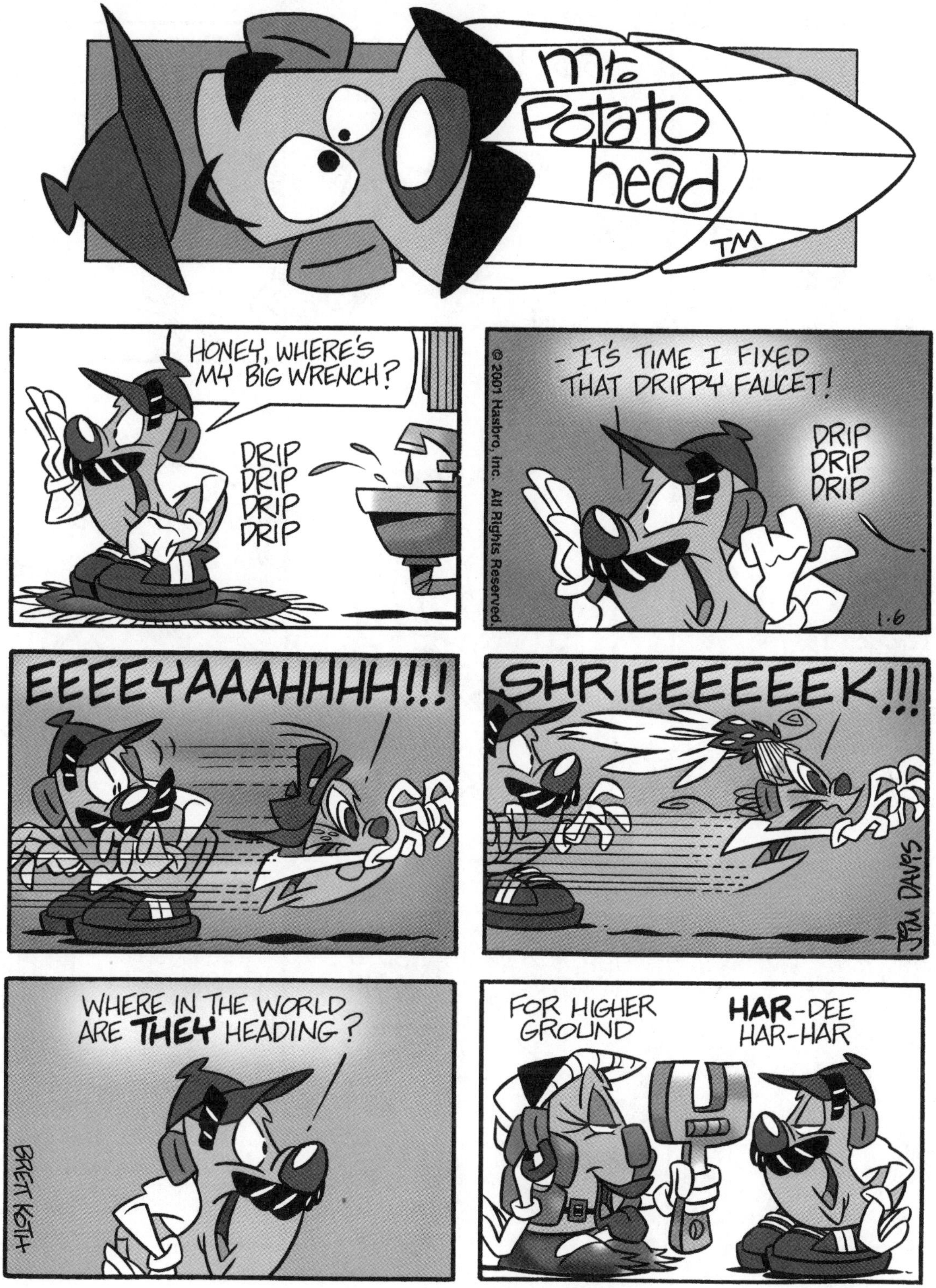

Mr. Potato head
TM
HONEY, WHERE'S MY BIG WRENCH?
DRIP DRIP DRIP DRIP
© 2001 Hasbro, Inc. All Rights Reserved.
- IT'S TIME I FIXED THAT DRIPPY FAUCET!
DRIP DRIP DRIP
1-6
EEEEYAAAHHHH!!!
SHRIEEEEEEEK!!!
JIM DAVIS
WHERE IN THE WORLD ARE **THEY** HEADING?
BRETT KOTH
FOR HIGHER GROUND
HAR-DEE HAR-HAR

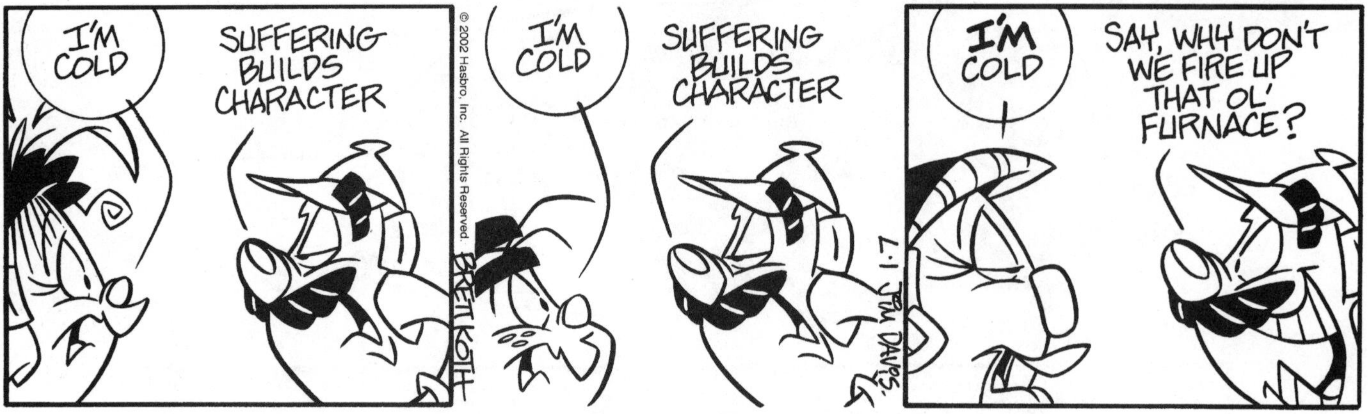
© 2002 Hasbro, Inc. All Rights Reserved.
I'M COLD
SUFFERING BUILDS CHARACTER
I'M COLD
SUFFERING BUILDS CHARACTER
I'M COLD
SAY, WHY DON'T WE FIRE UP THAT OL' FURNACE?
BRETT KOTH
JIM DAVIS 1.7

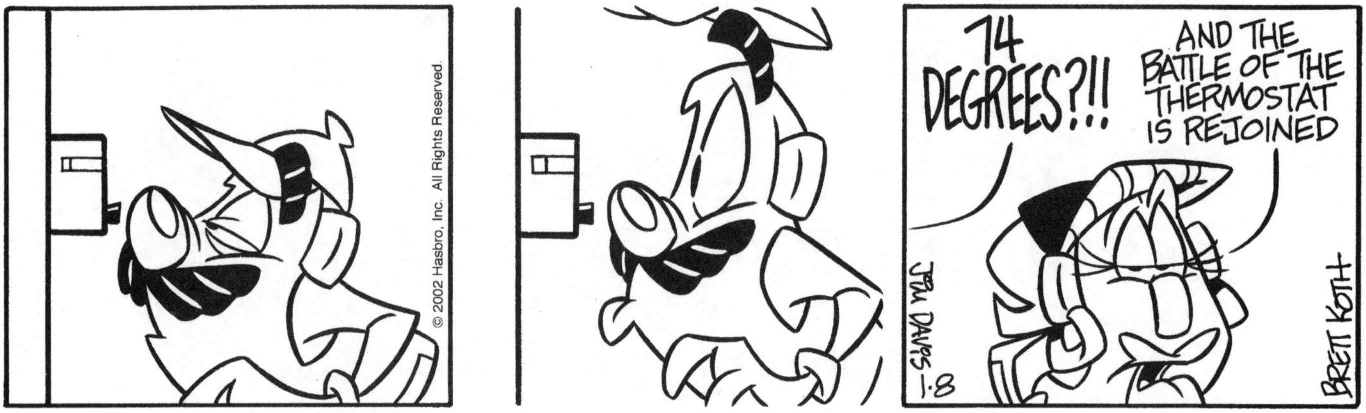
© 2002 Hasbro, Inc. All Rights Reserved.
74 DEGREES?!!
AND THE BATTLE OF THE THERMOSTAT IS REJOINED
JIM DAVIS 1.8
BRETT KOTH

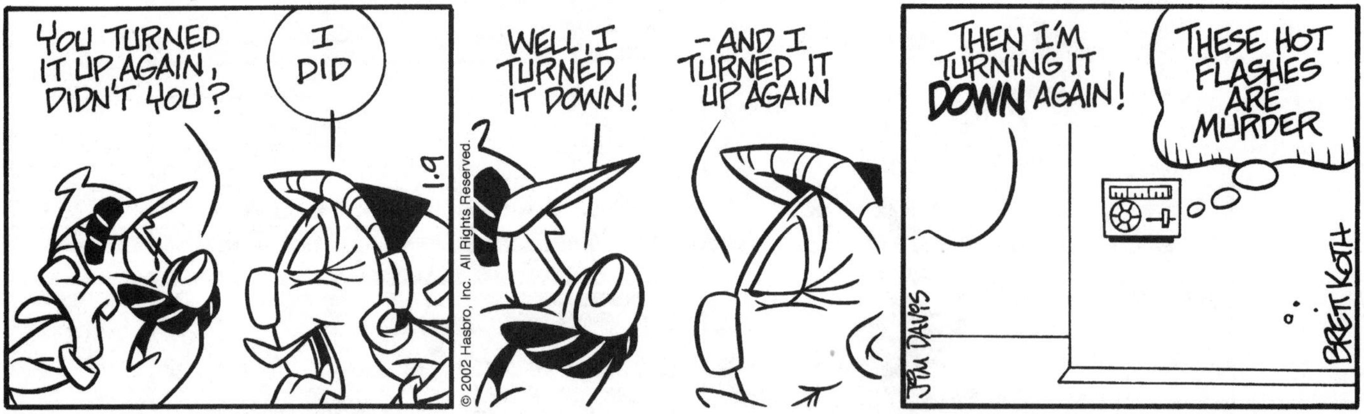
YOU TURNED IT UP AGAIN, DIDN'T YOU?
I DID
1.9
© 2002 Hasbro, Inc. All Rights Reserved.
WELL, I TURNED IT DOWN!
- AND I TURNED IT UP AGAIN
THEN I'M TURNING IT **DOWN** AGAIN!
THESE HOT FLASHES ARE MURDER
JIM DAVIS
BRETT KOTH

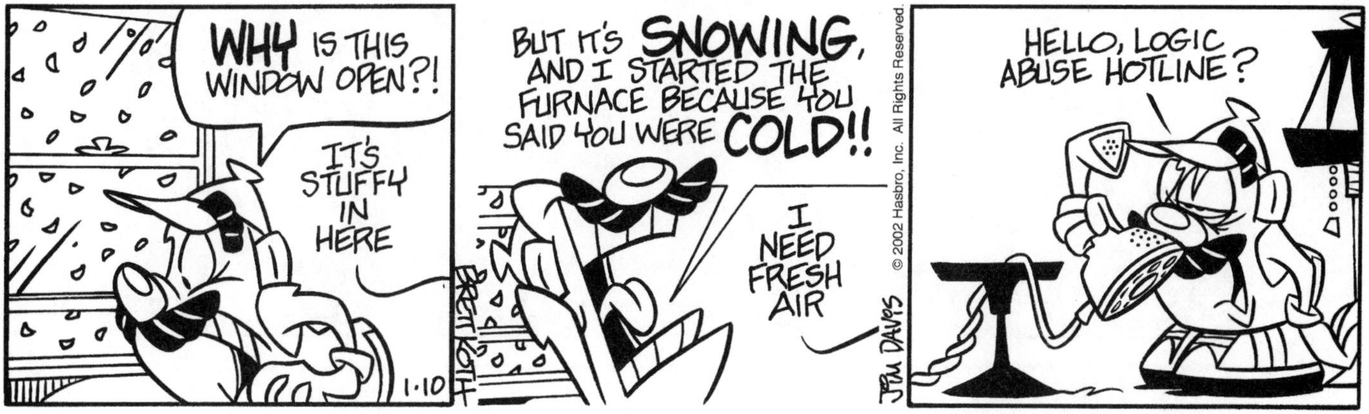
WHY IS THIS WINDOW OPEN?!
IT'S STUFFY IN HERE
BUT IT'S SNOWING, AND I STARTED THE FURNACE BECAUSE YOU SAID YOU WERE COLD!!
I NEED FRESH AIR
HELLO, LOGIC ABUSE HOTLINE?
© 2002 Hasbro, Inc. All Rights Reserved.

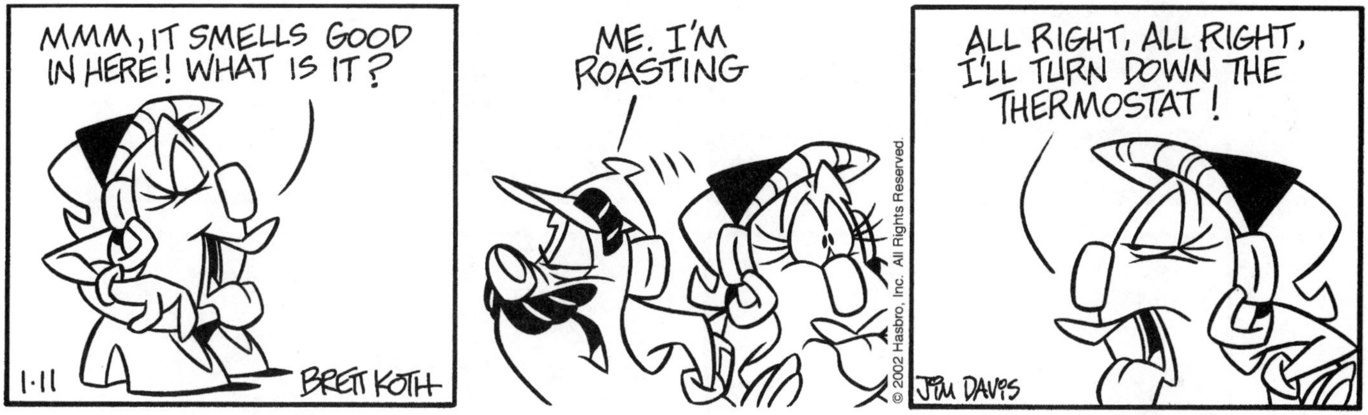
MMM, IT SMELLS GOOD IN HERE! WHAT IS IT?
ME. I'M ROASTING
ALL RIGHT, ALL RIGHT, I'LL TURN DOWN THE THERMOSTAT!
© 2002 Hasbro, Inc. All Rights Reserved.

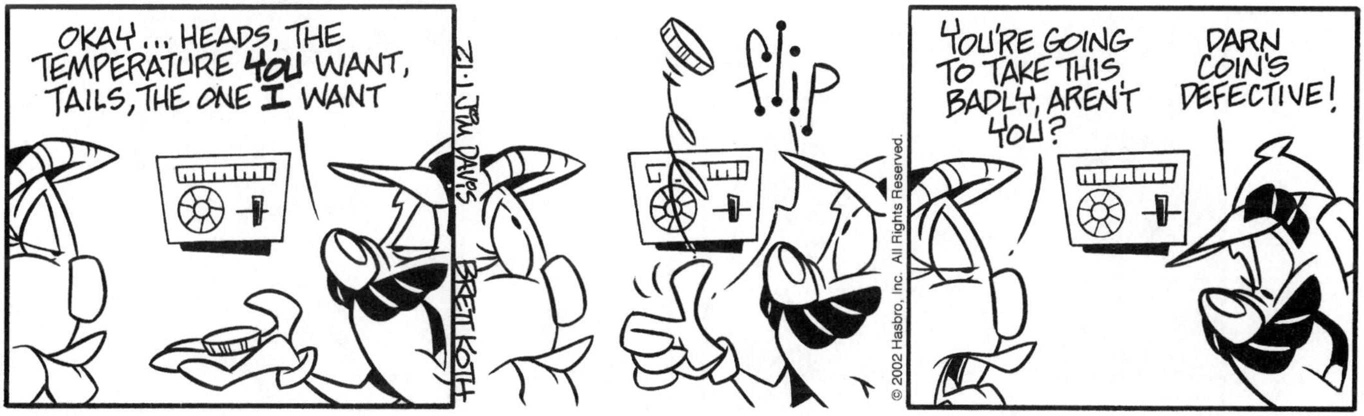
OKAY... HEADS, THE TEMPERATURE YOU WANT, TAILS, THE ONE I WANT
flip
YOU'RE GOING TO TAKE THIS BADLY, AREN'T YOU?
DARN COIN'S DEFECTIVE!
© 2002 Hasbro, Inc. All Rights Reserved.

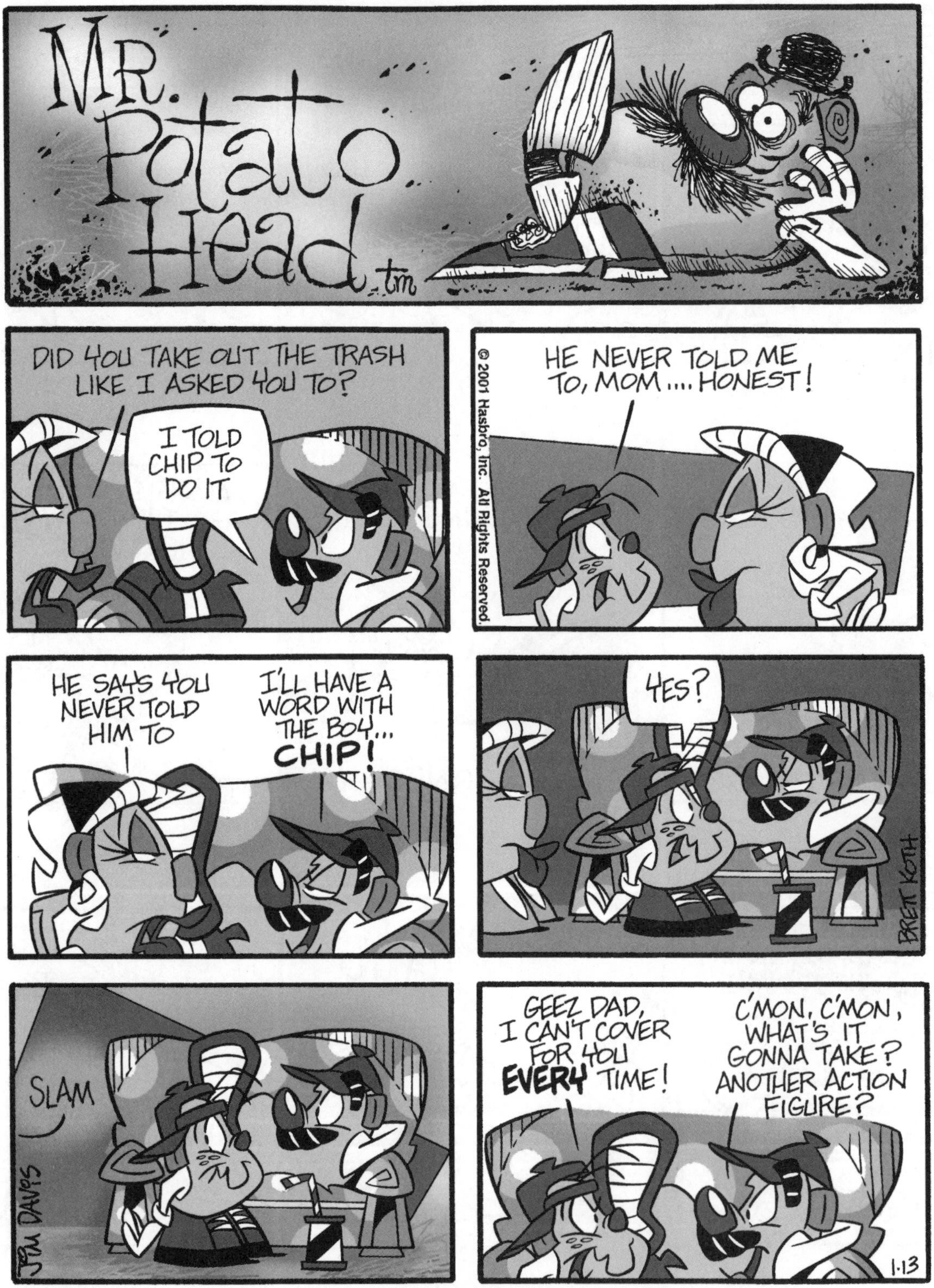
MR. Potato Head tm
DID YOU TAKE OUT THE TRASH LIKE I ASKED YOU TO?
I TOLD CHIP TO DO IT
© 2001 Hasbro, Inc. All Rights Reserved.
HE NEVER TOLD ME TO, MOM .... HONEST!
HE SAYS YOU NEVER TOLD HIM TO
I'LL HAVE A WORD WITH THE BOY... CHIP!
YES?
BRETT KOTH
SLAM
JIM DAVIS
GEEZ DAD, I CAN'T COVER FOR YOU EVERY TIME!
C'MON, C'MON, WHAT'S IT GONNA TAKE? ANOTHER ACTION FIGURE?
1.13

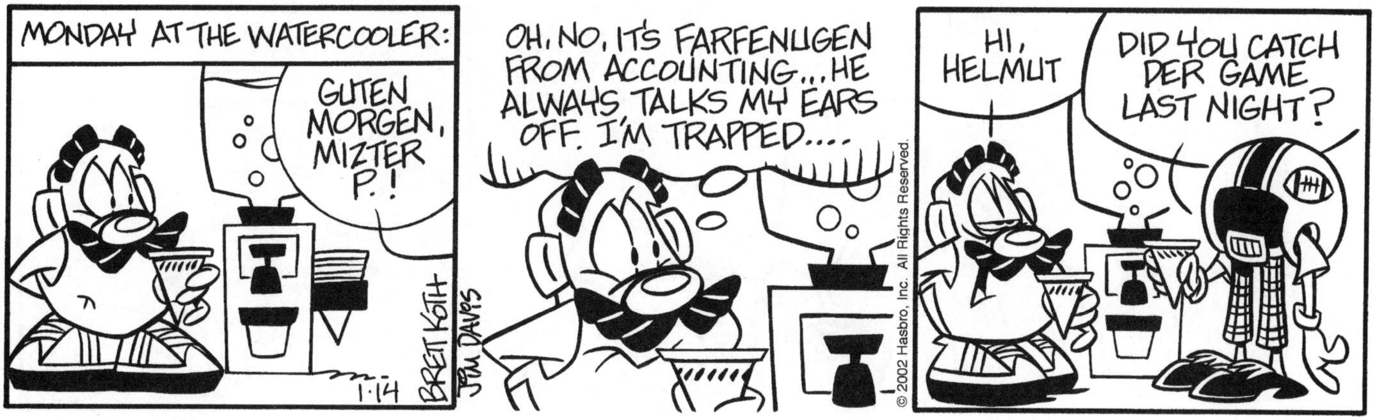
MONDAY AT THE WATERCOOLER:
GUTEN MORGEN, MIZTER P.!
1·14
BRETT KOTH
JIM DAVIS
OH, NO, IT'S FARFENUGEN FROM ACCOUNTING... HE ALWAYS TALKS MY EARS OFF. I'M TRAPPED....
© 2002 Hasbro, Inc. All Rights Reserved.
HI, HELMUT
DID YOU CATCH DER GAME LAST NIGHT?

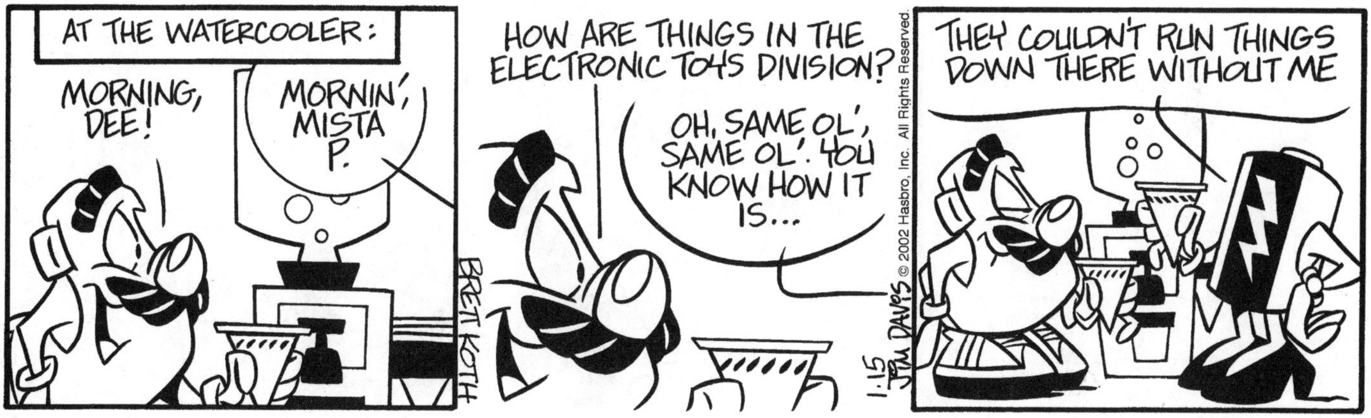
AT THE WATERCOOLER:
MORNING, DEE!
MORNIN', MISTA P.
BRETT KOTH
HOW ARE THINGS IN THE ELECTRONIC TOYS DIVISION?
OH, SAME OL', SAME OL'. YOU KNOW HOW IT IS...
1·15
JIM DAVIS
© 2002 Hasbro, Inc. All Rights Reserved.
THEY COULDN'T RUN THINGS DOWN THERE WITHOUT ME

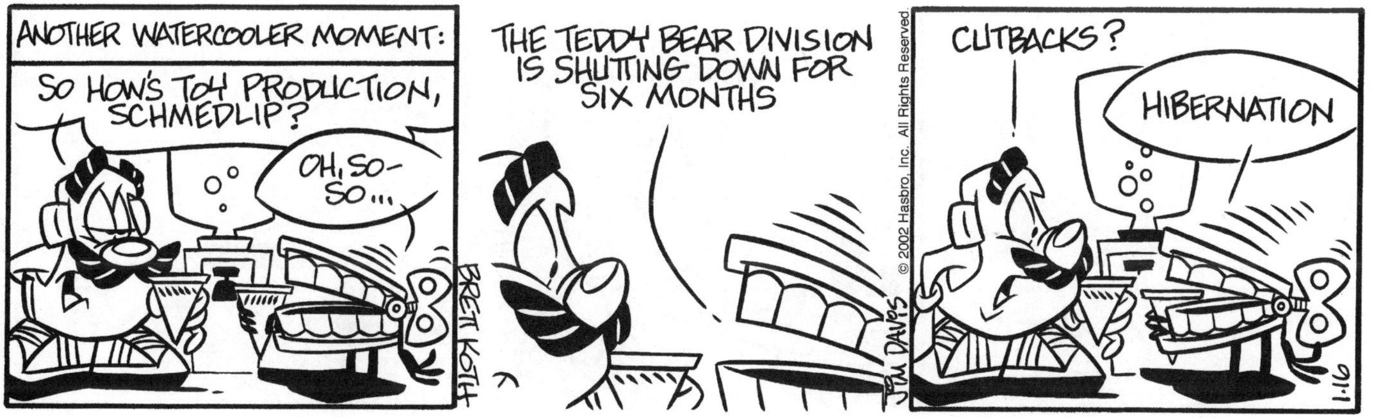
ANOTHER WATERCOOLER MOMENT:
SO HOW'S TOY PRODUCTION, SCHMEDLIP?
OH, SO-SO...
BRETT KOTH
THE TEDDY BEAR DIVISION IS SHUTTING DOWN FOR SIX MONTHS
JIM DAVIS
© 2002 Hasbro, Inc. All Rights Reserved.
CUTBACKS?
HIBERNATION
1·16

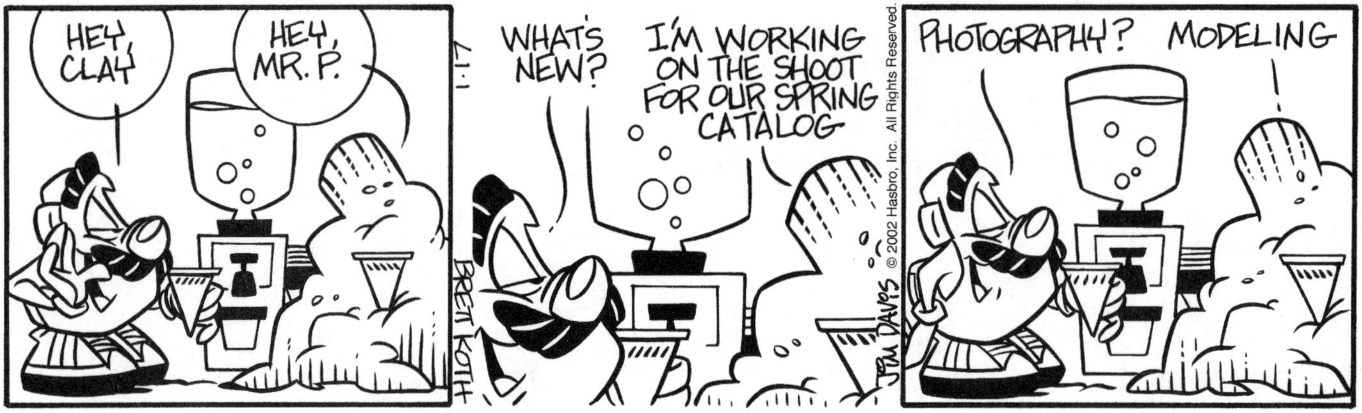
HEY, CLAY
HEY, MR. P.
1.17
WHAT'S NEW?
I'M WORKING ON THE SHOOT FOR OUR SPRING CATALOG
PHOTOGRAPHY? MODELING
BRETT KOTH
JIM DAVIS

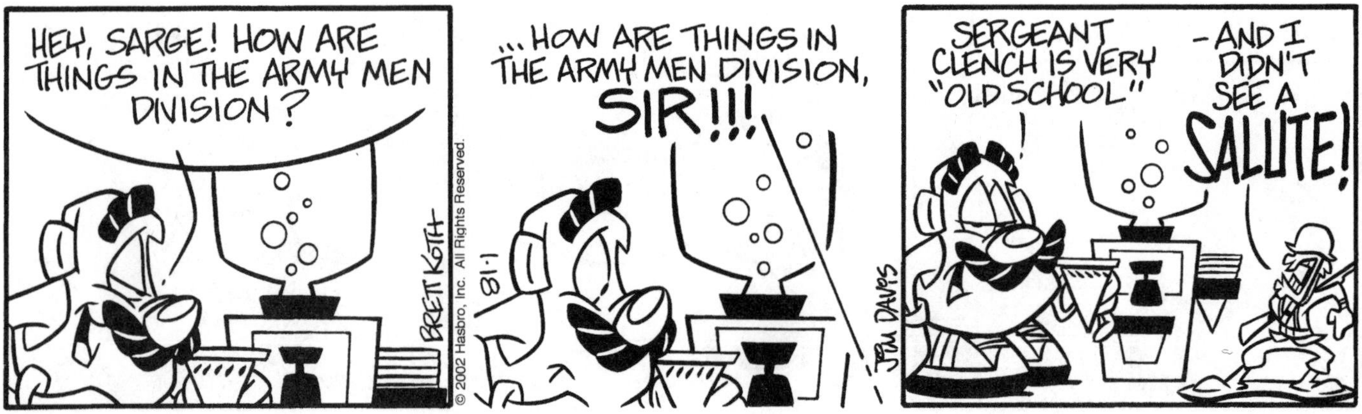
HEY, SARGE! HOW ARE THINGS IN THE ARMY MEN DIVISION?
...HOW ARE THINGS IN THE ARMY MEN DIVISION, SIR!!!
1.18
SERGEANT CLENCH IS VERY "OLD SCHOOL"
-AND I DIDN'T SEE A SALUTE!
BRETT KOTH
JIM DAVIS

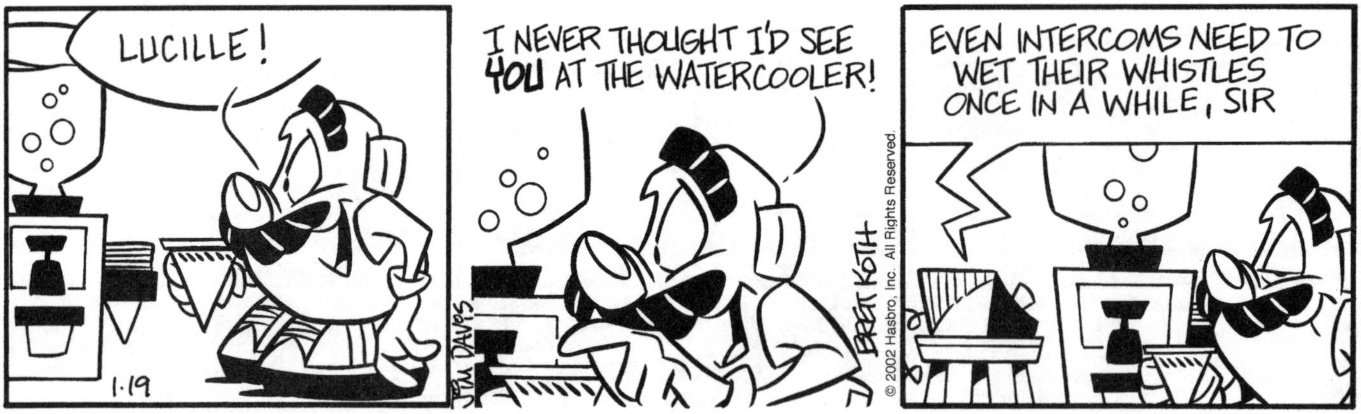
LUCILLE!
1.19
I NEVER THOUGHT I'D SEE YOU AT THE WATERCOOLER!
EVEN INTERCOMS NEED TO WET THEIR WHISTLES ONCE IN A WHILE, SIR
JIM DAVIS
BRETT KOTH

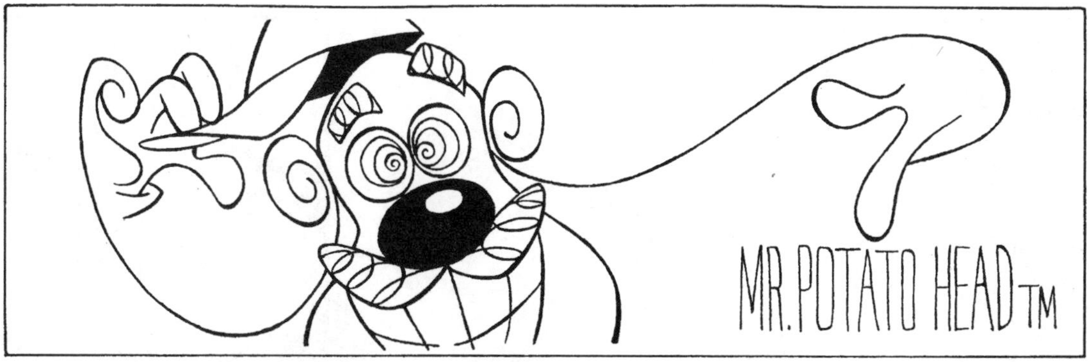
MR. POTATO HEAD TM

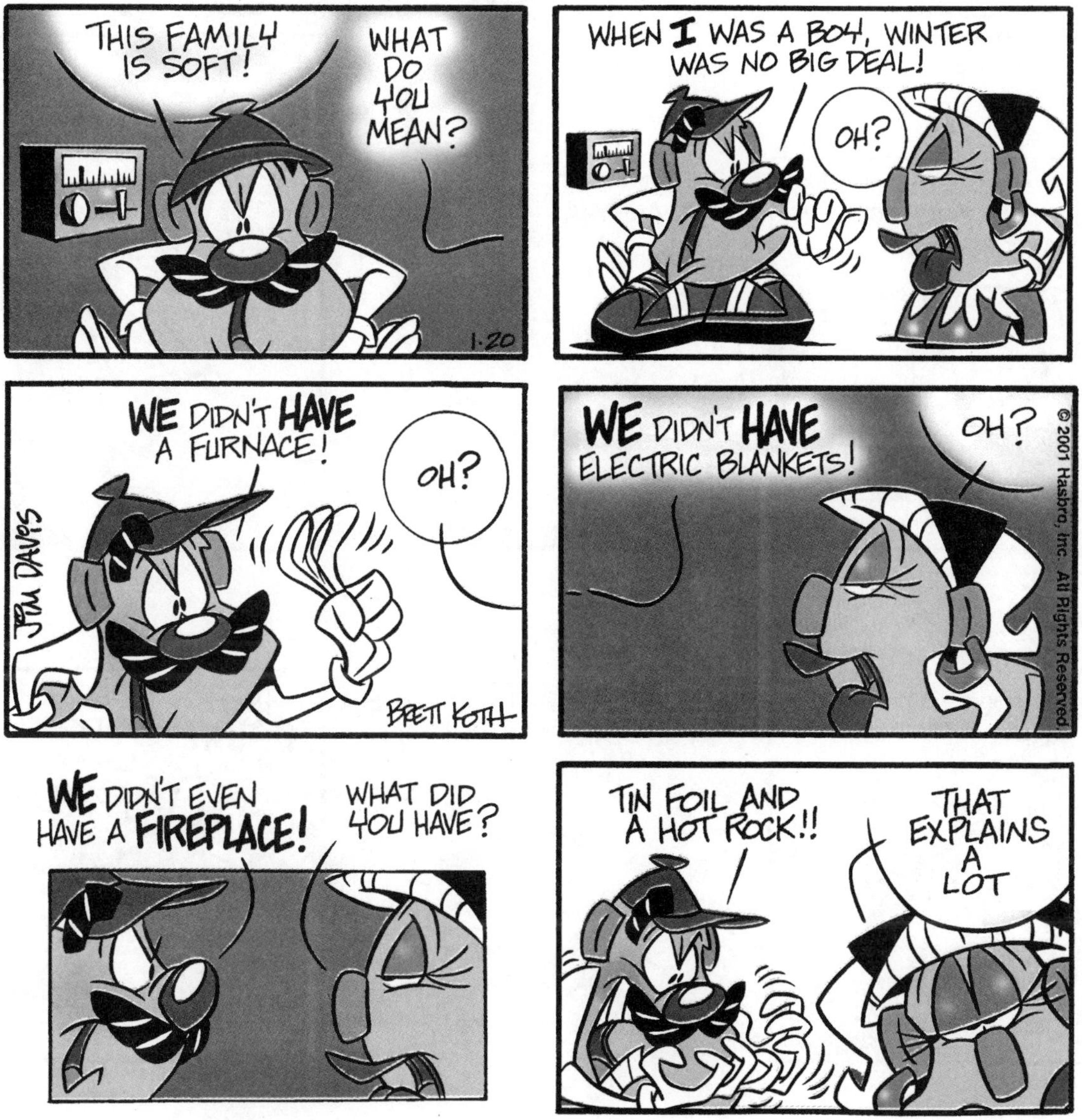
THIS FAMILY IS SOFT!
WHAT DO YOU MEAN?
1.20
WHEN I WAS A BOY, WINTER WAS NO BIG DEAL!
OH?
WE DIDN'T HAVE A FURNACE!
OH?
JIM DAVIS
BRETT KOTH
WE DIDN'T HAVE ELECTRIC BLANKETS!
OH?
© 2001 Hasbro, Inc. All Rights Reserved.
WE DIDN'T EVEN HAVE A FIREPLACE!
WHAT DID YOU HAVE?
TIN FOIL AND A HOT ROCK!!
THAT EXPLAINS A LOT

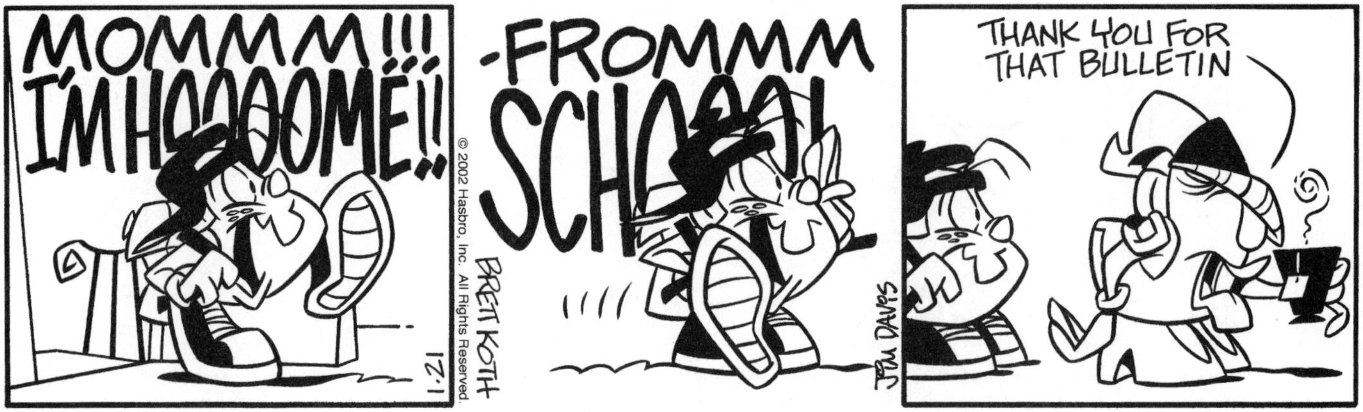
MOMMM!!!
I'M HOOOOME!!
-FROMMM
SCH
THANK YOU FOR THAT BULLETIN
© 2002 Hasbro, Inc. All Rights Reserved.
BRETT KOTH
1·21
JIM DAVIS

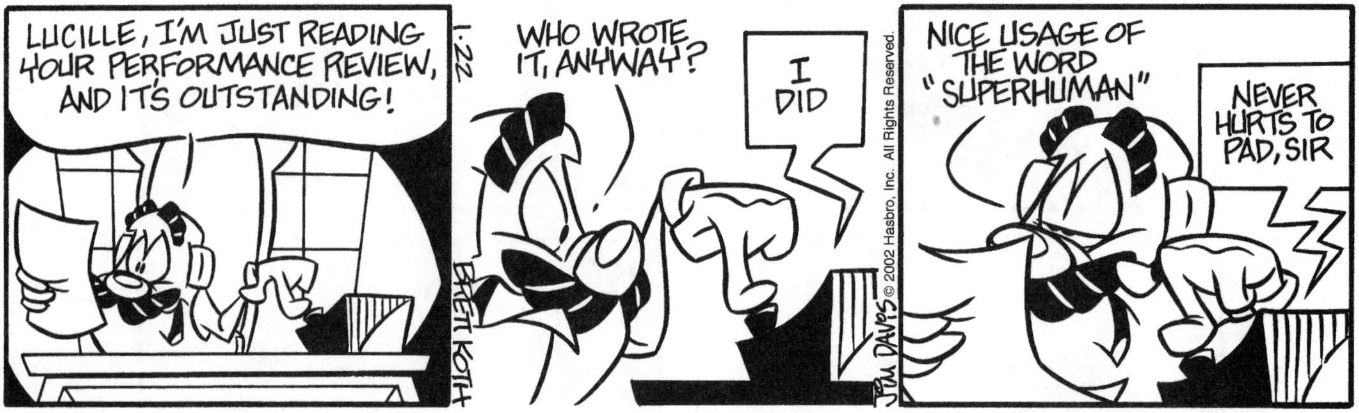
LUCILLE, I'M JUST READING YOUR PERFORMANCE REVIEW, AND IT'S OUTSTANDING!
1·22
WHO WROTE IT, ANYWAY?
I DID
NICE USAGE OF THE WORD "SUPERHUMAN"
NEVER HURTS TO PAD, SIR
BRETT KOTH
JIM DAVIS
© 2002 Hasbro, Inc. All Rights Reserved.

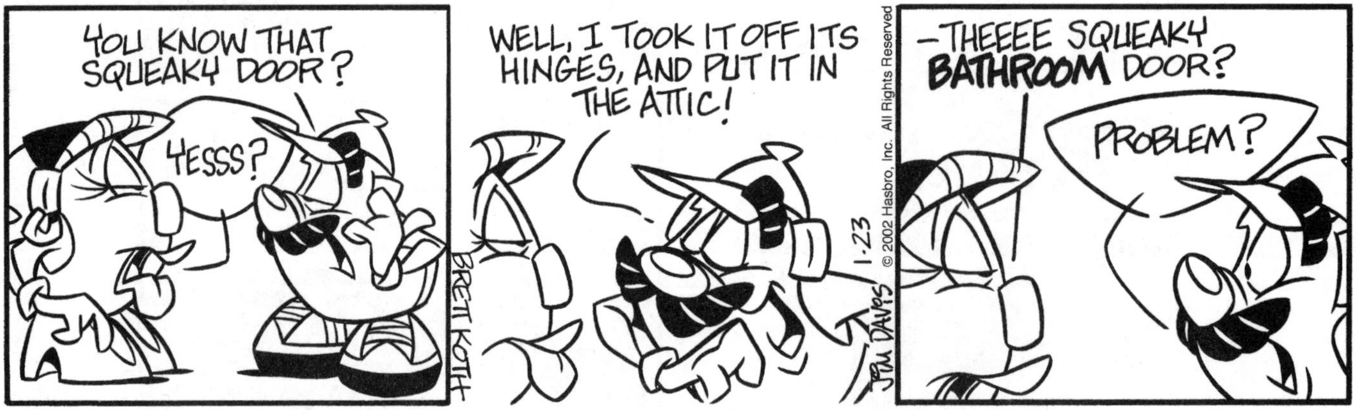
YOU KNOW THAT SQUEAKY DOOR?
YESSS?
WELL, I TOOK IT OFF ITS HINGES, AND PUT IT IN THE ATTIC!
-THEEEE SQUEAKY BATHROOM DOOR?
PROBLEM?
BRETT KOTH
1·23
JIM DAVIS
© 2002 Hasbro, Inc. All Rights Reserved

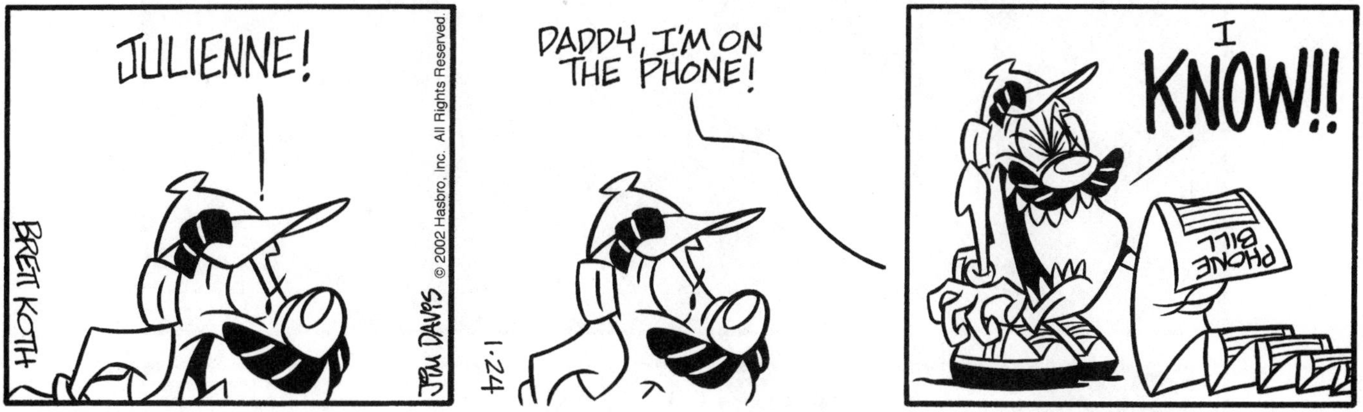
JULIENNE!
DADDY, I'M ON THE PHONE!
I KNOW!!
PHONE BILL

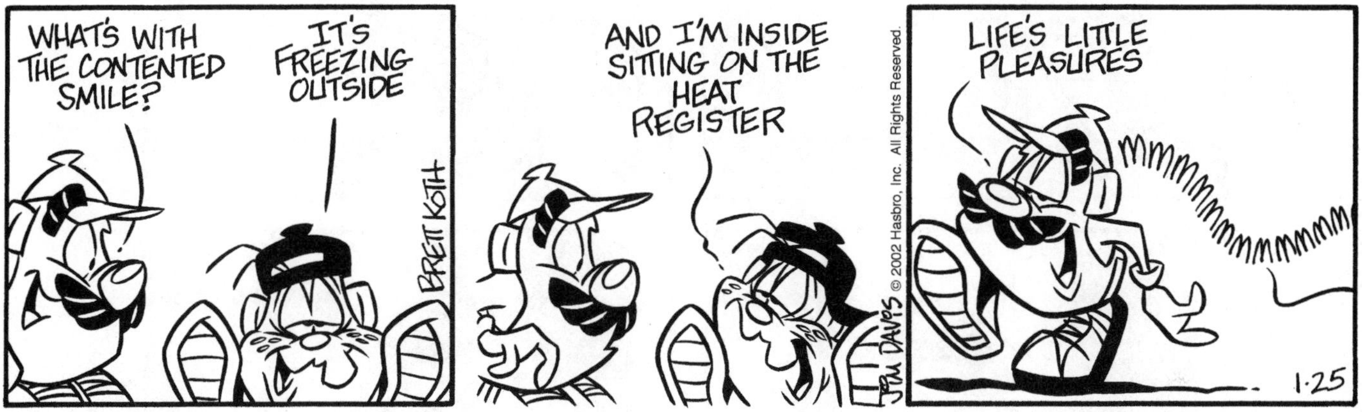
WHAT'S WITH THE CONTENTED SMILE?
IT'S FREEZING OUTSIDE
AND I'M INSIDE SITTING ON THE HEAT REGISTER
LIFE'S LITTLE PLEASURES
MMMMMMMMMMMMMMMMM

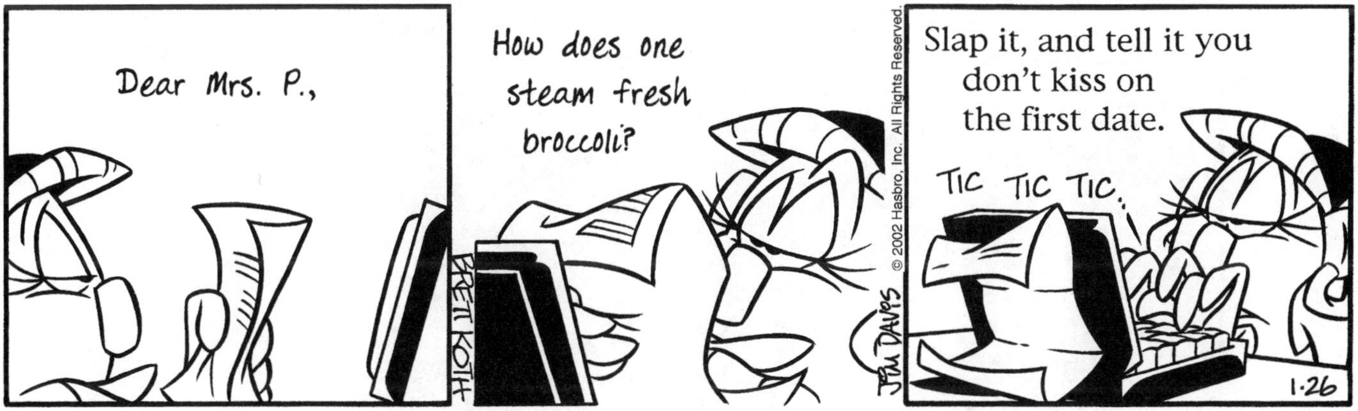
Dear Mrs. P.,
How does one steam fresh broccoli?
Slap it, and tell it you don't kiss on the first date.
TIC TIC TIC...

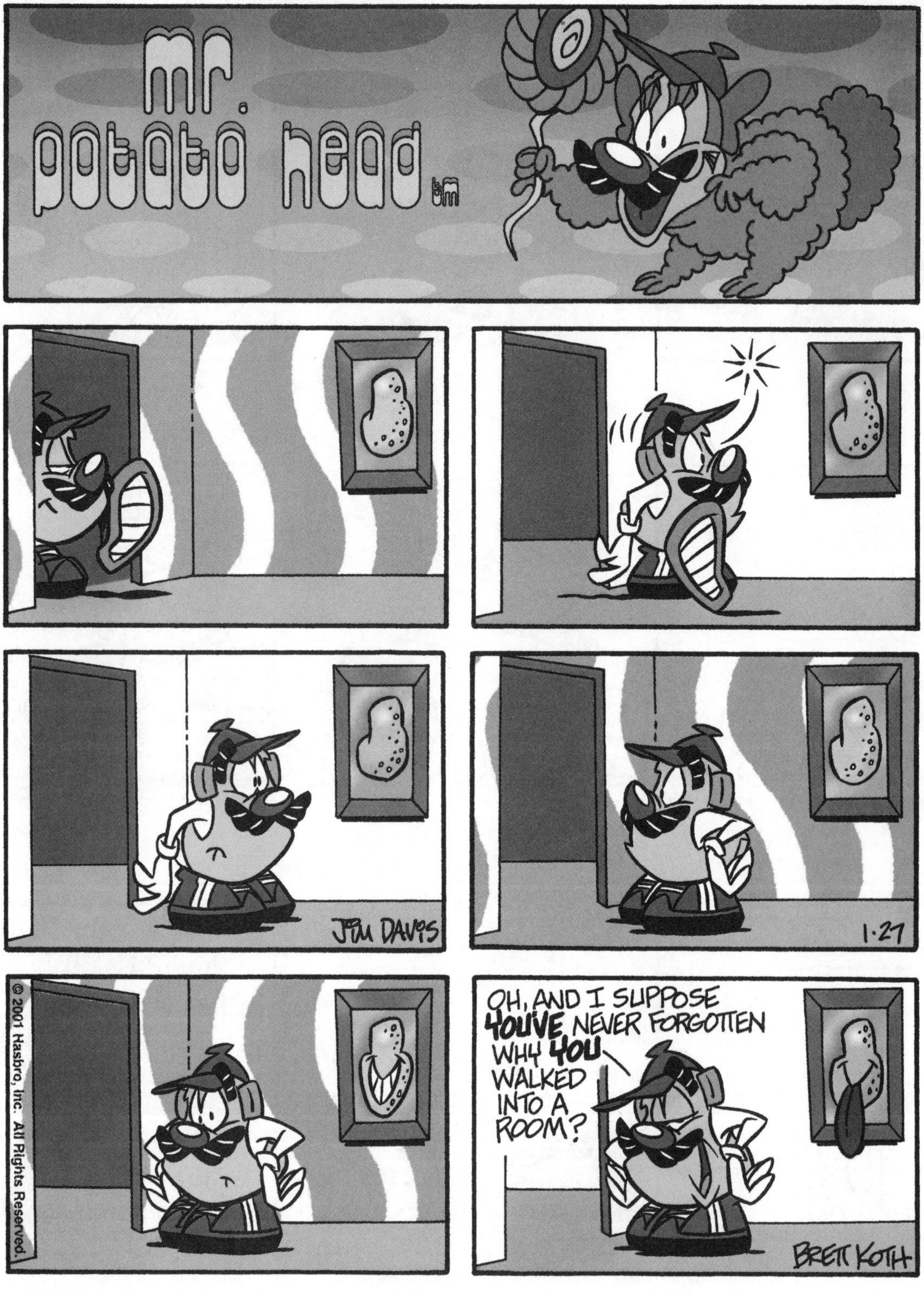
mr. potato head
JIM DAVIS
1·27
© 2001 Hasbro, Inc. All Rights Reserved.
OH, AND I SUPPOSE YOU'VE NEVER FORGOTTEN WHY YOU WALKED INTO A ROOM?
BRETT KOTH

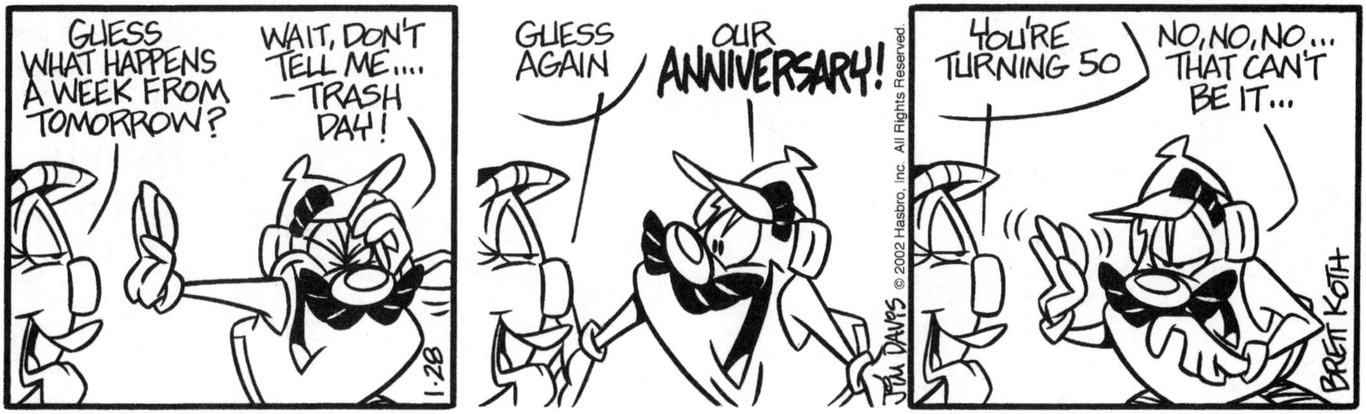
GUESS WHAT HAPPENS A WEEK FROM TOMORROW?
WAIT, DON'T TELL ME.... —TRASH DAY!
GUESS AGAIN
OUR ANNIVERSARY!
YOU'RE TURNING 50
NO, NO, NO... THAT CAN'T BE IT...
1·28
JIM DAVIS
BRETT KOTH
© 2002 Hasbro, Inc. All Rights Reserved.

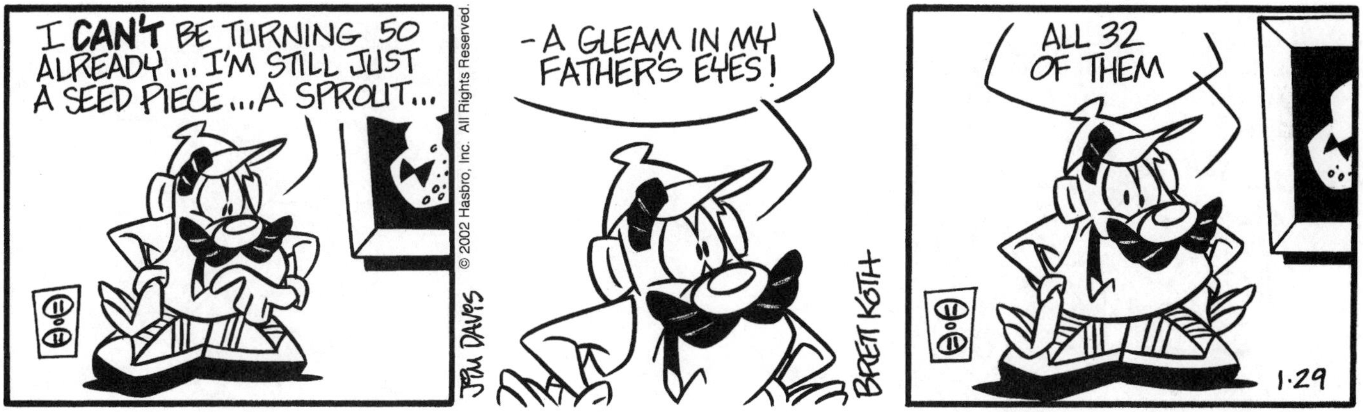
I CAN'T BE TURNING 50 ALREADY... I'M STILL JUST A SEED PIECE... A SPROUT...
—A GLEAM IN MY FATHER'S EYES!
ALL 32 OF THEM
1·29
JIM DAVIS
BRETT KOTH
© 2002 Hasbro, Inc. All Rights Reserved.

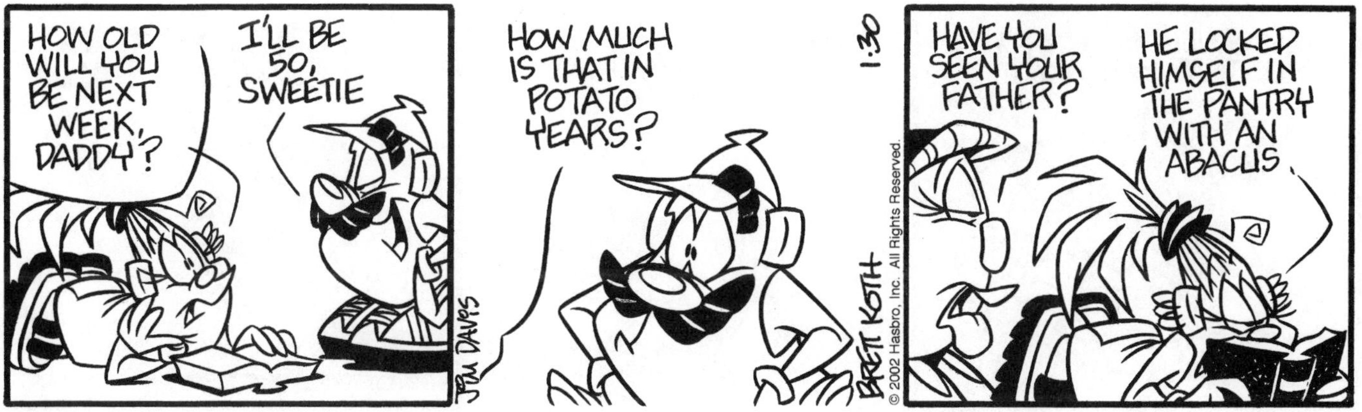
HOW OLD WILL YOU BE NEXT WEEK, DADDY?
I'LL BE 50, SWEETIE
HOW MUCH IS THAT IN POTATO YEARS?
HAVE YOU SEEN YOUR FATHER?
HE LOCKED HIMSELF IN THE PANTRY WITH AN ABACUS
1·30
JIM DAVIS
BRETT KOTH
© 2002 Hasbro, Inc. All Rights Reserved.

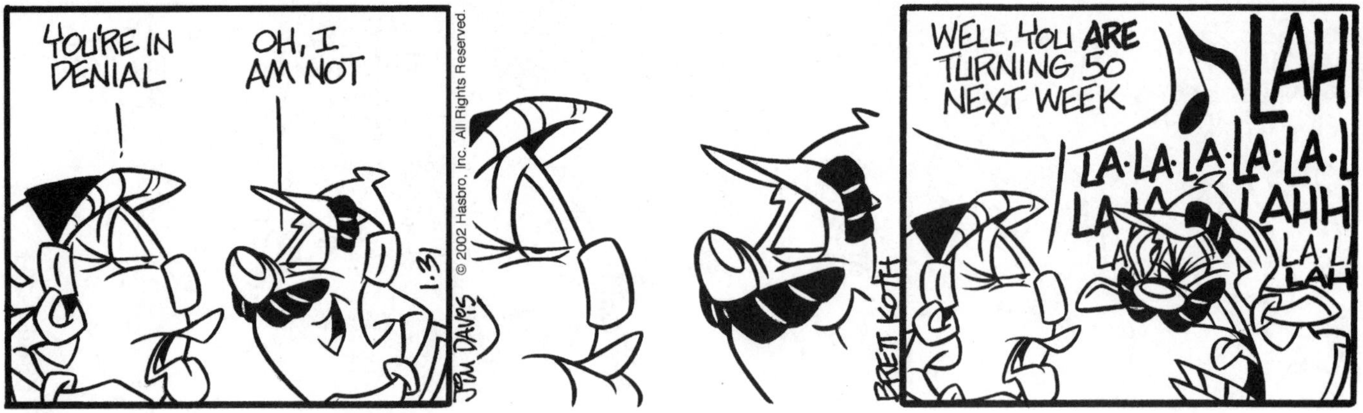
YOU'RE IN DENIAL
OH, I AM NOT
WELL, YOU **ARE** TURNING 50 NEXT WEEK
LAH
LA·LA·LA·LA·LA·L
LAHH
LA·L
LAH
1-31
JIM DAVIS
BRETT KOTH

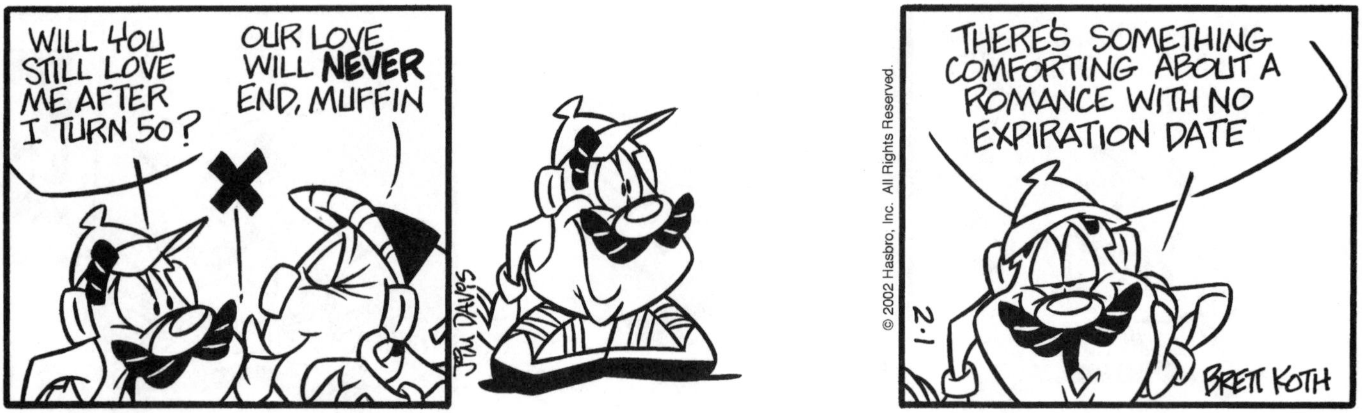
WILL YOU STILL LOVE ME AFTER I TURN 50?
OUR LOVE WILL **NEVER** END, MUFFIN
THERE'S SOMETHING COMFORTING ABOUT A ROMANCE WITH NO EXPIRATION DATE
2-1
JIM DAVIS
BRETT KOTH

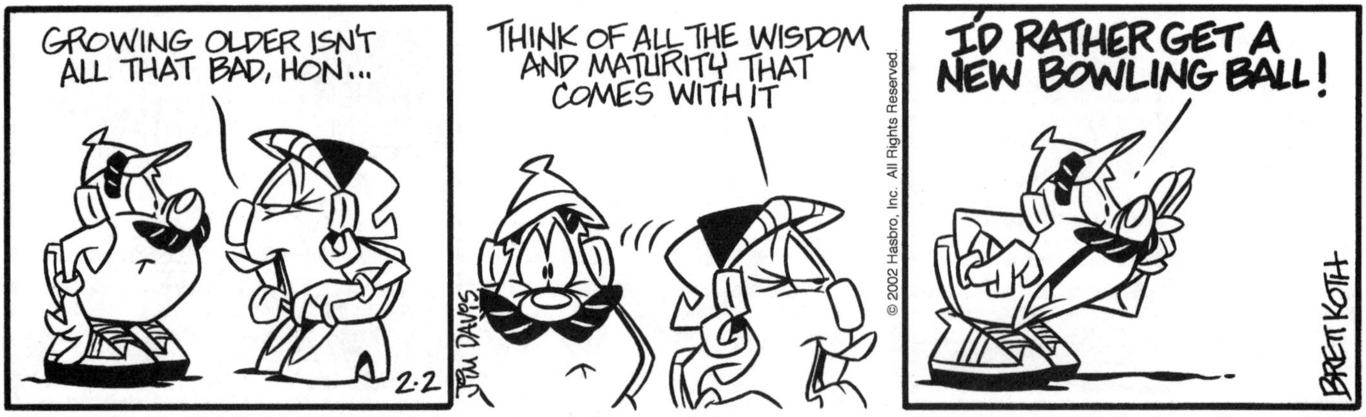
GROWING OLDER ISN'T ALL THAT BAD, HON...
THINK OF ALL THE WISDOM AND MATURITY THAT COMES WITH IT
I'D RATHER GET A NEW BOWLING BALL!
2-2
JIM DAVIS
BRETT KOTH

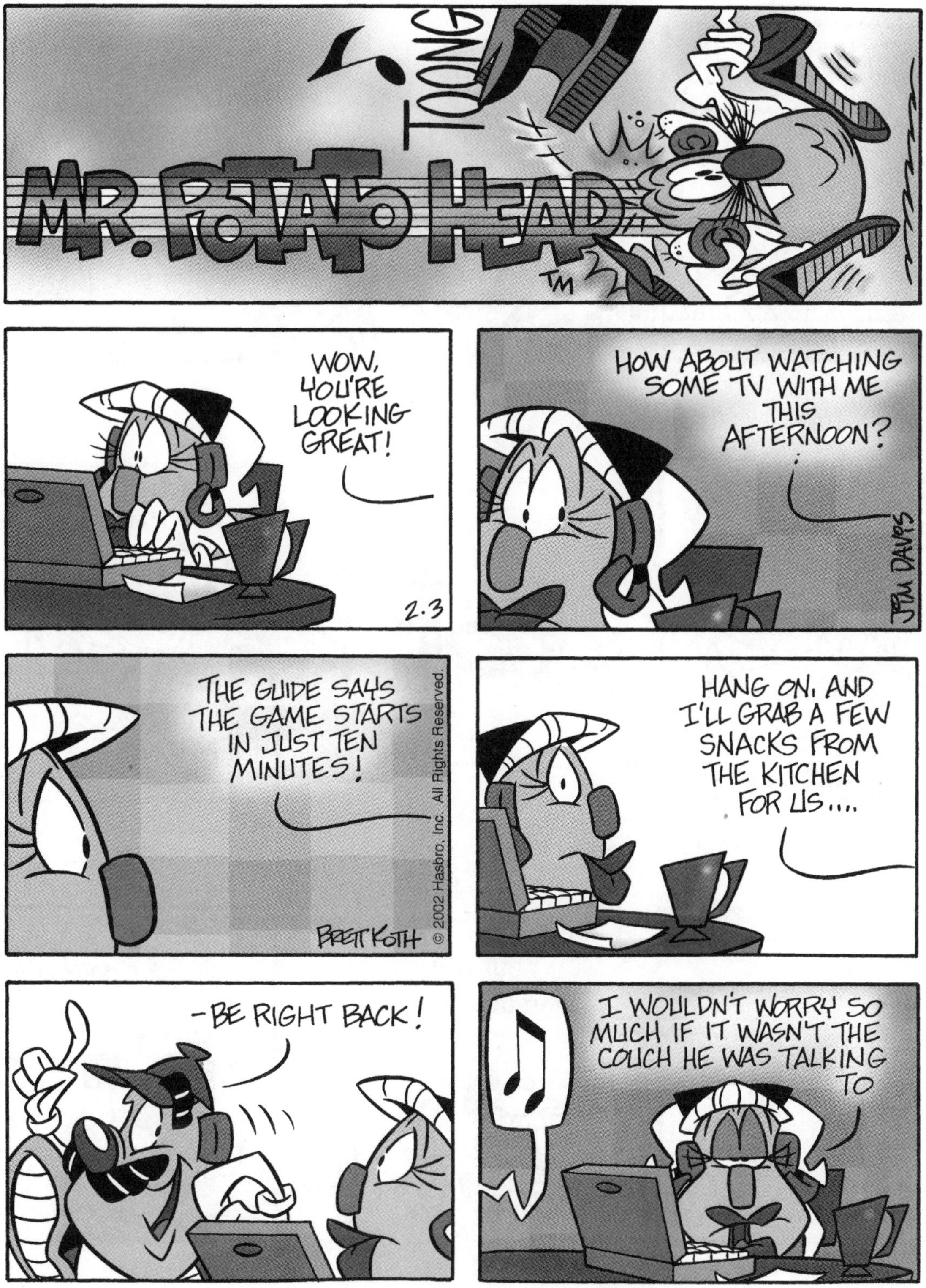
TOONG
MR. POTATO HEAD TM
WOW, YOU'RE LOOKING GREAT!
2.3
HOW ABOUT WATCHING SOME TV WITH ME THIS AFTERNOON?
JIM DAVIS
THE GUIDE SAYS THE GAME STARTS IN JUST TEN MINUTES!
BRETT KOTH
© 2002 Hasbro, Inc. All Rights Reserved.
HANG ON, AND I'LL GRAB A FEW SNACKS FROM THE KITCHEN FOR US....
-BE RIGHT BACK!
I WOULDN'T WORRY SO MUCH IF IT WASN'T THE COUCH HE WAS TALKING TO

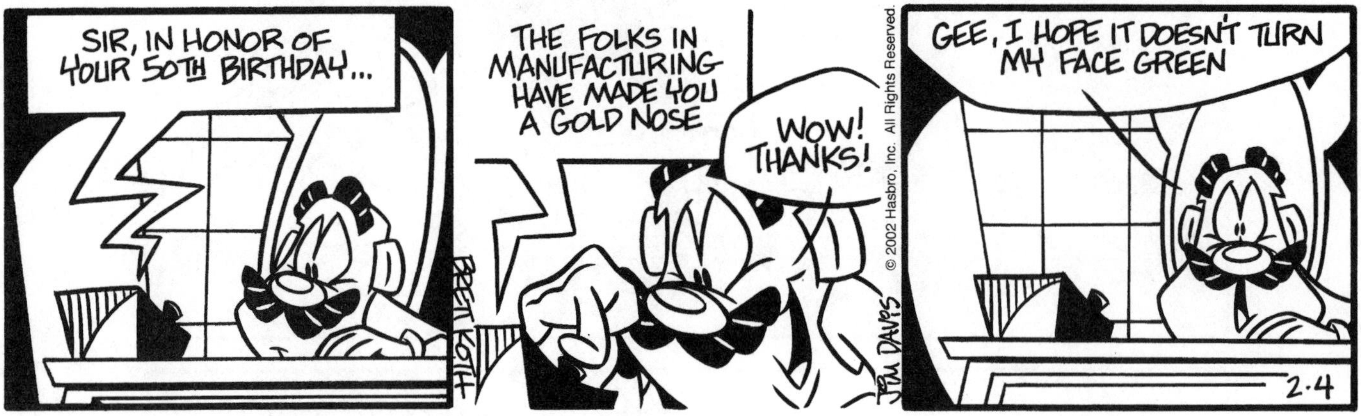
SIR, IN HONOR OF YOUR 50TH BIRTHDAY...
THE FOLKS IN MANUFACTURING HAVE MADE YOU A GOLD NOSE
WOW! THANKS!
GEE, I HOPE IT DOESN'T TURN MY FACE GREEN
BRETT KOTH
JIM DAVIS
© 2002 Hasbro, Inc. All Rights Reserved.
2·4

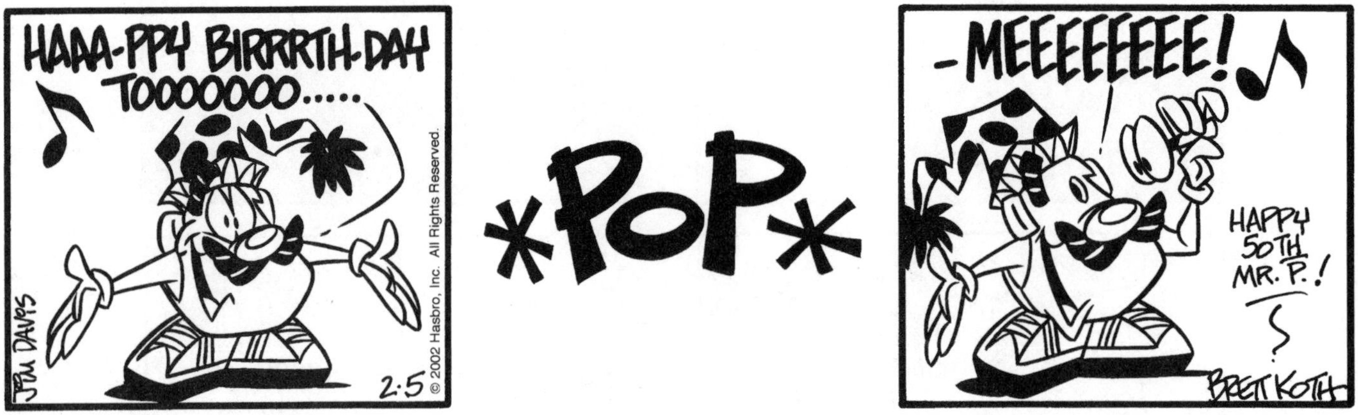
HAAA-PPY BIRRRTH-DAY TOOOOOOO.....
POP
-MEEEEEEEE!
HAPPY 50TH MR. P.!
JIM DAVIS
BRETT KOTH
© 2002 Hasbro, Inc. All Rights Reserved.
2·5

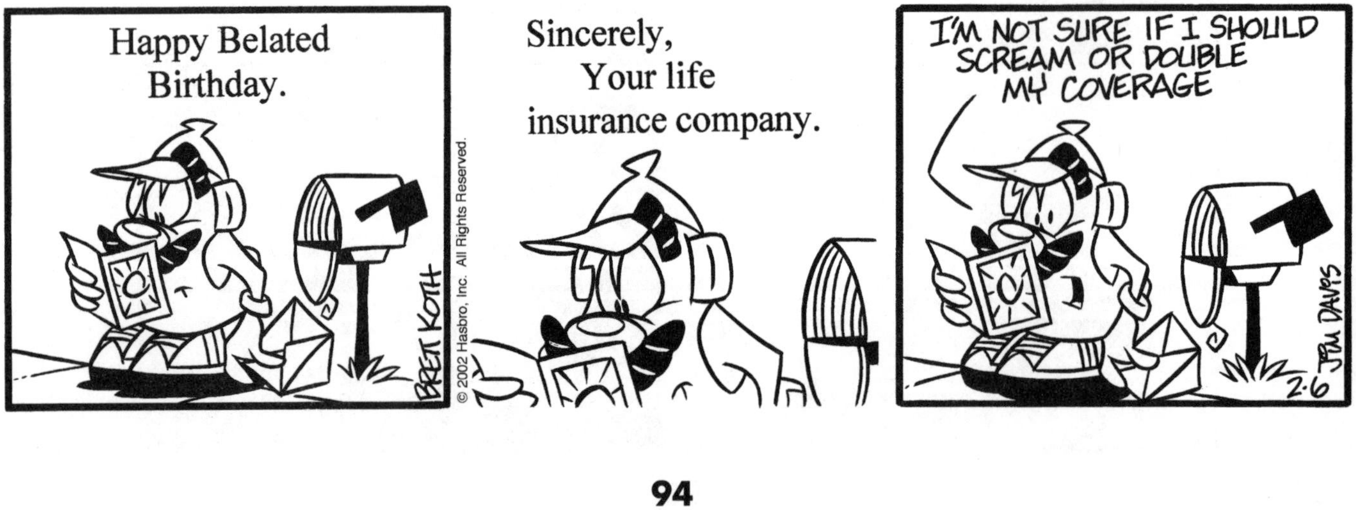
Happy Belated Birthday.
Sincerely, Your life insurance company.
I'M NOT SURE IF I SHOULD SCREAM OR DOUBLE MY COVERAGE
BRETT KOTH
JIM DAVIS
© 2002 Hasbro, Inc. All Rights Reserved.
2·6

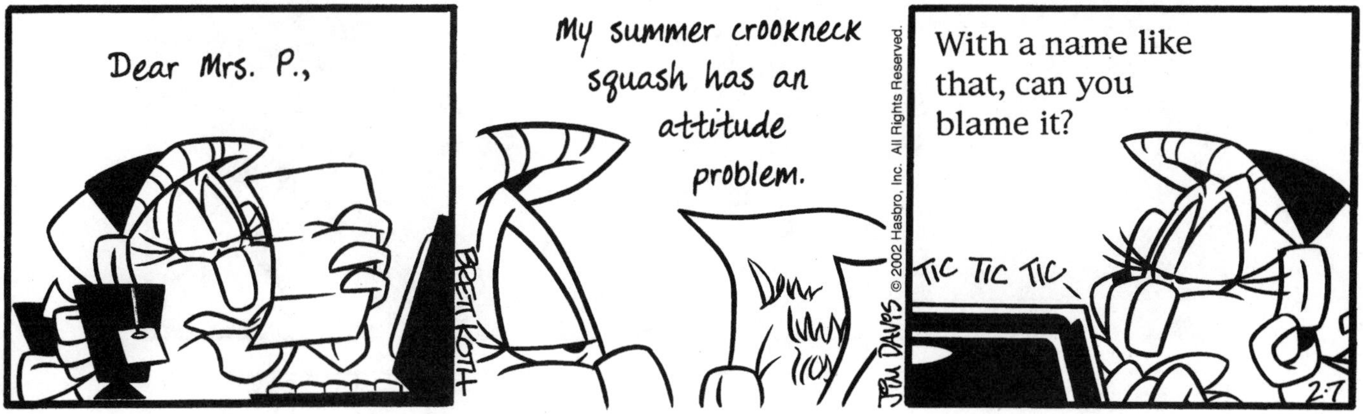
Dear Mrs. P.,
My summer crookneck squash has an attitude problem.
BRETT KOTH
JIM DAVIS © 2002 Hasbro, Inc. All Rights Reserved.
TIC TIC TIC
With a name like that, can you blame it?
2-7

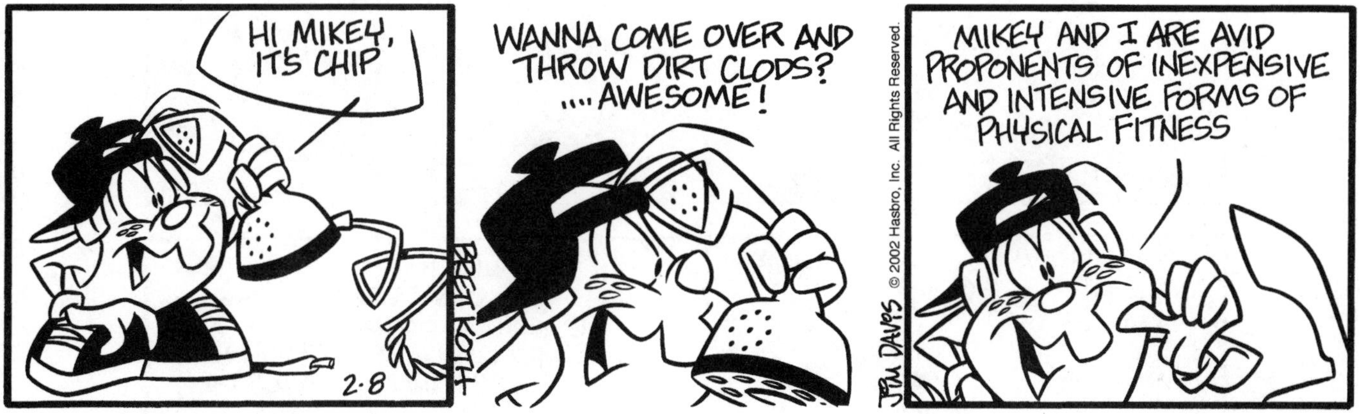
HI MIKEY, IT'S CHIP
2-8
WANNA COME OVER AND THROW DIRT CLODS? ....AWESOME!
BRETT KOTH
JIM DAVIS © 2002 Hasbro, Inc. All Rights Reserved.
MIKEY AND I ARE AVID PROPONENTS OF INEXPENSIVE AND INTENSIVE FORMS OF PHYSICAL FITNESS

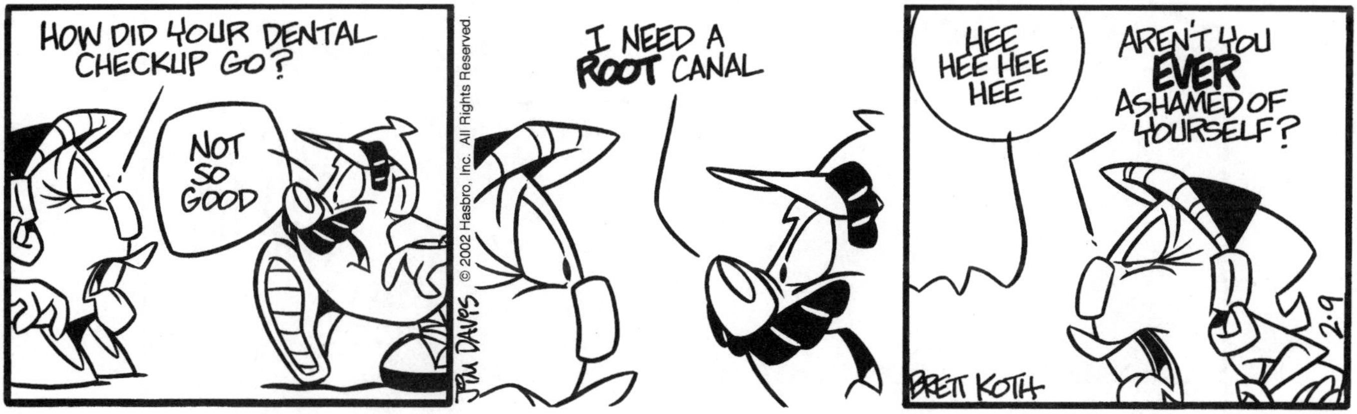
HOW DID YOUR DENTAL CHECKUP GO?
NOT SO GOOD
JIM DAVIS © 2002 Hasbro, Inc. All Rights Reserved.
I NEED A **ROOT** CANAL
HEE HEE HEE HEE
AREN'T YOU **EVER** ASHAMED OF YOURSELF?
BRETT KOTH
2-9

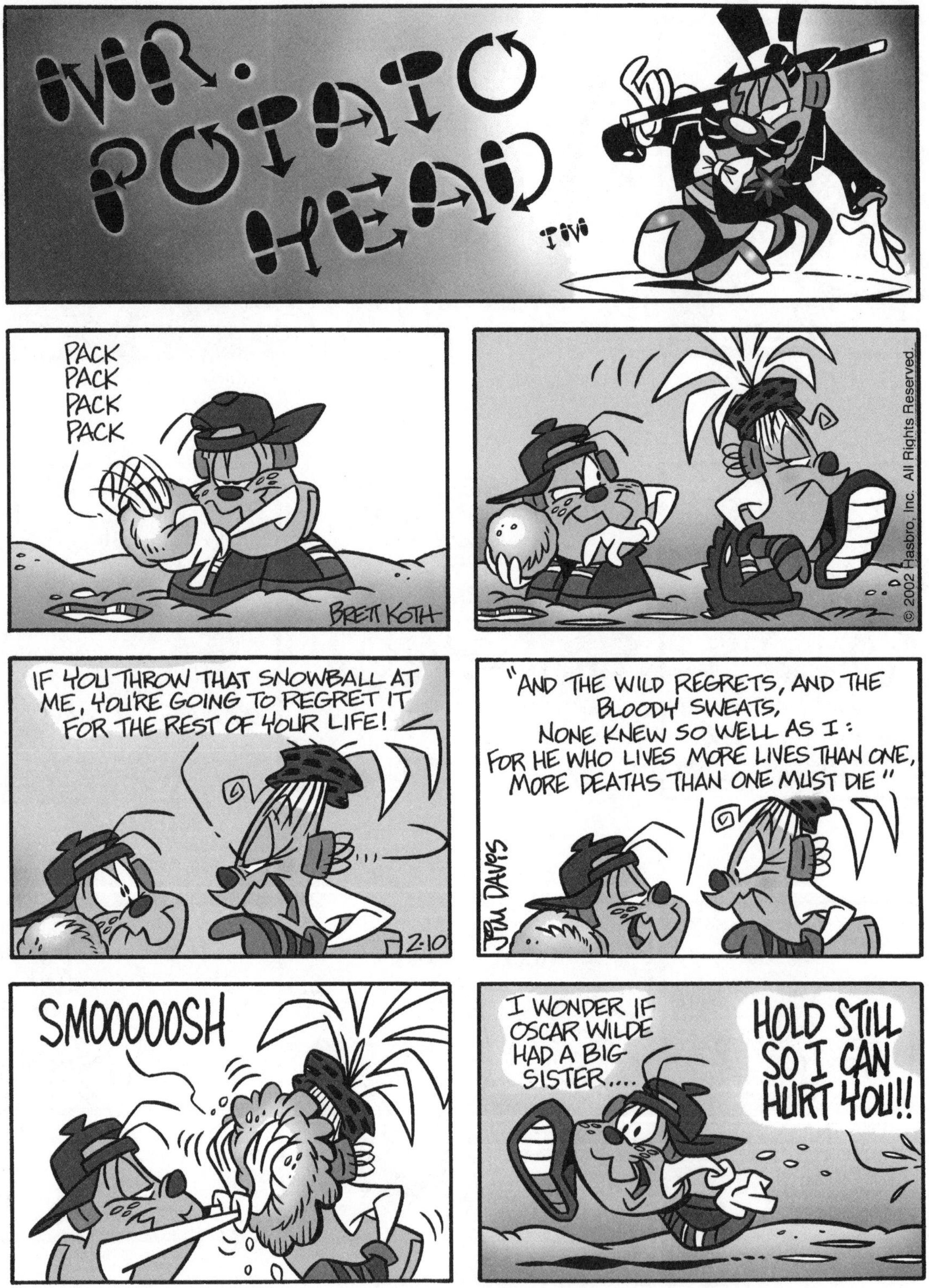
MR. POTATO HEAD
PACK PACK PACK PACK
BRETT KOTH
© 2002 Hasbro, Inc. All Rights Reserved.
IF YOU THROW THAT SNOWBALL AT ME, YOU'RE GOING TO REGRET IT FOR THE REST OF YOUR LIFE!
2·10
"AND THE WILD REGRETS, AND THE BLOODY SWEATS, NONE KNEW SO WELL AS I: FOR HE WHO LIVES MORE LIVES THAN ONE, MORE DEATHS THAN ONE MUST DIE"
JIM DAVIS
SMOOOOOSH
I WONDER IF OSCAR WILDE HAD A BIG SISTER.....
HOLD STILL SO I CAN HURT YOU!!

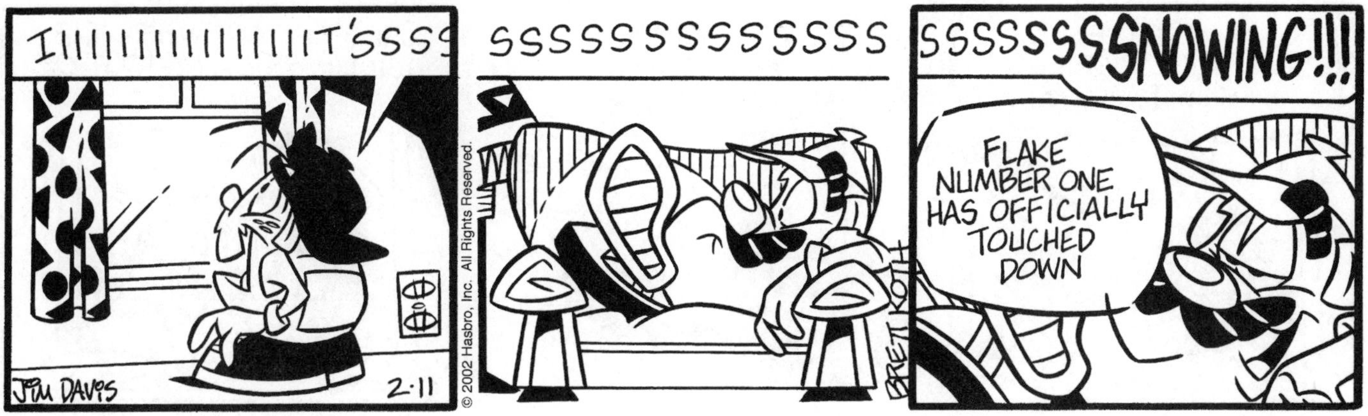
IIIIIIIIIIIIIIIIT'SSSS SSSSSSSSSSSSSS SSSSSSSSNOWING!!!
FLAKE NUMBER ONE HAS OFFICIALLY TOUCHED DOWN
JIM DAVIS
2·11
© 2002 Hasbro, Inc. All Rights Reserved.
BRETT KOTH

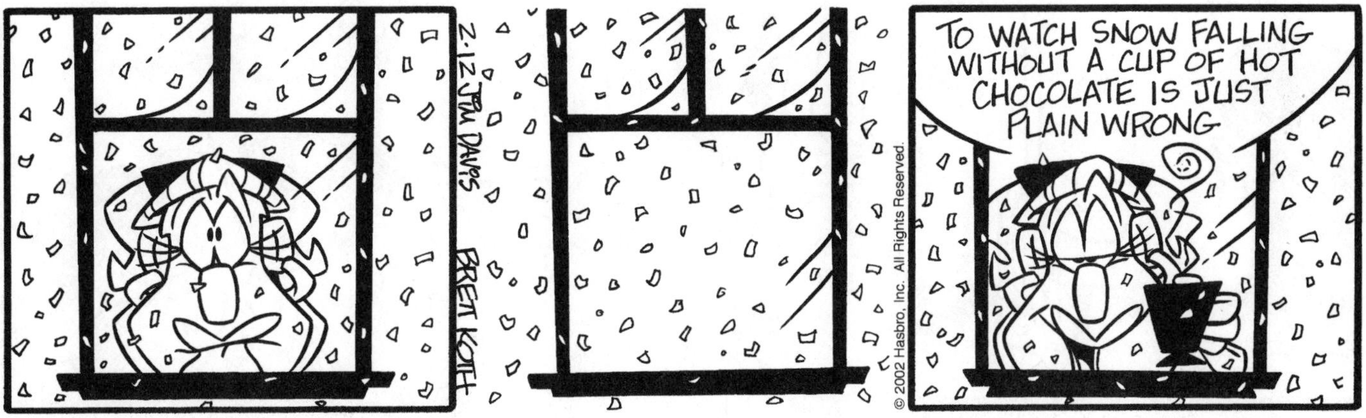
2·12 JIM DAVIS
BRETT KOTH
© 2002 Hasbro, Inc. All Rights Reserved.
TO WATCH SNOW FALLING WITHOUT A CUP OF HOT CHOCOLATE IS JUST PLAIN WRONG

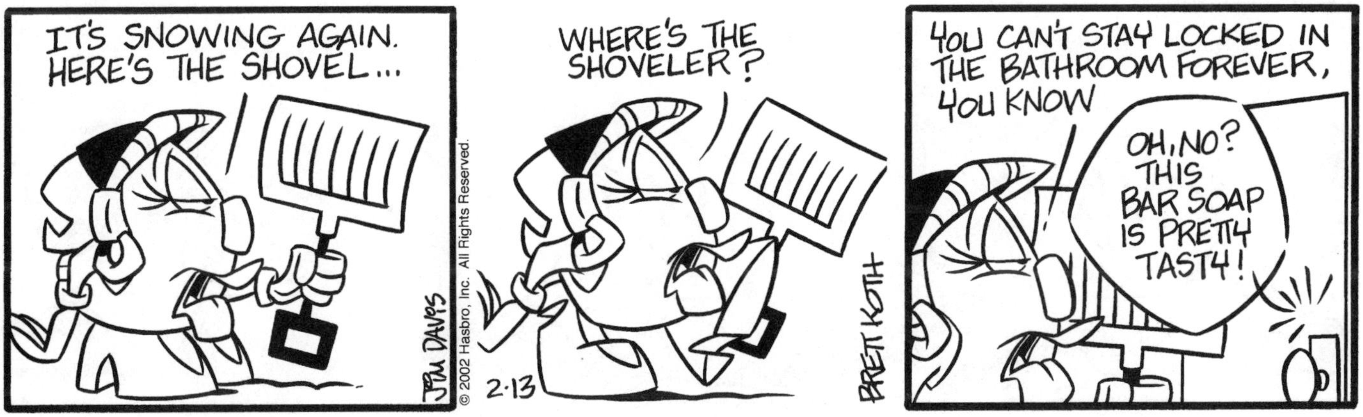
IT'S SNOWING AGAIN. HERE'S THE SHOVEL...
JIM DAVIS
© 2002 Hasbro, Inc. All Rights Reserved.
WHERE'S THE SHOVELER?
2·13
BRETT KOTH
YOU CAN'T STAY LOCKED IN THE BATHROOM FOREVER, YOU KNOW
OH, NO? THIS BAR SOAP IS PRETTY TASTY!

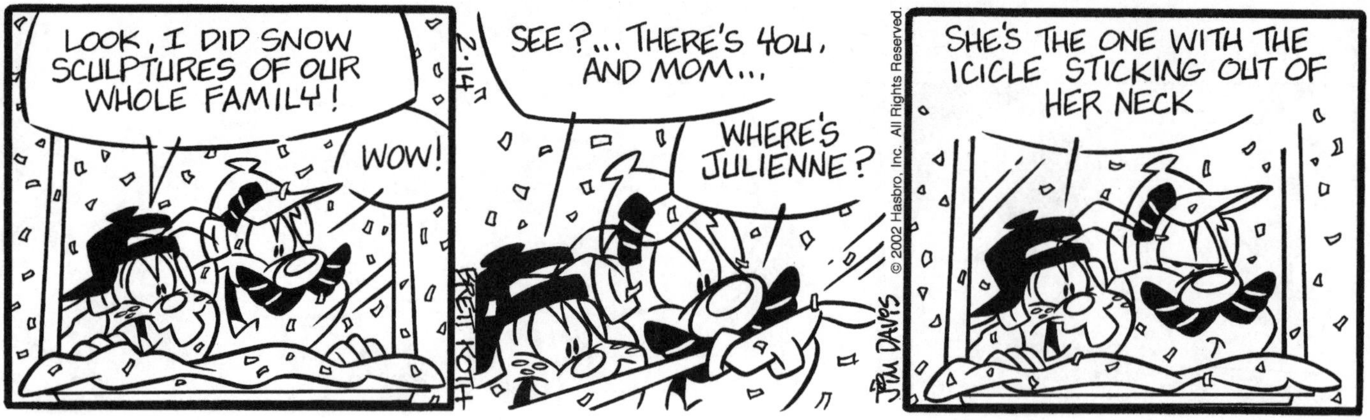
LOOK, I DID SNOW SCULPTURES OF OUR WHOLE FAMILY!
WOW!
2.14
SEE?... THERE'S YOU, AND MOM...
WHERE'S JULIENNE?
SHE'S THE ONE WITH THE ICICLE STICKING OUT OF HER NECK

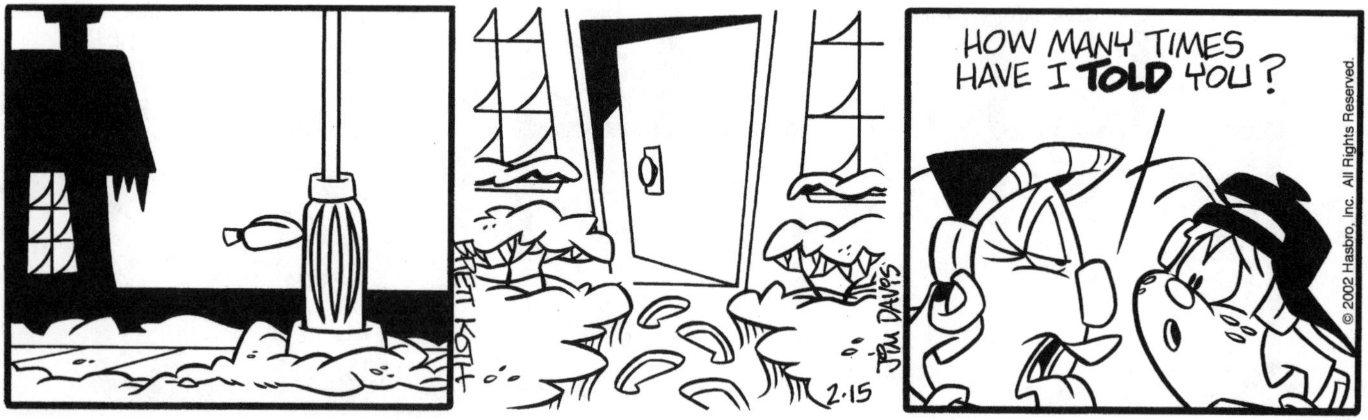
2.15
HOW MANY TIMES HAVE I **TOLD** YOU?

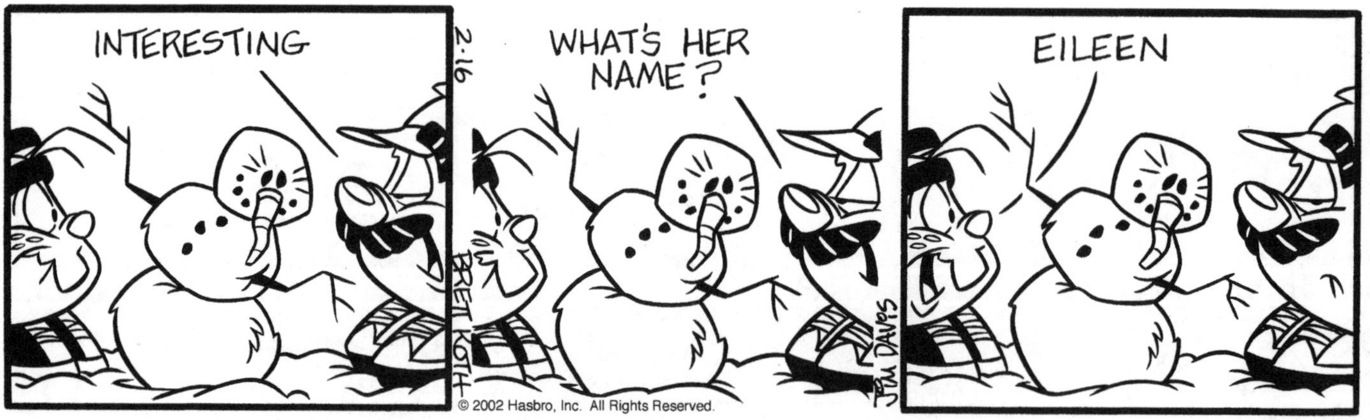
INTERESTING
2.16
WHAT'S HER NAME?
EILEEN

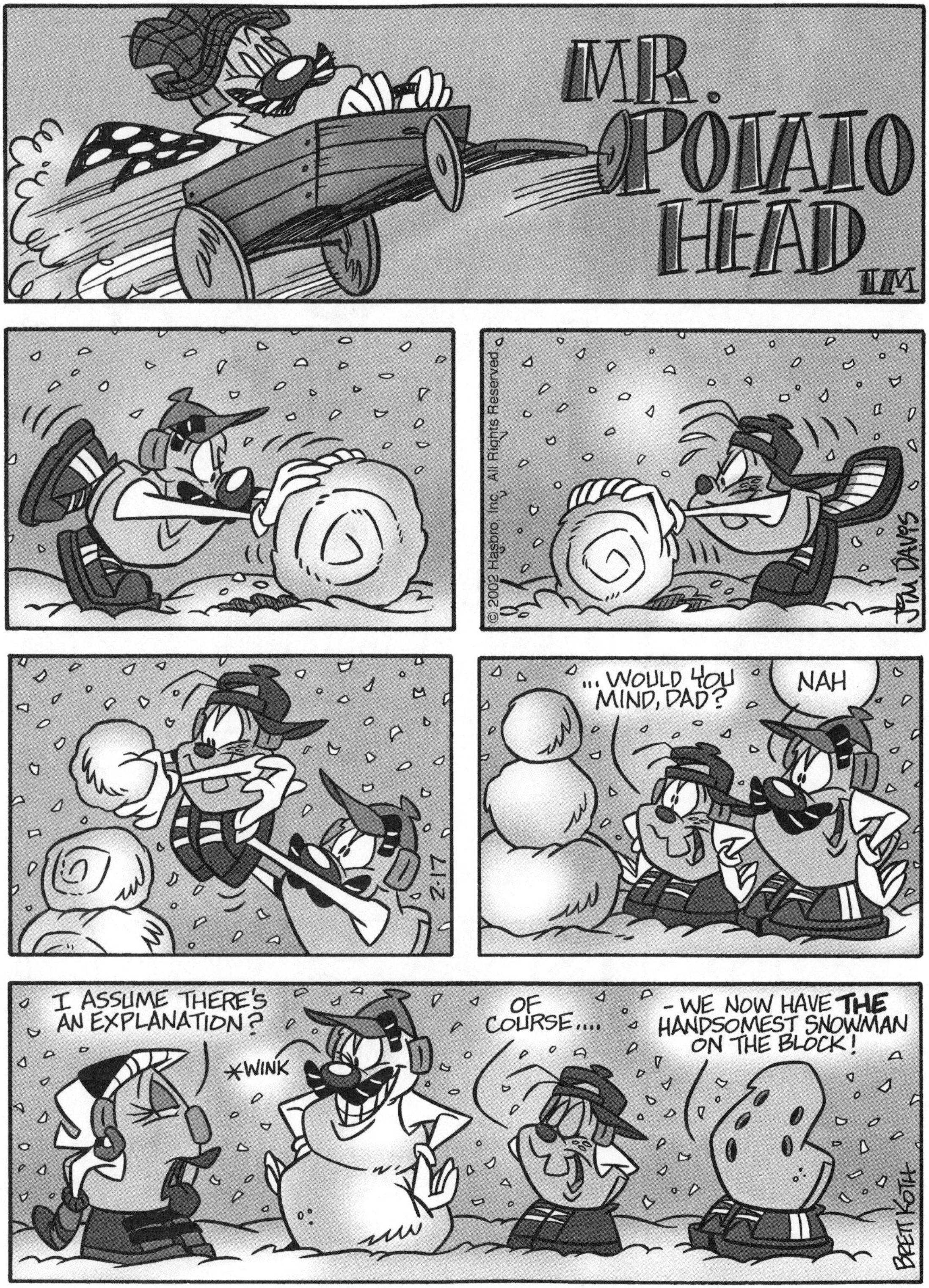
MR. POTATO HEAD TM
© 2002 Hasbro, Inc. All Rights Reserved.
JIM DAVIS
2-17
... WOULD YOU MIND, DAD?
NAH
I ASSUME THERE'S AN EXPLANATION?
*WINK
OF COURSE....
- WE NOW HAVE THE HANDSOMEST SNOWMAN ON THE BLOCK!
BRETT KOTH

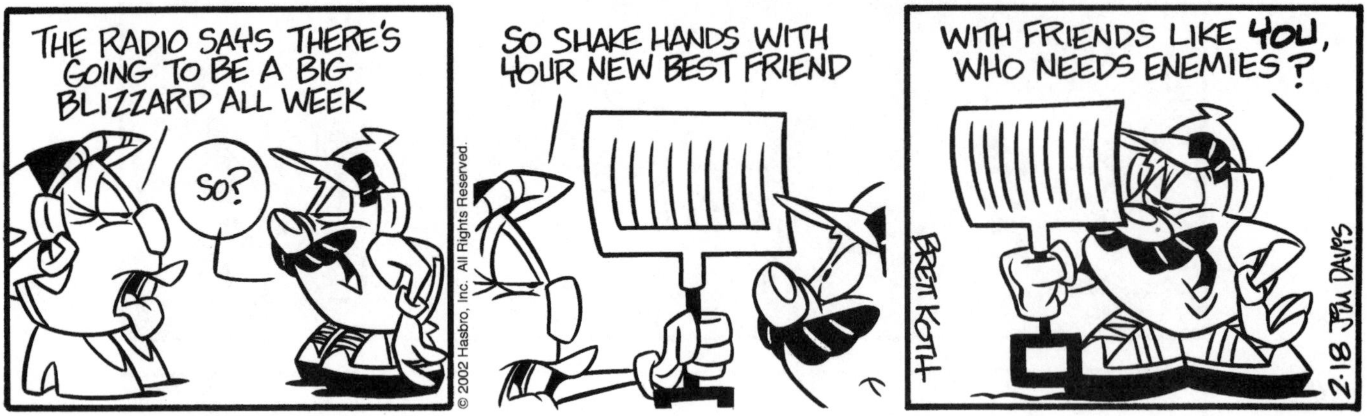
THE RADIO SAYS THERE'S GOING TO BE A BIG BLIZZARD ALL WEEK
SO?
SO SHAKE HANDS WITH YOUR NEW BEST FRIEND
WITH FRIENDS LIKE YOU, WHO NEEDS ENEMIES?
© 2002 Hasbro, Inc. All Rights Reserved.
2·18

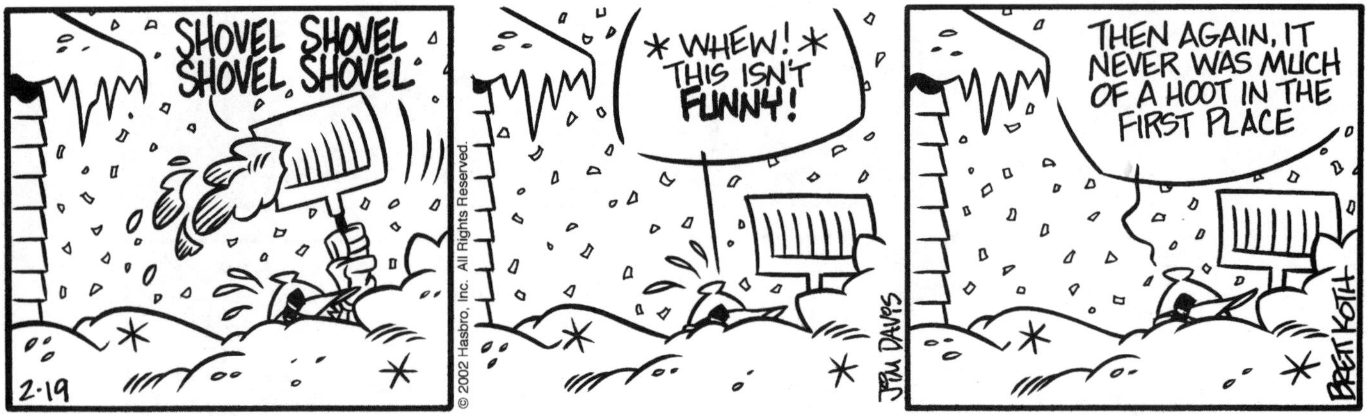
SHOVEL SHOVEL SHOVEL SHOVEL
WHEW! THIS ISN'T FUNNY!
THEN AGAIN, IT NEVER WAS MUCH OF A HOOT IN THE FIRST PLACE
© 2002 Hasbro, Inc. All Rights Reserved.
2·19

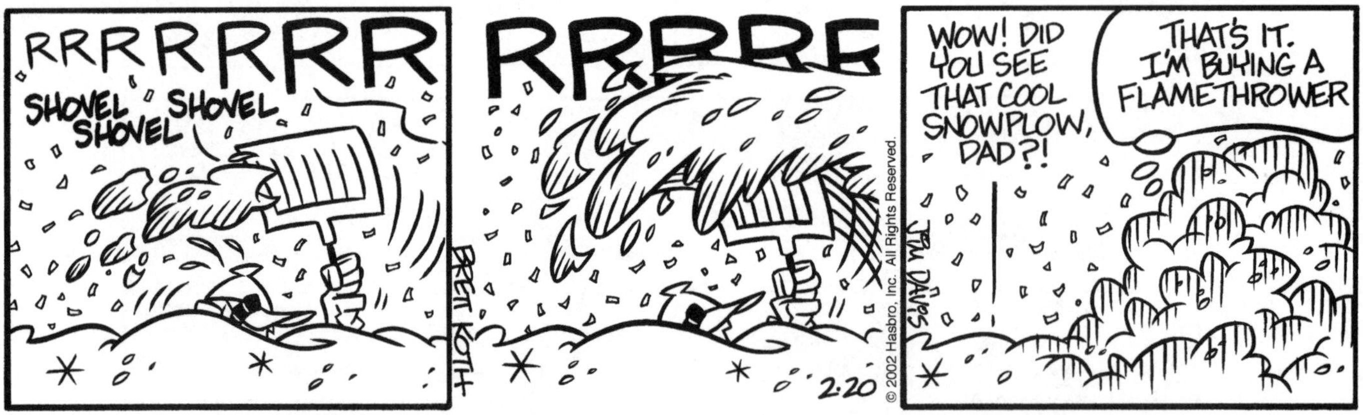
RRRRRRRR
SHOVEL SHOVEL SHOVEL
RRRRR
WOW! DID YOU SEE THAT COOL SNOWPLOW, DAD?!
THAT'S IT. I'M BUYING A FLAMETHROWER
© 2002 Hasbro, Inc. All Rights Reserved.
2·20

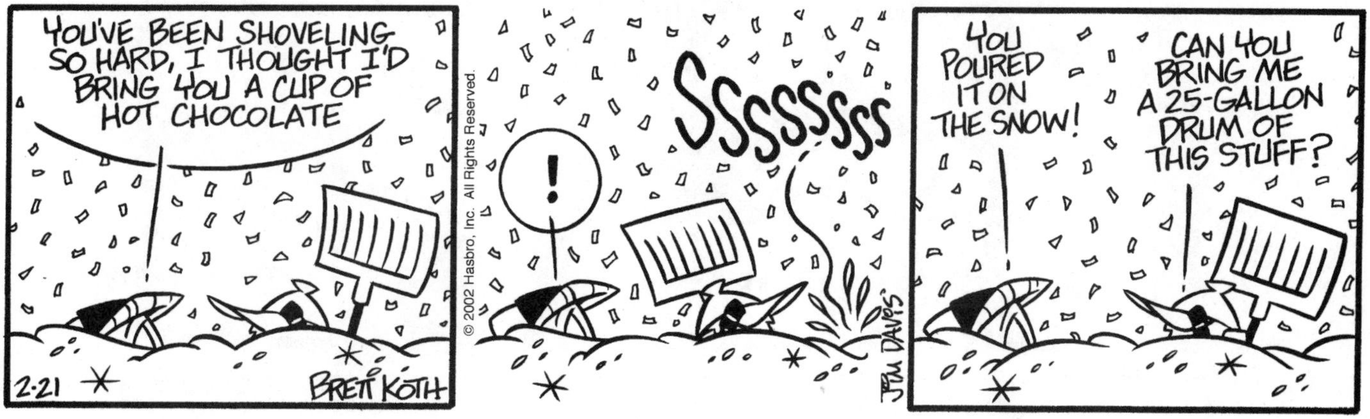
YOU'VE BEEN SHOVELING SO HARD, I THOUGHT I'D BRING YOU A CUP OF HOT CHOCOLATE
!
SSSSSSSS
YOU POURED IT ON THE SNOW!
CAN YOU BRING ME A 25-GALLON DRUM OF THIS STUFF?

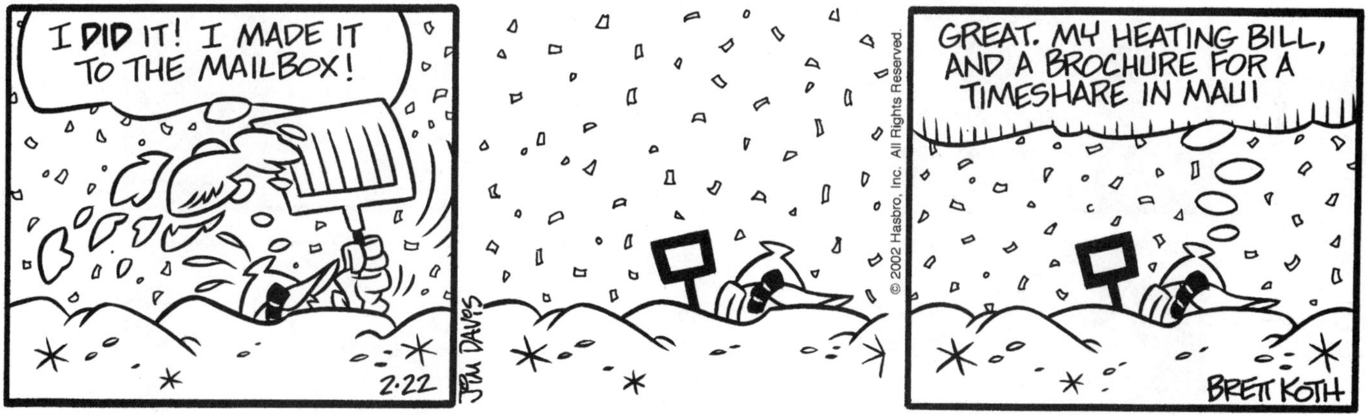
I DID IT! I MADE IT TO THE MAILBOX!
GREAT. MY HEATING BILL, AND A BROCHURE FOR A TIMESHARE IN MAUI

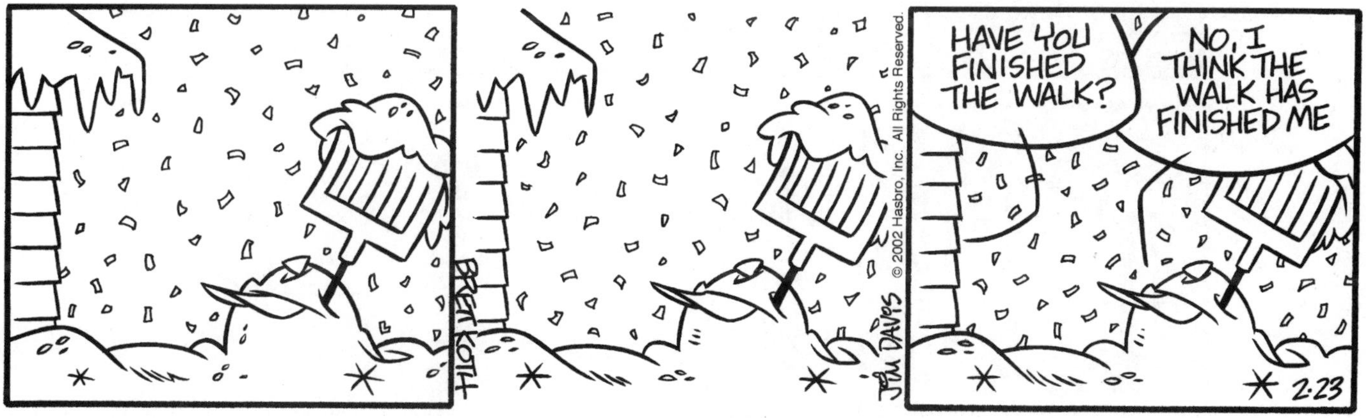
HAVE YOU FINISHED THE WALK?
NO, I THINK THE WALK HAS FINISHED ME

MR. POTATO HEAD ™
2-24
© 2002 Hasbro, Inc. All Rights Reserved.
JIM DAVIS
THUNK
THAT SCREAM SOUNDED LIKE A WOUNDED ANIMAL!
MORE LIKE A WOUNDED VEGETABLE
FIRST AID
BRETT KOTH

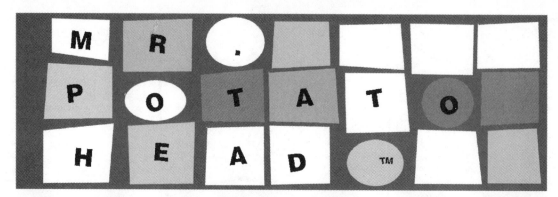

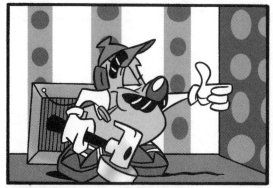

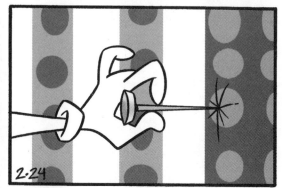

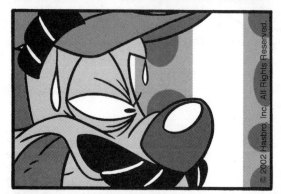

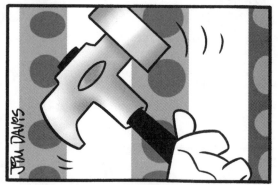

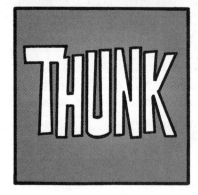

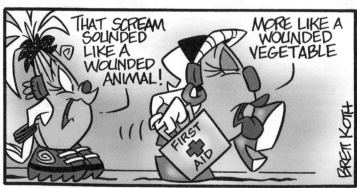

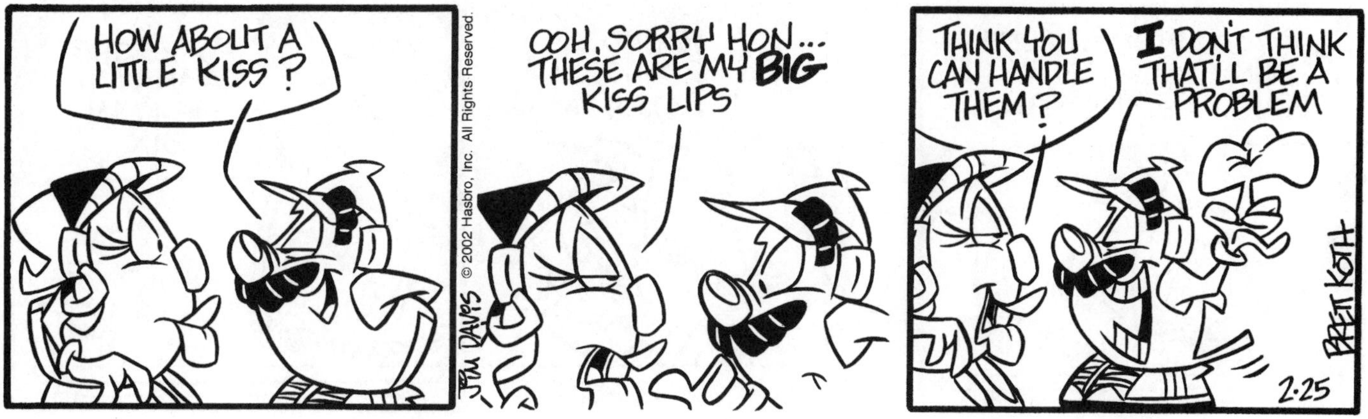
HOW ABOUT A LITTLE KISS?
OOH, SORRY HON... THESE ARE MY BIG KISS LIPS
THINK YOU CAN HANDLE THEM?
I DON'T THINK THAT'LL BE A PROBLEM
JIM DAVIS
© 2002 Hasbro, Inc. All Rights Reserved.
BRETT KOTH
2·25

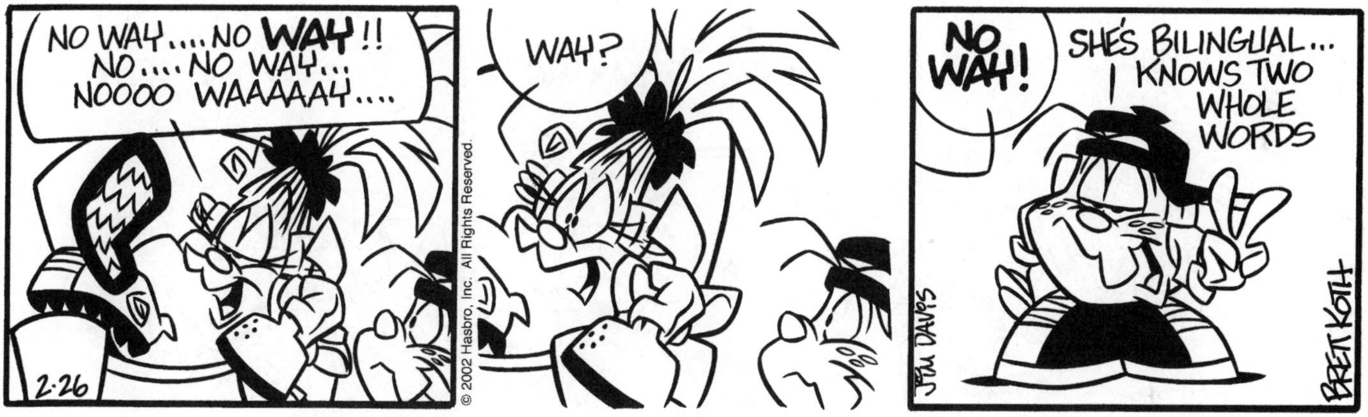
NO WAY.... NO WAY!! NO.... NO WAY... NOOOO WAAAAAY....
2·26
© 2002 Hasbro, Inc. All Rights Reserved.
WAY?
NO WAY!
SHE'S BILINGUAL... KNOWS TWO WHOLE WORDS
JIM DAVIS
BRETT KOTH

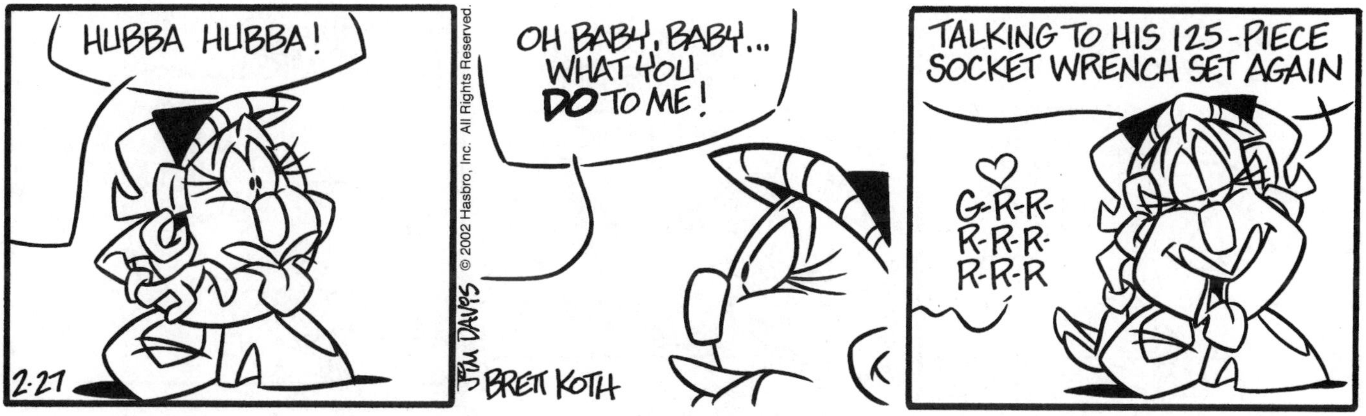
HUBBA HUBBA!
2·27
JIM DAVIS
© 2002 Hasbro, Inc. All Rights Reserved.
BRETT KOTH
OH BABY, BABY... WHAT YOU DO TO ME!
TALKING TO HIS 125-PIECE SOCKET WRENCH SET AGAIN
G-R-R-R-R-R-R-R-R

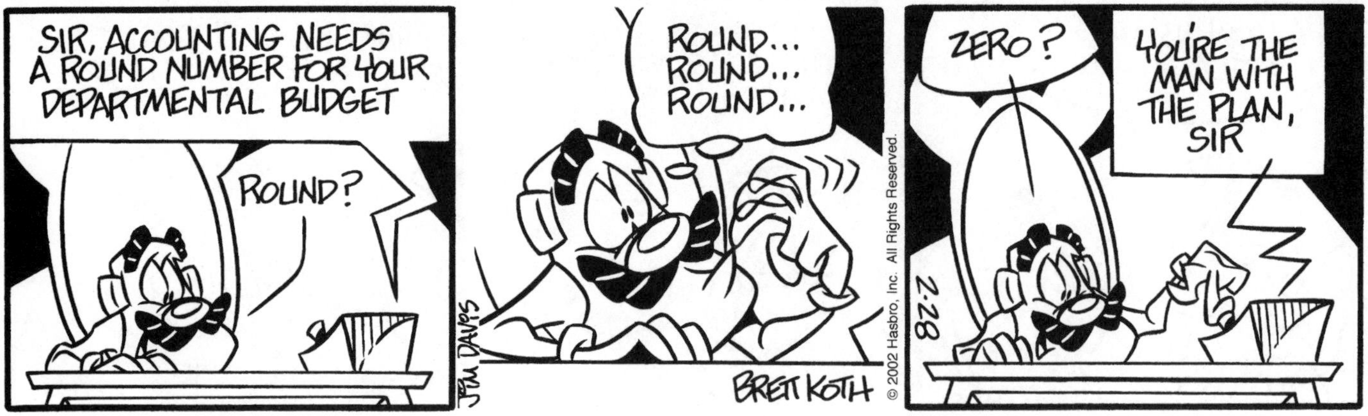
SIR, ACCOUNTING NEEDS A ROUND NUMBER FOR YOUR DEPARTMENTAL BUDGET
ROUND?
ROUND... ROUND... ROUND...
ZERO?
YOU'RE THE MAN WITH THE PLAN, SIR
JIM DAVIS
BRETT KOTH
2-28
© 2002 Hasbro, Inc. All Rights Reserved.

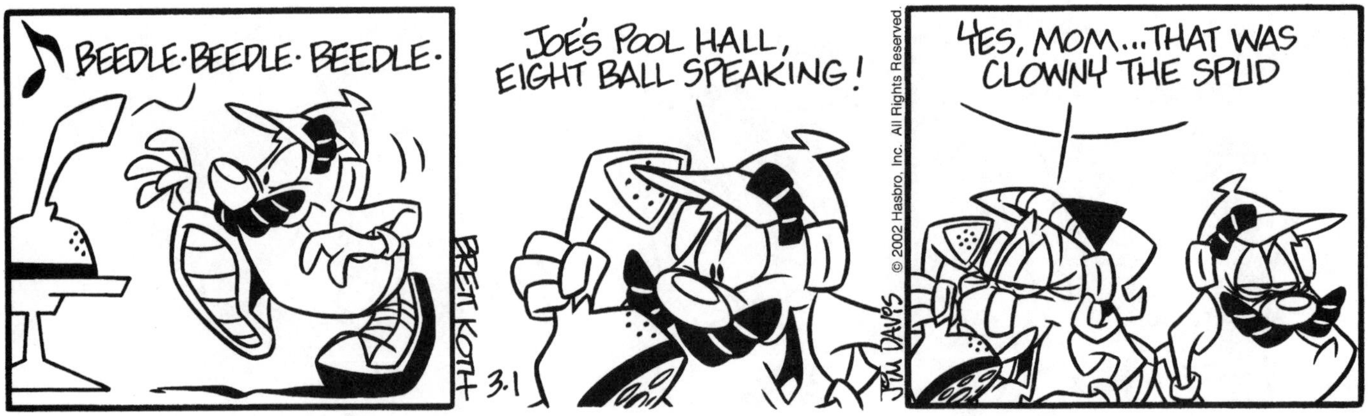
BEEDLE·BEEDLE·BEEDLE·
BRETT KOTH
3.1
JOE'S POOL HALL, EIGHT BALL SPEAKING!
JIM DAVIS
© 2002 Hasbro, Inc. All Rights Reserved.
YES, MOM...THAT WAS CLOWNY THE SPUD

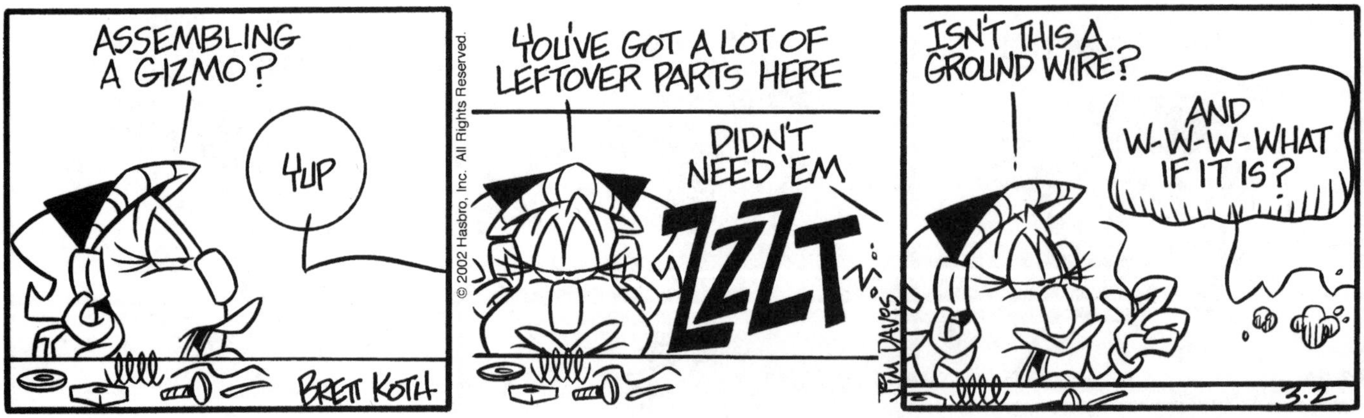
ASSEMBLING A GIZMO?
YUP
BRETT KOTH
© 2002 Hasbro, Inc. All Rights Reserved.
YOU'VE GOT A LOT OF LEFTOVER PARTS HERE
DIDN'T NEED 'EM
ZZZT
JIM DAVIS
ISN'T THIS A GROUND WIRE?
AND W-W-W-WHAT IF IT IS?
3-2

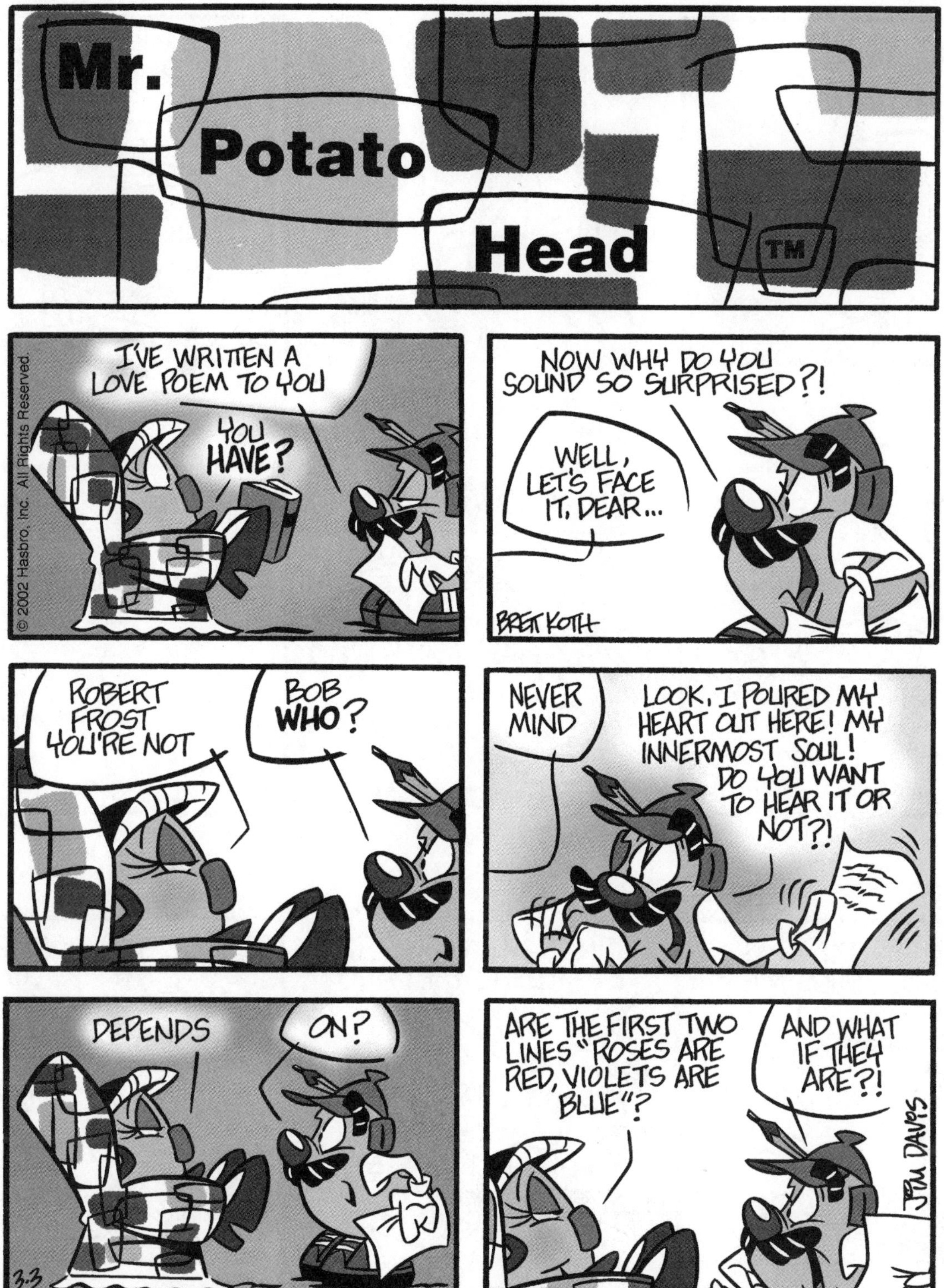
Mr. Potato Head ™
© 2002 Hasbro, Inc. All Rights Reserved.
I'VE WRITTEN A LOVE POEM TO YOU
YOU HAVE?
NOW WHY DO YOU SOUND SO SURPRISED?!
WELL, LET'S FACE IT, DEAR...
BRET KOTH
ROBERT FROST YOU'RE NOT
BOB WHO?
NEVER MIND
LOOK, I POURED MY HEART OUT HERE! MY INNERMOST SOUL! DO YOU WANT TO HEAR IT OR NOT?!
DEPENDS
ON?
3-3
ARE THE FIRST TWO LINES "ROSES ARE RED, VIOLETS ARE BLUE"?
AND WHAT IF THEY ARE?!
JIM DAVIS

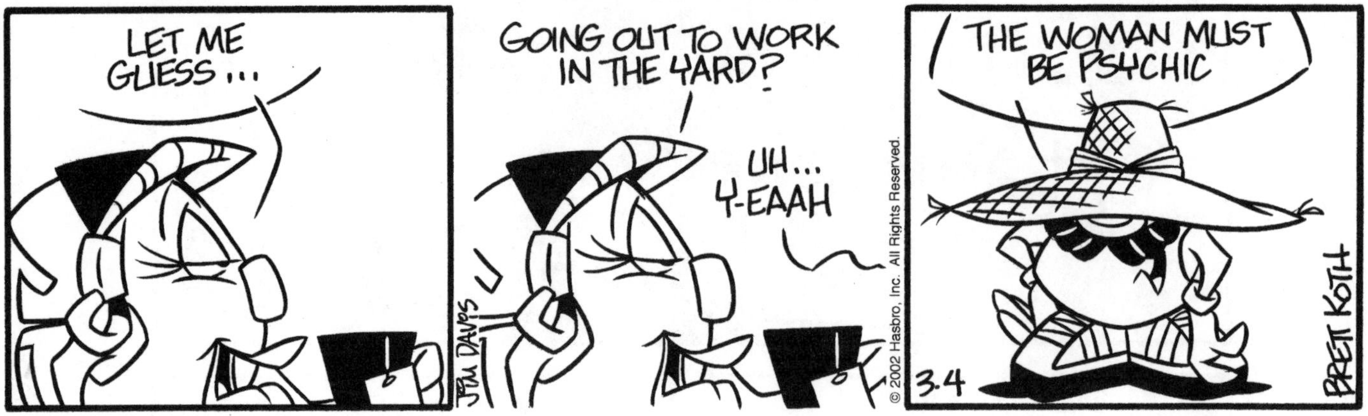
LET ME GUESS...
GOING OUT TO WORK IN THE YARD?
UH... Y-EAAH
THE WOMAN MUST BE PSYCHIC
© 2002 Hasbro, Inc. All Rights Reserved.
JIM DAVIS
BRETT KOTH
3-4

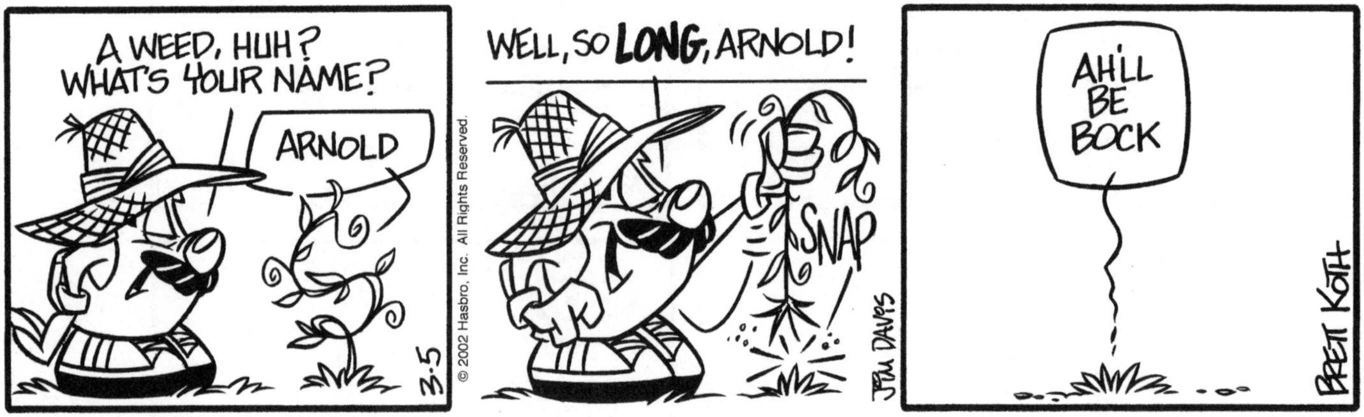
A WEED, HUH? WHAT'S YOUR NAME?
ARNOLD
WELL, SO **LONG**, ARNOLD!
SNAP
AH'LL BE BOCK
© 2002 Hasbro, Inc. All Rights Reserved.
JIM DAVIS
BRETT KOTH
3-5

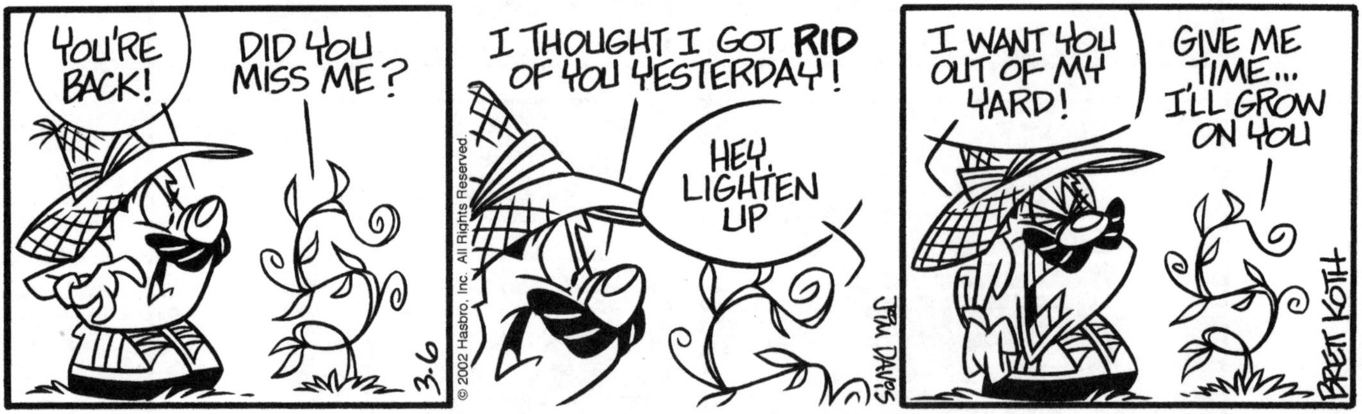
YOU'RE BACK!
DID YOU MISS ME?
I THOUGHT I GOT **RID** OF YOU YESTERDAY!
HEY, LIGHTEN UP
I WANT YOU OUT OF MY YARD!
GIVE ME TIME... I'LL GROW ON YOU
© 2002 Hasbro, Inc. All Rights Reserved.
JIM DAVIS
BRETT KOTH
3-6

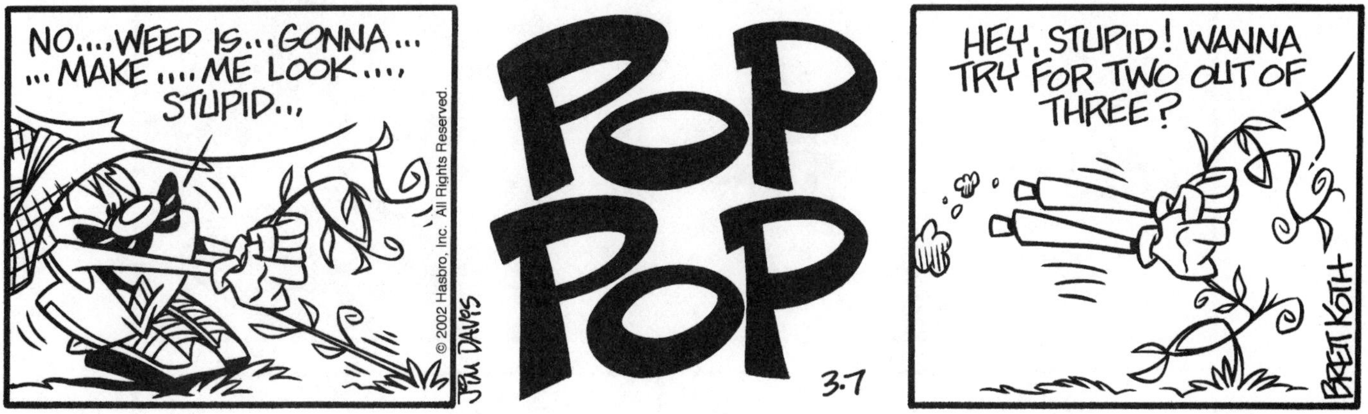
NO....WEED IS...GONNA... ...MAKE....ME LOOK...., STUPID...,
© 2002 Hasbro, Inc. All Rights Reserved.
JIM DAVIS
POP POP
3-7
HEY, STUPID! WANNA TRY FOR TWO OUT OF THREE?
BRETT KOTH

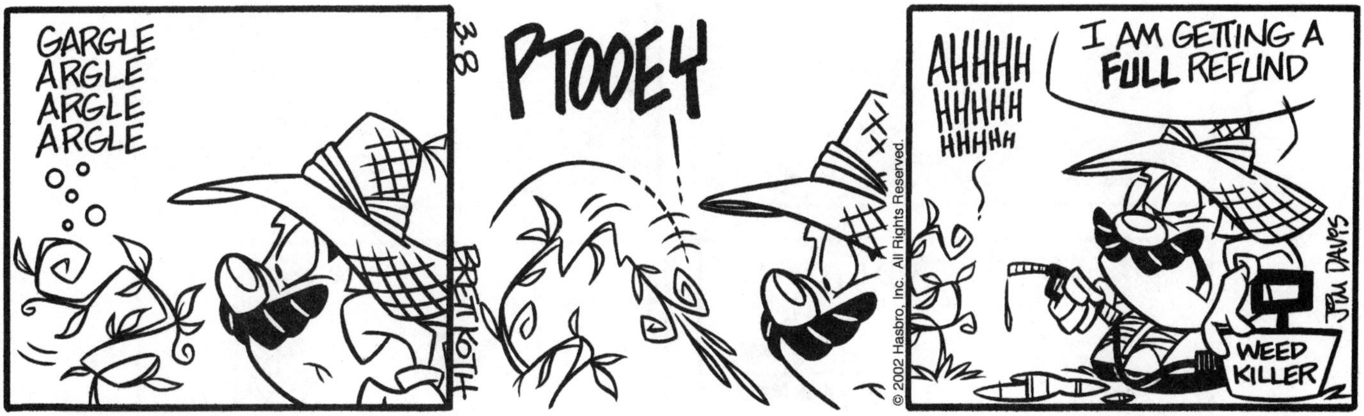
GARGLE ARGLE ARGLE ARGLE
3-8
BRETT KOTH
PTOOEY
© 2002 Hasbro, Inc. All Rights Reserved.
AHHHH HHHHH HHHHH
I AM GETTING A **FULL** REFUND
JIM DAVIS
WEED KILLER

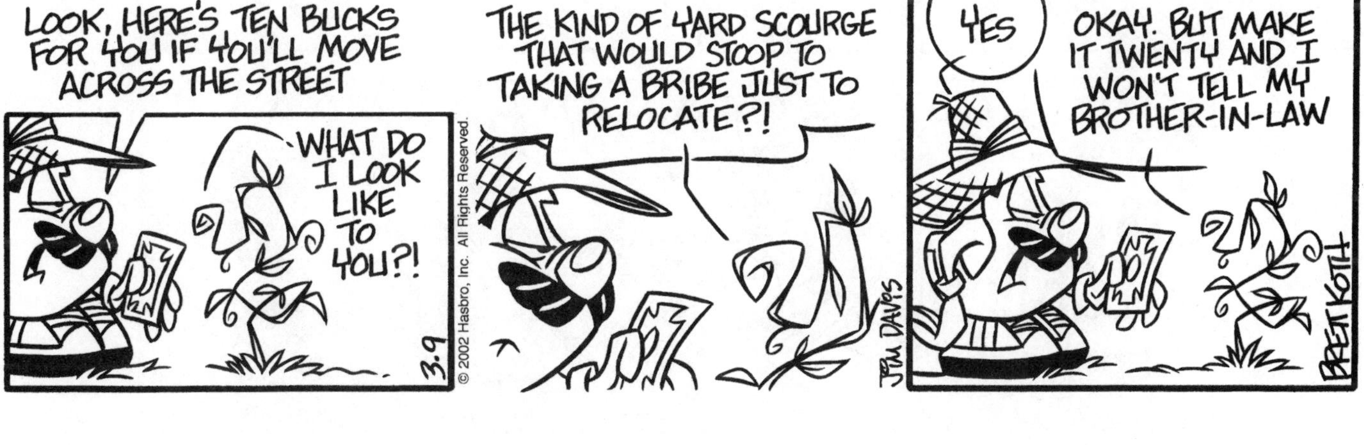
LOOK, HERE'S TEN BUCKS FOR YOU IF YOU'LL MOVE ACROSS THE STREET
WHAT DO I LOOK LIKE TO YOU?!
3-9
© 2002 Hasbro, Inc. All Rights Reserved.
THE KIND OF YARD SCOURGE THAT WOULD STOOP TO TAKING A BRIBE JUST TO RELOCATE?!
JIM DAVIS
YES
OKAY. BUT MAKE IT TWENTY AND I WON'T TELL MY BROTHER-IN-LAW
BRETT KOTH

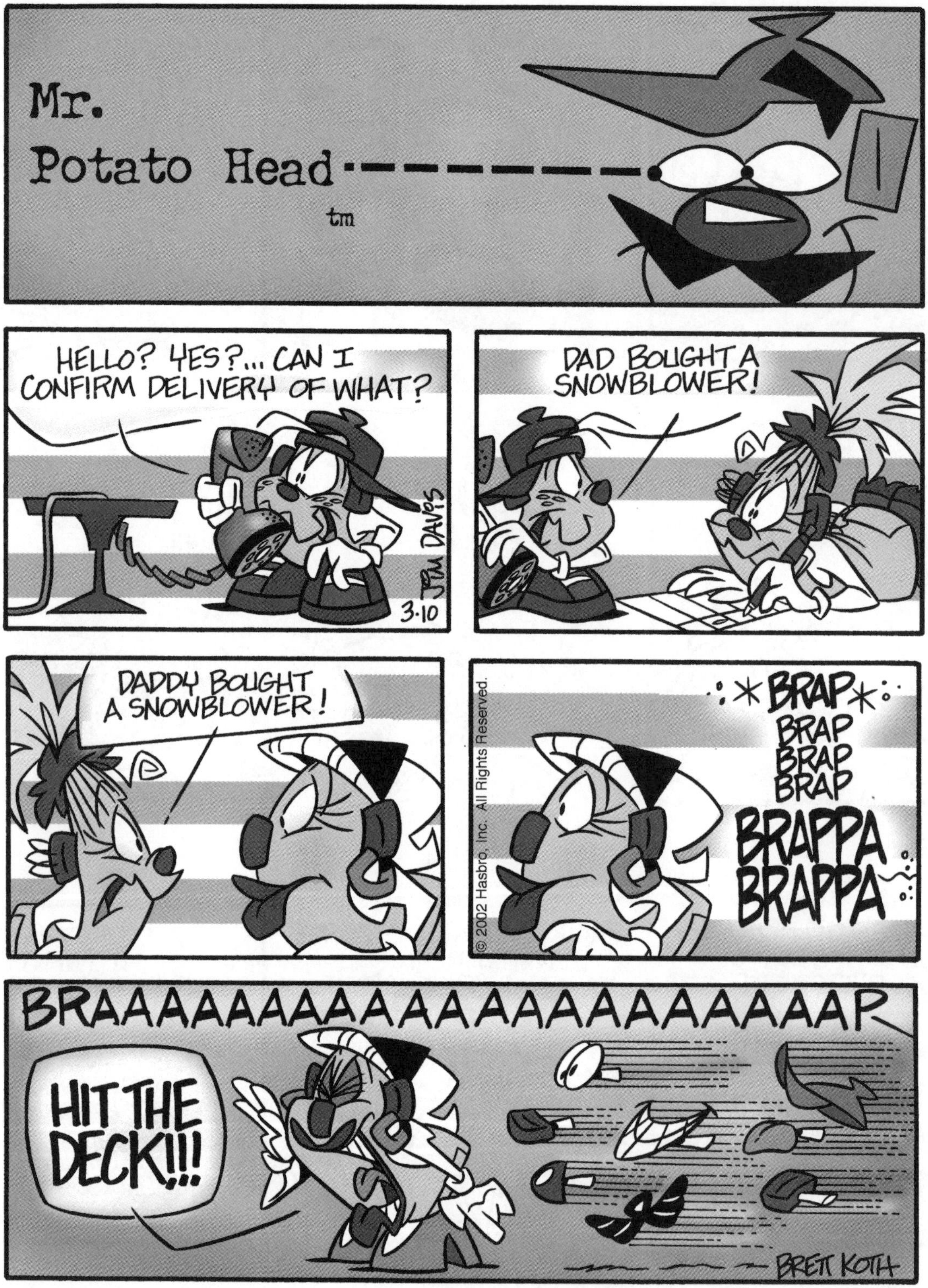
Mr. Potato Head
tm
HELLO? YES?... CAN I CONFIRM DELIVERY OF WHAT?
JIM DAVIS
3.10
DAD BOUGHT A SNOWBLOWER!
DADDY BOUGHT A SNOWBLOWER!
© 2002 Hasbro, Inc. All Rights Reserved.
BRAP BRAP BRAP BRAP
BRAPPA BRAPPA
BRAAAAAAAAAAAAAAAAAAAAAAP
HIT THE DECK!!!
BRETT KOTH

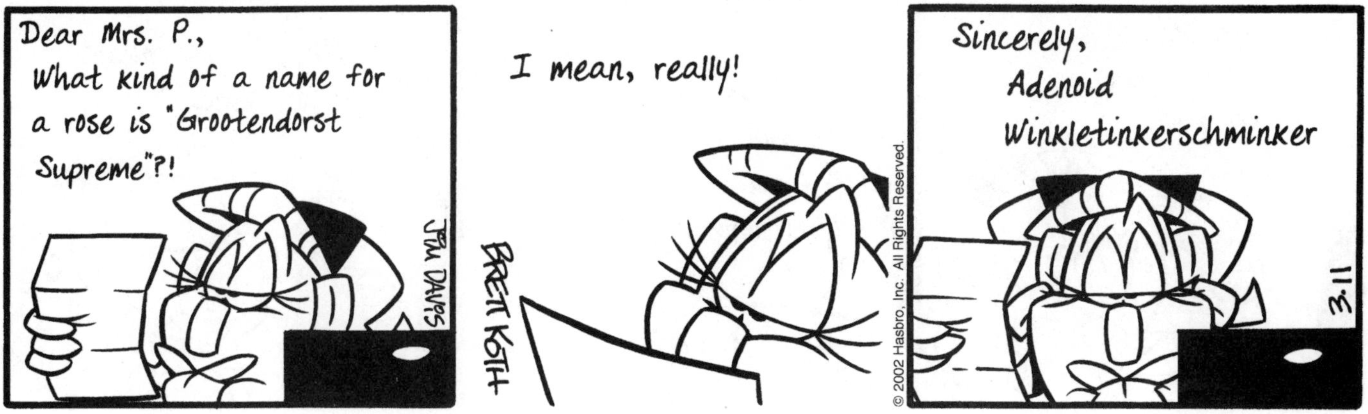
Dear Mrs. P.,
What kind of a name for a rose is "Grootendorst Supreme"?!
I mean, really!
Sincerely,
Adenoid Winkletinkerschminker
JIM DAVIS
BRETT KOTH
© 2002 Hasbro, Inc. All Rights Reserved.
3.11

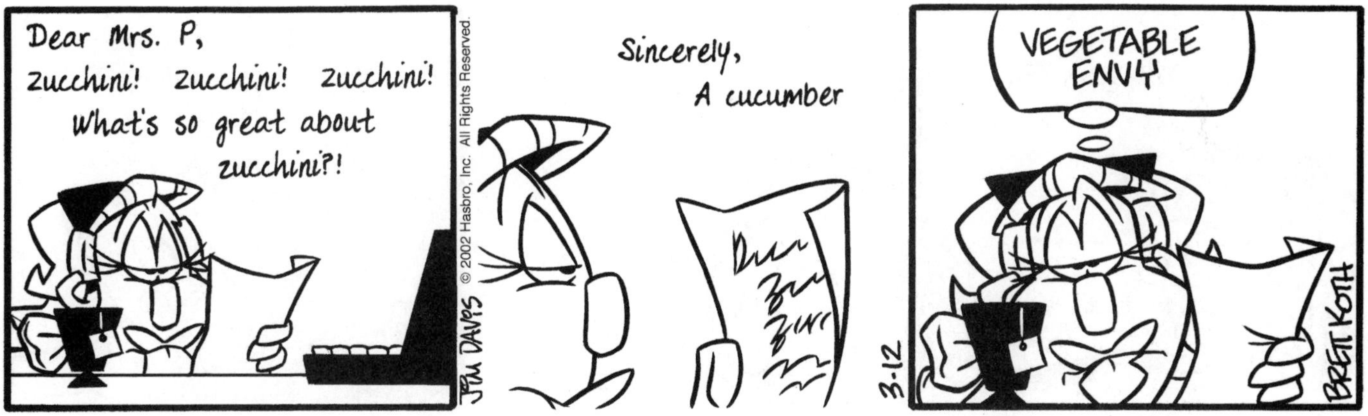
Dear Mrs. P,
zucchini! zucchini! zucchini! What's so great about zucchini?!
Sincerely,
A cucumber
VEGETABLE ENVY
JIM DAVIS
© 2002 Hasbro, Inc. All Rights Reserved.
3.12
BRETT KOTH

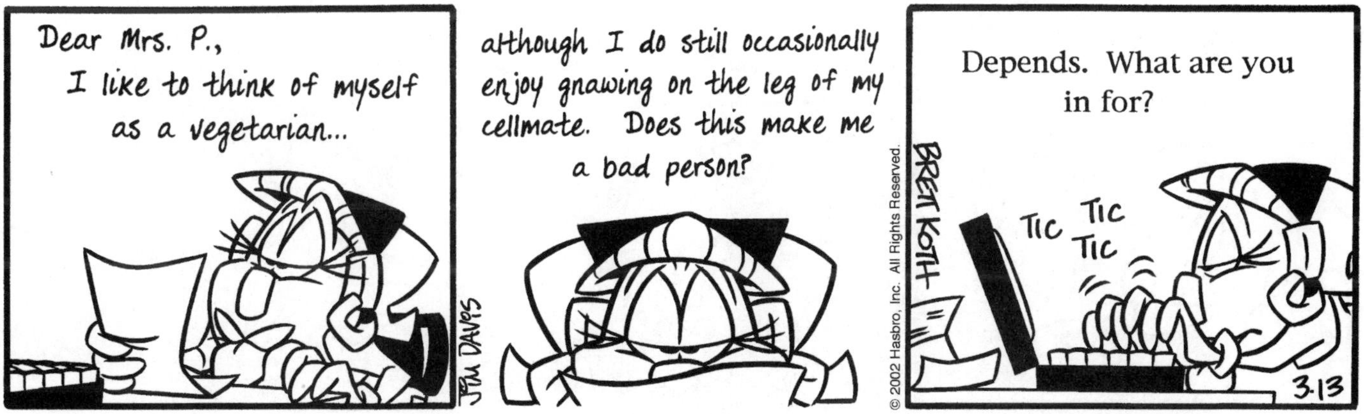
Dear Mrs. P.,
I like to think of myself as a vegetarian...
although I do still occasionally enjoy gnawing on the leg of my cellmate. Does this make me a bad person?
Depends. What are you in for?
TIC TIC TIC
JIM DAVIS
BRETT KOTH
© 2002 Hasbro, Inc. All Rights Reserved.
3.13

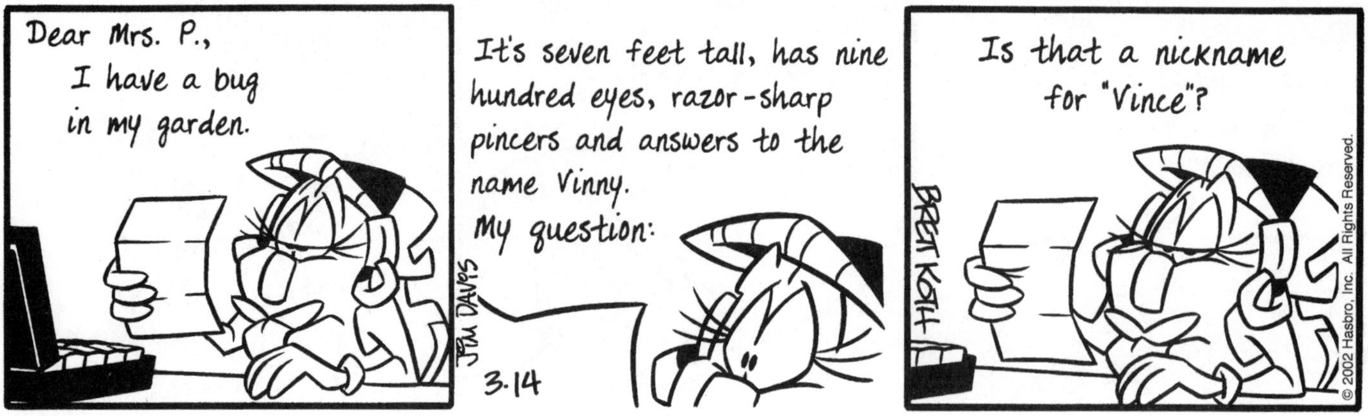
Dear Mrs. P.,
I have a bug in my garden.
It's seven feet tall, has nine hundred eyes, razor-sharp pincers and answers to the name Vinny.
My question:
Is that a nickname for "Vince"?
JIM DAVIS
3.14
BRETT KOTH
© 2002 Hasbro, Inc. All Rights Reserved.

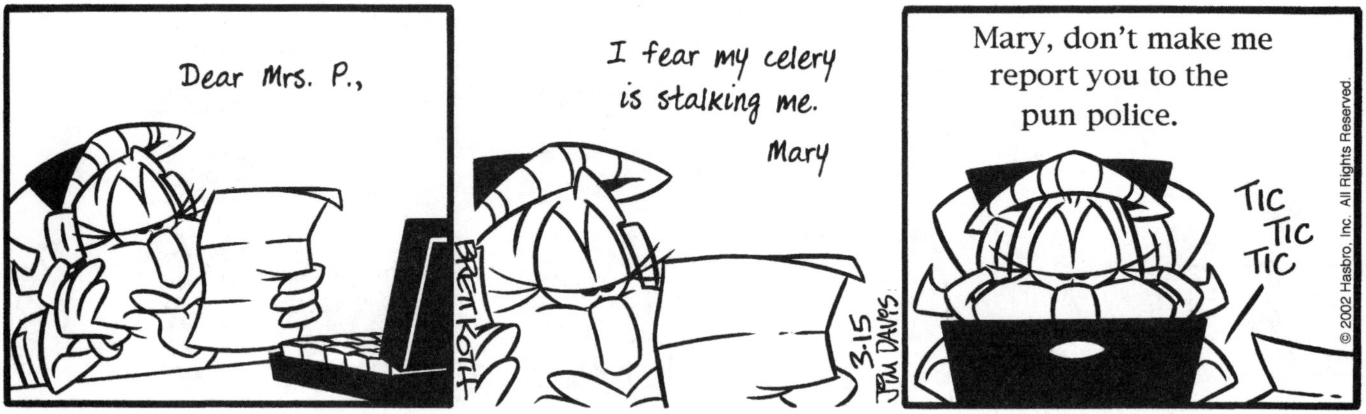
Dear Mrs. P.,
I fear my celery is stalking me.
Mary
Mary, don't make me report you to the pun police.
TIC
TIC
TIC
BRETT KOTH
3.15
JIM DAVIS
© 2002 Hasbro, Inc. All Rights Reserved.

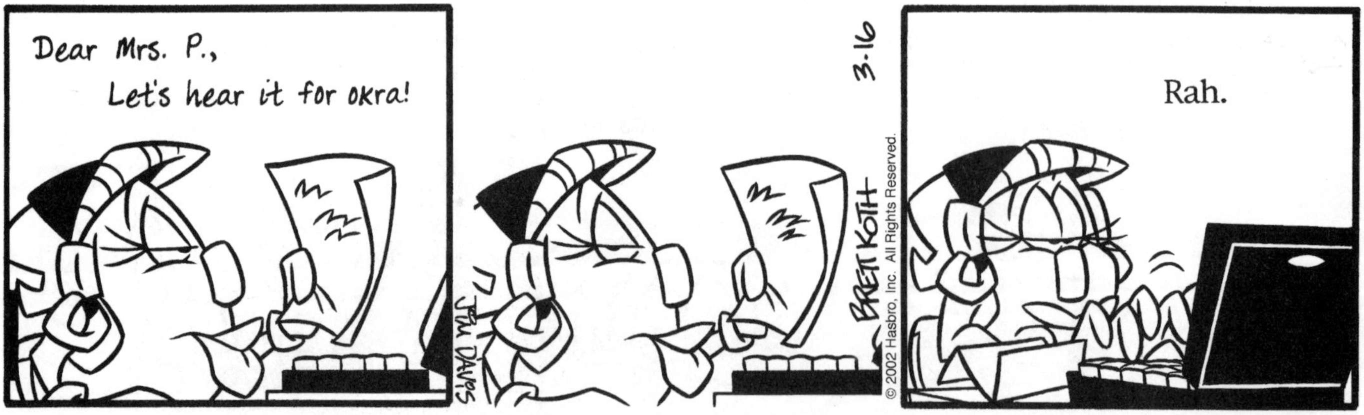
Dear Mrs. P.,
Let's hear it for okra!
Rah.
JIM DAVIS
3.16
BRETT KOTH
© 2002 Hasbro, Inc. All Rights Reserved.

MR. POTATO HEAD™

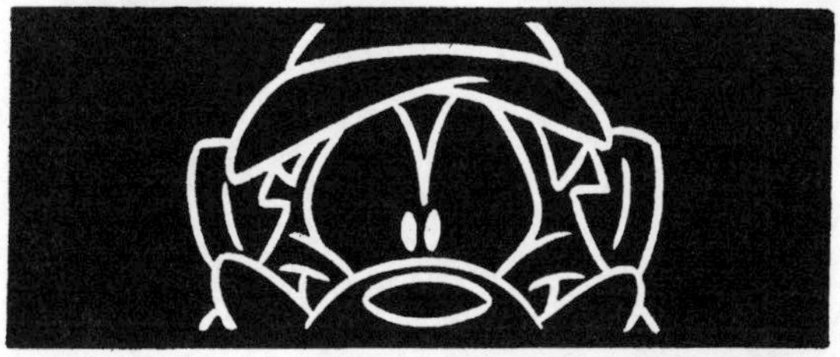

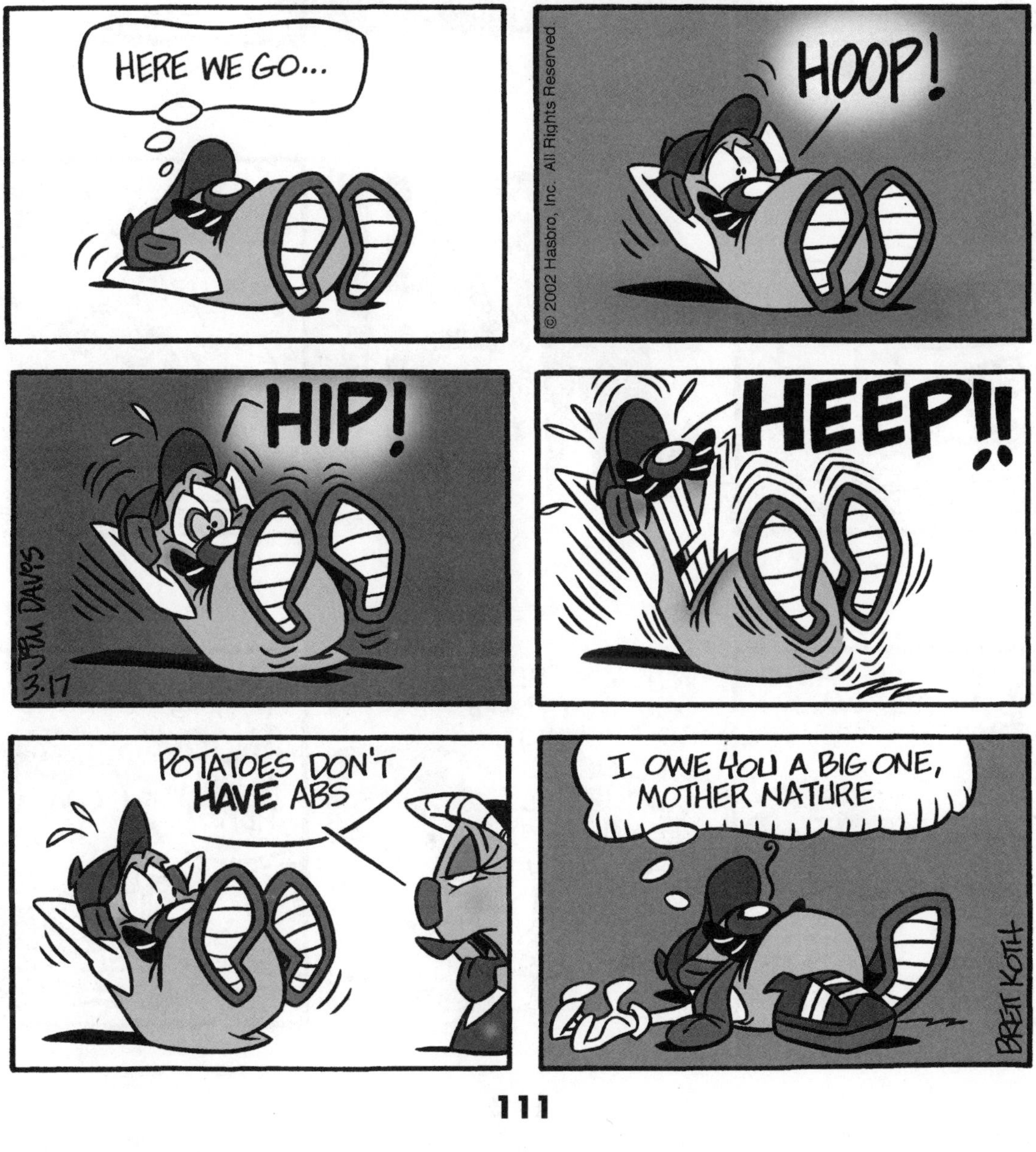
HERE WE GO...
© 2002 Hasbro, Inc. All Rights Reserved
HOOP!
HIP!
JIM DAVIS 3.17
HEEP!!
POTATOES DON'T **HAVE** ABS
I OWE YOU A BIG ONE, MOTHER NATURE
BRETT KOTH

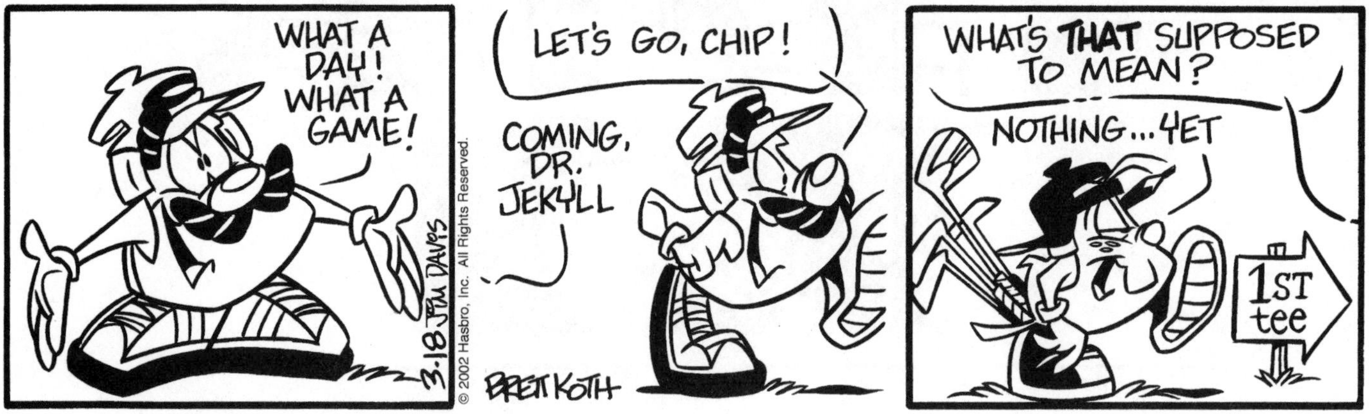
WHAT A DAY! WHAT A GAME!
3.18 JIM DAVIS
© 2002 Hasbro, Inc. All Rights Reserved.
LET'S GO, CHIP!
COMING, DR. JEKYLL
BRETT KOTH
WHAT'S **THAT** SUPPOSED TO MEAN?
NOTHING... YET
1ST tee

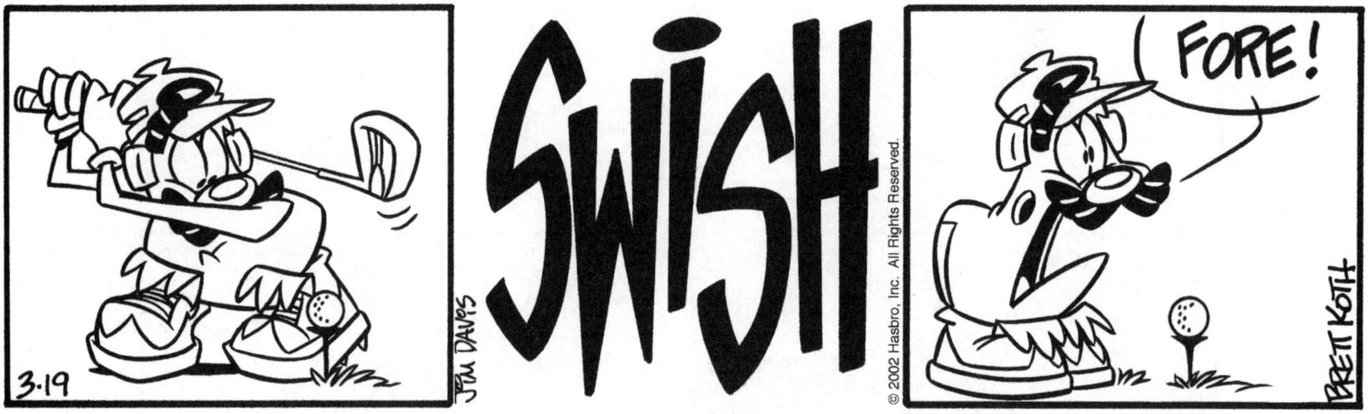
3.19
JIM DAVIS
SWISH
© 2002 Hasbro, Inc. All Rights Reserved.
FORE!
BRETT KOTH

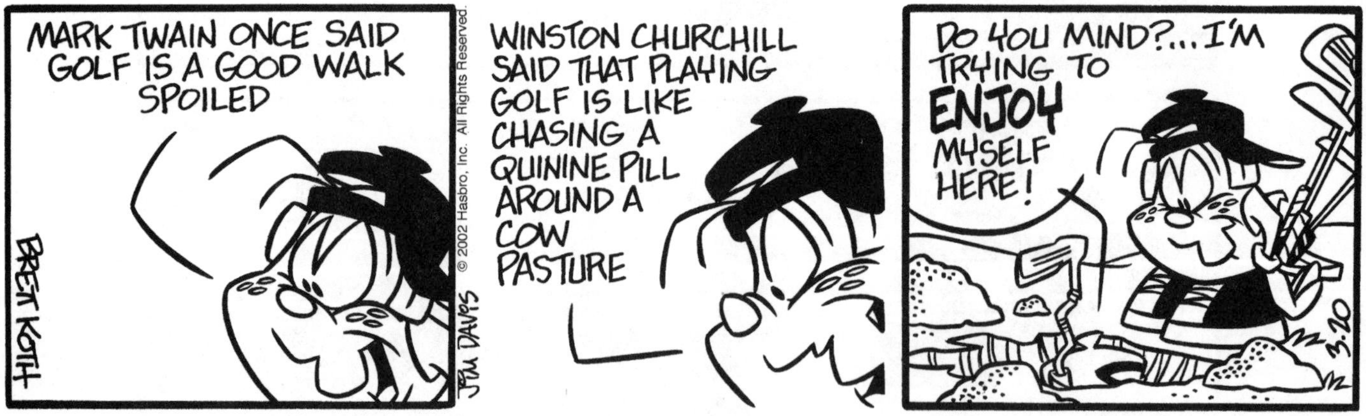
MARK TWAIN ONCE SAID GOLF IS A GOOD WALK SPOILED
BRETT KOTH
© 2002 Hasbro, Inc. All Rights Reserved.
JIM DAVIS
WINSTON CHURCHILL SAID THAT PLAYING GOLF IS LIKE CHASING A QUININE PILL AROUND A COW PASTURE
DO YOU MIND?... I'M TRYING TO **ENJOY** MYSELF HERE!
3.20

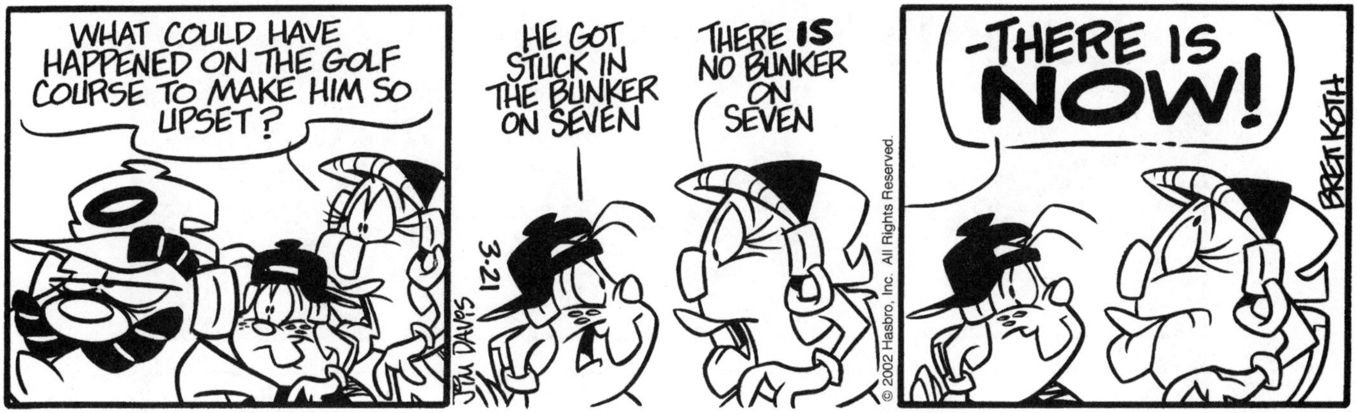
WHAT COULD HAVE HAPPENED ON THE GOLF COURSE TO MAKE HIM SO UPSET?
HE GOT STUCK IN THE BUNKER ON SEVEN
THERE **IS** NO BUNKER ON SEVEN
-THERE IS **NOW!**
3.21 JIM DAVIS
© 2002 Hasbro, Inc. All Rights Reserved.
BRETT KOTH

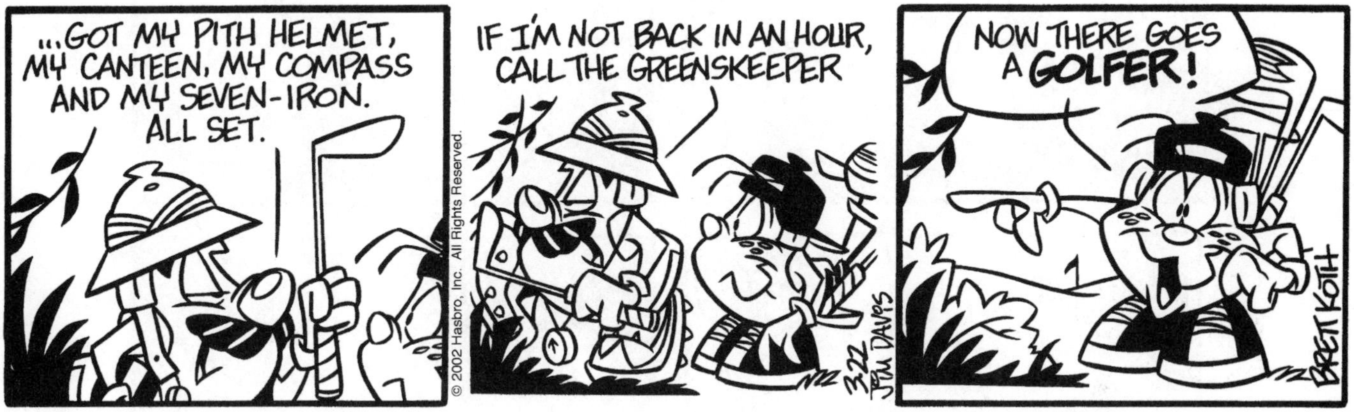
...GOT MY PITH HELMET, MY CANTEEN, MY COMPASS AND MY SEVEN-IRON. ALL SET.
© 2002 Hasbro, Inc. All Rights Reserved.
IF I'M NOT BACK IN AN HOUR, CALL THE GREENSKEEPER
3.22 JIM DAVIS
NOW THERE GOES A **GOLFER!**
BRETT KOTH

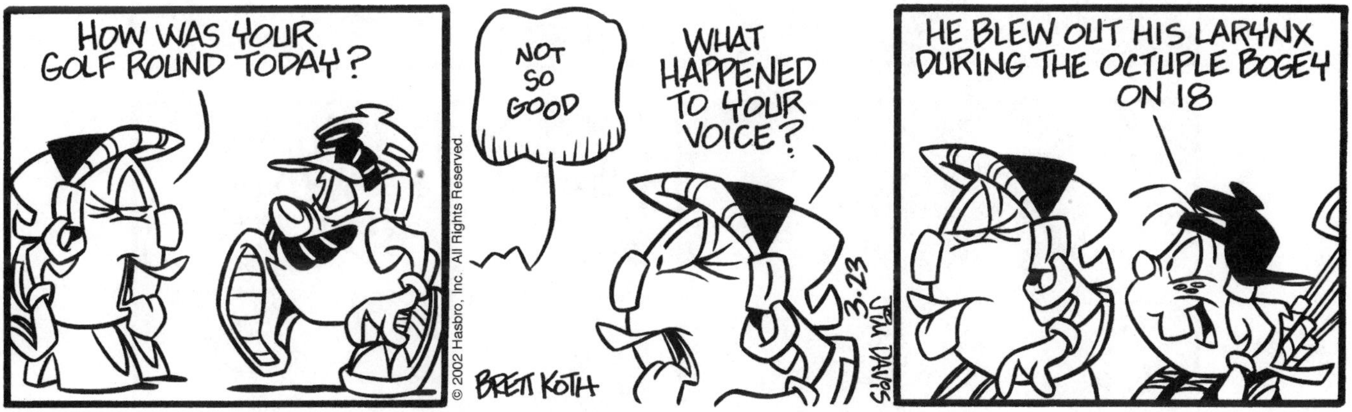
HOW WAS YOUR GOLF ROUND TODAY?
© 2002 Hasbro, Inc. All Rights Reserved.
NOT SO GOOD
WHAT HAPPENED TO YOUR VOICE?
BRETT KOTH
3.23 JIM DAVIS
HE BLEW OUT HIS LARYNX DURING THE OCTUPLE BOGEY ON 18

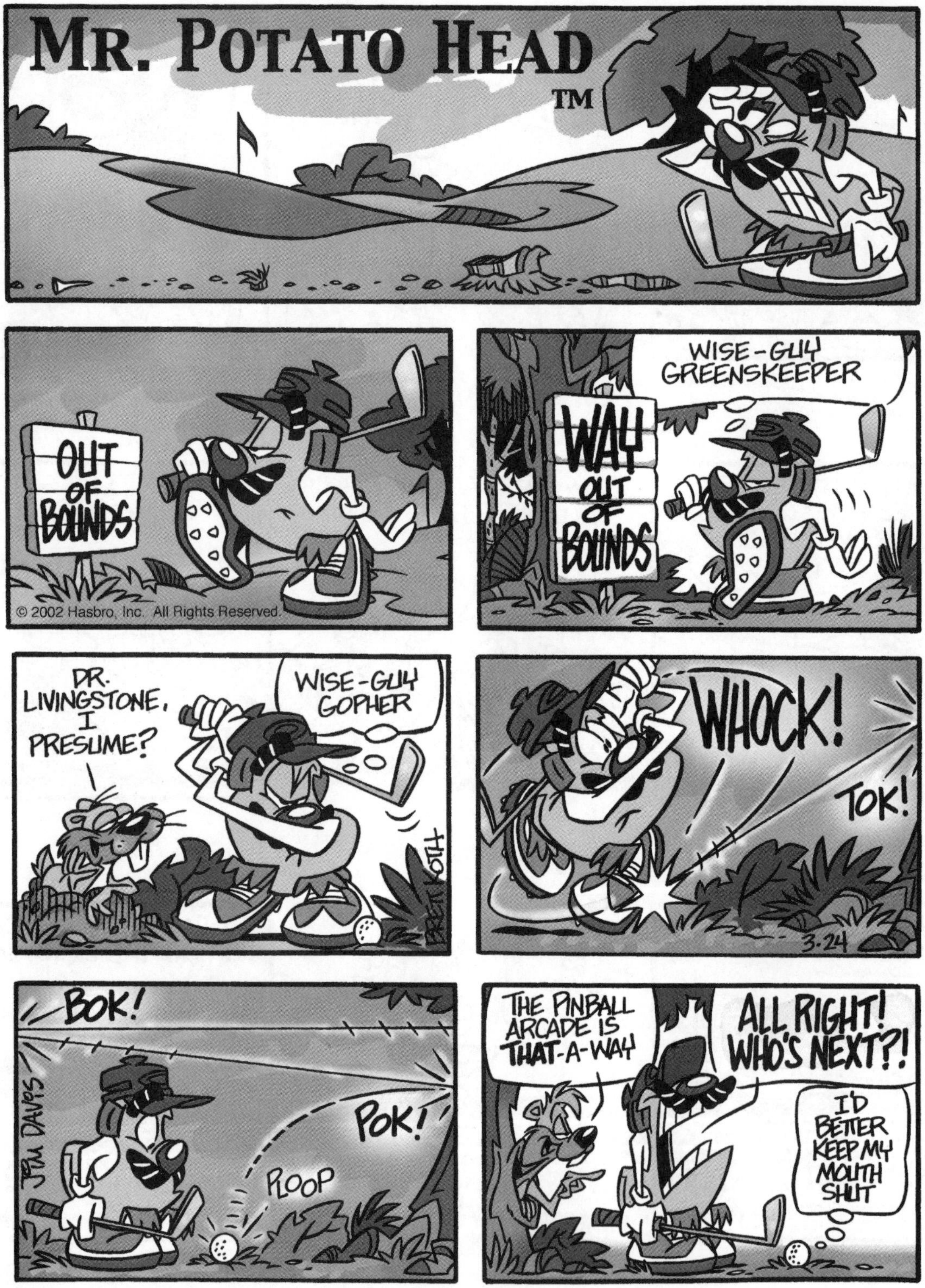
MR. POTATO HEAD
TM
OUT OF BOUNDS
© 2002 Hasbro, Inc. All Rights Reserved.
WISE-GUY GREENSKEEPER
WAY OUT OF BOUNDS
DR. LIVINGSTONE, I PRESUME?
WISE-GUY GOPHER
BRETT KOTH
WHOCK!
TOK!
3.24
BOK!
JIM DAVIS
POK!
PLOOP
THE PINBALL ARCADE IS THAT-A-WAY
ALL RIGHT! WHO'S NEXT?!
I'D BETTER KEEP MY MOUTH SHUT

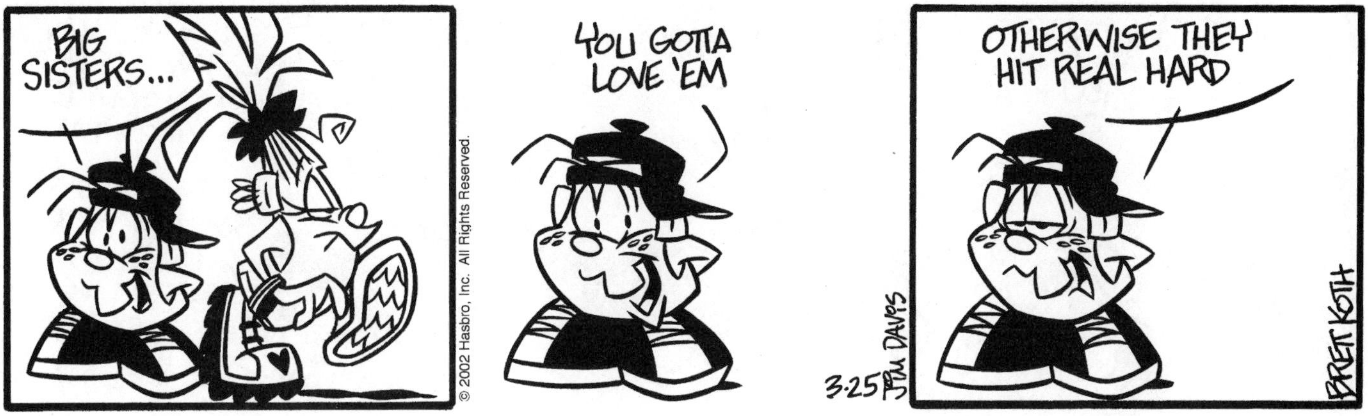
BIG SISTERS...
YOU GOTTA LOVE 'EM
OTHERWISE THEY HIT REAL HARD
© 2002 Hasbro, Inc. All Rights Reserved.

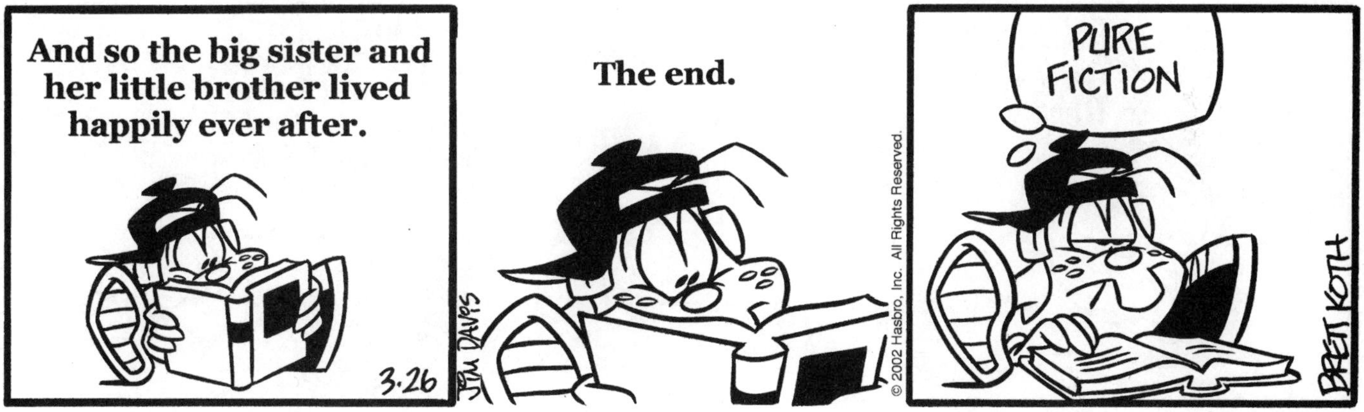
And so the big sister and her little brother lived happily ever after.
The end.
PURE FICTION
© 2002 Hasbro, Inc. All Rights Reserved.

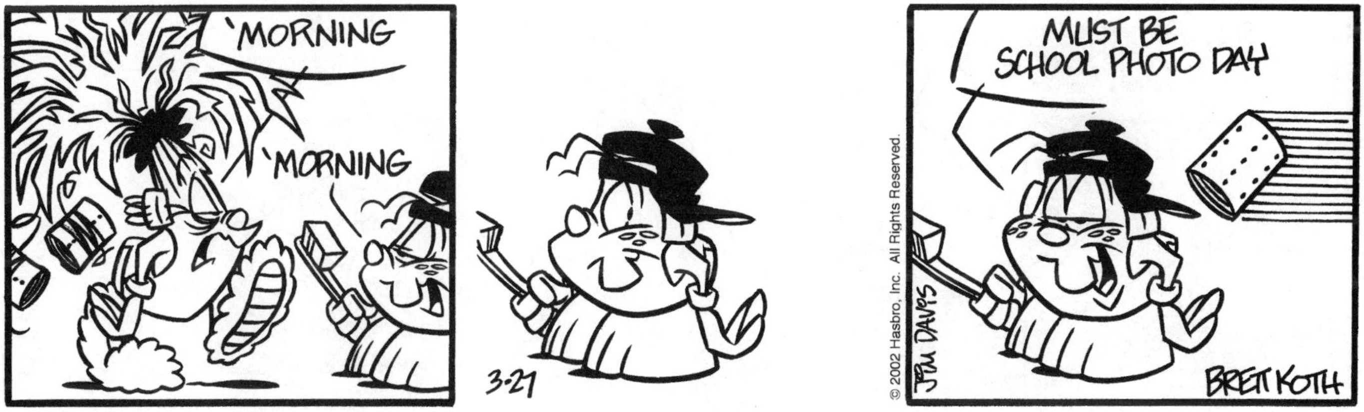
'MORNING
'MORNING
MUST BE SCHOOL PHOTO DAY
© 2002 Hasbro, Inc. All Rights Reserved.

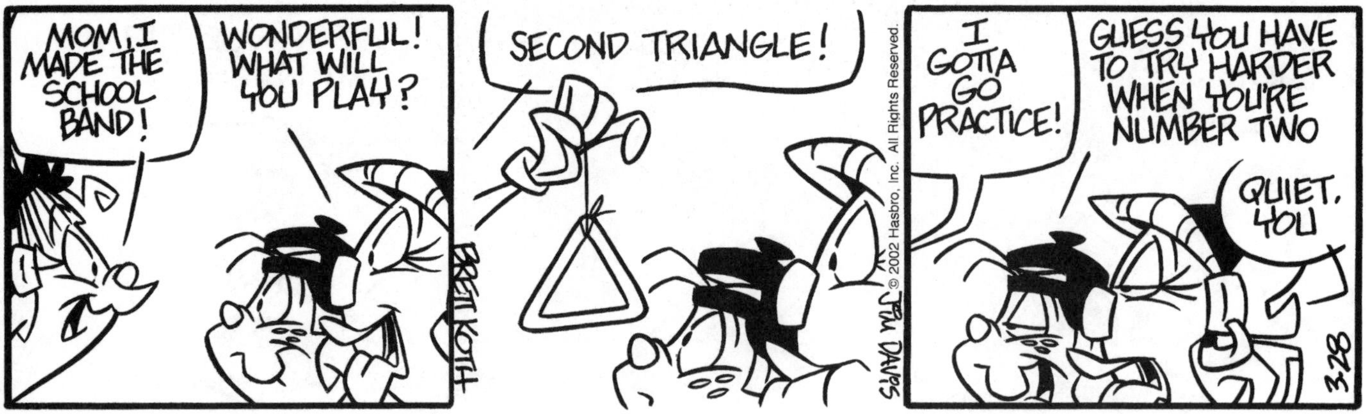
MOM, I MADE THE SCHOOL BAND!
WONDERFUL! WHAT WILL YOU PLAY?
BRETT KOTH
SECOND TRIANGLE!
JIM DAVIS
© 2002 Hasbro, Inc. All Rights Reserved.
I GOTTA GO PRACTICE!
GUESS YOU HAVE TO TRY HARDER WHEN YOU'RE NUMBER TWO
QUIET, YOU
3·28

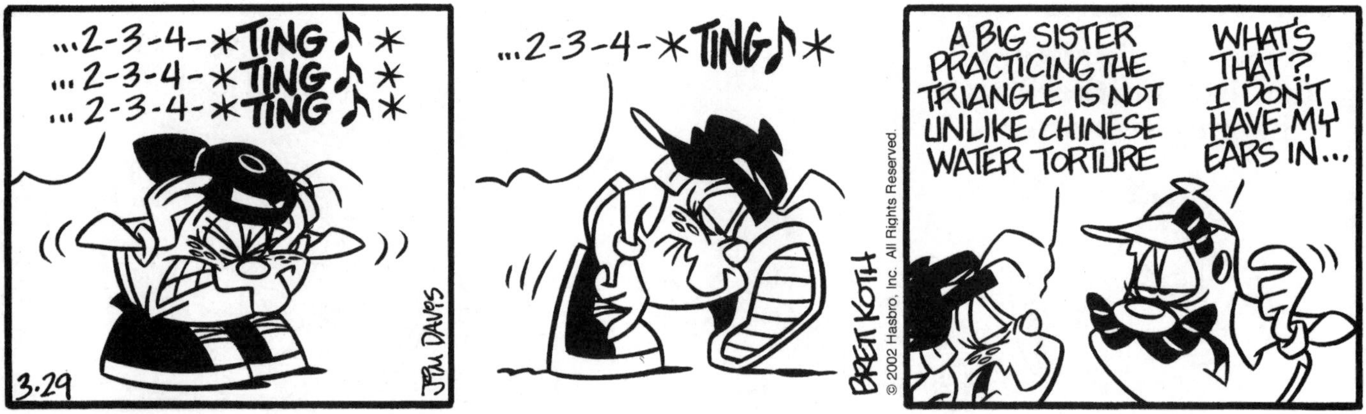
...2-3-4-*TING♪*
...2-3-4-*TING♪*
...2-3-4-*TING♪*
3·29
JIM DAVIS
...2-3-4-*TING♪*
BRETT KOTH
© 2002 Hasbro, Inc. All Rights Reserved.
A BIG SISTER PRACTICING THE TRIANGLE IS NOT UNLIKE CHINESE WATER TORTURE
WHAT'S THAT?, I DON'T HAVE MY EARS IN...

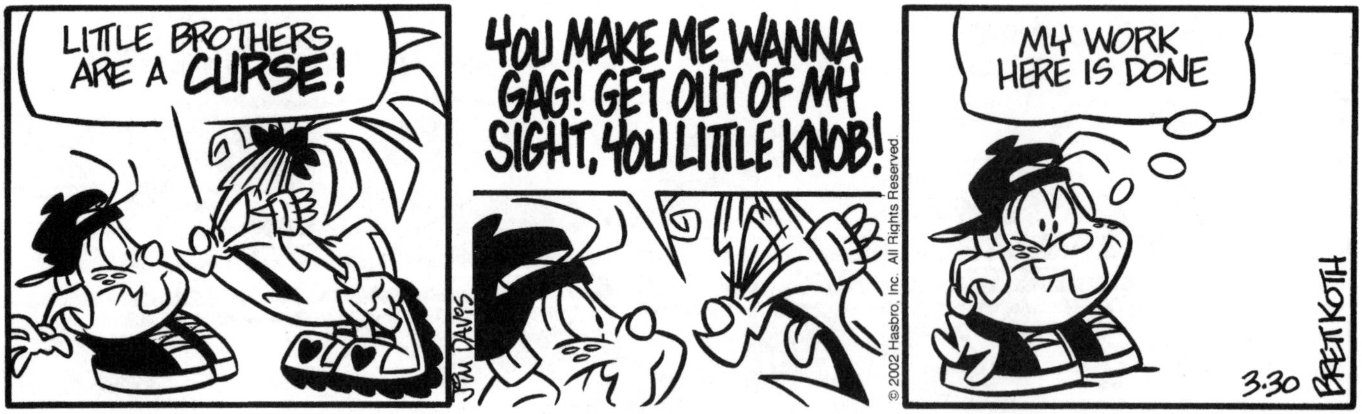
LITTLE BROTHERS ARE A CURSE!
JIM DAVIS
YOU MAKE ME WANNA GAG! GET OUT OF MY SIGHT, YOU LITTLE KNOB!
© 2002 Hasbro, Inc. All Rights Reserved.
MY WORK HERE IS DONE
3·30
BRETT KOTH

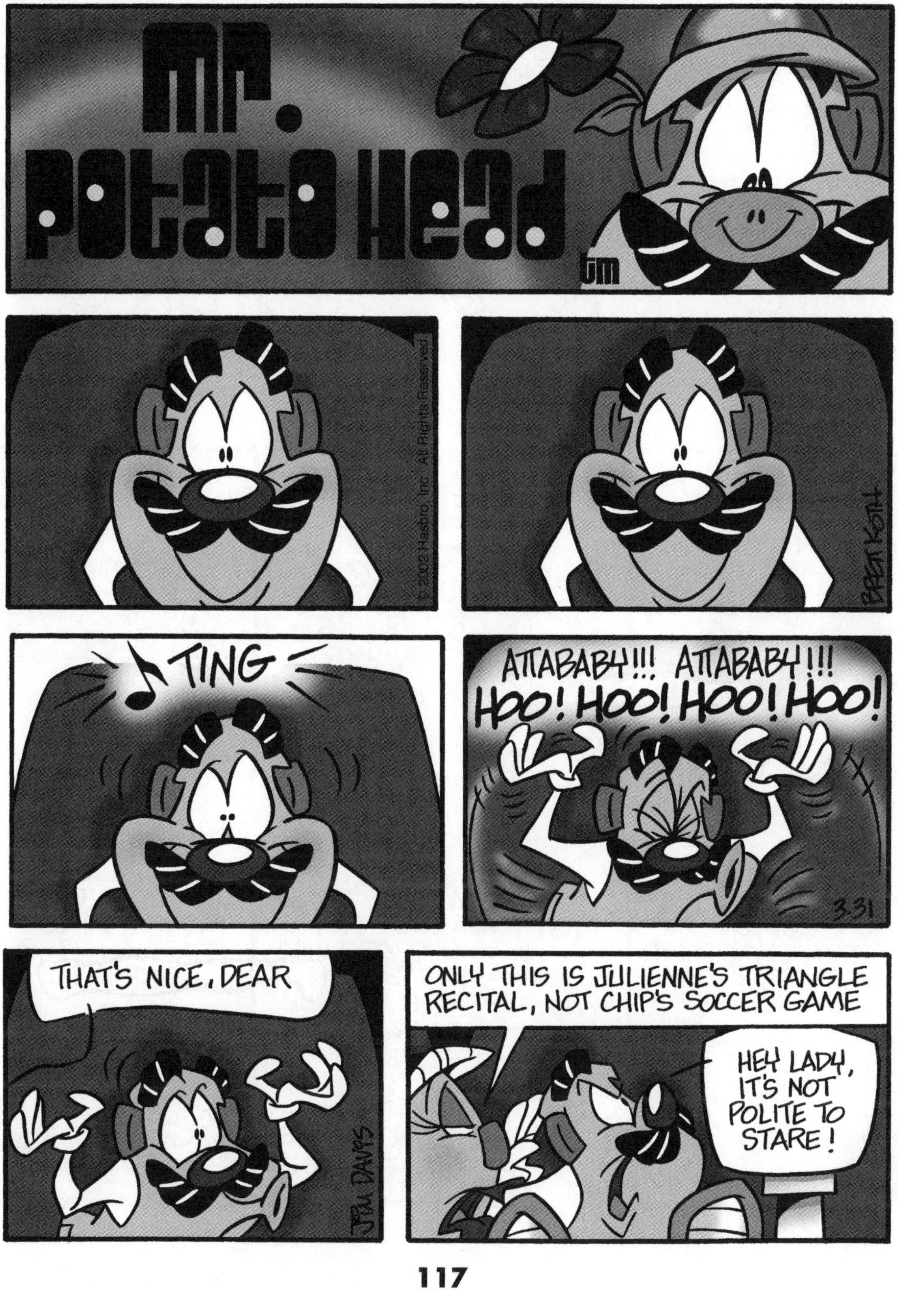

MR. POTATO HEAD
tm
© 2002 Hasbro Inc. All Rights Reserved
BRET KOTH
TING
ATTABABY!!! ATTABABY!!!
HOO! HOO! HOO! HOO!
3.31
THAT'S NICE, DEAR
JIM DAVIS
ONLY THIS IS JULIENNE'S TRIANGLE RECITAL, NOT CHIP'S SOCCER GAME
HEY LADY, IT'S NOT POLITE TO STARE!

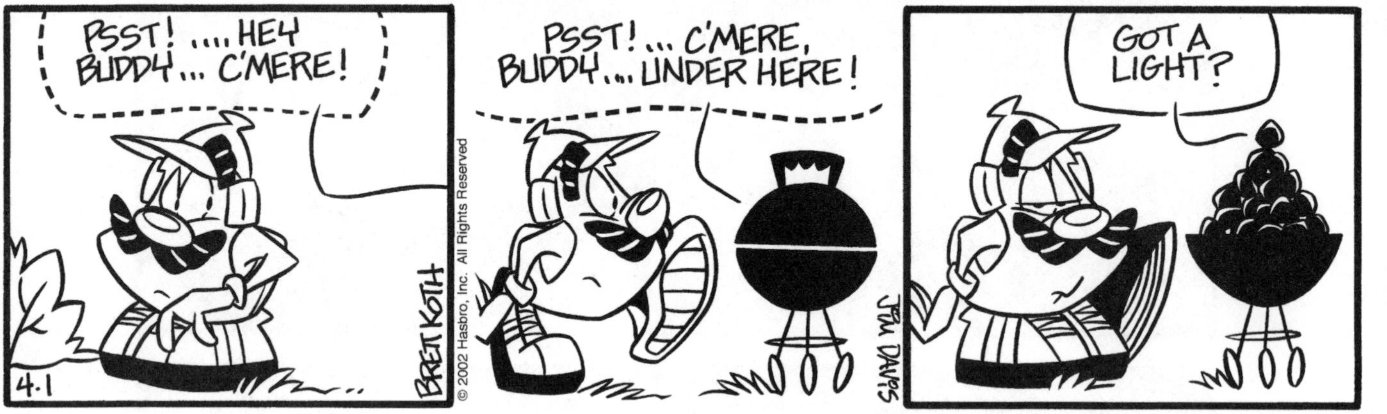
PSST! .... HEY BUDDY... C'MERE!
4.1
BRETT KOTH
© 2002 Hasbro, Inc. All Rights Reserved
PSST! ... C'MERE, BUDDY.... UNDER HERE!
JIM DAVIS
GOT A LIGHT?

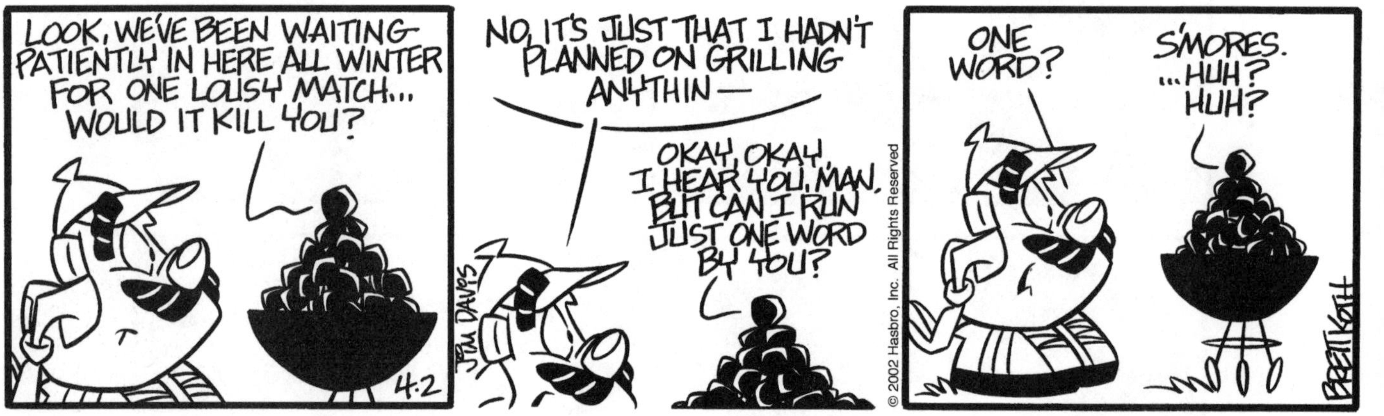
LOOK, WE'VE BEEN WAITING PATIENTLY IN HERE ALL WINTER FOR ONE LOUSY MATCH... WOULD IT KILL YOU?
4.2
JIM DAVIS
NO, IT'S JUST THAT I HADN'T PLANNED ON GRILLING ANYTHIN—
OKAY, OKAY, I HEAR YOU, MAN, BUT CAN I RUN JUST ONE WORD BY YOU?
© 2002 Hasbro, Inc. All Rights Reserved
ONE WORD?
S'MORES. ...HUH? HUH?
BRETT KOTH

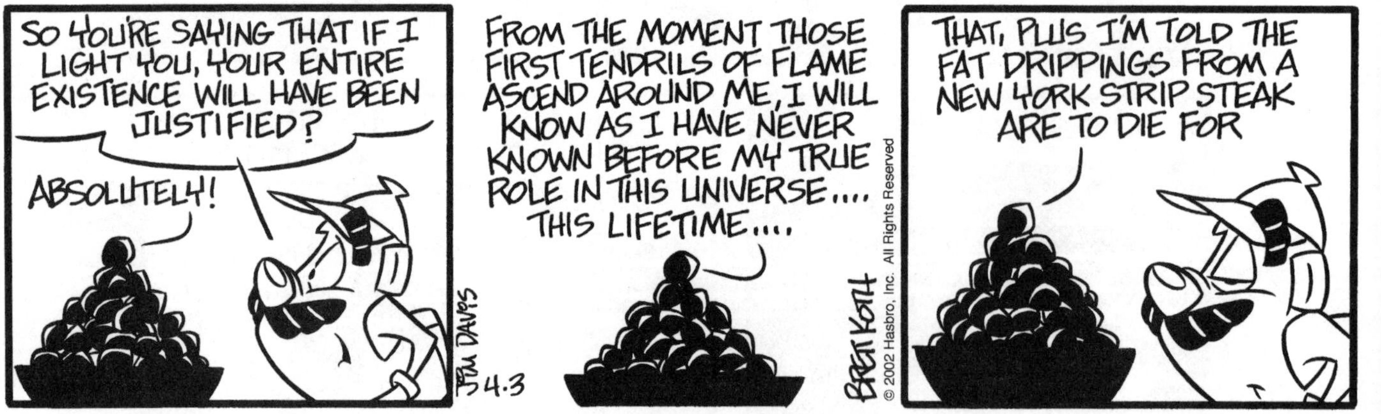
SO YOU'RE SAYING THAT IF I LIGHT YOU, YOUR ENTIRE EXISTENCE WILL HAVE BEEN JUSTIFIED?
ABSOLUTELY!
JIM DAVIS
4.3
FROM THE MOMENT THOSE FIRST TENDRILS OF FLAME ASCEND AROUND ME, I WILL KNOW AS I HAVE NEVER KNOWN BEFORE MY TRUE ROLE IN THIS UNIVERSE.... THIS LIFETIME....
BRETT KOTH
© 2002 Hasbro, Inc. All Rights Reserved
THAT, PLUS I'M TOLD THE FAT DRIPPINGS FROM A NEW YORK STRIP STEAK ARE TO DIE FOR

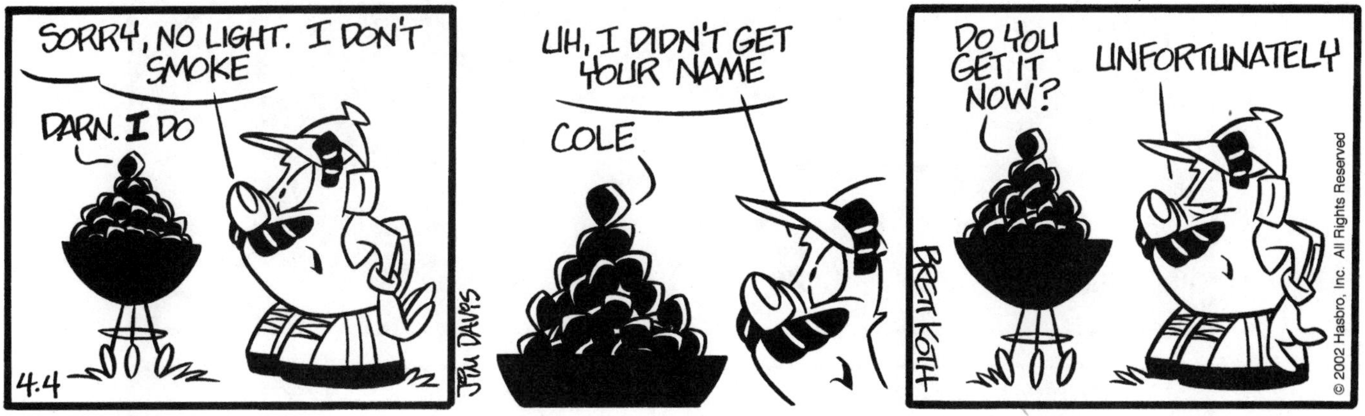
SORRY, NO LIGHT. I DON'T SMOKE
DARN. I DO
4.4
UH, I DIDN'T GET YOUR NAME
COLE
DO YOU GET IT NOW?
UNFORTUNATELY
© 2002 Hasbro, Inc. All Rights Reserved

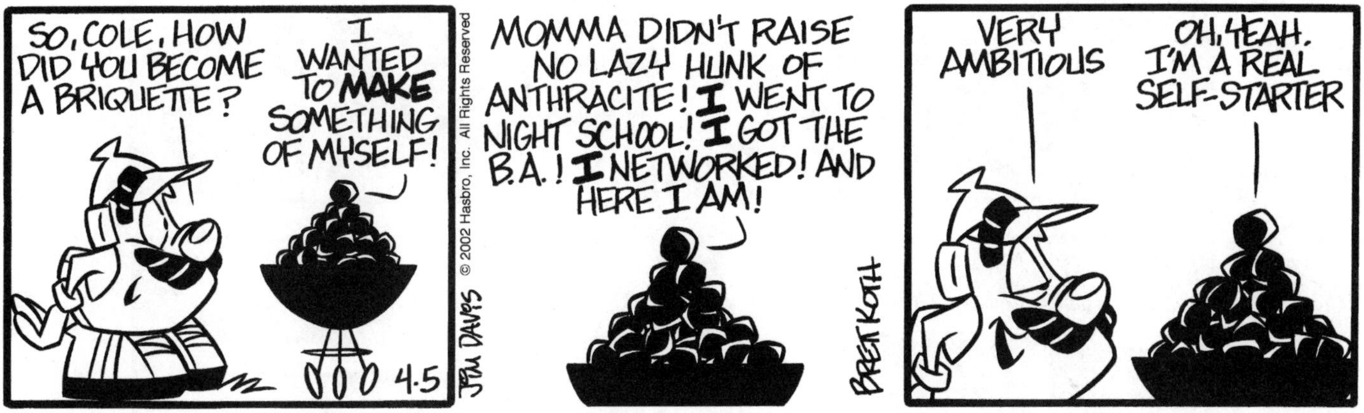
SO, COLE, HOW DID YOU BECOME A BRIQUETTE?
I WANTED TO MAKE SOMETHING OF MYSELF!
4.5
© 2002 Hasbro, Inc. All Rights Reserved
MOMMA DIDN'T RAISE NO LAZY HUNK OF ANTHRACITE! I WENT TO NIGHT SCHOOL! I GOT THE B.A.! I NETWORKED! AND HERE I AM!
VERY AMBITIOUS
OH, YEAH. I'M A REAL SELF-STARTER

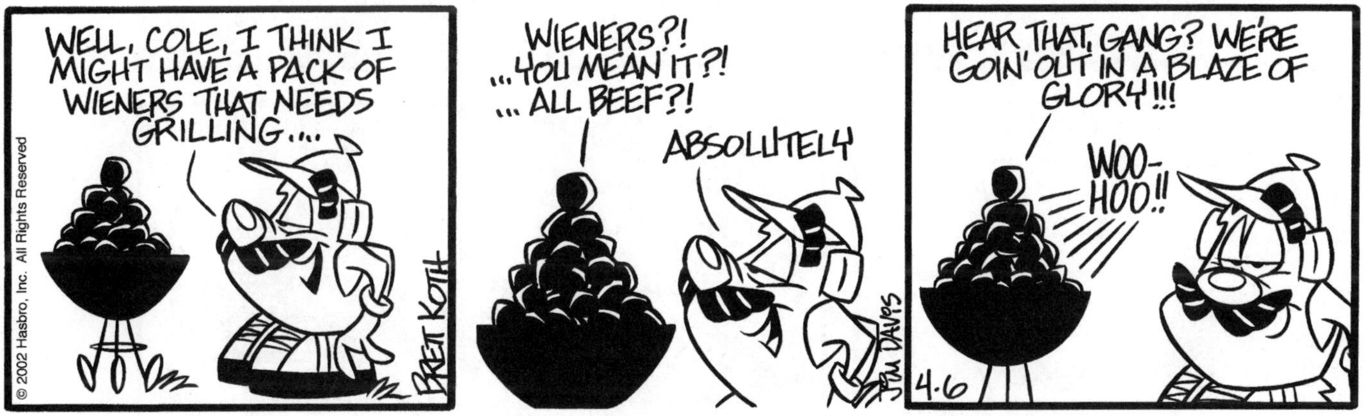
WELL, COLE, I THINK I MIGHT HAVE A PACK OF WIENERS THAT NEEDS GRILLING....
© 2002 Hasbro, Inc. All Rights Reserved
WIENERS?! ...YOU MEAN IT?! ... ALL BEEF?!
ABSOLUTELY
HEAR THAT, GANG? WE'RE GOIN' OUT IN A BLAZE OF GLORY!!!
WOO-HOO!!
4.6

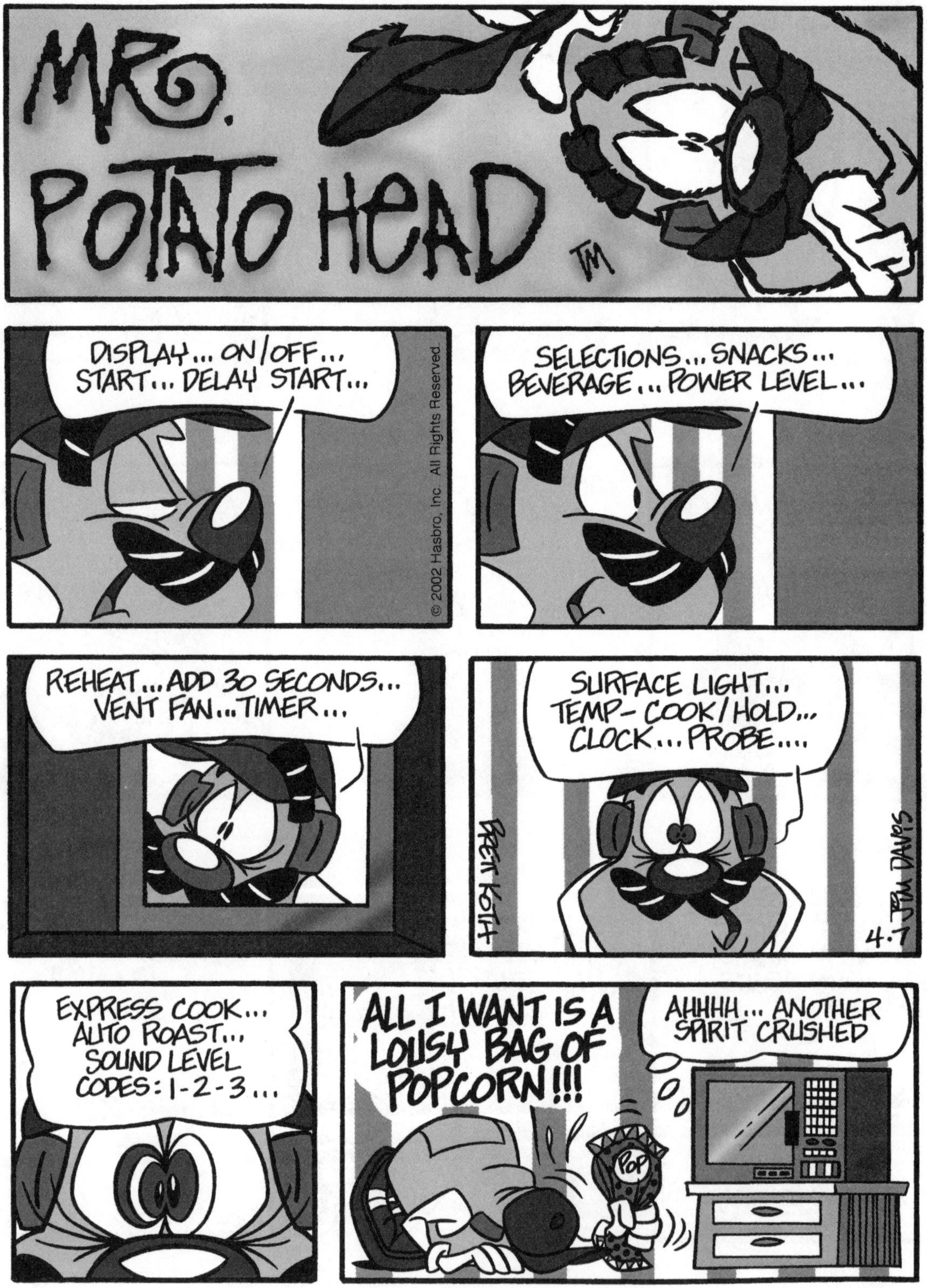
MR. POTATO HEAD TM
DISPLAY... ON/OFF... START... DELAY START...
© 2002 Hasbro, Inc. All Rights Reserved.
SELECTIONS... SNACKS... BEVERAGE... POWER LEVEL...
REHEAT...ADD 30 SECONDS... VENT FAN...TIMER...
SURFACE LIGHT... TEMP- COOK/HOLD... CLOCK... PROBE....
BRETT KOTH
JIM DAVIS
4-7
EXPRESS COOK... AUTO ROAST... SOUND LEVEL CODES: 1-2-3...
ALL I WANT IS A LOUSY BAG OF POPCORN!!!
AHHHH... ANOTHER SPIRIT CRUSHED
POP

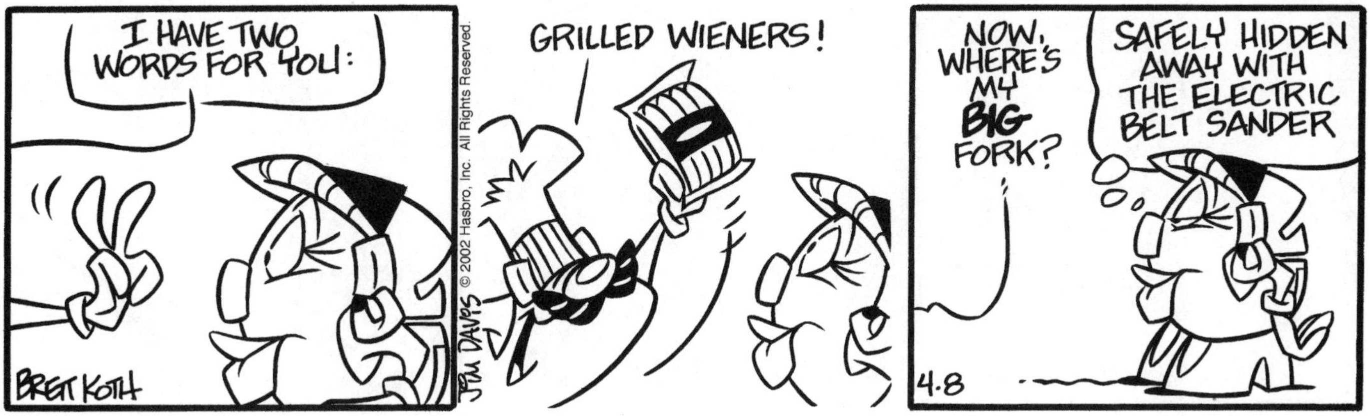
I HAVE TWO WORDS FOR YOU:
BRETT KOTH
JIM DAVIS © 2002 Hasbro, Inc. All Rights Reserved.
GRILLED WIENERS!
NOW, WHERE'S MY BIG FORK?
SAFELY HIDDEN AWAY WITH THE ELECTRIC BELT SANDER
4.8

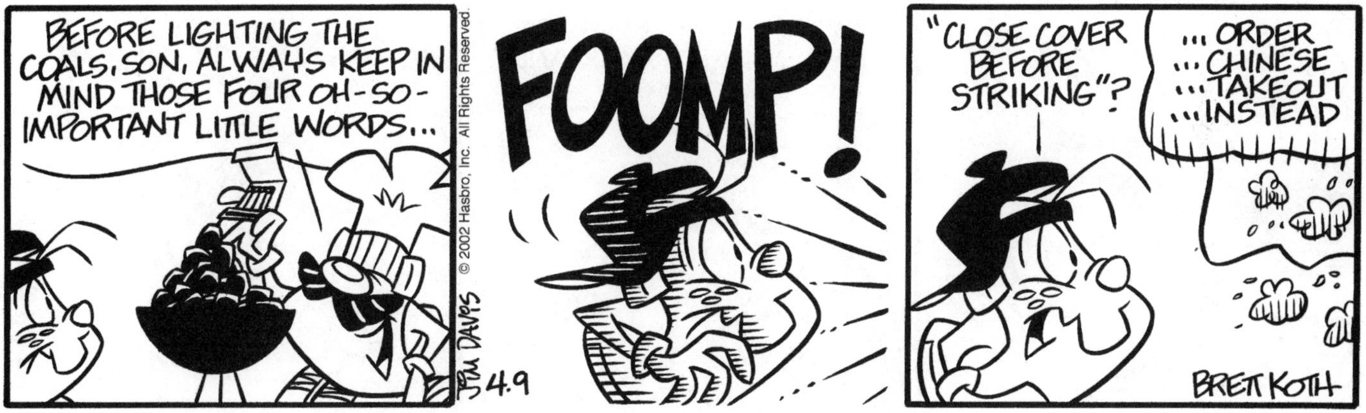
BEFORE LIGHTING THE COALS, SON, ALWAYS KEEP IN MIND THOSE FOUR OH-SO-IMPORTANT LITTLE WORDS...
JIM DAVIS 4.9 © 2002 Hasbro, Inc. All Rights Reserved.
FOOMP!
"CLOSE COVER BEFORE STRIKING"?
...ORDER ...CHINESE ...TAKEOUT ...INSTEAD
BRETT KOTH

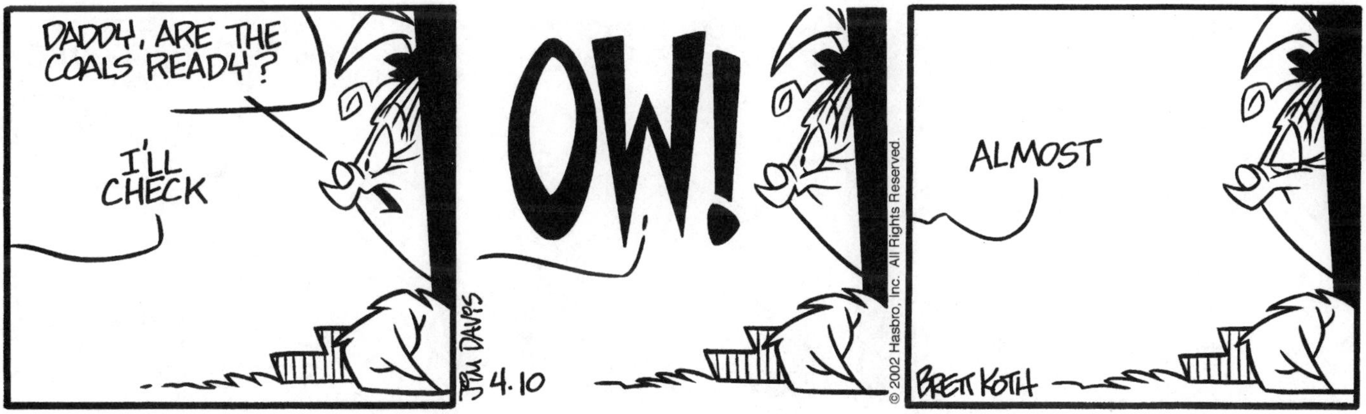
DADDY, ARE THE COALS READY?
I'LL CHECK
JIM DAVIS 4.10
OW!
© 2002 Hasbro, Inc. All Rights Reserved.
ALMOST
BRETT KOTH

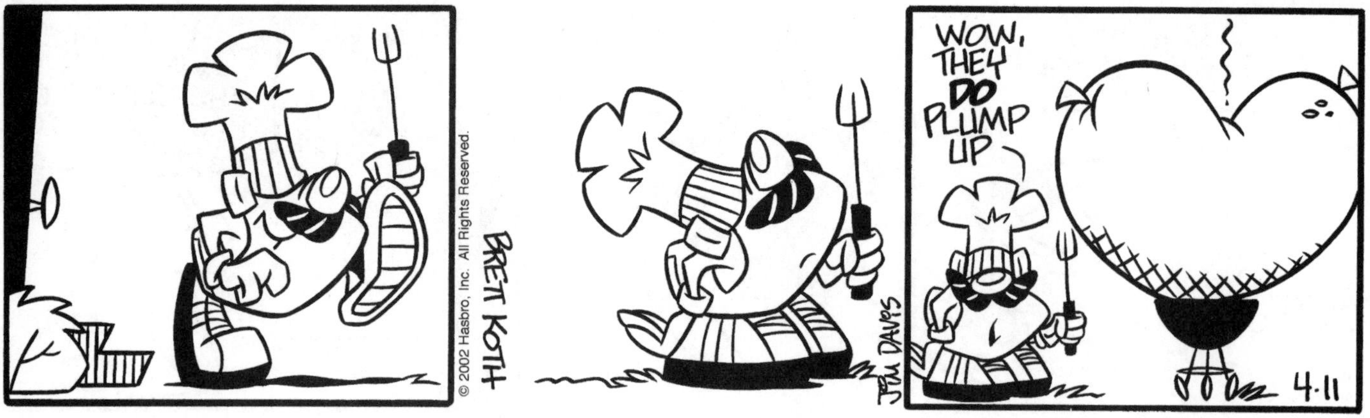
WOW, THEY DO PLUMP UP
4·11
© 2002 Hasbro, Inc. All Rights Reserved.

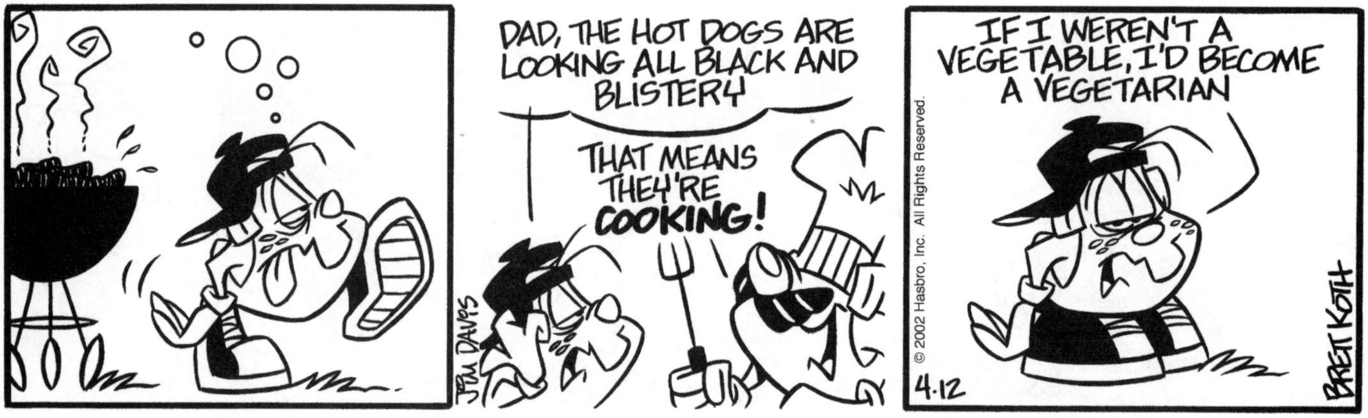
DAD, THE HOT DOGS ARE LOOKING ALL BLACK AND BLISTERY
THAT MEANS THEY'RE COOKING!
IF I WEREN'T A VEGETABLE, I'D BECOME A VEGETARIAN
4·12
© 2002 Hasbro, Inc. All Rights Reserved.

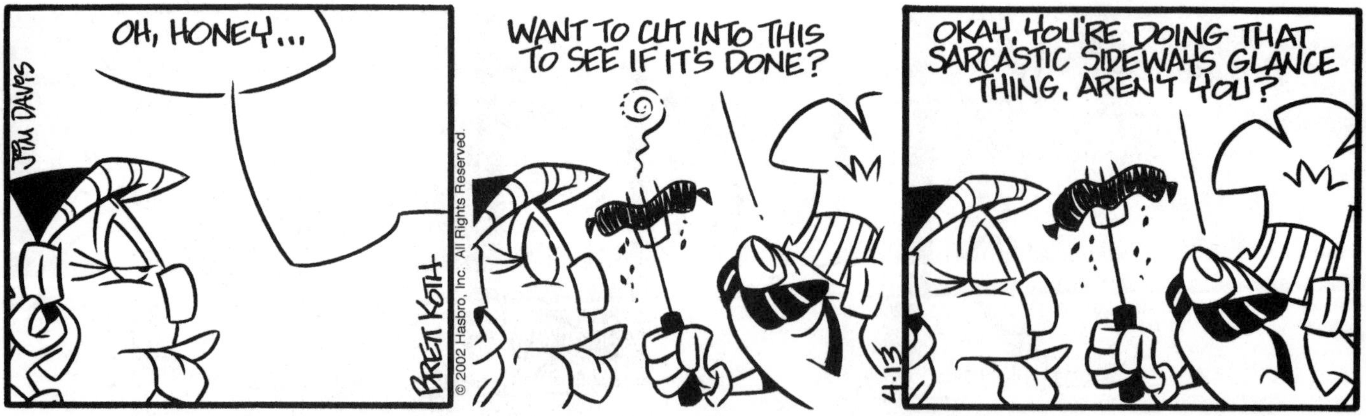
OH, HONEY...
WANT TO CUT INTO THIS TO SEE IF IT'S DONE?
OKAY, YOU'RE DOING THAT SARCASTIC SIDEWAYS GLANCE THING, AREN'T YOU?
4·13
© 2002 Hasbro, Inc. All Rights Reserved.

MR POTATO HEAD TM
DIP
© 2002 Hasbro, Inc. All Rights Reserved.
CHIPS, DIP....
JIM DAVIS
4-14
COMFY PILLOW, TV REMOTE....
...COOL BEVERAGE, PROGRAM GUIDE AND MY FAVORITE CORK COASTER!
AHHHHHHHHHHH
WHO SAYS MEN CAN'T ACCESSORIZE?
DIP
BRETT KOTH

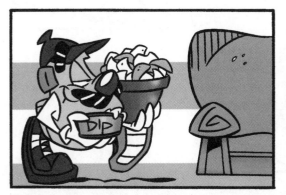

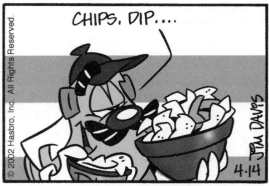

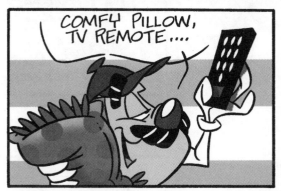

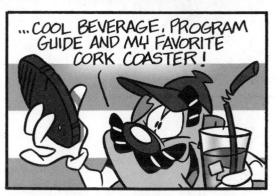

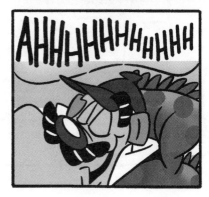

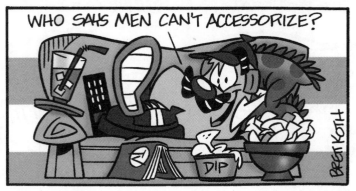

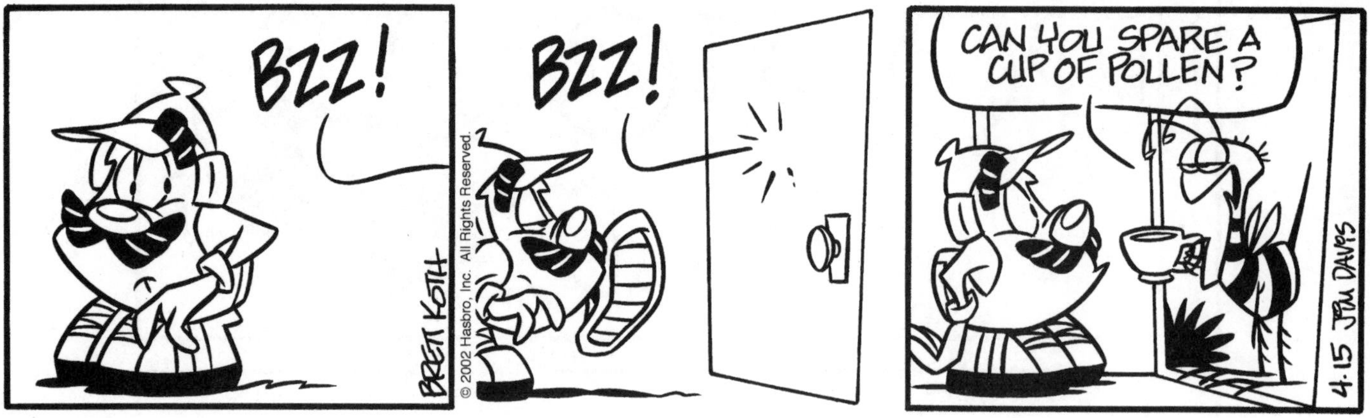
BZZ!
BZZ!
CAN YOU SPARE A CUP OF POLLEN?
BRETT KOTH
© 2002 Hasbro, Inc. All Rights Reserved.
4.15 JIM DAVIS

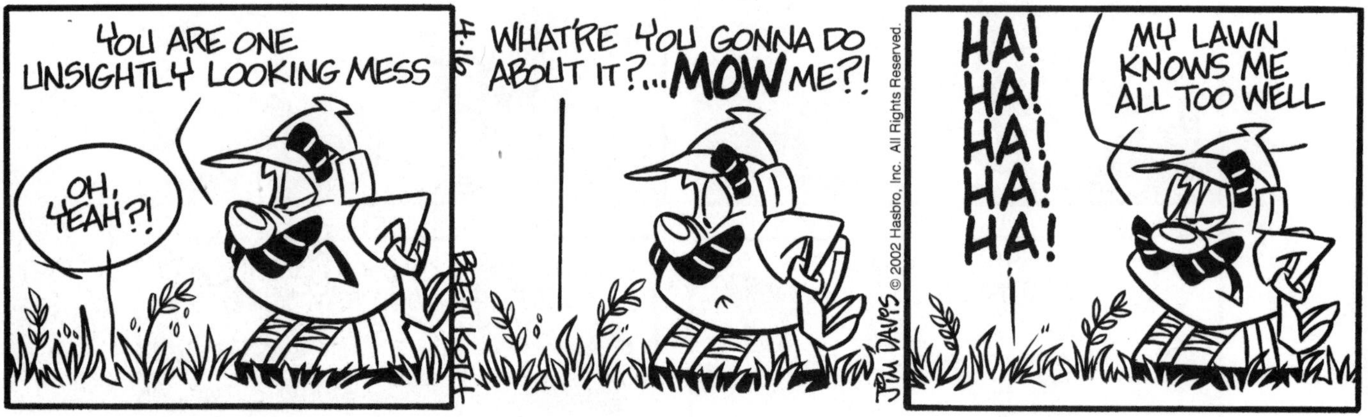
YOU ARE ONE UNSIGHTLY LOOKING MESS
OH, YEAH?!
WHAT'RE YOU GONNA DO ABOUT IT?...MOW ME?!
HA! HA! HA! HA! HA!
MY LAWN KNOWS ME ALL TOO WELL
4.16
BRETT KOTH
JIM DAVIS
© 2002 Hasbro, Inc. All Rights Reserved.

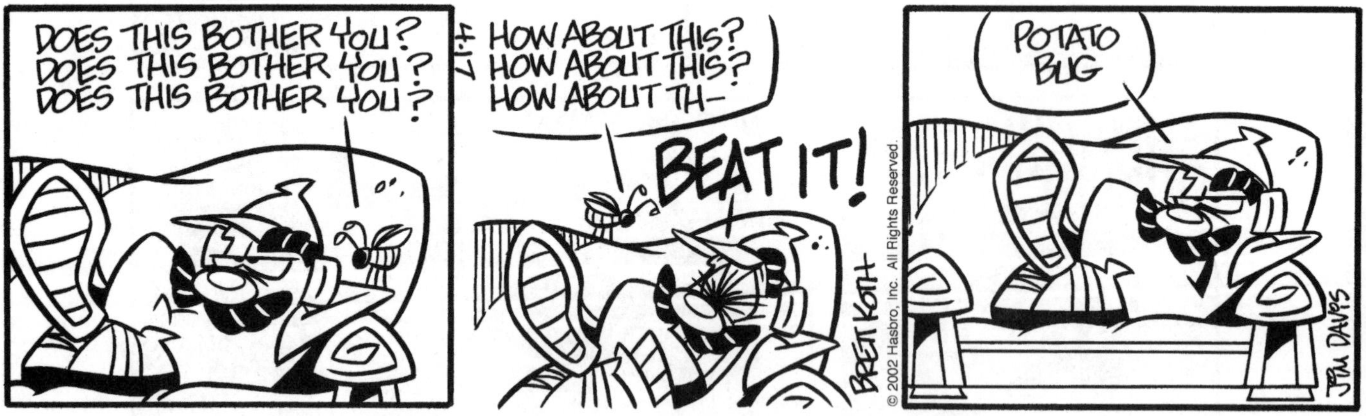
DOES THIS BOTHER YOU? DOES THIS BOTHER YOU? DOES THIS BOTHER YOU?
HOW ABOUT THIS? HOW ABOUT THIS? HOW ABOUT TH-
BEAT IT!
POTATO BUG
4.17
BRETT KOTH
© 2002 Hasbro, Inc. All Rights Reserved.
JIM DAVIS

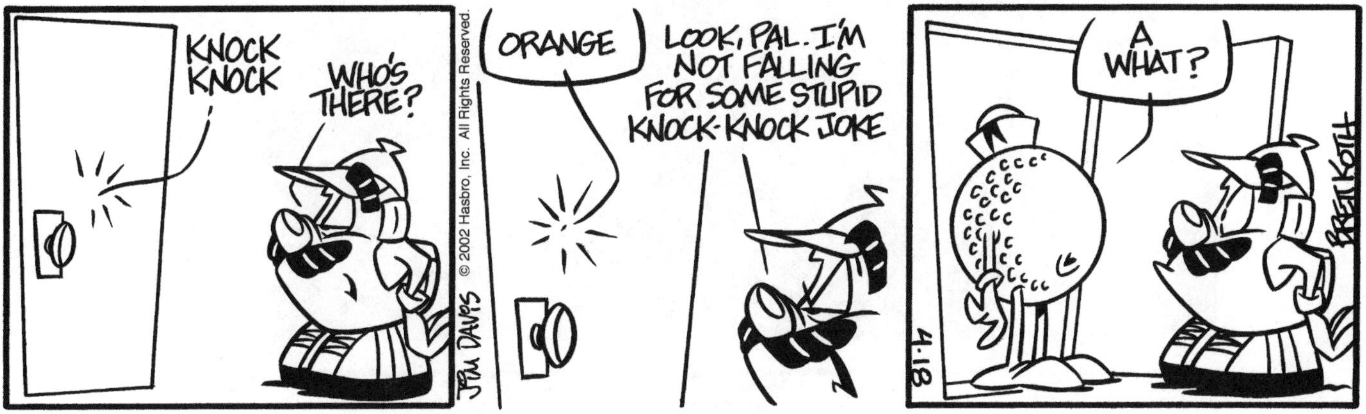
KNOCK KNOCK
WHO'S THERE?
© 2002 Hasbro, Inc. All Rights Reserved.
JIM DAVIS
ORANGE
LOOK, PAL. I'M NOT FALLING FOR SOME STUPID KNOCK-KNOCK JOKE
A WHAT?
4·18
BRETT KOTH

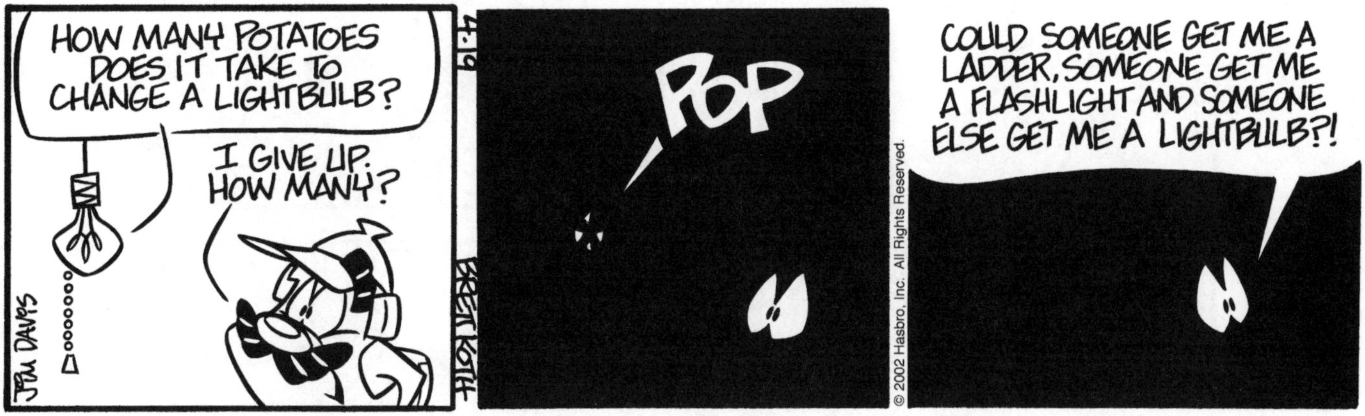
HOW MANY POTATOES DOES IT TAKE TO CHANGE A LIGHTBULB?
I GIVE UP. HOW MANY?
JIM DAVIS
4·19
BRETT KOTH
POP
© 2002 Hasbro, Inc. All Rights Reserved.
COULD SOMEONE GET ME A LADDER, SOMEONE GET ME A FLASHLIGHT AND SOMEONE ELSE GET ME A LIGHTBULB?!

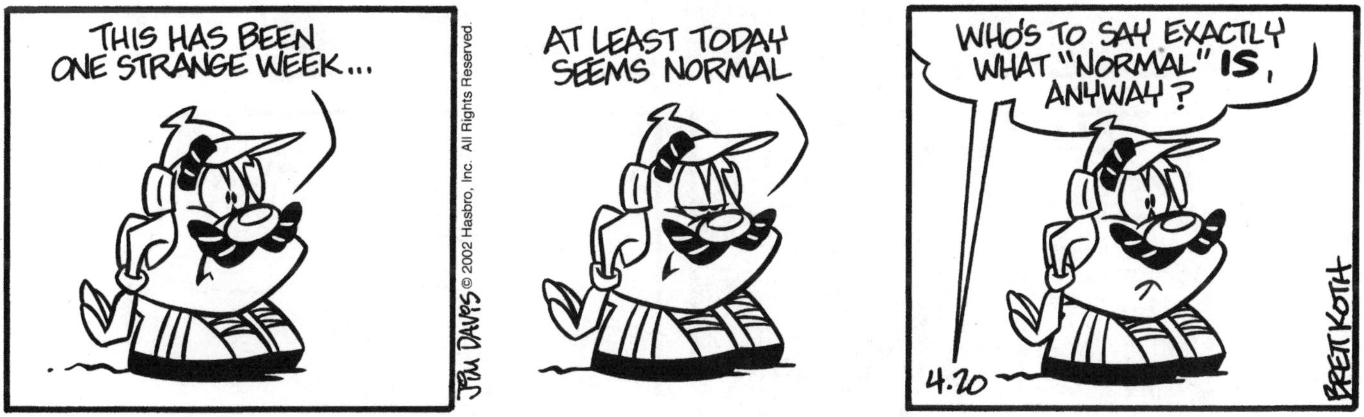
THIS HAS BEEN ONE STRANGE WEEK...
JIM DAVIS © 2002 Hasbro, Inc. All Rights Reserved.
AT LEAST TODAY SEEMS NORMAL
WHO'S TO SAY EXACTLY WHAT "NORMAL" IS, ANYWAY?
4·20
BRETT KOTH

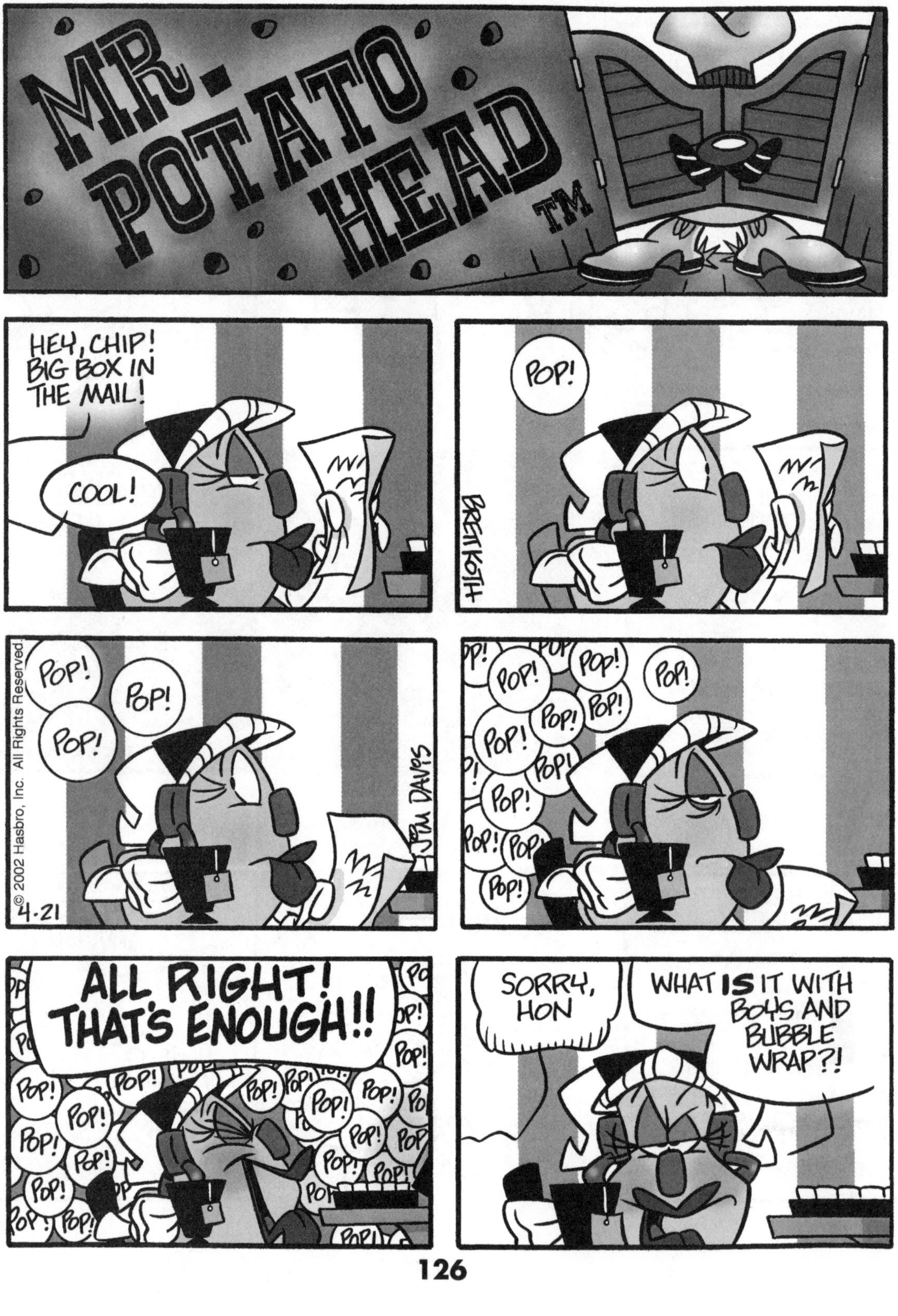
MR. POTATO HEAD
TM
HEY, CHIP! BIG BOX IN THE MAIL!
COOL!
POP!
BRETT KOTH
POP!
POP!
POP!
© 2002 Hasbro, Inc. All Rights Reserved.
4-21
JIM DAVIS
POP!
ALL RIGHT! THAT'S ENOUGH!!
POP!
SORRY, HON
WHAT IS IT WITH BOYS AND BUBBLE WRAP?!

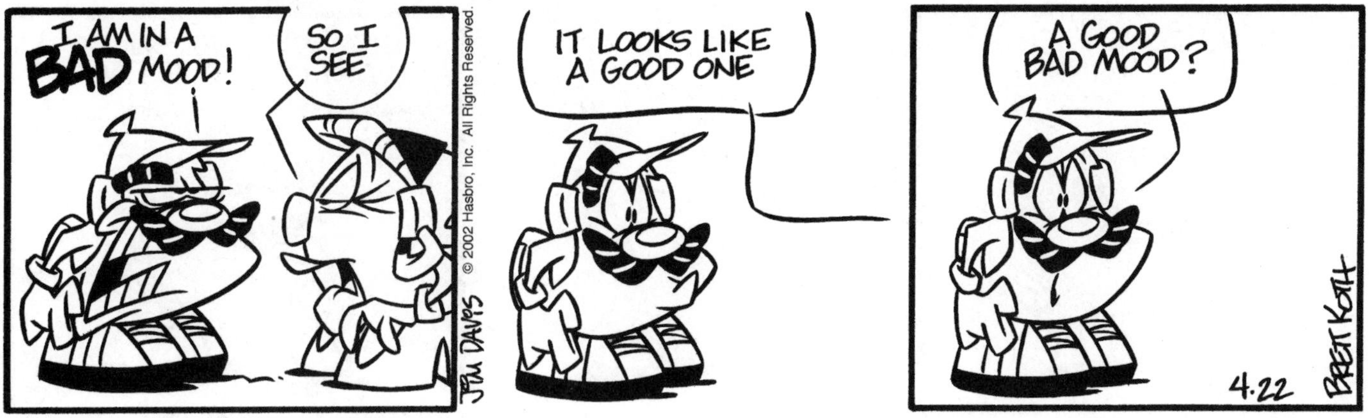
I AM IN A BAD MOOD!
SO I SEE
IT LOOKS LIKE A GOOD ONE
A GOOD BAD MOOD?
JIM DAVIS
© 2002 Hasbro, Inc. All Rights Reserved.
4.22
BRETT KOTH

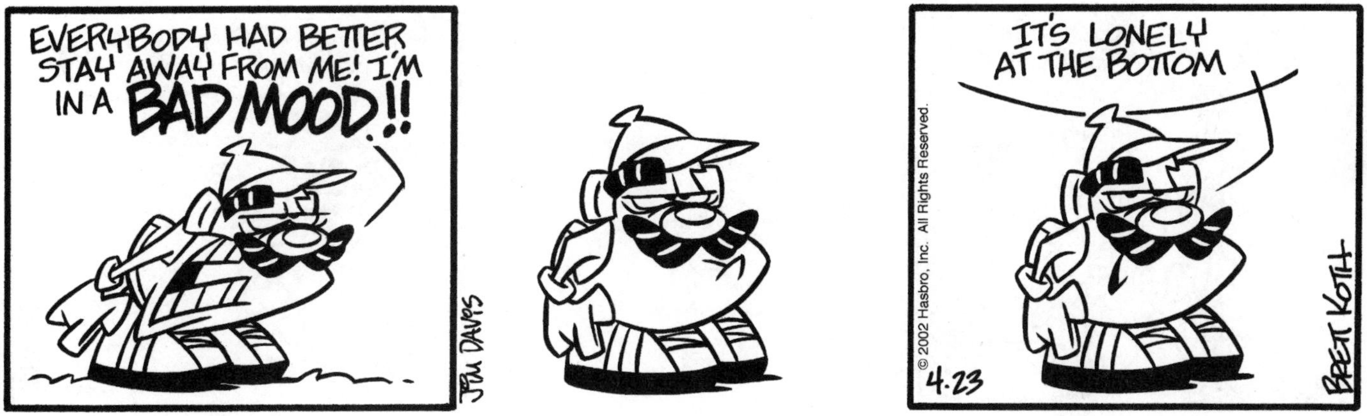
EVERYBODY HAD BETTER STAY AWAY FROM ME! I'M IN A BAD MOOD!!
IT'S LONELY AT THE BOTTOM
JIM DAVIS
© 2002 Hasbro, Inc. All Rights Reserved.
4.23
BRETT KOTH

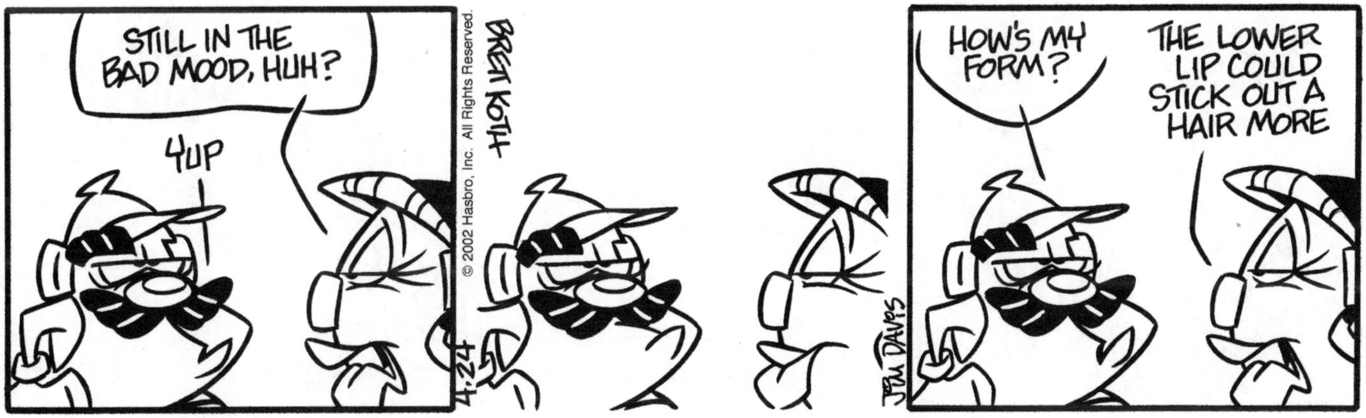
STILL IN THE BAD MOOD, HUH?
YUP
HOW'S MY FORM?
THE LOWER LIP COULD STICK OUT A HAIR MORE
© 2002 Hasbro, Inc. All Rights Reserved.
BRETT KOTH
4.24
JIM DAVIS

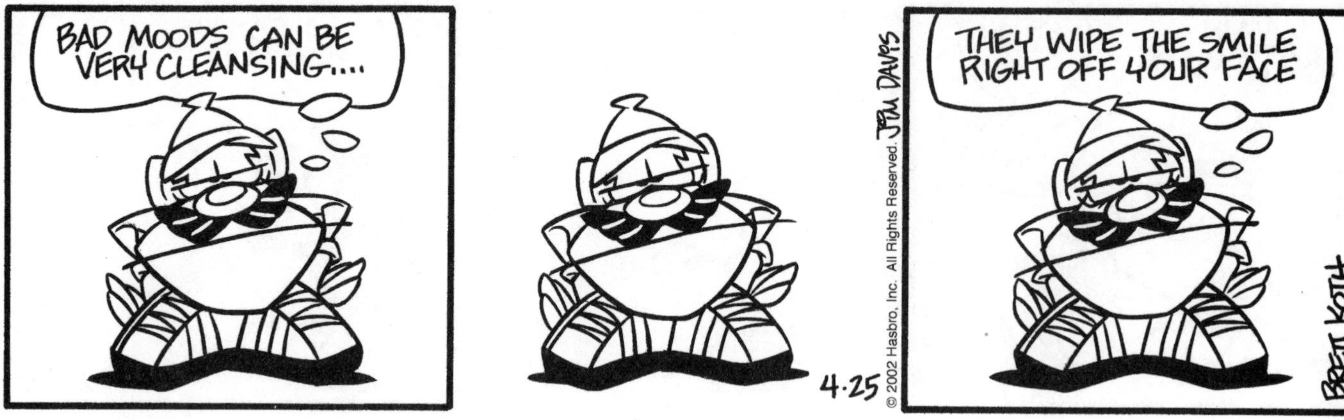
BAD MOODS CAN BE VERY CLEANSING....
THEY WIPE THE SMILE RIGHT OFF YOUR FACE
4·25
© 2002 Hasbro, Inc. All Rights Reserved.
JIM DAVIS
BRETT KOTH

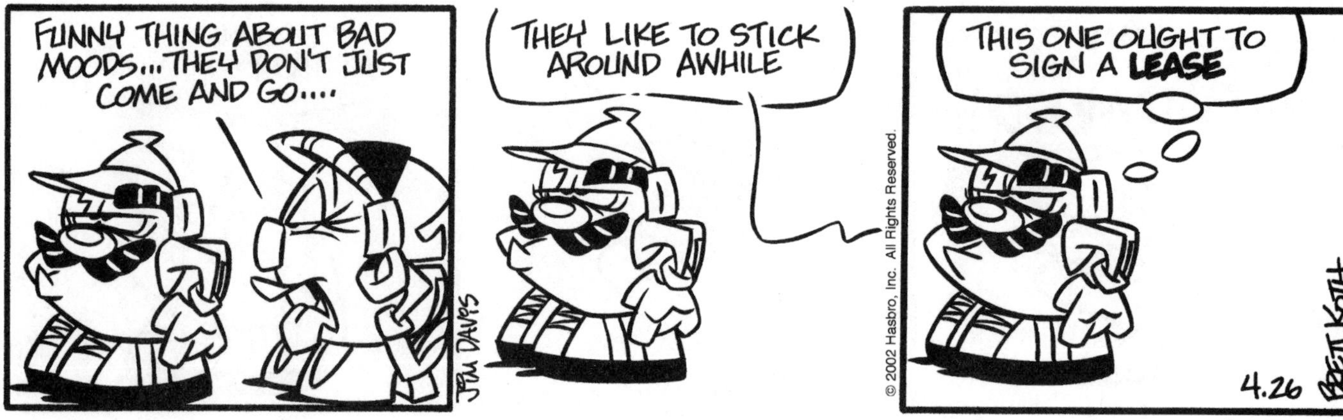
FUNNY THING ABOUT BAD MOODS... THEY DON'T JUST COME AND GO....
THEY LIKE TO STICK AROUND AWHILE
THIS ONE OUGHT TO SIGN A **LEASE**
4.26
© 2002 Hasbro, Inc. All Rights Reserved.
JIM DAVIS
BRETT KOTH

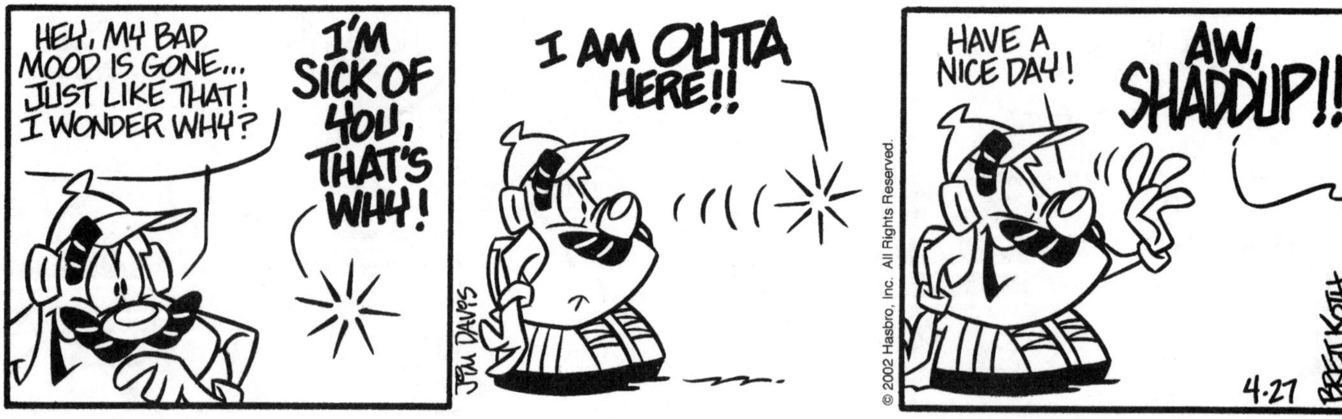
HEY, MY BAD MOOD IS GONE... JUST LIKE THAT! I WONDER WHY?
I'M SICK OF YOU, THAT'S WHY!
I AM OUTTA HERE!!
HAVE A NICE DAY!
AW, SHADDUP!!
4·27
© 2002 Hasbro, Inc. All Rights Reserved.
JIM DAVIS
BRETT KOTH